SCOTLAND: HER STORY

SCOTLAND

HER STORY

THE NATION'S HISTORY BY
THE WOMEN WHO LIVED IT

Edited by
Rosemary Goring

BIRLINN

First published in 2018 by
Birlinn Limited
West Newington House
10 Newington Road
Edinburgh
EH9 1QS

www.birlinn.co.uk

ISBN 978 178027 531 4

British Library Cataloguing in Publication Data
A catalogue record for this book is available from the British Library.

Typeset by Biblichor Ltd, Edinburgh
Printed and bound by Clays Ltd, Elcograf S.p.A.

For Margaret and Jenny

Contents

Acknowledgements

The first thought when undertaking a project such as *Scotland: Her Story* is: where to start? Closely followed by, where to draw a line? The same questions apply to these acknowledgements. The anthologist accumulates debts like a rookie at the roulette table. In that sense, such a book is a group effort, in the widest sense, and I offer my grateful thanks to all those who, wittingly or otherwise, helped in its compilation. Their fingerprints are all over it though, of course, omissions, oversights and misinterpretations are entirely my responsibility.

In trawling for material I have relied heavily upon Strathclyde University Library and its unfailingly helpful staff; made many raids upon the shelves of the Mitchell Library in Glasgow, Glasgow Women's Library, Edinburgh Central Library Scottish Department and the National Library of Scotland. Countless happy hours have been spent among their collections, where I have often found myself distracted by temptingly titled books or promising new avenues of enquiry. To all the librarians in these institutions, many thanks.

Scotland: Her Story is only the most recent and smallest stone on a mountainous cairn. In gathering the contents, I have called upon the research and knowledge of eminent historians whose own work has drawn on first-person narratives, which served as signposts for further exploring. Though far less well-known now than in her heyday, the avid compiler of historical vignettes, Agnes Mure Mackenzie, has been a first port of call, her bite-sized histories of the country – the four-volume *Scottish Pageant* – as fascinating and kaleidoscopic today as when first published. Other rich sources include T. C. Smout and Sydney Wood's *Scottish Voices* for its reading list alone, Alan Orr Anderson's crystal-clear translations of medieval documents in *Early Sources of Scottish History* and *Scottish Annals from English Chroniclers*, Gordon Donaldson's *Sources for Scottish Historical Documents*, Louise Yeoman's *Reportage Scotland*, and the extensive and comprehensive oral histories of the indefatigable Ian MacDougall, who has quite literally given a voice to the nation's people. To these must be added all those memoirists and diarists, famous and unheard of, brilliant and banal, whose works capture their own times and make them sing.

I am most grateful to Alan McLean, QC, for the entry on the Tumbling Lassie, and the background material that puts this extraordinary case in context;

to Ingrid Thomson, archivist at Glamis Castle, for pointing me to the journal of the much abused 9th Countess of Strathmore; and to playwright Jo Clifford, for so willingly agreeing to write about her experience, to a tight deadline, while finishing a new work of her own. Also, to Allan Hunter for a stream of good ideas, more than I could ever hope to include.

Andrew Simmons, my editor at Birlinn, has been a model of insight and calm, as nerveless and good-humoured at the controls as a Spitfire pilot under fire. Copy-editor Helen Bleck has a raptor's eye, and swooped on more than a few errors and glitches. Thanks also to the behind-the-scenes team at Birlinn – Jan Rutherford, Vikki Reilly, Jim Hutcheson, Neville Moir, Kristian Kerr, Hester Chatterton and, of course, the indomitable Hugh Andrew. They are the hardest-working, most upbeat publishing crew I have ever had the pleasure of working with. A huge thank you, too, to illustrator Saskia Cameron for achieving the near-impossible and distilling the essence of a multi-faceted book into a striking cover image.

Finally, I am indebted to my husband and in-house librarian Alan Taylor, not just for his books, but for suggestions, criticisms, hoovering and home-brewed coffee so strong it brought long-dead synapses back to life. He also compiled the index – heroic.

Introduction

To read most histories of Scotland – indeed of most countries – you'd be forgiven for thinking that women are a recent invention. From the earliest records to the Victorian age – and in some cases well into our own times – the archives show a country largely run for and by men. For far too long, in everyday life women were kept in the wings, just as in illuminated manuscripts we were consigned to the margins, alongside decorative flowers and tim'rous, cowering beasties. For those of us who grow peppery at the woeful absence in historical accounts of one half of the population, it is not good for our blood pressure to trawl through Church and court records, treasurers' receipts, royal charters, property deeds or the works of chroniclers, themselves always male. It is like going for a walk in the countryside where laid out before you are hills and trees and rivers, to find there is no birdsong, no barking dogs or frolicking lambs. The scene is partial, incomplete, and for that reason eerily empty.

Scotland: Her Story is an attempt to put women back into the picture, and to add depth and colour to the often monochrome portrait of the past. To this end, I have worked like a metal detectorist, reading my way across acres of recorded history, hoping for the dancing needle or high-pitched tone that would alert me to something worth digging out. From the early centuries, sadly, there was woefully little. To have any chance of being documented in the Middle Ages or before, a woman had to be a member of the aristocracy, or else the victim or perpetrator of an outrageous crime. The nuns of Coldingham monastery in 870 who, under their abbess's instruction, sliced off their own noses and top lips rather than be raped by rampaging Vikings, would doubtless have preferred to live in peace than make it so gruesomely into the archives. Their bloody appearance is a rare moment when women are glimpsed in such mortally dangerous situations, and acting with the same high courage as men whose names are remembered. Of course, if you are by nature optimistic, then neglect of women's affairs might suggest that whatever happened to them was for the most part less extreme and noteworthily nasty. It seems to me more probable, unfortunately, that unless they were servants of the Church, or had royal connections, women's fates, be they miserable or glorious, were simply not deemed worthy of comment. Not, that is, until the witchhunts began. In that shameful period, females of all classes suddenly found themselves in the spotlight, most of them innocent victims of hysteria and prejudice. Their persecution was, tragically, the reverse side of the coin. As in centuries before and after, women were seen by the authorities as potentially dangerous and subversive, especially those who did not conform by marrying, or who were too temptingly attractive, or dabbled in the supernatural, or were healers, eccentric, or simply old, poor and haggard. All of them were fair game at a time when popular feeling was roused against the wiles of woman-kind and their potentially ruinous allure.

Witches are a special case, a brief parting of the curtain on an ugly scene. It is not until the nineteenth century that we first catch sight of those such as the young girls and women who worked down the mines in Ormiston in East Lothian. When they were interviewed by a commission on child labour, officials could scarcely believe what they heard. The mournful voices of these underground toilers are among the most powerfully affecting you'll ever find. They emerge fleetingly from the gloom, like waifs in *Les Misérables*, but in their piteous descriptions of what they endured you can catch the echo of thousands more like them who were all but enslaved, whether working in the mines, or in factories, or on the land. And this, it's worth remembering, in one of the best-educated and most God-fearing countries in Europe.

For much of the past two millennia, it has been kings, nobles, bishops, Kirk ministers and latterly politicians who have dictated the terms by which the country was controlled, whether in laws passed or unwritten rules of behaviour designed at least in part to keep wives and daughters in their place. What insight we get into women before the early modern period is almost always from writings and documents composed by men, the self-appointed arbiters of what was to be recorded, and what to be forever forgotten or overlooked. Thus the lives of the vast majority of womenfolk, before the seventeenth century, go largely unseen and unheard. It is a telling silence. Those who have no voice are, by implication, powerless. The same *omertà* holds for the poor and the uneducated of either gender, conditions that pertained to the bulk of the country well into the sixteenth century, when literacy slowly began to spread. Children, both girls and boys, have also passed under a cloak of invisibility, their thoughts and names evaporated as if they never existed. By this measure, you could say that far more than half of Scotland's history has been forever lost.

The question all this raises, of course, is of how we define history. Is it the rigid backbone of the body politic, formed by the major political and religious events that have shaped our nation – the succession of kings, queens and regents, the treaties and charters by which alliances and enemies were made?

Is it the battles and murders, the ideologies and crusades, the enterprises, expeditions and inventions on which our present fortunes were founded? That certainly is how it was taught in my schooldays. We learned of the Roman invasions, and the Pictish fight-back. We marvelled at the tenacity of Robert the Bruce, though there was no mention of the appalling reprisals his female supporters suffered. We were thrilled by stories of Mary, Queen of Scots, who alone brought a sense of glamour and immediacy to the concept of sitting on the throne. But the tragic outcome for this mercurial and perennially fascinating woman was insidiously used to underline the point that women were not to be trusted to hold the reins of power. We could be fickle, mendacious and weak. Above all, when it came to men, we too often were, in Muriel Spark's phrase, 'bad pickers', for which the country was made to suffer.

I have included several episodes from Mary Stuart's extraordinary story, though in a life so dramatic there were many others which equally deserved a space. To view Scotland's history through the eyes of women without placing her centre stage would be to underplay the impact she made. In her own time, her good fortune in having a son, while Elizabeth I remained childless, ultimately led to the Union of Crowns under James VI in 1603 and thereby, some have argued, to the Union of Parliaments in 1707. Yet her significance has lived on beyond these dynastically and politically momentous events. Mary's chequered career, in which she made too many dubious alliances and miscalculations, has indelibly shaped ideas of women and leadership, initially for the worse, but recently more generously and hopefully. Unlike her ardent rival Elizabeth I, the Scottish queen could never be accused of quashing sentiment in pursuit of her aims. In remaining true to herself, nurturing her profound piety and rich imagination, and rarely curbing her emotional volatility, Mary Stuart never lost sight of her birthright, and her entitlement to govern. Even at the very end, with her head on the block, she retained her dignity in a way that has awed and inspired women ever since. Despite the dreadful errors of judgement she made, she is a peerless example of persistent hope, and the embodiment of a nobility that refused to surrender to self-pity. While certainly no role model, she used all her powers, for good and ill. Scotland would have been a more interesting and cultured place had there been more royal women like her.

Compared with the high drama of this queen's sorrowful tale, it is no wonder more ordinary women have barely registered. Until recent decades men have been the architects of Scotland, whether at Bannockburn, Flodden or the Somme, or during the violent upheavals of the Reformation and the Killing Years of the Covenanting period and the ongoing legacy of sectarianism, or while making a living by crofting, fishing and farming, or in factories, banks and offices. Women played a role – and some of them are thankfully caught in the act – but their part was almost always viewed as secondary. It was not, however, negligible. The outraged housewives of Glasgow and Edinburgh in 1637, for instance, who rounded on priests who dared preach from Laud's Book of Common Prayer, hint at a truth that contemporary historians have long known: the fact that their deeds are rarely found in print does not mean that women held a minor position. Quite the reverse. As a result, by the time our actions are routinely found in print, and we are giving our own accounts of what we have seen and done, our influence has likewise grown.

As if to keep step with women's increasing participation in the running of the country, our understanding of history has expanded exponentially, and it is within this context that *Scotland: Her Story* must be viewed. Those hoping for a crammer of the key points in our past will be disappointed. Too often women had nothing to do – so far as the record goes – with affairs of state. This is the problem with looking at history as witnessed by women. Just as men-only narratives offer a limited truth, so does the all-female version. Even so, it is hoped that this overview will fill some of the gaps and point to a richer shared heritage. It might also suggest a way of augmenting the male component of history too, since the low status of women has been echoed in the frequent neglect of the ordinary man's contribution.

In the past half century, thanks to the work of social and economic historians, the subject that Professor Tom Devine calls 'the Queen of Disciplines' is no longer predominantly a litany of dates, laws and charters, of competing rulers, leaders and soldiers, of shifting borders and switching loyalties. It has a more generous and subtle purview. The experience of being alive is now recognised as fundamental to fathoming the past. Consequently, *Scotland: Her Story* tries to tease out the contribution of women to the country's evolution, and to chart, where possible, developments or innovations as observed or initiated by women. Some of the most momentous events are seen only from the sidelines, but what a view this nevertheless gives. One such is the testimony of a widow whose house was near Culloden battlefield. Wild-eyed Jacobite soldiers who had hacked and burned their victims to death in the grounds of her house insisted on showing her what they had done, knowing full well her sympathies were with the other side. Thirty years earlier, the wife of a captured Jacobite aristocrat showed bravery to match any advancing soldier as she attempted to liberate him from the Tower of London the night before his execution. Just as dauntless were the nurses working on the front lines in the Great War.

Yet while always aware of trying to reflect pivotal moments of history, my focus has equally been on capturing the ways in which women and their mothers and daughters actually lived. Entries have been selected for the light they throw on their times as well as on their own distinctive situation, one person's experience mirroring the many. Thus the manner in which well-off families educated their girls, as seen in a bill for a term's schooling at an eighteenth-century Edinburgh dame school, or the first frank discussions of how best to maintain a sexual rapport in marriage, as intimated by Marie Stopes, are as crucial for deciphering our past as the deployment of armies, attachés and spies. History lies as much in what Jessie Kesson called the 'sma' perfect' as in the stand-off between global leaders. It is found in the tumble-down ruins of cottages in Caithness and Sutherland, where crofters were evicted in favour of sheep, as well as in the tumultuous tides of international affairs. Despite the bellowing nature of much political discourse, history is also made on the seemingly humdrum home front: young Grizel Baillie smuggling out food from the dinner table to feed her father, who was in hiding in an underground church vault in fear of his life; a liberal Edinburgh lawyer's wife setting up the first benefit society for women; Glasgow wives vehemently protesting rent rises while their men were away at war; a Communist couple adopting a black baby, and then another; a schoolgirl facing down one of the country's most eminent lawyers as she made a stand against sectarian bigotry.

This is not to suggest that women's history is on the small scale while men's is monumental, but it is to accept that since for centuries only a fraction of us have been in a position to wield authority in the public sphere, it is therefore inevitable that our ideas and actions have been conducted more within the domestic realm. Even those who defied their own times (and their private inhibitions) to follow their calling, such as the mathematician Mary Somerville, had to do so while overseeing their home and making sure the children were being cared for. Just as Jane Austen hid her writing whenever visitors came into the room, Somerville had to break off midway through algebraic calcula-tions to provide refreshments for unexpected guests with every appearance of pleasure. That in winter she had to work in the drawing room because there was no fireplace in her 'little room', says as much about her self-esteem as about the cost of coal.

The net of history in which women are caught, even fleetingly, is no less important than that of men, but it has been given far less emphasis. For those concerned, falling in love, getting married, having a baby – or a miscarriage or abortion – are, for a time at least, as important as international events. These are crucial components of women's history, and I have tried to represent them as fully as possible. For that reason, the book gives a protracted, roaring account of modern childbirth, which is how history began and will continue.

At various points, regardless of whether they were wives or mothers, women have sparked medical and educational revolutions, social and economic advances, and led the vanguard in the arts or sciences. Sometimes they have been heroic in just keeping the household running. As the cookery-school founder Mrs Margaret MacKirdy Black wrote in the preface to her manual of how to keep house,

> people cannot prosecute business with great energy, or study with much enjoyment or profit, if there are worries at home, or muddle and discomfort there. This is quite apparent to all, and though it seems a matter of minor importance compared with the great interests and objects that have to be carried on out of doors, yet if the household machinery is out of order, or not moving smoothly, the derangement may be carried forward till very important interests are disturbed.

Jane Welsh Carlyle's compendious letters are a running commentary on the state of her Victorian household and her marriage to the brilliant but moody historian Thomas Carlyle. By turns sardonic and witty, thoughtful and soul-searching, they show the ways in which highly intelligent women were held, if not precisely captive, then confined, allowed to flicker like candles rather than blaze like a fire. But some were able to shine far from the confines of the scullery and parlour – Mary Slessor, for instance, whose courage as a missionary in Nigeria makes for electrifying reading. There are countless examples of women defying the odds and emerging triumphant, yet this should come as no surprise. In fact, while it is frustrating for us today to know nothing of the existence and achievements of generations of womenfolk before our time, for their contemporaries I suspect they always knew they were capable of great things. Women might not have found their deeds immortalised in ink or on monuments, but to their families and friends, those with exceptional skill, determination and stamina did not go unnoticed. Ian Niall's description of the Herculean work done by nineteenth-century farmers' wives in the course of a day makes you tired just to read it. The chutzpah of a pioneer such as Susan Allison, who in the 1860s started married life in a cabin as the only white woman in the wilds of British Columbia, is staggering. She was no more remarkable, though, than Dundee's mill-workers, whose day began in the factory, and continued when they returned home for a second shift of shopping, cleaning, feeding and caring. Their champion Mary Brooksbank was just as intrepid, standing up to the authorities to demand better conditions, and prepared to be sent to the cells for it. Or there was Elsie Inglis, who refused to sit at home sewing when soldiers at the Western and

Russian fronts needed field hospitals. And Winnie Ewing, SNP MP, who endured such persistent and aggressive sexism on the back benches at Westminster it almost made her ill. And Judy Murray, who put everything she had to give into helping her sons become world-class tennis players and in so doing brought a touch of stardust to Scotland.

You do not, however, need to have the soul of Joan of Arc to be part of the vast panorama of our past. History is made in quieter moments too. Whether it's the ale women, whose popular trade was governed by strict laws, or soldiers' wives and prostitutes who, as camp followers, were never far from the sides of their men, or those paupers and criminals who ended up in the poorhouse, their presence is felt. Perhaps the most notable of these, whose name was never recorded, is the Tumbling Lassie, an acrobat whose employer claimed he had bought her. The sensational prosecution he raised to retain ownership, in 1687, was the first in which human rights were invoked, thereby setting the girl free. The Tumbling Lassie disappeared into her own future, but her case marked a new awareness of individuals' worth, regardless of their status.

That there is such scant trace of those who were witnesses to previous centuries makes one all the more grateful for whatever scraps can be found. Here, then, I have drawn for the early centuries on what little official documentation there is. Much of it is too dry or convoluted to print. The revolutionary Education Act of 1560, for example, which made provision for girls as well as boys to be given a rudimentary education, is as thrilling to read as the small print on a parking ticket. Even so it is possible in occasional vivid passages to find footprints of a few of the women who helped shape the Middle Ages and the centuries to 1700. Thereafter the sources improve, from Church and court registers to private correspondence and memoirs. Official documents in the form of government surveys and reports continue to be useful into the twentieth century, from descriptions of conditions in asylums and hospitals, to prisons and schools. By the eighteenth century the pickings grow much richer, and we do not have to rely so heavily on men's judgement of what deserves a mention. From this period, a handful of well-educated women are writing their own accounts, among them the brilliant society figure Lady Anne Barnard. She might not rival Jane Carlyle as a literary stylist, but unlike Jane she travelled extensively, and made an impression wherever she went. As diaries and journals and letters like hers slowly appear, women emerge from behind the arras. There is, for example, the disturbing testimony given by the Countess of Strathmore to the cruelty inflicted on her by her sadistic husband; even worse was the treatment meted out to Lady Rachel Grange, who was abducted and kept prisoner for years on her husband's instructions. This was a heinous crime that would have gone unnoticed but for two anguished letters she smuggled out. The following century there are amorous missives from the genteel Madeleine Smith, acquitted of murdering her lover, although the not-proven verdict speaks for itself. Around the same time the so-called Factory Girl, Ellen Johnston, left an understandably overwrought memoir. It must stand as one of the very earliest accounts – inevitably oblique – of sexual abuse. Her ordeal over several years was so appalling it made her contemplate suicide. Hardly more cheerful, though written with astonishing spirit, is the diary kept by Mary Milne, from Selkirk, when she was the cook for Elsie Inglis's hospital unit in Russia. Thereafter memoirs and autobiographies came into their own, whether by politicians like Katharine Murray, Duchess of Atholl, the country's first female MP, or Jess Smith's recollections of her traveller family's experiences. Yet there remain tantalising gaps. Where, for instance, are those intrepid women who worked behind enemy lines? Where is a refugee's journal, or a GP's trove of letters? If any exist I would be delighted to include them in future editions of this book.

Newspapers can sometimes fill the breach, offering plain testimony to women's affairs, from suffragettes to musicians. Far more vivid, though, are the oral testimonies collected in particular by the tireless historian Ian MacDougall. Thanks to him, and others of his ilk, we hear first-hand what it was like to work at the pithead, or on a dairy farm, or in a snooty Edinburgh department store.

Inevitably there are gaps – some conscious, others simple oversight. This is not, for instance, intended as a surrogate biographical dictionary. Nor have I included every occasion where women have broken the glass ceiling, such as the first female Kirk minister, who was ordained in 1969, or the first to take advantage of Muirfield Golf Course reversing its ban on female members (at the time of writing, a woman has yet to enter Muirfield clubhouse in her own right). With the Kirk, I have included instead the ordeal of a minister drummed out after she was raped. This is not to deny that the Church of Scotland has fully embraced women leaders, as has the Scottish Episcopal Church, but to show that the prejudice against women, fomented at the Reformation, has not yet been eradicated, whether in this institution, or in many other corners of the country.

Interest and readability have been the guiding principles behind everything included, so to ease the flow, I have not included ellipses to indicate words or sentences jumped over in many pieces, especially the older sections. Those wishing to read the original passages in full will find details in the list of sources. There have also been many discarded items. Where a notable experience or event has been tediously or colourlessly or inaccurately described, it has fallen regrettably by the wayside. In one instance, I could not find the piece I was looking for, so I asked for it to be written for this book especially. Hence the reflections of playwright Jo Clifford on the long, painful process of changing her identity from that of a man to a woman. I hope this powerful insight into the changing nature of womanhood and gender, along with all the other pieces, compensates for any absences.

Gathering the material for *Scotland: Her Story* has been eye-opening. On one hand, it has been intensely galling to see the persistent sidelining and belittling of women down the ages. But such is the interest in the exploits of those included, and the range of fields in which they have distinguished themselves, by the time I had gathered all these pieces my feeling was not of resentment or disappointment, but of the highest respect and, on occasion, awe. Inevitably there are criminals, cheats, abusers and bullies, but they are heavily outweighed by women of principle and character. What stands out is the stamina and fortitude of those who either excelled in the area of life into which they were born, or were determined to make their way on a bigger stage. That the world was so hostile to women of talent – and women in general – was the biggest hurdle they had to surmount. It could be dispiriting to reflect how many had to remake the wheel every time, but it is better to be inspired by admiring those who refused to be downcast. Thanks to sheer bloodymindedness, the only Scottish footballer to have played in a World Cup-winning side – for Italy – is Rose Reilly, who as a child would not be bawled off the pitch, and would not accept that the beautiful game was for boys alone. While speaking of sport, the definition of Scottish for the purposes of inclusion, an issue familiar to managers picking national teams, is broad. It includes those who are Scottish by marriage, by residence and 'by formation'.

With Reilly, as with many within these pages, a lifetime of hard work seems to be the common denominator. Added to this is resilience, and an awareness that they could not depend on anyone but themselves either to get on, or simply to survive. Women in Scotland these past 1,300 years have proved stoical, determined and fiercely resistant to being patronised, put down or silenced. From the early Middle Ages to today, when we occupy the highest positions of state, *Scotland: Her Story* reflects the gradual but sustained advance towards a situation where equality of opportunity and status is a given. We are not quite there yet and, sadly, gender is not the only bar to progress, or to achieving what we would wish. A child aspiring to be a pianist or a veterinary surgeon cannot snap her or his fingers to make their wish come true. Much – too much – depends still on upbringing and wealth, or the lack of them. Yet if

Scotland: Her Story can be said to demonstrate one thing – a message that can be passed, like the Olympic torch, from one century to the next, and from one woman to another – it is the overriding importance of talent and personality in making history happen.

Rosemary Goring
August 2018

SCOTLAND: HER STORY

THE FINAL LETTER WRITTEN BY
MARY, QUEEN OF SCOTS

8 February 1587

This final letter, written by Mary, Queen of Scots to Henri III, King of France hours before her beheading, is among the most powerful ever sent. In many ways it is a model of a historical document, conveying the author's personality – dignified, angry, sorrowful but neither remorseful nor afraid. Those traits were the mark of a ruler who continues to fascinate, because for all its seeming openness, what this missive does not reveal is whether or not the charges for which she was imprisoned were true. Unless new evidence comes to light, those facts went with her to the grave. Mary Stuart was gifted and complicated, an erratic monarch, devout Catholic, talented writer and linguist, and an uncowed captive, who never once conceded that she was anything but a woman wronged. As with many of the eye-witness accounts that follow in this collection, her perspective is vividly immediate and compelling. That it is biased is inevitable, as are almost all contemporary records, no matter how objective they may at first appear. It is for readers to glean what they can, and let their imaginations fill in the gaps.

Sire, my brother-in-law, having by God's will, for my sins I think, thrown myself into the power of the Queen my cousin, at whose hands I have suffered much for almost twenty years, I have finally been condemned to death by her and her Estates. I have asked for my papers, which they have taken away, in order that I might make my will, but I have been unable to recover anything of use to me, or even get leave either to make my will freely or to have my body conveyed after my death, as I would wish, to your kingdom where I had the honour to be queen, your sister and old ally.

Tonight, after dinner, I have been advised of my sentence: I am to be executed like a criminal at eight in the morning. I have not had time to give you a full account of everything that has happened, but if you will listen to my doctor and my other unfortunate servants, you will learn the truth, and how, thanks be to God, I scorn death and vow that I meet it innocent of any crime, even if I were their subject. The Catholic faith and the assertion of my God-given right to the English crown are the two issues on which I am condemned, and yet I am not allowed to say that it is for the Catholic religion that I die, but for fear of interference with theirs. The proof of this is that they have taken away my chaplain, and although he is in the building, I have not been able to get permission for him to come and hear my confession and give me the Last Sacrament, while they have been most insistent that I receive the consolation and instruction of their minister, brought here for that purpose. The bearer of this letter and his companions, most of them your subjects, will testify to my conduct at my last hour. It remains for me to beg Your Most Christian Majesty, my brother-in-law and old ally, who have always protested your love for me, to give proof now of your goodness on all these points: firstly by charity, in paying my unfortunate servants the wages due them – this is a burden on my conscience that only you can relieve: further, by having prayers offered to God for a queen who has borne the title Most Christian, and who dies a Catholic, stripped of all her possessions. As for my son, I commend him to you in so far as he deserves, for I cannot answer for him. I have taken the liberty of sending you two precious stones, talismans against illness, trusting that you will enjoy good health and a long and happy life. Accept them from your loving sister-in-law, who, as she dies, bears witness of her warm feeling for you. Again I commend my servants to you. Give instructions, if it please you, that for my soul's sake part of what you owe me should be paid, and that for the sake of Jesus Christ, to whom I shall pray for you tomorrow as I die, I be left enough to found a memorial mass and give the customary alms.

> This Wednesday, two hours after midnight.
> Your very loving and most true sister, Mary R
> To the most Christian king, my brother-in-law and old ally

AWAKE FOR SIN

The Venerable Bede, before 683

Entering the cloisters was a popular choice in the early Middle Ages, but not all who took holy orders did so because of religious conviction. It was often simply the best option for daughters who could not or did not want to find a husband and had no hopes of any inheritance to keep them in old age. Ebba, or Aebbe, who founded monasteries at Ebchester and St Abb's as well as at Coldingham, was a princess, the daughter of Aethelfrith, King of Bernicia. She was deeply pious, but unable to control those in her charge. The chilly outpost of Coldingham monastery, by the North Sea, housed monks and nuns together, and suffered the perhaps inevitable problem this raised. Even the saintly St Cuthbert, when visiting, was said to have struggled with temptation. Here Bede records the ascetic Adamnan's warning to the abbess.

In these times the monastery of virgins which they name Coldingham . . . was consumed by fire through fault of carelessness. And yet all who know have been very easily able to perceive that it happened from the wickedness of them who dwelt in it, and especially of those who seemed to be the greater.

But there lacked not a reminder to the guilty of God's mercy, that corrected by it they might like the Ninevites turn from them the anger of the just Judge by fasting, tears and prayers. For there was in that monastery a man of the race of the [Irish] Scots, Adamnan by name, who led a life in continence, and greatly devoted to prayers to God; so that except on Sunday and on the fifth day of the week he never partook of any food or drink, and often passed whole nights awake fully in prayer.

It chanced that on a certain day he had gone out a considerable way from that monastery, one of the brethren accompanying him, and was returning after finishing his journey. And when he approached the monastery and beheld its building rising aloft, the man of God burst into tears, and betrayed in the expression of his face the sorrow of his heart. And his companion perceiving it asked him why he did thus. But he replied, 'All these buildings which thou seest, public and private, very soon is it that fire shall consume them and turn them to ashes.'

And hearing this [his companion,] so soon as they entered the monastery, took heed to relate it to the mother of the congregation, Ebba by name. But she was naturally disturbed by such a prediction, and called the man to her, and very diligently inquired the matter of him, and how he knew of this.

And he said:– 'Recently, while occupied by night with vigils and psalms, I saw suddenly standing before me one of the unknown countenance. And since I was terrified by his presence, he told me not to fear; and addressing me as in a friendly voice he said, 'Thou dost well, who hast chosen in this time of the quiet of night not to indulge in sleep, but to continue in vigils and prayers.' And I said, 'I know that it is very needful for me to continue in salutary vigils, and to pray to God industriously for pardon for my sins.' And he rejoined, 'Thou sayest truth, because both for thee and for many others there is need to atone with good works for their sins. For indeed I have visited in order all this monastery, and have looked into the houses and beds of each, and have found no one of all save thee busied with the welfare of his soul; but all of them, both men and women, are either sunk in dull sleep or awake for sin. For even the small houses which were made for prayer or for reading are turned into lairs of banquettings, potations, gossiping and other allurements.

'Also the virgins dedicated to God, spurning respect for their profession, so often as they have leisure employ themselves in the making of fine raiment with which either to deck themselves like brides, to the danger of their condition, or to attract to themselves the friendship of strange men. And hence deservedly a heavy punishment has been prepared in raging flames for this place and its inhabitants.'

And the abbess said:– 'and wherefore wert thou not willing sooner to reveal to me this discovery?' And he answered, 'I was afraid, through respect for thee, lest perchance thou shouldst be too greatly distressed. And yet thou hast this consolation, that this disaster will not arrive in thy days.'

And when this vision was made known, for a few days the inhabitants of the place began somewhat to be afraid, and to chastise themselves, pausing in their crimes. But after the death of the abbess they returned to their former defilement so, nay they did more wickedly. And when they said 'Peace and security,' suddenly they were visited by the penalty of the aforesaid retribution.

VIKING INVADERS ARE REPELLED
Matthew Paris, 870

Viking invaders were terrifyingly brutal, but when her priory was threatened, Abbess Ebba of Coldingham matched them for ferocity and courage. After the destruction of Coldingham monastery by fire two centuries earlier, it had been rebuilt, and by the later ninth century was most probably a nunnery. Ebba the Younger, as she was known, must have been a charismatic figure, because what she asked of her nuns, in order to save them from rape, was extreme. Chronicler Matthew Paris describes the horrific scene.

In the year of the Lord 870 an innumerable host of Danes landed in Scotland; and their leaders were Inguar and Hubba, men of terrible wickedness and unheard-of bravery. And they, striving to depopulate the territories of all England, slaughtered all the boys and old men whom they found, and commanded that the matrons, nuns and maidens should be given up to wantonness.

And when such plundering brutality had pervaded all territories of the kingdoms, Ebba, holy abbess of the cloister of Coldingham, feared that she too, to whom had been instructed the care of government and pastoral care, might be given up to the lust of pagans and lose her maiden chastity, along with the virgins under her rule; and she called together all the sisters into the chapter-house, and burst into speech in this wise, saying, 'Recently have come into our parts the wickedest pagans, ignorant of any kind of humanity; and roaming through every part of this district they spare neither the sex of woman nor the age of child, and they destroy churches and churchmen, prostitute nuns, and break up and burn everything they come upon. Therefore if you decide to acquiesce in my advice, I conceive a sure hope that by divine mercy we may be able to escape the fury of the barbarians and to preserve the chastity of perpetual virginity.'

And when the whole congregation of virgins had undertaken with sure promises that they would in all things obey the commands of their mother, that abbess of admirable heroism showed before all the sisters an example of chastity not only advantageous for those nuns but also eternally to be followed by all succeeding virgins: she took a sharp knife and cut off her own nose and upper lip to the teeth, offering a dreadful spectacle of herself to all beholders. And since the whole congregation saw and admired this memorable deed, each one performed a similar act upon herself, and followed the example of her mother.

And after this had so taken place, when next morning dawned, the most wicked brigands came upon them, to give up to wantonness the holy women, and devoted to God; as also to plunder the monastery itself and burn it down in flames. But when they saw the abbess and each of the sisters so horribly mutilated, and saturated with their blood from the soles of their feet to their crowns, they retired from the place with haste, for it seemed to them too long to stay even for a short space there. But as they retired thence the aforesaid leaders commanded their evil satellites to set fire to and burn down the monastery with all its offices and with the nuns themselves.

And so the execution was fulfilled by the servants of iniquity, and the holy abbess and all the virgins with her attained most holily to the glory of martyrdom.

QUEEN MARGARET'S SAINTLY WAYS
Turgot of Durham, c. 1070s

Born in exile in Hungary, around 1045 the English Princess Margaret arrived in England as a girl, but was obliged to flee to Scotland following the Norman Conquest. Known as Margaret of Wessex, she married Malcolm III of Scotland, a most rambunctuous and brutal soldier, whose behaviour was rather at odds with her extreme piety. Appearances may have been deceptive, however, because Margaret's Christian habits

*appear to have tamed his wildest excesses (except when he was on the battlefield). She
also introduced religious reforms that were considered far-sighted, especially in helping to
align the Scottish Church with European practices. Turgot, the Bishop of St Andrews,
was a close associate of the royal family, and later wrote Margaret's biography. As this
passage suggests, she could be steely and stubborn. She died in 1093, days after her
husband's death in battle, and was canonised in 1250. After the Reformation her relics
were scattered. There is a grisly irony in the fact that for a time, Mary, Queen of Scots
was in possession of her head, to help her safely through childbirth. After it fell into the
hands of the Jesuits it was later lost, like many other relics, during the French Revolution.*

For repressing all evil in herself, there was great gravity in her joy and something
noble in her anger. Her mirth was never expressed in immoderate laughter;
when angry she never gave way to fury. Always angry with her own faults, she
sometimes reproved those of others with that commendable anger tempered
with justice which the Psalmist enjoined, when he says, 'Be angry and sin not.'

'O my children,' she would say, 'fear the Lord; for they that fear Him shall
not want anything that is good; and if you love Him, He will give you, my
darlings, prosperity in this life and eternal felicity with all the saints.'

On Maundy Thursday and at High Mass [her husband Malcolm] used to
make an offering of gold coins, and some of these she would often piously
steal and give away to the beggar who was importuning her for alms. Often
indeed the King, who was quite aware of what she was doing, though he
pretended not to know anything about it, was greatly amused at this kind of
theft, and sometimes, when he caught her in the act with the coins in her
hand, would jocularly threaten to have her arrested, tried and condemned.

[During her all-night devotions] nine orphan little children, who were utterly
destitute, she caused to be brought in to her at the first hour of the day in order
that she might feed them. For she ordered soft food, such as little children delight
in, to be prepared for them daily; and when the little ones were brought to her,
she did not think it beneath her to take them on her knee and make little sups for
them, and to place them in their mouths with the spoons she herself used.

While this was going on, it was the custom to bring three hundred poor
people into the hall, and when they had been seated round it in order, the
King and Queen came in, and the doors were shut by the servants, for with
the exception of the chaplains, certain religious, and a few attendants, no
one was permitted to witness their alms-givings. The King on the one side,
and the Queen on the other, waited upon Christ in the person of His
poor, and with great devotion served them with food and drink.

MATILDA RELUCTANTLY WEARS THE VEIL

Edmer, 1100

Princess Matilda, originally christened Edith by her parents Queen Margaret and Malcolm III, caused controversy when she agreed to marry Henry I, King of England. She had been raised by nuns in English monasteries, and took to wearing a veil because she did not want to accept any of the men her father suggested as husbands. The ploy was almost her undoing. This extract comes from the disingenuous testimony she gave to Anselm, the Archbishop of Canterbury, to prove that she had never taken her vows. Only when that fact was established could she legitimately wed.

'But yet,' said she, 'I do not deny that I have worn the veil. For, when I was a girl, and trembled under the rod of my aunt Christina, whom thou knowest well, she, in order to save my body from the raging lust of the Normans, – who lurked at that time in wait for every one's shame, – used to put a black hood over my head; and if I threw it off, used often to torture as well as dishonour me with cruel lashings and with too revolting taunts.

'And although I endured this hood in her presence, moaning and trembling, yet so soon as I could withdraw from her sight I was wont to seize it, fling it to the ground, and trample on it with my feet, and thus, though foolishly, to rage in the hatred with which I burned against it.

'In this way and no other, my conscience to witness, was I veiled. Yet if any say that I was consecrated, the truth about that too may be gathered from this, that (as many still surviving knew) my father's anger was kindled when he chanced to see me veiled, although in such manner as I have said: he lifted his hand and caught the veil, rent it in pieces, and called down God's hatred upon the one who put it upon me, asserting that he would rather have destined me to be earl Alan's wife [possibly Alan Rufus or Alan the Black] than to consort with nuns.'

A HOUSE FULL OF LEPERS

Aelred of Rievaulx, 1100

For all her loathing of the veil, it seems her mother's selfless behaviour remained a powerful influence on Matilda.

One deed of hers I shall relate, which I have heard from the mouth of the oft-to-be-mentioned and never-to-be forgotten king David.

'While I served,' said he, 'as a youth in the king's court, doing on a certain night I know not what in my dwelling with my friends, I was called by her and came to the queen's chamber. And behold the house was full of lepers, and the queen stood in the midst; and after laying aside her cloak, and putting on a linen covering, she poured water into a basin, and began to wash and to dry their feet; and after drying them to press them with both hands, and to kiss them.

'And when I said to her, "What dost thou, O my lady? Truly if the King knew this, he would never deign to kiss with his lips thy mouth, polluted with the corruption of lepers' feet."

'Then she said smiling, "Who knows not that the feet of the eternal King are to be preferred to a mortal king's lips? – I indeed have called thee, dearest brother, that thou mayst learn from my example to perform such things; take therefore the basin, and do as thou seest me do."

'At this word I was great afraid, and replied that in no wise could I endure it. So she persisted in her task, and I, guilty one, laughing returned to my friends.'

A MUCH-MALIGNED WIFE

William of Malmesbury, 1107

This short note seems to conceal a wealth of misery on both sides of an expedient marriage. It took place when, after the death of King Edgar, his brother Alexander succeeded to the throne. Henry I of England, keen to maintain good relations with his neighbour, used one of his many illegitimate children, Sybilla of Normandy, as a diplomatic pawn. However, Malmesbury appears to have been either misinformed or merely reflecting his own opinion of the queen, as all other accounts suggest the pair were happily married.

When Edgar succumbed to his destined fate, Henry allied to himself his successor, Alexander, giving him his illegitimate daughter in marriage. Of her while she lived [Alexander] had no offspring, so far as I know; and when she died before him, he grieved not much for her. For the woman lacked (so it is said) what might have been desired of her, either in modesty of manners or in refinement of person.

❦

A NURSEMAID WITNESSES HORROR

Orderic Vital, c. 1115

At the time of this grisly story, David, youngest son of Margaret and Malcolm III, and future King of Scotland, was Prince of the Cumbrians. Around the year 1113 he married Maud, Countess of Huntingdon.

Now his first-born offspring, of male sex, was cruelly slain by a certain miserable cleric, who for an unheard-of crime which he had committed among the Norwegians had been punished by the loss of his eyes and the cutting off of feet and hands. For there, after receiving the sacraments, when the people had retired, he struck a certain priest while he celebrated mass a strong blow with a great knife in the abdomen; and horribly scattering his intestines, sacrificed him upon the altar.

He was afterwards received by Earl David in England, for the love of God, and sufficiently sustained in food and clothing, along with a child, his daughter: and as if wishing to caress the two-year-old son of his benefactor, he cruelly thrust him with the iron fingers he used, being maimed; and thus, by instigation of the devil, without warning scattered the entrails of the suckling between the hands of his nurse. And thus was done to death the eldest child of David.

Therefore [the cleric] was bound to the tails of four wild horses and when they pulled vigorously in different directions, he was torn asunder, for the terror of miscreants.

❦

KING MALCOLM'S MOTHER GOES TOO FAR
William of Newburgh, 1153

Malcolm IV of Scotland was widely regarded as a preternaturally pious figure, despite being so young. English chronicler William of Newburgh described him hyperbolically as shining 'in the midst of a barbarous and perverse race like a heavenly star'. To his peers, apparently, he 'appeared as a monk'. This account suggests that even his mother felt he needed to gain a little worldly wisdom.

But upon the advance of youth he lacked not some who, sent by Satan, recking as nothing the loss of chastity in themselves, with wicked daring and poisonous persuasion urged him to the experience of carnal pleasure. But he, already desiring to follow the Lamb wherever he should go, had with his whole bosom inhaled the zeal for holy integrity, and knew that this treasure was to be cherished in the frail flesh as if in an earthen vessel; and at first the unbecoming persuasions of his contemporaries, and even of those whom he held in the place of masters, and then, when yet they held not their peace, so checked them with a certain authority by word and countenance that none of them henceforth dared try such things with him again.

But the enemy, urged on by jealousy, repulsed in this laid stronger snares for the godly child. He employed the mother, to insinuate to him the hidden poison as the counsel of motherly kindness; and not only to allure him by blandishments but even to instigate him by commands, urging him to be a King, not a monk; and showing that a girl's embraces best befitted his age and body. Constrained rather than conquered by his mother's import unity, he appeared to consent, not to distress his parent.

She gladly, standing by the bedside of her reclining son, placed by his side a beautiful and noble virgin, without opposition from him. When the accomplices had gone out and he had obtained solitude, fired by the flame of charity rather than of lust he rose immediately, and for the whole space of the night left the royal couch to the virgin, and slept upon the pavement [floor], covered with a cloak. Since he was found thus in the morning by the attendants, and the maiden's testimony followed, the virginity of both was declared.

When his mother afterwards employed either reproof or blandishments, by a certain authority of the constancy of his mind, he constrained her, so that she thought not to venture further in this matter.

QUEEN MARGARET'S ONGOING INFLUENCE
Roger Hoveden, 1199

More than a century after her death, and long before her official canonisation, the influence of Queen Margaret lived on.

In the same year, when William King of Scots, was in the purpose of coming into England with an army, he went to the tomb (which is at Dunfermline) of St Margaret, formerly queen of the Scots, and passed the night there. And being warned in his dreams by a divine oracle not to invade England with an army, he allowed his army to return home.

A QUEEN RUNS FOR HOME
Flores Historiarum, *13 February 1261*

The Queen Margaret referred to here was the daughter of Henry III, and the wife of Alexander III who, after her death in 1275, was notorious for his womanising. In an era when childbirth was a daunting and often fatal ordeal, who can blame her for wanting the comfort of home and the presence of her mother, Eleanor of Provence, as she prepared to have her first child?

During the same days Queen Margaret of Scotland bore her firstborn daughter in the castle of Windsor, where she had made a prolonged stay with her mother.

And learning this the Scots took it very ill that their queen should have been delivered outside of her own realm; for they had been altogether ignorant when she departed that she was so near to her confinement. For she had carefully hidden this from them and from the king, that thus regaining her native soil she might the more gladly fulfil the desire of child-birth.

RULES FOR ALE WOMEN

Leges Quatuor Burgorum, 13th century

Although the ordinary classes of women did not hold positions of public authority, they played a part in the running of towns and villages, providing some of the day-to-day necessities. Since ale was generally drunk in preference to water, being much cleaner and safer than water from town wells and streams, ale women were important figures. Regulation of the trade was strict, as the following edict shows. An ale-wand was the piece of peeled willow branch that hung outside the premises indicating that ale was sold within.

Quhat woman that wil brew ale to sell sal brew al the yeir throw eftir the custom of the toun, and gif scho dois nocht, scho sal be suspendit of hir office be the space of a yeir and a day. And scho sal maik guid ale and dois agane the custom of the toun and convikkit of it, scho sal gif til her merciment [fine] viii s. or than thole the law of the toun, that is to say, be put on the kuk-stule [ducking stool], and the ale sal be gevin to the puir folk the twa part and the thrid part send to the brethir of the hospital . . . And ilk browstar sal put hir ale-wand outwith hir hous at hir window or abune hir door, that it may be seeabil comounlie til all men, the quhilk [which] gif scho dois nocht, scho sal pay for hir defalt iiid.

THE MAID OF NORWAY'S FATE IS FEARED

Bishop William Fraser, 7 October 1290

The succession to the throne was a thorny issue since Alexander III died suddenly with no surviving children, in a fall from his horse. His eldest child, Margaret, had married the King of Norway and her three-year-old daughter, also Margaret, had been confirmed as his heir. Not all agreed, however, and long before the maid set out for Scotland, Robert the Bruce and John de Balliol were staking claims for the Crown. When Bishop William Fraser wrote this letter to Edward I, who was acting as broker between all these factions, his anxiety was palpable. Unknown to him, the (by then) seven-year-old Maid of Norway was already dead. His worries were well founded. Her arrival ought to have signalled the start of a new era of union with (and possible submission to) England, because it had been agreed that she would marry Edward I's son and heir, Edward of Caernarfon. Instead, news of her demise thwarted Edward's hopes and triggered the Wars of Independence, in which Robert the Bruce eventually prevailed. Years after the Maid of Norway's death, a woman arrived at the Norwegian court claiming to be the long-lost princess. Demonstrably a fraud, she was burned at the stake. At the point at which the bishop writes, however, there is still hope that she has survived.

Your ambassadors and we set ourselves to hasten our steps towards the parts of Orkney to confer with the ambassadors of Norway for receiving our Lady the Queen, and for this we had prepared our journey. But there sounded through the people a sorrowful rumour that our said Lady should be dead, on which account the kingdom of Scotland is disturbed and the community distracted. And the said rumour being heard and published, Sir Robert de Brus, who before did not intend to come to the foresaid meeting, came with a great following to confer with some who were there. But what he intends to do or how to act, as yet we know not. But the Earls of Mar and Atholl are already collecting their army; and some other nobles of the land join themselves to their party and on that account there is fear of a general war and a great slaughter of men, unless the Highest, by means of your industry and good service, apply a speedy remedy.

My Lords the Bishop of Durham, Earl Warenne and I heard afterwards that our foresaid Lady recovered of her sickness, but she is still weak; and therefore we have agreed amongst ourselves to remain about Perth, until we have certain news by the knights who are sent to Orkney, what is the condition of our Lady – would that it may be prosperous and happy; and if we shall have the accounts which we wish concerning her and which we await from day to day, we will be ready to set forth for those parts, as is ordained, for carrying out the business committed to us to the best of our power. If Sir John de Balliol comes to your presence we advise you to take care so to treat with him that in any event your honour and advantage be preserved. If it turn out that our foresaid Lady has departed this life (may it not be so), let your excellency deign if you please to approach towards the March [the border], for the consolation of the Scottish people and for saving the shedding of blood, so that the faithful men of the kingdom may keep their oath inviolate, and set over them for King him who of right ought to have the succession, if so be that he will follow your counsel. May your excellency have long life and health, prosperity and happiness.

Given at Leuchars on Saturday the morrow of Saint Faith the Virgin, in the year of our Lord 1290.

WARRANT FOR THE COUNTESS
OF BUCHAN'S CAPTURE

1306

Isabella MacDuff, Countess of Buchan, was Robert the Bruce's second cousin. Her husband John Comyn reviled Bruce for murdering his cousin, Red Comyn, in 1306, and switched sides to the English. The countess remained loyal and was determined to be present at Bruce's coronation at Scone, on 25 March, at which by hereditary right she was to place the crown on his head. In carrying out her clan duties (albeit a day late), she infuriated her husband, who had to be restrained from killing her by King Edward I. He, instead, wished her to be imprisoned in public in a cage, as 'a spectacle and eternal reproach'. She endured this punishment for four years, before being relocated to better quarters but it is presumed she died while still in captivity. Other women supporters of Bruce suffered appalling reprisals for their allegiance.

It is ordained and commanded, by letters under the Privy Seal, to the Chamberlain of Scotland or to his Lieutenant at Berwick on Tweed, that in one of the turrets within the Castle in the same place, in the place where it seems to him most suitable, he shall make a cage of strong lattice, of fuist and bars, well strengthened with iron, in the which he shall put the Countess of Buchan.

And that he cause her to be so well and surely guarded in that cage that she cannot get out. And that he appoint one woman, or two, of the said city of Berwick, English, who shall be free of suspicion, to serve the said Countess with food and drink and other things which are needful in that dwelling.

And that he has her so well and straitlay guarded in that cage that she speak to no one, neither man nor woman, who is of the Scottish nation, nor to any other, nor shall they have access to here save only the woman or women assigned to her, and those who guard her.

And that the cage shall so be made that the said Countess shall have the concession of a privy, but that this shall be so well and firmly constructed that it shall cause no danger in the matter of guarding the said Countess.

And that he who shall have her in keeping be charged to answer for it, body for body, and that he shall have an allowance for expenses.

In the same manner it is ordered that Mary, sister of Robert Bruce, formerly Earl of Carrick, shall be sent to Roxburgh, to keep there in the castle in a cage. Also Marjorie, the daughter of Robert Bruce, shall be delivered in Messire

Henry de Percy, to put her in England in safe-keeping, and also Christina, the sister of the said Robert Bruce, who was the wife of Christopher de Seton, to be put in guard in England in the same manner.

WEDDING LIST

Exchequer Rolls of Scotland, 17 July 1328

This inventory from the marriage of David II and Johanna of England, at Berwick-upon-Tweed, offers a fascinating glimpse of luxury in a hardscrabble age. As well as revealing the habits of high society it also marks an attempt by Robert the Bruce to make peace with England after Edward II's death the year before. David was Bruce's four-year-old son, and Johanna the seven-year-old sister of the newly crowned Edward III. This rare period of tranquillity was short-lived. On Robert the Bruce's death the following year, conflict once more resumed.

Item, to buying 23 pieces of coloured cloth, and 23 pieces of striped cloth, for the robes of the knights at the wedding at Berwick, £173 9s 2d. And for 20 pieces of cloth for the squires, and 16 pieces for the sergeands, £90. And for 41 surcoats of miniver, £63 10s 6d. And for 24 surcoats of vair, £22 16s. And for 73 surcoats of strandling, and 7 surcoats of squirrel, and 100 hoods of miniver, £64 5s 6d. And for 100 surcoats of budge, 40 hoods of budge, £17 10s. And for 4,200 ells of canvas, 1,270 ells of linen, 345 ells of napery, 687 ells of towelling, £108 14s 7d. And for 4,360 pounds of almonds, 600 pounds of rice, 40 loaves of sugar, weighing 378 pounds, £53 18s. And for 180 pounds of pepper, 55 pounds of mace, 27 pounds of cloves, 10 pounds of nutmegs, 5 pounds of grain of Paradise, 3 pounds of cicovalens, £36 5s 2d. And for 2 pounds of spikenard, 8 pounds of colouring for the food, 74 pounds of cinnamon, 55 pounds of galingale, 43 pounds of saffron, 70 pounds of cooking-sugar in barrels, 70 pounds of cummin, 1 bale of ginger weighing 180 pounds, 1 pound of dragées, 204 pounds of sweets, 41 pounds of special sweets, £53 9s 7d.

And for 13 pieces of wax, weighing two hundred stones, £51 13s 6d. And for twenty casks of wine, £75. And for 1 cask of vinegar, 2 pipes of verjuice, 2 pipes of olive oil, 1 pipe of honey, 2 barrels of mustard, 7 barrels of eels, containing 2,200, two casks of white fish, £24 15s 6d. And for three large cooking pans, seven large ladles, four large copper baking tins, with the necessary chains, and three large gridirons, for all of which [the Chamberlain] must otherwise account, £20 2s. And to Peter 'of the machines' for buying and bringing over these things from Flanders to Scotland, under contract made with him at the rate of two shillings in the pound, £85 11s.

Total of all this, £941 6d.

A MOTHER'S IMPOSSIBLE CHOICE
John Major, July 1333

When Edward I laid siege to Berwick, hostages were taken to make sure the town kept its promise of surrendering if they were not relieved by the Scots by 19 July. One hostage was Thomas Setoun, son of Berwick's governor. Somehow the Scots managed to get supplies through the cordon, and Governor Setoun therefore insisted the terms of the deal remained intact. But the English saw it otherwise.

Whereupon the enemy hanged Thomas Seton, their hostage, on a high gallows in the sight of his parents, believing that by the death of their son and heir, his parents, especially his loving mother, would be brought to surrender the town at once to the English. But this high-hearted woman ranked the town and her country's freedom above her son's life.

BLACK AGNES DEFEATS THE ENGLISH
Liber Pluscardensis, *1338*

On 13 January 1338, Agnes, Duchess of Dunbar and March, was alone in Dunbar castle with her servants and guards when the English attacked. This raid, under the command of William Montagu, the 1st Earl of Salisbury, was intended to help wrest the throne from David Bruce on behalf of Edward Balliol. Instead they were thwarted by a woman who appears to have had no fear. With her husband away fighting in the Scottish army, she withstood siege for five months, using her wits to bamboozle the enemy. At one point legend has it that the English troops produced Agnes's brother with a noose around his neck. Go ahead, she said, telling them if they carried out their threat she would then inherit the earldom of Moray. Known as Black Agnes because of her dark hair and complexion, she is an inspiration and not just to those of us raised in Dunbar. Some even say they have seen her walking the castle ruins — although this part of town does have an abundance of pubs.

On the 13th [January], the castle of Dunbar was besieged by Sir William Montagu, Earl of Salisbury, and by the Earl of Arundel, leaders of the army of the King of England: for half a year they were there, assailing that castle with divers engines, but they could do nothing against it. Nor was any other captain in command there but the Countess of March, commonly called Black Annes [Agnes] of Dunbar, who defended the besieged castle most laudably: who also was most wise, diligent, and cautious. She herself, in mockery of the English, would in the sight of all dust with a fair cloth the place where a stone from their engines had struck the ramparts.

The King of England, hearing that they gained little there, sent a strong force to their aid, but the column was broken up, put to flight, and destroyed by Sir Laurence Preston, who however was himself wounded in the mouth by a spear, and died on the field, his men not knowing of it.

After this, the Earl of Salisbury, who took very ill the severe defeats inflicted by the Scots lords on the English troops who were coming to his aid, and wishing to attack the said castle more powerfully, had constructed a certain engine called a Sow, and brought it up to the walls of Dunbar Castle. Which, when Black Annes saw, she said to the Earl Montagu, 'Montagu, for all the power that thou may, ere long time pass, I shall gar thy Sow farrow against her will.' And with that she made a very large engine in the Castle, flinging huge stones, which flying night and day from the walls, shattered the said Sow and almost all who were within it, broke the heads of many, and forced them altogether to give up the attack: and she captured and brought into the Castle all their siege gear with their engines and provision.

Now the Earl of Salisbury had two armed galleys guarding the harbour of the sea to those within. But a noble and valiant man, Alexander de Ramsay, venturing one dark night to the fortress of the Bass [the Bass Rock], unseen by the galleys, brought back a supply of provisions from that place. For which thing he deserved both praise and reward, for on his return he overpowered and slew many of the foreigners who were watching and listening before the Castle.

On the next day, Black Annes ordered to be presented to the said Earl, who was sore pressed for victual, a great abundance of bread of fine wheat flour and noble wine. Which when the Earl saw, he despaired of taking the Castle: so, treating by a third person with a certain porter of the Castle, he agreed with him, for a great sum of gold, to open to him, under cover of night, one of the secret posterns of the Castle, so that he might enter with his men. With the consent of the Countess, who feigned not to know of it, this was arranged, and one night (when one part of the gold had been received) the said postern gate was opened, as had been promised. Into which when the Earl moved to enter, one of his followers, named Coupland, suspecting a plot, suddenly dragged back the said Earl from the doorway, and by the violent movement found himself inside the door, which was closed at once by the falling of that sliding door which in French is called portculisse. So the Earl escaped, and Coupland was taken, and Black Annes, standing on the wall, called out to him mockingly, 'Adieu, adieu, Monsieur Montagu!'

After all this, news came from the King of England that the mortal war between him and the King of France had been revived and so, on the sixteenth day of June, having seen the letters bidding him leave all and return to England, he withdrew without ceremony, taking no leave of his hostess.

MURDER OF JAMES I

(?) One of Queen Joan's ladies-in-waiting, 20 February 1427

James I, second son of Robert III, was imprisoned for eighteen years in the Tower of London by Henry IV, although by the final years of his captivity he was treated more like a guest than a hostage. When, in 1424 at the age of twenty-nine, he was released, he returned to Scotland with his wife Joan Beaufort and began to impose his authority on the over-powerful nobility. Executing rivals and forfeiting their lands made him serious enemies, and his murder was carried out by his uncle, Walter Stewart, the Earl of Atholl — who believed he had a right to the throne — and Sir Robert Graham, with the assistance of Robert Stewart, the king's chamberlain (who was Atholl's grandson). A talented musician and writer, James appears to have allowed his love of the arts to impair his judgement on the evening of his death, when he neglected to give a hearing to a woman reputedly with second sight. James's killers came for him when he was staying at Blackfriars, the royal lodging in Perth. This account is a trans- lation by the scribe John Shirley of the original Latin version, which was probably given, in part at least, by one of the queen's companions. She may have been Katharine Douglas, who tried to prevent the traitors breaking in by barring a door with her arm, which was shattered as a result. Afterwards, Queen Joan was utterly savage in dealing with the murderers.

So both after supper and long into quarter of the night, in the which the Earl of Athol and Robert Stewart were about the King, where they were occupied at the playing of the chess, at the tables, in reading of romances, in singing and piping, in harping, and in other honest solaces of great pleasure and disport. Therewith came [a] woman of Ireland that cleped [called] herself a divineress, and entered the King's court till she came straight to the King's chamber door she knocked till at last the usher opened the door, marvelling of the woman's being there that time of the night, and asking her what she would. 'Let me in, sir,' quoth she, 'for I have something to say and tell unto the King, for I am the same woman that not long agone desired to have speech with him at the Leith when he should pass the Scottish Sea.' The usher went in and told him of the woman. 'Yea,' quoth the King, 'let her come tomorrow.'

The usher came again to the chamber door to the said woman, and there he told her that the King was busy in playing, and bid her come again upon the morrow. 'Well,' said the woman, 'it shall repent you all that ye will not let me speak now with the King.' Thereat the usher laughed and held her a fool, charging her to go her way.

Within an hour the King asked for the voidee [parting cup] and drank and every man departed and went to rest. Then Robert Stewart that was right familiar with the King and had all his commandments in the chamber, was the last that departed: and he knew well the false purveyed treason and was consented thereto, and therefore left the King's chamber door open, and had bruised and blundered the locks of them in such wise that no man might shut them. And about midnight he laid certain planks and hurdles over the ditches of the ditch that environed the garden of the chamber, upon which the said traitors entered. That is to say Sir Robert Graham, with other of his coven unto the number of three hundred persons: the King that same time standing in his nightgown [dressing gown], all unclothed save his shirt, his cap, his comb, his kerchief, his furred pinsons [slippers], upon the form and the foot-sheet [the cloth on which he stood to undress], so standing afore the chimney, playing with the Queen and other ladies and gentlewomen with her, cast off his nightgown for to have gone to bed. But he harkened and heard great noise without and great clattering of harness, and men armed, with great sight of torches. Then he remembered him, and imagined anon that it should be the false traitorous knight, his deadly enemy, Sir Robert Graham: and suddenly the Queen, with all the other ladies and gentlewomen, ran to the chamber door and found it open; and they would have shut it but the locks were so blundered that they neither could nor might shut it. The King prayed them to keep the said door as well as they might, and he would do all his might to keep him to withstand the false malice of his traitors and enemies, he supposing to have brasten [broken] the farments of the chamber windows, but they were so square and so strongly soldered in the stones with molten lead that they might not be brasten for him without more and stronger help. For the which cause he was ugly astonished and in his mind could think on no other succour but start to the chimney and take the tongs of iron that men righted the fire with in time of need, and under his feet he mightily brast up a plank of the chamber floor and therewithal covered him again and entered low down among the ordure of the privy, that was all of hard stone and none window nor issue thereupon save a little square hole even at the side of the bottom of the privy, that at the making thereof of old time was left open to cleanse and ferme the said privy, by the which the King might well have escaped, but he made to let stop it well three days afore, hard with stone, because that when he played there at the paume [indoor tennis played with the palm] the balls that he played with oft ran in at that foul hole.

And so there was for the King no rescue nor remedy, but there he must abide, alas the while! The traitors without laid at the chamber doors with crows, with levers, and with axes, that at the last they brake up all and entered, because the door was not fast shut, with swords, axes, glaives, bills, and other terrible and fearful weapons. Among the great press of which traitors there was a fair lady sore hurt in the back, and other gentlewomen hurt and sore wounded. With the which the ladies and all the women made a sorrowful skyre [scream] and ran away for the hideous fear of those boistous [*sic*] and merciless men of arms. The traitors furiously passed forth into the chamber, and found the Queen so dismayed and abashed of that horrible and fearful governance that she could neither speak nor withdraw her; and as she stood there sore astonished, like a creature that had lost her kindly reason, one of the traitors wounded her villainously and would have slain her, ne had not been one of Sir Robert Graham's sons, that thus spake to him and said, 'What will ye do, for shame of yourself, to the Queen? She is but a woman. Let us go and fetch the King.' And then, not witting well what she did or should do for that fearful and terrible affray, fled in her kirtle, her mantle hanging about her; the other ladies in a corner of the chamber crying and weeping all distrait, made a piteous and lamentable noise.

And there the traitors sought the King in all the chamber about, in the withdrawing chambers, in the litters, and under the presses, the forms, the chairs, and all other places; but long they busily sought the King, but they could not find him, for they neither knew nor remembered the privy. The King, hearing of long time no noise nor stirring of the traitors, weened and deemed that they had all been gone, and cried to the women that they should come with sheets and draw him up out of that unclean place of the privy. The women at his calling came fast to the privy door that was not shut, and so they opened it with labour, and as they were aboutward to help up the King, one of the ladies, called Elizabeth Douglas, fell into the privy to the King. Therewith, one of the false traitors, called Robert Chambers, supposed verily since they could not find in none of the said chambers the King, that he had of necessity hidden him in the privy: and therefore he said to his fellows, 'Sirs,' quoth he, 'whereto stand we thus idle and lose our time, as for the cause that we be come for hither. Come on forth with me, and I shall readily tell you where the King is.' For this same Thomas [*sic*] Chambers had been afore right familiar with the King, and therefore he knew all the privy corners of these chambers; and so he went forth straight to the same privy where the King was, and perceived and saw how a plank of the floor was broken up, and lift it up with a torch and looked in, and saw the King there and a woman with him. Saying to his fellows, 'Sirs, the spouse is found wherefore we be come and all this night have carolled here.' Therewithal, one of the said tyrants and traitors, cleped [called] Sir John Hall, descended down to the King, with a great knife in his hand, and the King, doubting him sore of his life, caught him mightily by the shoulders and with full great violence cast him under his feet, for the King was of his person and nature right manly strong. And seeing another of that Hall's brothers that the King had the better of him, went down also for to destroy the King: and anon as he was there descended, the King caught him manly by the neck and cast him above that other and so he defouled them both under him that all a long month after men might see how strongly the King had holden them by the throats, and greatly the King struggled with them for to have bereaved them of their knives, by the which labour his hands were all for-cut. But an the King had been in any wise armed, he might well have escaped this matter, by the length of his fighting with those two false traitors: for if the King might any while longer have saved himself, his servants and much other people of the town by some fortune should have had some knowledge therefor, and so have come to his succour with help. But alas the while, it will not be.

Therewithal that odious and false traitor Sir Robert Graham, seeing the King laboured so sore with those two false traitors which he had cast under his feet, and that he waxed faint and was weary, and that he was weaponless, the more pity was, descended down also unto the King, with an horrible and mortal weapon in his hand. And then the King cried him mercy. 'Thou cruel tyrant,' quoth Graham to him. 'Thou hadst never mercy of lords born of thy blood, ne of none other gentlemen that came in thy danger, therefore no mercy shalt thou have here.' Then said the King, 'I beseech thee that for the salvation of my soul, ye will let me have a confessor.' Quoth the said Graham, 'Thou shalt never have other confessor but this same sword.' And therewithal he smote him through the body, and therewithal the good King fell down. And then the said Graham, seeing his King and sovereign lord infortuned with so much disease, anguish, and sorrow, would have so left, and done him no more harm. The other traitors above, perceiving this, said unto Sir Robert, 'We behote thee faithfully, but if thou slay him or thou depart, thou shalt die for him on our hands doubtless.' And then the same Sir Robert, with the other two that descended first down, fell upon that noble prince, and in full horrible and cruel wise they murdered him. Alas for sorrow that so immeasurably cruelty and vengeance should be done to that worthy prince, for it was reported by true persons that saw him dead, that he had sixteen deadly wounds in his breast, without many another in divers places of his body.

BOLD WOMEN

Don Pedro de Ayala, 1498

Spain's diplomat at the court of James IV was a sharp observer, but generous in spirit. His comment on the boldness of women is echoed in many foreign travellers' notes.

The women are courteous in the extreme. I mention this because they are really honest, though very bold. They are absolute mistresses of their houses, and even of their husbands, in all things concerning the administration of their property, income as well as expenditure. They are very graceful and handsome women. They dress much better than here [England], and especially as regards the head-dress, which is, I think, the handsomest in the world.

ROYAL WEDDING

John Young, 8 August 1503

Henry VIII's sister Margaret Tudor was only thirteen when she arrived in Edinburgh to marry James IV. It was a strategically astute union, allowing both sides to think they had secured the better deal. Margaret's father, Henry VII, foresaw his son taking both crowns, while the Scots viewed the alliance as a way potentially of securing a claim for the Stuart dynasty upon the English throne. It is said that when first shown a portrait of her future husband Margaret was not impressed, and that when they met, she insisted he shave off his mossy beard. This report was written by the Somerset herald, John Young, who travelled with the princess's retinue on its glittering procession north. This set out on 8 July, and only reached Scotland, at Lambertonkirk, on 1 August, one week before the nuptials. Young recounts the day when finally Margaret reached Edinburgh, carried on a litter.

Half of the way the King came to meet her, mounted upon a bay horse, running as he would run after a hare, accompanied of many gentlemen. The said horse was trapped in a demi-trapping of cloth of gold. Upon the neck was a fringe of thread of gold. The saddle and the harness were of that same, except the harness of the head, which was of silver and gilt. Great buttons with loops of thread of gold as well to the said trappings to the bridle. His stirrups gilt. The King wore a jacket like to the trapping. The lists of the said border were of purple velvet furred with fine black budge, his doublet of violet satin, his hose of scarlet, his shirt bound about of fine pierrery and pearls, his spurs gilt and long. At the coming of the Queen he made her very humble obeisance in leaping down off his horse and kissed her in her litter. This done, he mounted again, and each one being put in order as before, a gentleman usher bore the Sword before him. The said sword covered with a scabbard of purple velvet, which was written upon with pearls, *God me Defend*. The like on the pommel and the cross and the chape also.

After him came the Archbishop of Glasgow, the Bishop of Moray, and the Earl Bothwell, accompanied of many gentlemen that brought him a courser, his harness of cloth of gold and of crimson velvet furred with marten. The King being always nigh to the Queen in devising with her, there came a gentleman that brought him a courser, his harness of cloth of gold and of crimson velvet interlaced all about of white and red. Upon the horse was a page in a jacket of blue damask, upon the which horse the King mounted without putting his foot with the stirrup, in the presence of them all. After, he caused the said gentleman to mount behind him, for to assay if his courser would bear behind or not.

But because that he was not dressed he came down off the said horse and punted upon the palfrey [horse] of the said Queen, and the said Queen behind him, and so rode through the said town of Edinburgh.

Nigh thereby was in order the Lord Hamilton, cousin of the said King, with many other lords, knights, and gentlemen to the number of two hundred horses well appointed. Some in jackets of cloth of gold, or velvet, and of damask figured with gold and of many colours. In likewise others were in jackets of camlet [silk and camel hair] and many of them wore very good chains.

And by him rode the Master of his Horse, named Companes Gascon, very well appointed, conveying five young gentlemen of honour, all arrayed in jackets half parted of cloth of gold figured and of blue velvet, mounted upon coursers, and others honestly appointed.

In the midst of the town was a cross, new painted, and nigh to that same was a fountain, casting forth of wine, and each one drank who would. The town of Edinburgh was in many places hanged with tapestry, the houses and windows were full of lords, ladies, gentlemen and gentlewomen, and in the streets were so great a multitude of people without number that it was a fair thing to see . . . and in the churches of the said town, bells rang for mirth.

A LONELY BRIDE WRITES TO HER FATHER
Margaret Tudor, 1503

The early months of Margaret's marriage to James IV were not easy, as her older husband appeared to prefer the company of associates such as Thomas Howard, the Earl of Surrey. Ten years later, this seasoned soldier and politician was to lead the English army to victory at the Battle of Flodden, where James met his end. If Margaret's father, Henry VII, replied to this complaining letter, it would not have been to offer sympathy but to remind her of her role as Queen Consort and prime ally of the English court.

Sir, as for news I have none to send, but that my lord of Surrey is in great favour with the King here, that he cannot forbear the company of him no time of the day. He and the Bishop of Moray ordereth everything as nigh as they can to the King's pleasure: I pray God it may be for my hearts's ease in time to come. They call not my chamberlain to them which I am sure will speak better for my part than any of them that be of that counsel. And if he speak anything for my cause, my Lord of Surrey hath such words unto him that he dare speak no further. God send me comfort to his pleasure, and that I and mine that be left here with me be well entreated, such ways as they have taken. For God's sake, sir, hold me excused that I write not myself to your grace, for I have no leisure this time, but with a wish I would I were with your grace, now, and many times more, when I would answer. As for this that I have written to your grace, it is very true, but I pray God I may find it well for my welfare hereafter. No more to your grace at this time, but our Lord have you in his keeping. Written with the hand of your humble daughter, –

Margaret

🌿

AFTER FLODDEN

Proclamation by town council of Edinburgh, 10 September 1513

The Battle of Flodden was a calamity for the country in every respect. With an esti-mated 10,000 men dead, including James IV and his son Alexander, women had to step into their shoes, from the dowager queen to the widow of the customs and excise officer in Edinburgh, not to mention the countless ordinary roles of farming, fishing and building. This proclamation by the town council was written the day after the battle, before the full extent of the disaster was known. Its view of what women are capable of is not flattering.

The X day of September, we do you to wit, for as Miele as thair is and greit rumour now laitlie risen within the toun, touching our Soverane Lord and his army, of the quhilk we understand that thair is cumin na veritie as yit, quhair-foir we chairge straitlie and commandis, in our Soverane Lordis name and the Presidentis, for the Provost and Bailzeis within thus Burgh, that all maneir of persounis, nybouris within the samyn, haif readie thair fensabill geir and wapponis for weir, and compeir thairwith to the said Presidentis at jowing of the comoun bell, for the keiping and defens of the toun against thaim that wald invaid the samyn.

And also chairgis that all wemen and speciallie vagaboundis that they pass to thair labouris, and be nat sein upoun the gait clamourand and cryand, under the pain of banisching of thair persounis but favouris: and that the third, wemen of guid, pass to the Kirk and pray, quhen tyme requiris, for our Soverane Lord and his army, and nybouris being thairat.

🌿

DOWAGER QUEEN STANDS HER GROUND

Letter to Lord Dacre, 1515

*Margaret Tudor became Regent of Scotland after her husband James IV's death at
Flodden, as he had decreed. When she remarried, Parliament – which had never liked
the idea of a female regent – immediately revoked her role and insisted she hand over
the young King James V, who was three, and his infant brother. It was the start of an
acrimonious and worrying time for the dowager queen, seeing her in midnight flight to
England to protect herself, her children and her soon-to-be-born daughter. Lord Thomas
Dacre, Warden General of the English Marches and the man to whose house she fled,
was a long-standing friend of Margaret as well as James, despite being on the enemy
side. One of his associates wrote to him, describing the scene below as it unfolded at
Stirling Castle.*

And when she saw the lords within three yards of the gates, she bade them
stand, and demanded the cause of their coming. They told her they had
come from the Duke and Parliament to demand 'deliverance of the King and
his brother'.

   Without hesitation, she defied them: And then she caused the portcullis
be letten down, and made answer, saying that the castle was her own feoff-
ment, given to her by the King her late husband and that her said late husband
had made her protectrix, and given her authority to have the keeping and
government of her said children, wherefore she could in no wise deliver
them to any person.

A PRIORESS'S DOUBLE LIFE

Marquis of Dorset, April 1524

Muriel Spark's novel, The Abbess of Crewe, *was a political satire on Watergate. Her
vision of a convent filled with secret recording machines might seem far-fetched, but as
this letter to Henry VIII from the English warden of the East and Middle Marches
suggests, espionage flourished within ecclesiastical walls. In the same year as this report,
another spy, the prioress at nearby Eccles, succeeded in wrecking the Scottish Regent's
plans for an expedition against England. The question this request raises is whether the*

Coldstream prioress got her intelligence from Margaret Tudor and, were that so, was it given unwittingly or in full knowledge of how it would be used?

Please it your most noble Grace to be advertised that of late the Queen's Grace of Scotland your sister wrote her especial letters of request as well unto my lord your Lieutenant as to me, to forbear and save from burning a poor religious house of nuns called Coldstream, the Prioress whereof Her Grace reporteth to be very good and kind unto her. Whereupon both my Lord Lieutenant and I have granted her request, and have so written unto her Grace accordingly. Another cause which moved us the sooner to assure the said house, was by cause the Prioress thereof is one of the best and assured spies we have in Scotland, for which cause we may not spare her.

MARY OF GUISE IS MOCKED

John Knox, 1554

When Mary of Guise, mother of Mary, Queen of Scots, was appointed Regent while her daughter was raised in safety at the French court, she met the same resistance as had Margaret Tudor. Some men simply could not abide the thought of a woman in charge of the country. The incendiary preacher John Knox's remarks here are a rehearsal for his later tract, 'The First Blast of the Trumpet Against The Monstrous Regiment of Women', in which he railed against females having power, insisting it went against the Bible.

The Dowager had to practise somewhat with her brethren, the Duke of Guise and the Cardinal of Lorraine, the weight whereof the Governor after felt: for shortly after her returning, was the Governor deposed of the government, (justly by God, but most unjustly by men), and she made Regent in the year of God 1554; and a crown put upon her head, as seemly a sight (if men had eyes) as to put a saddle upon the back of an unruly cow. And so began she to practise practice upon practice how France might be advanced, her friends made rich, and she brought to immortal glory . . . And in very deed, in deep dissimulation, to bring her own purpose to effect, she passed the common sort of women.

MARY STUART'S FIRST WEDDING

(?) A Scottish student in Paris, 24 April 1558

Mary Stuart's life began inauspiciously with the death of her father when she was newly born, but by the time she married the French dauphin, when she was fifteen, her future looked bright. Although fourteen-year-old Francis was what was euphemistically called 'weak-minded', there was genuine affection between them. The following year her husband was crowned Francis II, and she became Queen Consort of France. This fragment of a poem, thought to be by a Scottish university student in Paris, captures the happy-go-lucky feel of the day's celebrations, a mood one imagines the young queen shared. On this joyful occasion no one, least of all Mary, could have foreseen the troubled years that lay ahead.

[They scattered] gold and silver amang the pepill
on every side of the scaffald within the kirke. Whar
with qui potest capere capiat was sik yalping and
yeoling, sik calling and crying as, as the like (I
think) was never hard. Ther gentillmen tint
their clokis, gentilwemen ther fartingales
merchantmen ther gownes, maisters in art ther
hudis, studentis ther cornet cappis, and religious
men had ther scapilliries violently riven fra ther
shulders. Whar also amang the rest was a stout
yong baire futed freir of Sainct Francis ordir, the
whilk freir gat mair of the cast money than four of
his cumpanions. The whilk beand demandid
wharfor he did handill money contrary to his
profession: he answerid, hola my freindis hola,
content your selves, for gife Sanct Francis him
self war heir present this day whilk was the chief of
our profession, he wald put to his hand, as I have
done, and my comions, in handling and keping this [almis] mey (therby
    mening na cuvetou) to the laude of God, and honour of maist godly
    and triumphant marriage . . .

[To see the merchantment in ther] doublettis,
gounles, maisters in art hudles, and studentis with
many uthers caples, it was a merie sport for him
that tint nathing. And thane to heir thare

lamentation, it was na les sport. Some saing, I have
tint my cloke wurth ten crownes and gat but a
teston. Ane uther sais, alace my gowne was
pluckide fra my bak wurth six crownes, and gat but
5 sous. The third sais my purs is gane and 50
crowns in it and gat nathinge. I have gotine quod
ane uther a cuppill of gud crownes of the sonne and
tint nathinge. Wharfor I heringe and seing this gud
fellowes having sike gret tinsell for gredines
in getting of few pecis of monie, and specialy him
that tine his purs and 50 crownes in it and gat
nathing: I was forced, not alanerly to say with the
poet Virgil Quid non mortalia pectora cogis, auri
sacra fames

They scattered gold and silver amongst the people
on every side of the platform within the kirk. Where
with 'who could seize, let him seize it' there was such yelping and yowling,
such calling and crying, as the like, I
think, was never heard. There gentlemen lost
their cloaks, ladies their farthingales
merchants their gowns, masters of arts their
hoods, students their cornered caps and clerics
had their scapularies violently torn from their
shoulders. Amongst the rest was a stout
young bare-footed Franciscan friar,
who got more of the 'poor-oot' than four of
his companions. Being challenged
what he was doing handling money contrary to his
profession, he answered: 'Hola, my friends, Hola!
Content yourselves, for if Saint Francis himself
were present here this day, who was the chief of
our order, he would put out his hand as I have
done and my companions in handling and keeping this alms money
　　(thereby meaning that he was not being greedy) to the praise of God
　　and Honour of this most godly and triumphant marriage . . .

To see the merchants in the doublets
without their gowns, the masters of arts hoodless, and students with
many others capless, was merry sport for him

who lost nothing. And then to hear their
lamentation, it was no less sport, some saying 'I have
lost my cloak worth ten crowns, and got only a
teston [about a shilling]. Another says alas my gown was
plucked from my back worth six crowns and I got but
five sous [roughly, pennies]. The third says my purse is gone and 50
crowns in it and I got nothing. I have gotten, said
another, a couple of good crowns of the sun and
lost nothing. Wherefore, I hearing and seeing these good
fellows having such great loss for greediness
in getting a few pieces of money, and particularly him
who lost his purse and 50 crowns in it and got
nothing: I was forced, not alone, to say with the
poet Virgil 'Accursed greed for gold, what dost thou not drive hearts of
   men to do?'

YOUNG MARY'S BEAUTY

Pierre de Brantôme, 1561

*This French soldier and historian writes glowingly of the young Mary, Queen of Scots,
and was not unusual in being struck by her looks, intellect and attainments.*

And as her fair age grew, so she was seen in her great beauty and her great
virtues, increasing in such sort that, coming to fifteen years, her beauty began to
show its fair light in the full fair noon, and darken the sun when he shone forth
most strongly, so fair was the beauty of her body. And as for that of her mind, it
was even the same, for she was very learned in Latin, which she understood and
spoke very well, and was at pains to cause Antoine Fochain, of Channay in
Vermandois, to draw up for her a Rhetoric in French, so that she should better
understand French and be more eloquent in it; as she was, and better than if she
had been born in France. So it did one good to watch her speak, whether to the
highest or the lowest. And so long as she was in France, she kept always two
hours a day to study and read. Above all she loved poetry and poets.

Always, when she spoke with anyone, she used a very gentle, dainty, and
attractive speech, mingled at times with a most discreet and modest intimacy,
and specially with a most lovely grace.

Being dressed (as I have seen her) in the barbaric fashion of her country [i.e. Highland dress], she seemed in a mortal body and a rude and barbaric dress, a true goddess. Those who have seen her so dressed can confirm it in all truth, and those who have not can have seen her portrait so attired; so that I have seen it said to the Queen mother and the King that she showed herself still in that more fair, charming, and desirable than in any other. How then would she appear in state, in her fair and rich adornments, whether in the French or the Spanish fashion, or with an Italian cap, or in her other gear of the full white mourning, in which it was most fair to see her, for the white of her face with the white of her veil which should be victor.

She had yet more, that perfection to fire the world, a voice very sweet and good, for she sang very well, according her voice with a lute, which she touched so daintily with that fair white hand.

MARY, QUEEN OF SCOTS AND HER TURBULENT CLERIC
John Knox, 1565

Recalling Mary's return to Scotland from France in 1561 after she had been widowed, John Knox described it as a day when 'the very face of heaven . . . did manifestly speak what comfort was brought unto this country with her, to wit, sorrow, dolour, darkness and all impiety'. This unpromising start set the tone for their relationship. His account of one of many uncomfortable encounters he had with her shows how severely she was aggravated by his trenchant opinions and criticisms. Knox should be the patron saint of those who dare to speak truth to power, because he felt neither fear nor awe of her position. The outburst he records was occasioned by his objection to her plan to marry Henry Stuart, Duke of Albany, otherwise known as Lord Darnley. He was right to urge a rethink, as history has shown, but one suspects that, petted and admired and spoilt as she had always been by those at her court, Mary was reluctant to heed wiser counsel, especially from one so judgemental and self-righteous. Knox, as always, writes of himself in the third person – never a good sign.

The Queen in a vehement fume began to cry out, that never Prince was used as she was. 'I have,' said she, 'borne with you in all your rigorous manner of speaking, both against myself and against my uncles; yea, I have sought your favour by all possible means; I offered unto you presence and audience, whensoever it pleased you to admonish me, and yet I cannot be quit of you; I vow to God I shall be once revenged.' And with these words scarce could Murdock, her secret chamber boy, get napkins to hold her eyes dry, for the tears and the howling, besides womanly weeping, stayed her speech. The said John did patiently abide all the first fume, and at opportunity answered, 'True it is, Madam, your Grace and I have been at divers controversies, into the which I never perceived your Grace to be offended at me; but when it shall please God to deliver you from that bondage of darkness and error, wherein ye have been nourished, for the lack of true Doctrine, your Majesty will find the liberty of my tongue nothing offensive. Without the Preaching-place, Madam, I think few have occasion to be offended at me, and there, Madam, I am not master of myself, but must obey him who commands me to speak plain, and to flatter no flesh upon the face of the earth.'

'What have you to do,' said she, 'with my marriage? Or, what are you within the Commonwealth?' 'A subject born within the same,' said he, 'Madam; and albeit I be neither Earl, Lord, nor Baron within it, yet hath God made me (how abject that ever I be in your eyes) a profitable and useful member within the same; yea, Madam, to me it appertaineth no less, to forewarn of such things as may hurt it, if I foresee them, than it doth to any one of the nobility; for both my vocation and conscience craveth plainness of me; and therefore, Madam, to yourself I say, that which I spake in public, whensoever the nobility of this realm shall be content, and consent, that you be subject to an unlawful husband, they do as much as in them lieth to renounce Christ, to banish the Truth, to betray the freedom of this realm, and perchance shall in the end do small comfort to yourself.'

At these words, howling was heard, and tears might have been seen in greater abundance than the matter required. John Erskine of Dun, a man of meek and gentle spirit, stood beside, and entreated what he could to mitigate her anger, and gave unto her many pleasant words, of her beauty, of her excellency; and how that all the princes in Europe would be glad to seek her favours. But all that was to cast oil into the flaming fire. The said John stood still, without any alteration of countenance, for a long time, while that the Queen gave place to her inordinate passion; and in the end he said, 'Madam, in God's presence I speak, I never delighted in the weeping of any of God's creatures; yea, I can scarcely well abide the tears of mine own boys, whom my own hands correct, much less can I rejoice in your Majesty's weeping; But seeing I have offered unto you no just occasion to be offended, but have spoken the truth, as my vocation craves of me, I must sustain your Majesty's tears, rather than I dare hurt my conscience, or betray the

Commonwealth by silence.' Herewith was the Queen more offended, and commanded the said John to pass forth of the cabinet, and to abide farther of her pleasure in the chamber.

DAVID RICCIO'S ASSASSINATION
Sir James Melville, 9 March 1566

The shrewd diplomat James Melville was present in Holyrood when Mary's secretary, the Italian singer David Riccio, was murdered before her eyes. She was pregnant by Lord Darnley at the time. He is believed to have instigated, or at least agreed, to the deed, to cause a miscarriage and force the queen to make him next in line to the throne if she remained childless. Given the level of poisonous intrigue at court, and Darnley's lack of backbone, the enmity Riccio had aroused by being the queen's favourite, and privy to much confidential information, was perhaps reason enough for getting rid of him. This barbaric episode heralded the beginning of the end for Mary, resulting in a series of terrible decisions on her part that eventually brought her downfall. As this memoir shows, poor judgement on her part – not least in marrying Darnley – was in part also at the root of this.

Now ther cam heir in company with the ambassadour of Scavoy, ane David Ricio, of the contre of Piedmont, that was a merry fallow and a gud mucitien; and hir Maieste had thre varletis of hir chamber that sang thre partis, and wanted a beiss to sing the fourt part; therfor they tald hir Maieste of this man to be ther fourt marrow, in sort that he was drawen in to sing somtymes with the rest; and eftirwart when the ambassadour his maister retournit, he stayed in this contre, and wes retiret in hir Maiestes service as ane varlet of hir chamber. And efterwart when hir French secretary retired him self till France, this David obtenit the said office, and therby entrit in greter credit, and occupied hir Maiesteis ear of tymes in presens of the nobilite, and when ther was gretest conventions of the estatis; quhilk maid him to be sa invyed and hated that some of the nobilite wald glowm [frown] upon him, and some of them wald schulder him and schut hym by, when they entrit in the chamber, and fand him alwais speaking with hir Maieste. And some again addressit them unto him, and dependit upon hym; wherby in schort tym he becam very rich. Not without some fear, therefore, he lamented his estait unto me, and askit my consaill, how to behave hym self. I tald him, that strangers wer commonly envyed when they medlit over far in the affaires of forren contrees. I said again, that it wes thocht that the maist part of the affaires of the contre past throw his handis; and advysit him, when the nobilite wer present, to gif them place, and prey the Quenis Maieste to be content therwith. Quhilk he did, and said unto me efterwart, that the Quen wald not suffer him, bot wald nedis have him to use him self in the auld maner. Efterwart, seing the invy against the said David till increase, and that be his wrek hir Maieste mycht incure displesour, I tok occasion to enter with hir Maieste, and in maist humble maner schew her what advyse I had geven unto Seigneur David, as is abone specified. Hir Maieste said, that he medlit na farther bot in hir French wretingis and affaires, as hir uther Frenche secretary had done of before; and said, that wha ever fand falt therwith, sche wald not leave to do hir ordinary directions. Sche thankit me for my continuell cair, and promysed to tak sic gud ordour ther intill as the cause requyred. The K[ing – Darnley] wes wone to geve his consent over facely to the slauchter of seigneur David, quhilk the Lordis of Mortoun, Ruthven, Lindsay and uthers had devysit; that way to be masters of the court, and to stay the parlement. The King was yet very yong of yeares, and not weill experimented with the nature of this nation. It was supponit also that the Erle of Lenox knew of the said enterpryse, for he had his chamber within the palice; and sa had the Erles of Atholl, Bothewell, and Huntly, wha baith eschaiped be louping down out of a window, towardis the litle garding wher the lyons are lugit [lodged]. This vil act was done upon a Satterday [the 9.] of [March] in the year [1565] about sex houres. When the Quen was at hir supper in hir cabinet, a nomber of armed men entrit within the closs before the closing of the yetis, and tok the keyes from the porter. Ane part of them passit up throw the Kingis chamber, conducted be the Lord Ruthven and George Douglas the postulat [Postulate Bishop]; the rest remanit in the close, with drawen swerdis in ther handis, crying 'a Douglas, a Douglas,' for ther slougern; for it was in the glomyng of the evenyng. The King was past up to the Quen of before, and was leanin upon hir chair, when the Lord Ruthven entrit with his knappisca [headpiece] upon his head, and George the postulat entrit in with him and dyvers uther, sa rudly and unreverently, that the burd [table] fell, the candelis and meat and plaitis fell. Sr David tok the Quen about the waist, and cryed for marcy; bot George Douglas pluckit fourth the Kingis dager that wes behind his bak, and strak him first with it, leavyng it sticking within him. He geving gret skirlis and cryes, wes rudly reft from the Quen, wha culd not get him saif. He wes forceably drawen fourth of the cabi-net, and slain in the utter hall, and her Maieste keped as captyve . . . The nyxt mornyng, quhilk was Sonday, I was lettin fourth at the yet: for I lay therin.

SECRET CURE FOR SMALLPOX SCARS
Mary Stuart, May 1566

In this letter to her cousin Elizabeth, a month before she gave birth, Mary gives a glimpse of the dangers to which even royalty were prey. The English court had been so alarmed by the queen's near death the previous autumn that it encouraged her to marry, or in some way secure the succession. Elizabeth's face was relatively unscarred by the disease, but her faithful nurse and companion, Lady Mary Sidney, was not so lucky. When he got home from abroad, her husband Henry was appalled at the sight that greeted him: 'I lefte her a full fair Ladye in myne eye at least the fayerest, and when I retorned I found her as fowle a ladie as the smale pox could make her.'

So good has mingled so closely with evil that the occasion has been the sooner given me, on receipt of your letters, written with your own hand, to praise God for your health than time to regret your illness; which I do with my whole heart, and chiefly since I have heard the great danger you were in, and how you came off so cheaply that that fair face will lose nothing of its perfection.

Randolph begged me to send you some recipe to keep it from showing, which I could not have done as I would wish, for he who dressed me is dead, and was called Fernel, First Physician to the King: and he would never tell me the recipe for the water which he put on my face, after having opened it all with a lancet: and after all, it would be too late to use it. I am very sorry I did not know it sooner, for I would have sent you him whom I consider most excellent for this, who was my man, assuring you that I would never know of anything that would serve you, but that I would do it as a good sister should, so long as I know my love rewarded by such affection.

I have no doubt of this, trusting your promises and the constancy of that heart which you have given me in exchange for mine, which I think so well employed. And on this conclusion, not to trouble you with too long discourse, I will make an end, having informed you, by the same means, of the quieting of those disturbances which for a short time have troubled me – more for pity of those whom God has so far abandoned than from fear to fall into their danger: for I trust my subjects, who have shown themselves all that I could have desired, and I hope will be the better for so clear an example of the wrath of God, which has fallen on the wicked. I do not doubt that Randolph will have so amply given you all the news that I need not weary you with a longer letter, save to kiss your fair hands and pray God that He give you, Madame my good sister, most happy and long life, and the fortune wished you by

Your faithful and affectionate good sister and cousin forever.

MARIE R

ELIZABETH I HEARS OF MARY STUART'S NEWBORN SON

Sir James Melville, 19 June 1566

For the Virgin Queen, the arrival of Mary's son, who would one day become James VI and I, was no cause for celebration. As well as its dynastic implications, it was a source, it seems, of private chagrin.

All this whyll I lay within the castell of Edenbrough, preing nycht and day for hir Maiesteis gud and happy delyvery of a fair sonne. This prayer being granted, I was the first that was advertist be the Lady Boyn, in hir Maiesteis name, to part with deligence, the xix day of Junij in the year 1566, between ten and eleven houres before nun. The fourt day efter I was at Londoun, and met first with my brother; wha sent and advertist the secretary Cicill that same nycht of my commyng, and of the birth of the prince; willing hym to kep it up, untill my being at court to schaw it my self unto hir Maieste, wha was for the tym at Grenwitch; wher hir Maieste was in gret merines and dancing efter supper; bot sa schone as the secretary Cicill roundit [whispered] the newes in hir ear of the prince birth, all merines was layed asyd for that nycht; every ane that wer present marveling what mycht move sa sodane a chengement; for the Quen sat down with hir hand upon hir haffet [cheek]; and boursting out to some of hir ladies, how that the Quen of Scotlandis was leichter of a faire soune, and that sche was bot a barren stok.

RELATIONS IMPROVE BETWEEN MARY AND DARNLEY

Thomas Crawford, February 1567

Mary's previous dislike of her husband's vanity and volatility had by now turned to loathing and distrust. The pair were estranged and living apart when she visited Darnley in his family home in Glasgow, where he was recovering from serious illness (possibly smallpox or syphilis). In retrospect it seemed strange that she suddenly appeared willing for a rapprochement. The following is a version of the meeting observed by one of Darnley's servants, in which she persuades her husband to leave a place where he was well guarded.

He said he would never think that she 'who was hys owne propre fleshe,' would do him hurt, and if any other would, 'theye shuld bye it dere, unlesse they tooke him slepinge,' though he suspected none. So he desired her to bear him company, 'for she ever fownde som adoe, to drawe her sellfe from him to her owne lodginge, and woulde never abyde with him paste two houres at once.'

She was very 'pensiffe', and he found fault; and said he heard she had brought a litter with her. She said it was brought to carry him more softly than on horseback. He said a sick man should not so travel, 'in so colde weather.' She answered she would take him to Craigmiller to be with him 'and not farre from her sonne.'

He said he would go, if they might be at bed and board as husband and wife, and she to leave him no more: and if she promised this on her word, he would go where she pleased – without this, he would not go. She said if she had not been so minded, she would not have come so far, and gave him her hand and faith of her body, that she would love and use him as her husband. But before they could come together 'he must be purged and clensed of hys sicknesse . . . For she minded to give him the bathe at Craigmiller.'

Then she desired him to keep to himself the promise betwixt him and her: lest the lords thought not well of their sudden agreement, considering 'he and theye were at some wordes before.' He said he knew no cause why they should mislike it, and desired her not to move any against him, as he would 'stirre' none against her, and that they would work in one mind, or it would turn to inconvenience to both. She answered – 'She never sowght anye waie bye [page torn here] him, he was in faulte him sellfe.' He said his faults were published: but there were that made greater faults than ever he made, that he believed were unknown.

He then asked me what I thought of his voyage? I said I liked it not, for if she had desired his company, instead of to Craigmiller, she would have taken him to his own house in Edinburgh, rather than a gentleman's house 2 miles out of town – therefore my opinion was she took him more like a prisoner than her husband. He answered he thought little less himself: save the confidence he had in her promise only. Yet he would put himself in her hands, 'thowghe she showlde cutte hys throate'.

DARNLEY'S MURDER

Barbara Mertine and M. De Clarnault, 11 and 16 February 1567

On the night of 9 February 1567, a deafening explosion was heard from Kirk o' Field, near Holyrood Palace. Shortly afterwards, the strangled body of Lord Darnley, in his nightclothes, was found in the grounds. These witnesses evoke the terror of the night. It was to prove one of the most disreputable events in royal history. Following the blast – here called the 'crak' or crack, the prime suspect behind the murder was James Hepburn, Earl of Bothwell, to whom Mary was dangerously and indecorously close.

Feb. 11, Deposition on the King's murder
In presence of the Earls of Huntly, Cassillis, Caithness, Sutherland, Bishops of Galloway, Ros, Comptroller, Justice clerk, etc.
Barbara Mertine, sworn, etc., depones that before the 'crak rais,' she passed to the window of her house in the 'Freir wynd, fornentis' the Master of Maxwell's lodging, and heard 13 men come forth at the 'Freir (yett)' and pass to the Cowgait and up the Freir wynd. Then the 'Crak rais' and 11 men came forth, 2 of whom had 'cleir thingis' on them, and passed down the passage that 'cummies fra the Freirs' and so to the town. She cried on them as they passed, called them traitors, and said they had been at some 'evill turn'.

Feb. 16
Report of M. De Clarnault
That on Sunday the 9th about 7pm the Queen with the principal nobles at Court visited the King – stayed 2 or 3 hours, and then attended the marriage of one of her gentlemen, as she had promised; or it is thought she would have staid till midnight or 1 a.m., seeing their good agreement for 3 weeks past. She retired soon from the 'nopce,' [nuptials] to go to bed. And about 2 a.m. a

tremendous noise was heard, as if a volley of 25 or 30 cannon, arousing the whole town; and on her sending to know whence it came, they found the king's 'logis' totally destroyed (raze), and himself 60 or 80 'pas' from the house in a garden, dead, also his valet de chambre and a young page. One may imagine the distress and agony of this poor princess, such a misfortune chancing when her majesty and the King were on such good terms. It is well seen this unhappy affair proceeded from an underground mine: as yet the author is unknown.

※

MARRIAGE OF MARY AND THE EARL OF BOTHWELL

Diurnal of Occurents, 15 May 1567

After being acquitted of murder, Bothwell allegedly abducted Mary and carried her off to Dunbar Castle, where he raped her in order to ensure they married. It sounds violent and coercive, but a few days after their marriage, one courtier said that things were not what they seemed. There was much propaganda against Mary, however, and this was perhaps another slur. Or it may have been true. Either way, marrying Bothwell was political suicide. Elevating him to the rank of Duke of Orkney and Zetland was, for some, the last straw. This account suggests the wedding was a less than joyful affair.

Upoun the aucht day of the said moneth [May 1567] befoir none Marie, be the grace of God, quene of Scottis, wes proclamit in the palice of Halyrudhous, to be maryt with the said James, erle Bothwell . . .

Upoun the nynt day of the said moneth of May, our soverane ladie and the said erle Bothwell wes proclamit in the college kirk of Sanct Geill to be mariyt togidder.

Upoun the ellevint day of the said moneth, our soverane ladie and the said erle Bothwell come furth of the castell of Edinburgh and wes lugeit [lodged] in the abbay.

Upoun the tuelf day thairof betuix sevin and aucht houris at evin, James erle Bothwell wes maid duk of Orkney and Zetland, with greit magnificence, and four knychtis wes maid thairat; viz. James Cokburne of Langtoun, Patrik Quhitlaw of that Ilk, James Ormestoun of that Ilk and Alexander Hepburne of Beinstoun; and thair wes few or nane of the nobilitie thairat.

Upoun the fyftene day of May 1567 Marie, be the grace of God, quene of Scottis, wes maryt on James Duke of Orknay, erle Bothwell, Lord Haillis

Crichtoun and Liddisdail, great Admiral of Scotland, in the palice of Halyrudhous within the auld chappell, be Adame Bischope of Orkney, not with the mess bot with preitching, at ten houris afoir none. Thair wes not many of the nobilitie of this realme thairat, except the erle Crawfurd, the erle Huntly, the erle Sutherland, my lordis Abirbrothok [Arbroath], Olyphant, Flemynge, Glamis and Boyd, Johne Archbischope of Sanctandrois, the bischope of Denblane, the bischope of Ross, Orknay, with certane utheris small gentilmene quha awatit upone the said Duke of Orkney. At this marriage thair wes nathir plesour nor pastyme usit as use wes wont to be usit quhen princes wes maryt.

QUEEN IN CAPTIVITY
Mary Stuart, 28 May 1568

Mary's marriage to Bothwell divided her followers, and those who could not accept him as King Consort led their army against her at Carberry Hill on the outskirts of Musselburgh, on 15 June 1567. After negotiations, Mary conceded defeat, so long as Bothwell was allowed to go free. He fled, and she never saw him again. (He was eventually taken prisoner in Denmark, where he died after ten years spent in chains.) Mary was taken captive, first at Loch Leven, and then after an unsuccessful escape and another military defeat, at the Battle of Langside, she fled to England, thinking her cousin Elizabeth would come to her aid. While in protective custody in Carlisle Castle, she wrote to her cousin. She can have been under no illusion that she was in a desperate situation, yet her tone remains surprisingly sanguine. Clearly she still expected Elizabeth to take her side against her detractors, who believed she had conspired to murder Darnley. She was forced to abdicate in July, but under duress, since earlier she had stated: 'As for the resignation of my crown . . . I beg you not to weary me again, for I am resolved and deliberate rather to die than to do it: and the last word that I shall speak in my life shall be that of a Queen of Scots.'

Madame my good sister, I have received two of your letters, to the first of which I hope to make answer with my own mouth . . . Madame, I am grieved that the haste in which I wrote my last letter made me leave out, as I see by yours, the thing which chiefly moved me to write to you, and which is the main cause of my coming into your kingdom: which is that having been this long time prisoner, and as I have written already, unjustly treated,

I desired above all to come to you in person to make my complaint, as much for nearness of blood, likeness of rank, and profound friendship, as to clear myself in your sight of such slanderous words as they have dared to put forward against my honour, and also from the assurance I felt that beyond all these points, you would consider that, when they were banished for their crimes committed against me, at your request I recalled these ungrateful subjects and restored them to their former condition, to the detriment and prejudice of my own, as then was manifest. Thus since, in regard for you, I did what wrecked me, or came at least too near it, I may in justice turn to her who, meaning no ill, has caused the harm, so that she may repair the error which has ensued.

Notwithstanding, as below you promise me by your letters to take my just cause into your own hands until you have returned me to the state which it has pleased God to call me – I send for this purpose my cousin Milord Fleming, a faithful subject: so that, being by you assured of this, he may pass into France, and thank the King, Monsieur my good brother, for his offers and good offices, which I will reserve for another time, if I need them, as [I do those] of others in general, contenting myself with your aid and support, which I shall be no little bound, all my life, to recognise in all that is in my power.

If this is not the case (which I am certain will not be your doing, but that of some other whom I cannot judge, nor care to) at least I was certain that you would permit me, as freely as I came to throw myself into your arms as my chiefest friend, to seek aid, on your refusal, from the other princes and friends, my allies, according as it shall serve me without doing any prejudice to you, or to the old sworn friendship between us two. And whichever of these two you please shall be welcome to me – however much I prefer the one to the other – since, thank God, I do not lack good friends and neighbours in my just quarrel. Thus for me, all that matters is the delay, (to speak to you frankly as you do to me) I have already found somewhat harsh and strange, seeing that I have so frankly placed myself in your country, without conditions, and that, having stayed a fortnight in your castle, as almost a prisoner, I received no permission, when your councillors came, to go to you with my complaint, though I trusted you so much that I asked no more than to go to you and let you hear my true grievances.

Now, I beg you to think of what importance is my long delay; and not to be cause of my ruin (of which, thank God, there is no other sign) make me know indeed the sincerity of your natural affection to your good sister and cousin and sworn friend. Remember, I have kept my promise! I sent you my heart in a ring, and now I have brought you the real one, and my body with it, more surely to knit the knot that binds me to you.

Now, not to wrong the sufficiency of the bearer, in whom you may trust as in me, I will not weary you with longer discourse, save to present my affectionate remembrance to your good grace, and pray God to give you, Madame, in health, long and happy life.

From Carlisle, this xxviii of May.

Your very faithful and obliged, if it please you, good sister and cousin without charge.

MARIE R

A PENSION FOR JOHN KNOX'S WIDOW

General Assembly of the Church of Scotland, 1572

Margaret Knox, née Stewart, was a relative of Mary, Queen of Scots, who disapproved of her marriage to the widower John Knox. She was offended not by the disparity in age – she was seventeen and he fifty-four – but that her permission had not been asked. Margaret was Knox's second wife, and bore him three daughters before his death in November 1572. Shortly after, the General Assembly showed their gratitude for all he had done. Two years later Margaret married Sir Andrew Ker, the conspirator who had held a pistol to the queen's side as Riccio was stabbed, so that she could do nothing but watch.

The Assembly, remembering the long and faithful travels [labours] made in the work of God by umquhile John Knox, minister of Edinburgh, lately departed at the mercy of God, leaving behind him Margaret Stewart his relict, and his three daughters gotten on her, improvided for: And seeing that his long travels and deserts merit to be favourably remembered in his posterity, being also required most earnestly thereunto by my Lord Regent's Grace [the Earl of Morton], as his direct letters thereupon bear, have granted and consented to give, and by the tenour hereof grants, gives, consents, and dispones to the said Margaret Stewart, relict, and her three daughters of the said umquhile John Knox, the pension which he himself had in his time of the Kirk, and that for the year next approaching and following his decease, viz, of the year of God 1573 years, to their education and support, extending to 500 merks money, two chalders of wheat, six chalders bere, two chalders oats, to be uplifted for that year allanerlie, out of the samen assignations and places that he had it in his time. And therefore requires and in the name of God desires the Lords of the Council and Session to grant and give letters at instance of the said relict and bairns of the said umquhile John Knox, to cause them to be answered obeyed and paid of the said pension of the year foresaid, in the same form, and better if need be, as was granted to himself in his time.

THE EXECUTION OF MARY, QUEEN OF SCOTS

Robert Wingfield, 8 February 1587

When the end came, Mary had been kept captive for nineteen years, latterly in Fotheringay Castle under the unforgiving watch of the Calvinist Sir Amias Paulet. She had been shunted from one prison to another, and the effect it had on her health was cruel. After a brief few weeks in Carlisle, she was moved to Bolton Castle, and it was while here that she was confronted with the evidence from the so-called Casket Letters. Although unsigned, they were allegedly her correspondence with Bothwell. Mary always maintained they were forgeries. Whether this was true or not, they appeared to show her knowledge of, and collusion in, Darnley's killing. Thus, in July 1567, she was forced to abdicate and the throne passed to her son James VI, later James VI and I.

A potential rallying point for a Catholic restoration, she remained highly dangerous, and at no time did Elizabeth I ever grant her wish to meet. Perhaps believing she had nothing left to lose, Mary appeared to have agreed to a plot to kill Elizabeth. On discovery, this was all the excuse Elizabeth needed to get rid of her troublesome rival. This poignant description of the morning she went to the scaffold was written as a report for Lord Burghley, the Lord High Treasurer, and was most likely by courtier – and hired assassin – Robert Wingfield.

First, the said Scottish Queen, carried by two of Sir Amyas Paulett's gentlemen, the Sheriff going before her, came most willingly out of her chamber into an entry next the hall, at which place the Earl of Shrewsbury and the Earl of Kent, Commissioners for the execution, with the two governors of her person and divers knights and gentlemen did meet her, where they found one of the Scottish Queen's servants, named Melvin, kneeling on his knees, who uttered these words with tears to the Queen of Scots his mistress: 'Madam, it will be the sorrowfullest message that ever I carried, when I shall report that my Queen and dearest mistress is dead.' Then the Queen of Scots, shedding tears, answered him, 'You ought rather to rejoice than weep, for that the end of Mary Stewart's troubles is now come. Thou knowest, Melvin, that all this world is but vanity and full of troubles and sorrows: carry this message from me to my friends, that I die a true woman to my religion, and like a true Scottish woman and a true French woman. But God forgive them that have long desired my end; and He that is the true judge of all secret thoughts knoweth my mind, how that ever it hath been my desire to have Scotland and England united together. Commend me to my son, and tell him that I have not done any thing that may prejudice his kingdom of Scotland: and so, good Melvin, farewell,' and kissing him, she bade him pray for her.

Then she turned her to the Lords, and told them that she had certain requests to make of them. One was for a sum of money which she said Sir Amyas Paulett knew of, to be paid to one Curle her servant; next all her poor servants might enjoy that quietly which by her will and testament she had given unto them; and lastly that they might be all well intreated, and sent home safely and honestly into their countries. 'And this I conjure you, my lords, to do.'

Answer was made by Sir Amyas Paulett, 'I do well remember the money Your Grace speaketh of, and Your Grace need not to make any doubt of the not performance of your requests, for I do surely think they shall be granted.'

'I have,' said she, 'one other request to make unto you, my lords, that you will suffer my poor servants to be present about me at my death, that they may report when they come into their countries that I died a true woman unto my religion.'

Then the Earl of Kent, one of the Commissioners, answered, 'Madam, it cannot well be granted, for that it is feared lest some of them would with speeches both trouble and grieve Your Grace, and disquiet the company, of which we have already had some experience, or seek to wipe their napkins in some of your blood, which were not convenient.'

'My lord,' said the Queen of Scots, 'I will give my word and promise for them that they should not do any such thing as your lordship hath named. Alas, poor souls, it would do them good to bid me farewell. And I hope your mistress, being a maiden Queen, in regard of womanhood will suffer me to have some of my own people about me at my death. And I know she hath not given you so strict a commission but that you may grant me more than this, if I were a far meaner woman than I am.' And then (seeming to be grieved) with some tears uttered these words: 'You know that I am cousin to your Queen, and descended from the blood of Henry VII, a married Queen of France, and the anointed Queen of Scotland.'

Wherefore, after some consultation, they granted that she might have some of her servants, according to her Grace's request, and therefore desired her to make choice of half a dozen of her men and women. Who presently said that of her men she would have Melvin, her apothecary, her surgeon, and one other old man besides and of her women, those two that did use to lie in her chamber.

After this, she being supported by Sir Amyas's two gentlemen aforesaid, and Melvin carrying up her train, and also accompanied with all the lords, knights, and gentlemen aforenamed, the Sheriff going before her, she passed out of the entry into the great hall, with her countenance careless, importing rather mirth than mournful cheer, so she willingly stepped up to the scaffold which was prepared for her in the hall, being two feet high and twelve feet broad, with rails round about, hanged and covered with black also. Then, having the stool brought to her, she sat her down; by her, on the right hand, sat the Earl of Shrewsbury and the Earl of Kent, and on the left hand stood the Sheriff, and before her the two executioners; round about the rails stood knights, gentlemen, and others.

Then silence being made, the Queen Majesty's Commission for the execution of the Queen of Scots was openly read by Mr Beale, Clerk of the Council, and these words pronounced by the assembly, 'God save the Queen.' During the reading of which Commission the Queen of Scots was silent, listening unto it with as small regard as if it had not concerned her at all, and with as cheerful a countenance as if it had been a pardon from Her Majesty for her life; using as much strangeness [indifference] in word and deed as if she had never known any of the assembly, or had been ignorant of the English language.

Then one Dr Fletcher, Dean of Peterborough, standing directly before her, without the rail, bending his body with great reverence, began to utter this exhortation, following, 'Madame, the Queen's most excellent majesty, etc.,' and iterating these words three or four times, she told him, 'Mr Dean, I am settled in the ancient Catholic Roman religion, and mind to spend my blood in defence of it.' Then Mr Dean said, 'Madame, change your opinion and repent of your former wickedness, and settle your faith only in Jesus Christ, by Him to be saved.' Then she answered again and again, 'Mr Dean, trouble not yourself any more, for I am settled and resolved in this my religion, and am purposed therein to die.' Then the Earl of Shrewsbury and the Earl of Kent, perceiving her so obstinate, told her that since she would not hear the exhortation begun by Mr Dean, 'We will pray for Your Grace, that it stand with God's will that you may have your heart lightened, even at this last hour, with the true kingdom of God, and so die therein.' Then she answered, 'If you will pray for me, my lords, I will thank you: but to join in prayer with you I will not, for that you and I are not of one religion.'

Then the lords called for Mr Dean, who kneeling on the scaffold stairs began this prayer, 'O most gracious God and merciful Father, etc.,' all the assembly, saving the Queen of Scots and her servants, saying after him. During the saying of which prayer, the Queen of Scots sitting upon a stool, having about her neck an Agnus Dei, in her hand a crucifix, at her girdle a pair of beads with a golden cross at the end of them, a Latin book in her hand, began with tears and with loud and fast voice to pray in Latin; and in the midst of her prayers, she slided off from her stool, and kneeling, said divers Latin prayers, and after the end of Mr Dean's prayer, she, kneeling, prayed in English to this effect, for Christ His afflicted Church, and for an end of their troubles; for her son, and for the Queen's Majesty, that she might prosper and serve God aright. She confessed that she hoped to be saved by and in the blood of Christ, at the foot of whose crucifix she would shed her blood. Then said the Earl of Kent, 'Madam, settle Christ Jesus in your heart, and leave these trumperies.' Then she, little regarding or not at all, went forward with her prayers, desiring that God would avert His wrath from this Island, and that he would give her grief and forgiveness for her sins. These with other prayers she made in English, saying she forgave her enemies with all her heart that had long sought her blood, and desired God to convert them to the truth; and in the end of her prayer she desired all saints to make intercession for her to Jesus Christ, and so kissing the crucifix of her also, said these words, 'Even as Thy arms, O Jesu, were spread here upon the Cross, so receive me into Thy arms of mercy, and forgive me all my sins.'

Her prayer being ended, the executioners desired Her Grace to forgive them her death, who answered, 'I forgive you with all my heart, for now, I hope, you shall make an end of all my troubles.' Then they, with her two women, helping of her up, began to disrobe her of her apparel; then she laying the crucifix upon the stool, one of the executioners took from her neck the Agnus Dei, which she laying hands of, gave it to one of her women, and told the executioner he should be answered money for it. Then she suffered them, with her two women, to disrobe her of her chain of pomander beads and all other her apparel most willingly, and with joy rather than sorrow helped to make unready [undress] herself, putting on a pair of sleeves with her own hands which they had pulled off, and that with some haste, as if she had longed to be gone.

All this time they were pulling off her apparel, she never changed her countenance, but with smiling cheer she uttered these words, that she never had such grooms to make her unready, and that she never put off her clothes before such a company.

Then she being stripped of all her apparel saving her petticoat and kirtle, her two women beholding her made great lamentation, and crying and crossing themselves, prayed in Latin. She turning herself to them, embracing them, said these words in French, 'Ne criez vous, j'ai promis pour vous,' and so crossing and kissing them, bade them pray for her and rejoice, and not weep, for that now they should see an end of all their mistress' troubles.

Then she, with smiling countenance, turned to her men servants, as Melvin and the rest, standing upon a bench nigh to the scaffold, who sometimes weeping, sometimes crying out aloud, and continually crossing themselves, prayed in Latin, and crossing them with her hand bade them farewell, wishing them to pray for her even until the last hour.

This done, one of the women, having a Corpus Christi cloth lapped up three-corner-ways, kissing it, put it over the Queen of Scots' face, and pinned it fast to the caul of her head. Then the two women departed from her, she kneeling down upon the cushion most resolutely and without any token or fear of death, she spake aloud this psalm in Latin, 'In te Domine confide, non confundar in aeternum, etc.' Then groping for the block, she laid down her head, putting her chin over the block with both her hands, which holding there still, had been cut off had they not been spied. Then lying upon the block most quietly, and stretching out her arms, cried, 'In manu tuas, Domine,' three or four times. Then she lying very still upon the block, one of the executioners holding of her slightly with one of his hands, she endured two strokes of the other executioner his axe, she making very small noise or none at all, and not stirring any part of her from where she lay; and so the executioner cut off her head, saving one little gristle, which being cut in sunder, he lift up her head to the view of all the assembly, saying 'God save the Queen.'

Then her dressing of lawn falling off from her head, it appeared as grey as one of three score and ten years old, polled very short, her face in a moment by so much altered from the form she had when she was alive, as few could remember her by her dead face. Her lips stirred up and down for a quarter of an hour after her head was cut off.

Then Mr Dean said with a loud voice, 'So perish all the Queen's enemies,' and afterwards the Earl of Kent came to the dead body, and standing over it, said with a loud voice, 'Such an end of all the Queen's and the Gospel enemies.'

Then one of the executioners, pulling off her garters, espied her little dog, which was crept under her clothes, which could not be got forth by force, yet afterwards would not depart with the dead corpse, but came and lay between her head and her shoulders, which being imbrued with her blood was carried away and washed, as all things else were that had any blood was either burned or clean washed, and the executioners sent away with money for their fees, not having any one thing that belonged to her. And so, every man being commanded out of the hall, except the Sheriff and his men, she was carried by them up into the great chamber, lying ready for the surgeons to embalm her.

THE NORTH BERWICK WITCHES

Newes from Scotland, *1591*

In 1590, James VI and his new wife Anne of Denmark were almost shipwrecked on their way home to Scotland. A superstitious and neurotic man – with some reason, since his court was a viper's nest – James believed it when he was told witches had brewed up the storm. Measures were soon taken, in Denmark as well as Scotland, to rid the king and his people of such mortal danger. The anonymous pamphlet, Newes from Scotland, *from which this extract comes, was probably published in late 1591, following the two-year trial of the supposed witches. It is thought to have been written by James Carmichael, minister of Haddington, who might have been present at the trial. A fine piece of propaganda, prurience and prejudice, it shows the tense atmosphere of the times, in which no woman – nor some men – could feel safe, or dare offend, for fear of being labelled a witch. Court records across the country are filled with trials of witches, or accusations that sometimes come to nothing, well into the seventeenth century. This document is rare for being explicit about the means of torture used. In showing how Geillis Duncan was made to confess, it offers the only record of the origin of the protracted North Berwick witchhunt, in which seventy people were implicated. In all, between the sixteenth and eighteenth centuries – the last case was Janet Horne in 1727 – it is thought that around 4,000 women were executed as witches.*

Within the town of Tranent in the kingdom of Scotland there dwelleth one David Seton, who, being deputy bailiff in the said town, had a maidservant called Geillis Duncan, who used secretly to be absent and to lie forth of her master's house every other night. This Geillis Duncan took in hand to help all such as were troubled or grieved with any kind of sickness or infirmity, and in short space did perform many matters most miraculous. Which things, for asmuch as she began to do them upon a sudden, never having done the like before, made her master and others to be in great admiration, and wondered there at. By means whereof the said David Seton had his maid in some great suspicion that she did not those things by natural and lawful ways, but rather supposed it to be done by some extraordinary and unlawful means.

Whereupon her master began to grow very inquisitive, and examined her which way and by what means she was able to perform matters of so great importance: whereat she gave him no answer. Nevertheless, her master, to the intent that he might be better try and find out the truth of the same, did with the help of others torment her with the torture of the pilliwinks [thumbscrews] upon her fingers, which is a grievous torture, and binding or wrinching her head with a cord or rope, which is a most cruel torment also, yet she would not confess anything. Whereupon they, suspecting that she had been marked by the devil (as commonly witches are), made diligent search about her, and found the enemy's mark to be in her fore-crag, or fore part of her throat; which being found, she confessed that all her doings was done by the wicked allurements and enticements of the devil, and that she did them by witchcraft.

After her confession, she was committed to prison where she continued for a season; where immediately she accused these persons following to be notorious witches, and caused them forthwith to be apprehended one after another: viz. Agnes Sampson, the eldest of them all, dwelling in Haddington, Agnes Tompson of Edinburgh, Doctor Fian, alias John Cunningham, master of the school at Saltpans in Lothian . . . with innumerable others in those arts . . . Of whom some are already executed, the rest remain in prison to receive the doom of judgement at the king's Majesty's will and pleasure . . .

This aforesaid Agnes Sampson, which was the elder witch, was taken and brought to Holyroodhouse before the king's Majesty and sundry other of the nobility of Scotland, where she was straitly examined; but all the persuasions which the king's Majesty used to her with the rest of his council might not provoke or induce her to confess anything, but stood stiffly in denial of all that was laid to her charge. Whereupon they caused her to be conveyed away to prison, there to receive such torture as hath been lately provided for witches in that country.

And forays much as by due examination of witchcraft and witches in Scotland it hath lately been found that the devil doth generally mark them with a privy mark, by reason the witches have confessed themselves that the devil doth lick them with his tongue in some privy part of their body before he doth receive them to be his servants; which Mark commonly is given them under the hair in some part of their body whereby it may not easily be found out or seen, although they be searched. And generally so long as the mark is not seen to those which search them, so long the parties that hath the mark will never confess anything. Therefore by special commandment this Agnes Sampson had all her hair shaven off in each part of her body, and her head thrawn with a rope according to the custom of that country, being a pain most grievous, which she continued almost an hour, during which time she would not confess anything, until the devil's mark was found upon her privities; then she immediately confessed whatsoever was demanded of her, and justifying those persons aforesaid to be notorious witches.

Item, the said Agnes Sampson was after brought again before the king's Majesty and his council, and being examined of the meetings and detestable dealings of those witches, she confessed that upon the night of Allhollon Even last [Halloween], she was accompanied as well with the persons aforesaid as also with a great many other witches to the number of two hundred; and that all they together went to sea each one in a riddle or sieve, and went in the same very substantially with flagons of wine, making merry and drinking by the way in the same riddles or sieves, to the Kirk of North Berwick in Lothian . . .

Item, the said Agnes Sampson confessed that the devil being then at North Berwick Kirk attending their coming in the habit or likeness of a man, and seeing that they tarried over long, he at their coming enjoined them all to a penance, which was that they should kiss his buttocks in sign of duty to him; which being put over the pulpit bare, everyone did as he had enjoined them. And having made his ungodly exhortations, wherein he did greatly inveigh against the king of Scotland, he received their oaths for their God and true service towards him, and departed; which done they returned to sea, and so home again . . .

The said witches being demanded how the devil would use them when he was in their company, they confessed that when the devil did receive them for his servants, and that they had vowed themselves unto him, then he would carnally use them, albeit to their little pleasure, in respect of his cold nature; and would do so at sundry other time.

Post-script:

This strange discourse before recited, may perhaps giue some occasion of doubt to such as shall happen to read the same, and thereby coniecture that the Kings maiestie would not hazarde himselfe in the presence of such notorious witches, least therby might haue insued great danger to his person and the general state of the land, which thing in truth might wel haue bene feared. But to answer generally to such, let this suffice: that first it is well knowen that the King is the child & seruant of God, and they but seruants to the deuil, hee is the Lords annointed, and they but vesselles of Gods wrath: he is a true Christian, and trusteth in God, they worse than Infidels, for they onely trust in the deuill, who daily serue them, till he haue brought them to utter destruction. But heerby it seemeth that his Highnesse carted a magnanimious and undanted mind, not feared with their inchantmentes, but resolute in this, that so long as God is with him, hee feareth not who is against him. And trulie the whole scope of this treatise dooth so plainely laie open the wonderfull prouidence of the Almightie, that if he had not bene defended by his omnipotencie and power, his Highnes had neuer returned aliue in his voiage fro Denmarke, so that there is no doubt but God woulde as well defend him on the land as on the sea, where they pretended their damnable practise.

❦

JAMES VI'S VIEW OF WITCHES

1597

The following credulous account was published in James VI's own book on the subject of witches, Daemonologie *(1597). Fascinated and appalled by the thought of such female malevolence, the king treats the subject in the form of a dialogue between two characters. Their conclusions are chillingly predictable:*

Philomathes: What can be the cause that there are twentie women giuen to that craft, where ther is only one man?

Epistemon: The reason is easie, for as that sexe is frailer then man is, so is it easier to be in trapped in these grosse snares of the Deuill . . .

PRENUPTIAL CONTRACT

1598

This careful marriage contract is typical of the inheritance arrangements made in case the worst happened, and no male heir was produced. It was between Mark Ker, son of Sir John Ker of the Hirsel, in the borders, and Jean Hamilton, second daughter of Alexander Hamilton of Innerwick, near Dunbar.

Gif it sall happin thair be na airis maill (as God forbid) bot airis femell procreat betuixt the saidis Mar and his future spous; gif there be bot ane air femell the sowme of ten thowsand punds; gif there be twa airis femell the sowme of auchtene thowsand merkis to be equallie distributit betuixt thame; gif there be ma airis femell nor twa, the sowme of tuentiefour thowsand merkis to be equallie devydit and distributit amangis all the saidis airs femell.

ON BEASTS AND WOMEN

Sir Anthony Weldon, 1617

Written by one of the court who accompanied James VI and I on a visit to Scotland, this barbed observation is probably by Sir Anthony Weldon.

The air might be wholesome but for the stinking people that inhabit it; the ground might be fruitful had they wit to manure it. Their beasts be generally small, women only excepted, of which sort there are none greater in the whole world.

AN UNEXPECTED NIGHT–TIME VISITOR

John Taylor, the Water-Poet, 1618

Inspired to visit Scotland on learning that the playwright Ben Jonson was soon to do the same, Taylor enjoyed his jaunt, even though on one of his first nights in the country he was obliged to lodge in a house where the good-wife was giving birth. Towards the end of his travels, on his way south via Elgin, he had a memorable night in Brechin.

So after five and thirty dayes hunting and travell, I returning, passed by another stately mansion of the Lord Marquesses, called Straboggi [Strathbogie] and so to Breekin [Brechin], where a wench that was borne deafe and dumb came into my chamber at midnight (I being asleepe), and shee opening the bed, would faine have lodged with mee: but had I beene a Sardanapalus, or a Heliogabalus, I thinke that either the great travell over the mountaines had tamed me: or if not, her beautie could never have moved me. The best parts of her were, that her breath was as sweet as sugar-carrion, being very well shouldered beneath the waest; and as my hostesse tolde me the next morning, that shee had changed her maiden-head for the price of a bastard not long before. But howsoever, shee made such a hideous noyse, that I started out of my sleepe, and thought that the Devill had beene there: but I no sooner knew who it was, but I arose, and thrust my dumb beast out of my chamber; and for want of a locke or a latch, I staked up my doore with a great chaire.

EDINBURGH STYLE

Sir William Brereton, summer 1636

A Member of Parliament under Charles I, and later an army commander during the English Civil War, Brereton was a seasoned traveller, and wrote pithily about what he found. In the case of Scotland, it was generally filth and slatternliness: 'The people here are slothful,' he wrote, shortly after arriving in Edinburgh, 'that they fetch not fresh water every day, but only every other day, which makes their water much worse (especially to drink), which when it is at best is bad enough.' When not grumbling, he took careful note of women's apparel.

Touching the fashion of the citizens, the women here wear and use upon festival days six or seven several habits and fashions; some for distinction of widows, wives and maids, others apparelled according to their own humour and phantasy. Many wear (especially of the meaner sort) plaids, which is a garment of the same woollen stuff whereof saddle cloths in England are made, which is cast over their heads, and covers their faces on both sides, and would reach almost to the ground, but that they pluck them up, and wear them cast under their arms. Some ancient women and citizens wear satin straight-bodied gowns, short little cloaks with great capes, and a broad boun-grace [brim] coming over their brows, and going out with a corner behind their heads; and this boun-grace is, as it were, lined with a white stracht cambric suitable unto it. Young maids not married all are bareheaded; some with broad thin shag ruffs, which lie flat to their shoulders, and others with half bands with wide necks, either much stiffened or set in wire, which comes only behind . . .

THE BOOK OF COMMON PRAYER
IS ROUNDLY REJECTED

Henry Guthrie and Robert Baillie, 1637

When the Book of Common Prayer was introduced in Scotland, at the behest of Charles I, congregations were in uproar, and women were at the forefront of the furore. It had been written by the Scottish bishops, the king, and the Archbishop of Canterbury, William Laud, without any consultation with the Kirk's ministers. As a result the Scottish people felt this popish liturgy was being foisted upon them, and they rose against it. This depiction of the reaction in the capital is the source of the colourful story of Jenny Geddes lobbing her stool at David Lindsay, the Bishop of Edinburgh, when he dared read aloud from it. She is recorded as shouting, 'Villain, dost thou say mass at my lug?' This might be poetic licence, but certainly summed up the sentiment of the crowd, and Lindsay's coach was pelted with stones when he left the cathedral. The response in Glasgow was even more intemperate. Eight years later the Archbishop of Canterbury was executed for treason, doubtless not soon enough for such Protestant zealots. Revolts such as these led the following year to the Scottish National Covenant, and a period of intensely violent upheaval and civil war in England, Scotland and Ireland.

Edinburgh
Henry Guthrie, 16 July

They began the work in the city of Edinburgh, where upon the 16th of July, 1637 the ministers in their several pulpits made intimation that the next sabbath (being the 23rd) the service-book would be read in all the churches, extolling the benefit of it, and exhorting the people to comply with it. And that the work might be done in St. Giles's kirk with the greater solemnity, the bishop of Edinburgh came there himself from Holyroodhouse to assist at it. No sooner was the service begun, but a multitude of wives and serving women in the several churches, rose in a tumultuous way, and having prefaced awhile with despightful exclamations, threw the stools they sate on at the preachers, and thereafter invaded them more nearly, and strove to pull them from their pulpits, whereby they had much ado to escape their hands, and retire to their houses. And for the bishop (against whom their wrath was most bent) the magistrates found difficulty enough to rescue him. This tumult was taken to be but a rash emergent, without any predeliberation; whereas the truth is, it was the result of a consultation at Edinburgh in April, at which time Mr. Alexander Henderson came thither from his brethren in Fife, and Mr. David Dickson from those in the west country; and those two having communicated to my lord Balmerino and Sir Thomas Hope the minds of those they came from, and gotten their approbation thereto, did afterwards meet at the house of Nicholas Balfour in the Cowgate, with Nicholas, Eupham Henderson, Bethia and Elspa Craig, and several other matrons, and recommended to them, that they and their adherents might give the first affront to the book, assuring them that men should afterwards take the business out of their hands.

William Annan was a preacher from Ayr who made the mistake of using Laud's prayer book while visiting the city. This account is by one of the most famous ministers in Church history, who refused to use the Book of Common Prayer, and helped draw up the charges against Laud. He was also the one sent to invite Charles II to accept the Crown of Scotland.

Glasgow
Robert Baillie

At the outgoing of the church, about 30 or 40 of our honestest women, in one voyce, before the Bishope and Magistrats, did fall in rayling, cursing, scolding with clamours on Mr William Annan: some two of the meanest was taken to the Tolbooth. All the day over, up and down the streets where he went, he got threats of sundry in words and looks; bot after supper, whill needleslie he will goe to visit the Bishop, who had taken his leave with him, he is not sooner on the causey, at nine o'clok, in a mirk night, with three or four Ministers with him, but some hundredths of inraged women, of all qualities, are about him, with neaves [fists], and staves, and peats, (but) no stones: they beat him sore; his cloake, ruffe, hatt, were rent: however, upon his cryes, and candles set out from many windows, he escaped all bloody wounds; yet he was in great danger, even of killing. This tumult was so great, that it was not thought meet to search, either in plotters or actors of it, for numbers of the best qualitie would have been found guiltie.

DINNER RUINED

John Lauder, Lord Fountainhall, c. 1650

Campvere was Scotland's staple port in Holland. Shortly before this anecdote occurred, observed by a famous jurist and justice of the peace, the Kirk at Campvere was officially joined to that in Scotland, meaning many Scots passed through. As this fragment suggests, some made themselves more welcome than others.

How a hostess at Camphire [Campvere] served Mr Robert Macquaire, being there to dine with a great deal of other company, he was desired to seek a blessing: he began so long winded grace that the meat was all spoilt and cold ere he had done. The wife was wud angry. The next day he comes, the meat was no sooner put to the fire but she comes to Mr Robert and bids him say grace. 'What's your haste, Margaret? Is the meat ready?' 'No, sir, but it's laid to the fire, and ere ye have ended your grace it will be ready.'

HIDING FROM THE LAW

Grizel Murray, 1677

Songwriter Grizel Baillie (née Hume), famous for works such as 'Were na ma heart licht I wad dee', is the heroine of this piece. Taken from her daughter Grizel's memoir of her, it recounts the nerve-racking period when Grizel's father, Sir Patrick Hume, had to go into hiding, as a supposed conspirator in a plot to assassinate Charles II. The family home, Redbraes Castle, was occupied by government troops, and Hume hid in nearby Polwarth Church. In taking him provisions his daughter risked discovery, and not just his death but hers. The grandfather to whom Grizel junior refers in the first line is Robert Baillie of Jerviswood, who was implicated in the plot, and to whom Hume was close. He was executed in 1684 for treason. Grizel senior later married his son, George, the pair having formed an attachment at the age of twelve.

After persecution began afresh, and my grandfather Baillie again in prison, her father [Sir Patrick Hume] thought it necessary to keep concealed; and soon found he had too good reason for so doing; parties being continually sent out in search of him . . . No soul knew where he was, but my grandmother and my mother, except one man, a carpenter called Jamie Winter. By the assistance of this man, they got a bed and bed–clothes carried in the night to the burying-place, a vault under ground at Polwarth Church, a mile from the house; where he was concealed a month. She went every night by herself, at midnight, to carry him victuals and drink, and staid with him as long as she could to get home before day. Often did they laugh heartily, in that doleful habitation, at different accidents that happened. She at that time had a terror for a church-yard, especially in the dark but when engaged by concern for her father, she stumbled over the graves every night alone, without fear of any kind entering her thoughts, but for soldiers, and parties in search of him. The minister's house was near the church; the first night she went, his dogs kept such a barking, as put her in the utmost fear of a discovery; my grandmother sent for the minister next day, and upon pretence of a mad dog, got him to hang all his dogs. There was also difficulty of getting victuals to carry him, without the servants suspecting: the only way it was done was, by stealing it off her plate at dinner into her lap. Many a diverting story she has told about this. Her father liked sheep's head; and while the children were eating their broth, she had conveyed most of one into her lap; when her brother Sandy, the late Lord Marchmont, had done, he looked up with astonishment, and said, 'Mother, will ye look at Grisel; while we have been eating our broth, she has eat up the whole sheep's head.' As the gloomy habitation my grandfather was in, was not to be long endured but from necessity, they were contriving other places of safety for him; amongst others, particularly one under a bed which drew out, in a ground floor, in a room of which my mother kept the key. She and the same man worked in the night, making a hole in the earth, after lifting the boards; which they did by scratching it up with their hands, not to make any noise, till she left not a nail upon her fingers; she helping the man to carry the earth, as they dug it, in a sheet on his back, out at the window into the garden. He then made a box at his own house, large enough for her father to lie in, with bed and bed-clothes, and bored holes in the boards for air. When it had stood the trial, for a month, of no water coming into it her father ventured home, having that to trust to. After being at home a week or two one day, in lifting the boards, the bed bounced to the top, the box being full of water. In her life she was never so struck, and had near dropped down, it being at that time their only refuge. Her father, with great composure, said to his wife and her, he saw they must tempt Providence no longer, and that it was now fit and necessary for him to go off and leave them . . . They were then obliged to trust John Allan, their grieve, who fainted away when he was told his master was in the house, and that he was to set out with him on horseback before day, and pretend to the rest of the servants, that he had orders to sell some horses at Morpeth Fair. Accordingly, my grandfather getting out at a window to the stables, they set out in the dark. My grandfather, whose thoughts were much employed, and went on as his horse carried him, without thinking of his way, found himself at Tweedside, out of his road, and at a place not fordable, and no servant. He found means to get over, and get into the roads on t' other side, where, after some time, he met his servant, who showed inexpressible joy at meeting him, and told him, as he rode first, he thought he was always following him, till upon a great noise of the gallopping of horses after him, he looked about, and missed him. This was a party sent to his house to take him up; where they searched very narrowly, and possibly, hearing horses were gone from the house, suspected the truth, and followed. They examined this man, who, to his great joy and astonishment, missed his master, and was too cunning for them. . . . He immediately quitted the high road, after a warning by so miraculous an escape. He got to London through bye-ways, passing for a surgeon; he could bleed, and always carried lancets. From that he went to France, and travelled from Bourdeaux to Holland on foot; where he sent for his wife and ten children.

SOLDIERS' WIVES

Sir James Turner, 1683

Sir James Turner was a professional (and brutal) soldier from 1632 to 1684. During the savage Civil War he switched from Covenanter to Royalist, and was heavily involved in action. After Charles II came to the throne at the Restoration in 1660, he was knighted. Amongst his works are a military instruction manual called Pallas Armata. *It is rich in details of battle formations, and how to use pikes and swords. Almost as an aside he described the doughty women who followed armies rather than stay at home.*

Women who follow an Army may be ordered (if they can be ordered) in three ranks, or rather Classes, one below another. The first Classe be of those who are Ladies, and are the Wives of the General and other principal Commanders of the Army, who for the most part are carried in Coaches . . . The second Classe is of those who ride on Horseback, and these must ride in no other place than where the Baggage of the Regiment to whom they belong marches, but they are very oft extravagant, gadding here and there, and therefore in some places they are put in Companies, and have one or more to command and oversee them, and these are called in Germany, Hureweibles, Rulers or Marshals of the Whores. I have seen them ride, keep Troop, rank and file very well, after that Captain of theirs who led them, and a Banner with them, which one of the Women carried. The third Classe is of those who walk on foot, and are the wives of inferiour Officers and Souldiers; these must walk beside the Baggage of the several regiments to which they belong, and over them the several regimental marshals have inspection. As woman was created to be a helper to man, so women are great helpers in armies to their husbands, especially those of the lower condition: neither should they be rashly banished out of armies. They provide, buy, and dress, their husband's meat, when their husbands are on duty or newly come from it: they bring in fuel for the fire and wash their linens, and in such manner of employments a soldier's wife may be helpful to others and gain money to her husband and herself. Especially are they useful in camps and leaguers [as foragers]. At the long siege of Breda it was observed that the married soldiers fared better, looked more vigorously, and were able to do more duty than Batchellors; and all the spite was done the poor women, was to be called their husbands mules, but those who would have been glad to have had such mules themselves. Among all these kinds of Women in well order'd Armies, there are none but those who are married. If there be any else, upon examination made by the Minister, Priest or Consistory, they are put away with ignominy.

ABDUCTION!

Privy Council, 1684

This dramatic tale reads like a soap opera. Was the young heiress kidnapped by a money-grabbing opportunist, or was theirs a romance that prevailed despite severe opposition? As this vivid court record shows, the story changes depending on which side is doing the telling.

David Scott of Hedderwick, having only one daughter, called Jean Scott, who was his apparent heir, he was so tender of her education and so hopeful to have seen her married to his satisfaction, that he abstained from marriage upon that account these seven years by-past since her mother's death, and intended to have bestowed both his fortune and estate upon her if she had been suitably matched according to his inclination . . .

Nevertheless, Francis Ogilvie, Younger of Newgrange, and his accomplices, came to the said David Scott of Hedderwick's house, where his only daughter Jean was, and having taken advantage of his sickness, being then bedfast and having been so six months by ane fall from his horse, most of them being in arms, did under silence and cloud of night having first corrupted Margaret Neilson, a servant in the house, and bribed her did most unchristianly and inhumanly entice the said Jean Scott, being but about fourteen years of age, to go along with them as if it had been to see some curiosity or show, and did carry her hoodwinked from place to place for their own unwarrantable designs: whereof Lady Fintry, her grandmother, having notice, did follow after and overtake them at the Kirkton of Errol, and there rescued her grandchild from them and took her to be with herself. Notwithstanding whereof the said Francis Ogilvie and his brother and their accomplices did most violently invade and assault the grandmother, and because she made resistance according to her weak power on behalf of her grandchild, they did in a most inhumane manner first hold her by force and then tear her nightclothes from her head, and after this barbarous usage they violently took the child from her, and had the impudence to apply to the Lord Bishop of St Andrews for a warrant to marry them, which His Grace refused. They notwithstanding detained the person of the said Jean Scott in their custody, *tanquam in privato carcere* [as in a private prison], which abuses being contrair both to the law of God and Man, it is humbly expected from your lordships' justice that the said Francis Ogilvie and his brother and accomplices should be severely punished to the terror of others . . .

It is answered for the defenders that the complaint is altogether groundless and scandalous. The said Francis Ogilvie and Jean Scott having for several years contracted ane mutual and entire love and affection, and resolved to live and die together, the said Francis did patiently attend, expecting her father's consent and appropriation to the intended marriage: but the said Jean Scott, finding that her father's relations were endeavouring to force upon her another man, for whom she had no kindness, she wrote a letter to the said Francis, acquainting him therewith, and desiring him to meet her at ane particular place of her own appointment, and assured him that she should be ready waiting upon him, and should go with him wherever he himself pleased. Upon receipt of which letter, Francis Ogilvie did come with his brother and other two gentlemen, who were accidentally with him at the time, to the place appointed, and finding her there . . . he did ask her whether or not she was ready and willing to go with him as she had promised in her letter. She answered that she was most willing, and had come from her father's house with that intention and design. Thereupon the said Francis did allow her ane part of his horse (as in civility and kindness he was obliged) and went with her that night to the Laird of Balfour's house.

When they were at Balfour's house, the said Jean Scott did write ane letter to the Laird of Pitcur, entreating him to interfere [intervene] with the Bishop of Aberdeen for ane warrand to marry her with the said Francis: and the said Francis having gone to Pitcur with the said letter which she writ, her cousin german [cousin] the Laird of Brotherton did come to the said Jean, entreating her to go back: but she absolutely refused, declaring that she came away of purpose from her father's house to live and die with the said Francis, and should never part with him.

Thereafter, they came to the Kirkton of Errol, where the Lady Fintry did overtake them, to whom the said Jean Scott did frequently declare and repeat the foresaid deliberate design and inclination before the Lairds of Finshaven and Kinfauns and the parson of Errol: and after she had lyen with her grandmother all night and refused the next morning to turn back with her, the said Lady Fintry did abuse her with many opprobrious speeches, and thereafter fell a-beating the said Francis Ogilvie: and after he had received several strokes from her, he did at last hold her hands without any further incivility: and during the time when the said Lady Fintry was beating the said Francis, the said Jean Scott did run downstairs and rode away several miles (of purpose to be quit of her grandmother) before ever the said Francis Ogilvie removed from the place.

This being the true matter of fact, it is answered to the complaint, That David Scott the father did never intend to raise any such complaint, but on the contrair, finding that all this affair was done by his daughter's own contrivance, and that Francis Ogilvie acted nothing but what was proper and incumbent for a gentleman to do, he did send private advertisement for them to come and wait upon him at his own house in Montrose: but some of his relations, out of design to get his estate, and how on that account endeavoured to keep up a difference betwixt him and his daughter, being advertised of her coming, did go to David Scott's house and keep the doors shut and refuse them access: and this complaint was duly raised by them in the father's name . . .

And seeing that the said Francis Ogilvie and the said Jean Scott have such entire affection and complacency in each other, and that the pursuers themselves cannot allege any disparity in the marriage, and that he is content to provide and secure her in ane suitable jointure, he and the remenant defenders ought to be assoilzied [absolved] from this unjust and groundless complaint.

MARTYRS ON THE MUDFLATS
Patrick Walker, 11 May 1685

The trial and execution of the Wigtown Covenanters Margaret McLachlan or Lauchlison (or some variant of that name), who was sixty-two, and Margaret Wilson, who was eighteen, was exceptionally cruel. When accused of attending conventicles, they refused to recant their beliefs, and were condemned to die. Like others who adhered to the National Covenant, they would not accept the monarch as head of the Church. To set an example to others, these women were tied at the low-water mark on the mudflats of Wigtown Bay. As one commentator wrote, 'The old woman was bound furthest out, to bob like a fisher's float on every advancing wave . . .' This was intended to give the young woman time to renounce her convictions and save herself. But as Patrick Walker, who witnessed it, shows, she was resolute in her beliefs. Sir Robert Grierson of Lag was one of the commissioners who condemned the women for 'nonconformity', earning himself the title Cruel Lag.

The old woman was first tied to the stake, enemies saying, 'Tis needless to speak to that old damn'd bitch, let her go to hell.' But say they, 'Margaret, ye are young; if ye'll pray for the King, we will give you your life.' She said, 'I'll pray for salvation for all the elect, but the damnation of none.' They dashed her under the water, and pulled her up again. People looking on said, 'O Margaret, will ye say it?' She said, 'Lord, give him repentance, forgiveness, and salvation, if it be Thy holy will.' Lagg cry'd, 'Damn'd bitch, we do not want such prayers; tender the oaths to her.' She said, 'No, no sinful oaths for me.' They said, 'To hell with them, to hell with them, it is o'er good for them.' Thus suffered they that extraordinary and unheard-of-death.

WAITING FOR LOVE

Alexander Allardyce, c. 1680s

For many women, their only hope of financial security lay in marriage. One young widow evidently saw Bishop Robert Leighton, later Archbishop of Glasgow, as an excellent catch. Whether she ever found a second spouse is not known, but the divine remained a bachelor all his days.

A young woman, the widow of a minister in his diocese, took it into her head that the Bishop was in love with her. Thinking he was long in speaking his mind, she went to him in the Haining, a lonely walk by the waterside, where he used to meditate. Upon his asking her commands. 'Oh, my lord,' she said, 'I had a revelation last night.' 'Indeed,' answered he, 'What is it?' 'That your lordship and I were married together.' 'Have a little patience,' replied the Bishop, much abashed, 'till I have a revelation too.'

THE TUMBLING LASSIE

Court of Session, 13 January 1687

This brief record of a court case, discovered in the papers of John Lauder of Fountainhall, is one of the most interesting legal documents of the period. It is the first case to revolve around the concept of human rights in Scotland. Sadly, there is no record of the Tumbling Lassie's name. Even her nickname was added by Lauder as an afterthought. Sold by her mother, she was an acrobat in a performing group that included two people of colour – 'blackamoors' – whose manager, or owner, was so incensed when she ran away and found shelter with the borderers Scot of Harden and his wife that he sued them for the return of his property. The notes scribbled on the case by Lauder, possibly on the evening of the court hearing, included details such as that the Tumbling Lassie 'danced in all shapes'. She was clearly obliged to perform even when in pain, her master oiling her joints to that end. Lauder added that 'Physicians attested the employment of tumbling would kill her and bruise all her bowels.' According to Alan McLean QC, 'This is the earliest record I know of expert medical evidence being advanced in the Court of Session.' It is remarkable that despite this being a time of witch persecution and bloody judicial executions, when property was held so sacrosanct a thief could swing for an apple, there was near unanimity in dismissing the case, since 'we have no slaves in Scotland and mothers cannot sell their bairns'. This was not entirely true, given the feudal conditions under which some still worked, but the principle was deemed sound. Despite the Chancellor disagreeing, the Tumbling Lassie was set free and, one hopes, went on her way rejoicing.

January 13, 1687
REID against SCOT of Harden and his Lady
REID the mountebank pursues Scot of Harden and his Lady, for stealing away from him a little girl, called the tumbling-lassie, that danced upon his stage; and he claimed damages, and produced a contract, whereby he bought her from her mother for L.30 Scots. But we have no slaves in Scotland, and mothers cannot sell their bairns; and physicians attested the employment of tumbling would kill her; and her joints were now grown stiff, and she declined to return; though she was at least a prentice, and so could not run away from her master; yet some cited Moses' law, that if a servant shelter himself with thee against his master's cruelty, thou shalt surely not deliver him up. THE LORDS renitenti Cancellario [i.e. with the Chancellor dissenting] assoilzied [absolved] Harden on the 27th of January.

✤

A SERVANT'S RELIGIOUS AWAKENING
Elizabeth West, 9 October 1697

The interest in this account of a young woman's devotion lies partly in the rarity of a servant's journal. It might be no coincidence that the obviously educated Elizabeth West lived in Prestonpans, an East Lothian fishing town blighted by witchcraft accusations and trials in this and the previous century. It's estimated that eighty-one were found guilty of witchcraft here, a level of persecution and suspicion that must have left its mark. West's reflections in her diary, which she called Spiritual Exercises, *were no doubt genuine, but they were also perhaps intended as a record, should it be needed, of her blameless piety.*

When the minister came to serve the first table, the first words he uttered were 'What is thy request, Queen Esther, and it shall be granted thee.' O then, my heart cried out . . . 'O make me more holy than I have been, that the image of my Lord and Bridegroom may appear in my converse to the world. Let me have as near conformity to thee as ever was attained by any. I this day request for more help in reading thy holy word, for as yet it seems to me the darkest book ever I read. I also make request for my poor parents, as formerly, and all my Christian acquaintances, ministers and people, and for our land in general, that the Gospel might never depart from our land of Scotland. Come, purge thy church among us of everything that hinders thy appearance among the golden candlesticks. O Lord, grant me greater degrees of humility, both outward and inward, for I find self-conceit sometimes like to overcome me. I here, this day, promise to stand by thy cause, though persecutions should arise, and to lay down my life if thou call for it . . .'

I must confess that I had great liberty in seeking all those things, both in public and in secret. Oh, it was a comfortable day to me, wherein my interest in Christ was as visible letters before mine eyes! It is impossible for the tongue of men or angels to declare the joy and comfort I experienced, and wherein I gave myself to the Lord. In testimony hereof, I take myself to witness, and all in heaven and earth, that I am not mine own but the Lord's.

Written and subscribed at Prestonpans, Oct.9, 1697
Elizabeth West

FAMINE

Patrick Walker, 1690s

The failure of seven consecutive harvests in the early 1690s resulted in one of the most desperate times of hardship the country has ever known. During the 'Ill-Years', about a fifth of the population – around 200,000 people – went begging. Patrick Walker offers a horrifying picture of the times. This is taken from his biography of Mr Daniel Cargill, a Covenanting martyr whose many prophesies were believed by some – including Walker – to have come true in this disaster. The unimaginable distress of mothers unable to feed their children is harrowingly evoked.

These unheard-of manifold Judgments continued seven Years, not always alike, but the Seasons, Summer and Winter, so cold and barren, and the wonted Heat of the Sun so much withholden, that it was discernible upon the Cattle, flying Fowls and Insects decaying, that seldom a Fly or Gleg was to be seen: Our Harvests not in the ordinary Months; many shearing in November and December, yea, some in January and February; The Names of the Places I can instruct: Many contracting their Deaths, and losing the Use of their Feet and Hands sharing and working amongst it in Frost and Snow; and after all some of it standing still, and rotting upon the Ground, and much of it for little Use either to Man or Beast, and which had no Taste or Colour of Meal.

Meal became so scarce, that it was at Two Shillings a Peck, and many could not get it. It was not then with many, Where will we get Silver? but, Where will we get Meal for Silver? I have seen, when Meal was all sold in Markets, Women clapping their Hands, and tearing the Clothes off their Heads, crying, How shall we go home and see our Children die in Hunger? They have got no Meat these two Days, and we have nothing to give them.

Through the long Continuance of these manifold Judgments, Deaths and Burials were so many and common, that the Living were wearied in the Burying of the Dead. I have seen Corpses drawn in Sleds, many got neither Coffin nor Winding-sheet.

I have seen some walking about the Sun-setting, and Tomorrow about Six a-Clock in the Summer Morning found dead in their Houses, without making any Stir at their Death.

CHOOSING A WIFE

Sir John Clerk of Penicuik, 1700

This rather unromantic approach to marriage by a youthful lawyer and politician does at least show the extent to which couples by this age were able to select their partners. When eventually Clerk found his match, it lasted only a matter of months as his new wife died in childbirth at Christmas.

I was about 24 years of age when I was admitted an Advocat, and a little after my Father tried all the ways he could think of to have me marry with some prospect of real advantage with regard to my Fortune. He had projected a Wife for me, the Daughter of ——, but the Lady was not to my taste, and indeed it was happy for me to have stopt short in this Amour, for she proved the most disagreable woman I ever knew, 'tho otherways a nise enough conceity woman. The next attempt my Father made was for the Daughter of a certain Lord, afterwards an Earle, but before I made any advances that way, I found that she was engaged to a neighbouring Gentleman, Mr. C. of O., to whom she was afterwards married, and proved a very good Woman for the short time she lived. The third attempt of this kind was indeed a choise of my own, Lady Margaret Stuart, the eldest sister of the Earl of Galloway. This young lady was a very handsome woman, and for the most part bred up in Galloway, a stranger to the follies of Edin., and one with whom I thought I cou'd be very happy. We contracted a friendship and familiarity with one another in the space of 5 or 6 months. My Father was exceedingly pleased with the match, but wou'd contract very small things for a Lady of Quality to live on, viz., about 4000 ms. Scots yearly for our support during his life, and 4000 ms. for a joynture in case I hapned to die before her. The Earl her Brother scrupled much at this. However she was resolved to take her hazard, and we were married with the consent of all parties, on the 6th. of March, 1701.

❧

SCHOOL FEES

Elisabeth Stratoun, 1700

The cost of educating a young lady at school in Edinburgh was high, as this bill shows. Boys were generally sent to burgh and parish schools, while very young children and girls went to private schools under the charge of 'dames'. Miss Margaret Rose was fortunate in having a father enlightened enough to consider her education important, since even among the well-off this was not always the case. The curriculum offered at this upmarket establishment was narrow – reading, writing, dancing and sewing – but considered sufficient for the constrained lives its genteel pupils would eventually lead.

Accompt the Laird of Kilraick for his daughter, Miss Margaret Rose,
    for her board and education, to Elisabeth Stratoun

Imprimis, one quarter board, from the 2d September
    to the 2d of Decr., ...   £60 0 0

Item, Dancing, one quarter £14 10 0

Item, One quarter singing and playing, and virginalls, ...   £11 12 0

She having two Masters for playing, I payed a dollar more
    to the second then [*sic*] to the first.

Item, One quarter at wryting,   06 0 0

Item, For five writting books, ...   01 0 0

Item, For satine seame, and silk to her satine seame, ...   06 0 0

Item, One set of wax-fruits ...   06 0 0

Item, One looking glass that she broke, ...   04 16 0

Item, A frame for a satine seame, ...   01 10 0

Item, 2 dozen of linnen, for smoaks to her, at 2 shilling per eln, ...   07 4 0

Item, One quarter at wryting, which I payed befor she entered
    a boarder, from the 2d December 1699 to 2d March 1700, ...   06 0 0

Item, A glass for her sattine [*sic*] seame, ...   01 4 0

Summa   £125 16 0

Discharged by 'Elizabeth Stratoun, indweller in Edinburgh'

RAPE IN THE HIGHLANDS

Anonymous, (?) early 18th century

It's not certain when this Gaelic poem was written. What it reflects, however, is a culture in which women took a submissive, or pragmatic, attitude towards men.

> An cuala sibhs' a' mhoighdeann cheutach
> Air an tug Niall Ba[grave]n an éiginn
> Air taobh beinneadh ri latha gréineadh?
> 'S truagh, a righ, nach b' e mi fheéin i.
> Cha sraicinn broilleach do léineadh.
> Nan sracadh, gum fuaighinn fhéin i . . .

> Did you hear about the beautiful maiden
> Who was raped by fair-haired Neil
> On the mountainside on a sunny day?
> Pity that it was not me.
> I would not tear the front of your shirt.
> Or if I did, I would sew it up . . .

HOUSEHOLD ACCOUNTS

Sir John Lauder, c. 1700

These domestic accounts give a vivid picture of this high-ranking judge's household. (It was Lauder who kept the only record of the Tumbling Lassie.) That he was keen for his wife to be better educated perhaps suggests he wished her to share his love of books, but more likely indicates he wanted her to relieve him of keeping the household accounts. Her name was Marion Anderson and, as for Lauder, this was her second marriage. Drinkmoney, incidentally – earlier known as giltsilver – was a tip, or bonus. In these days a dollar was worth around £2 18s 0d or £2 16s 0d, a little less than three Scots pounds.

> Given in drinkmoney to my godfather's nurse, a dollar
> To the tailzeor for mending my cloaths, a shilling

Then given to my wife for the house, 10 dollars

Then for a pair of shoes, 1lb. 19s.

Payed to John Nicoll for a great bible, 17 shillings

Given for new wine, a shilling

A dollar and a halfe given to a man for teaching my wife writing and
    arithmetick, 4lb. 8s.

Item at Geo. Lauder's penny wedding, a dollar

Item to the fidlers, a 6 pence

Then given at the kirk door, halfe a dollar

For Broun's Vulgar errors, 6 shillings 6p.

Then given to my wife to buy linnen to make me shirts with, 2 dollars

Payed for a pair of gloves, 30 shil.

Item, given to my wife to help to buy black lace for hir goun, 2 dollars

Item, for wax and soap, 7 pence

For a quaire of paper, 9 pence

For a book against the commonly received tennents of witchcraft, 8 pence

On coffee and other things, 16 pence

Item, for a timber chair, 18 pence

Item, to the barber, 6 pence

Item, spent upon the race day, 3 shillings

For 4 comedies, viz., Love in a Nunnery, Marriage a la mode, Epsom
    Wells, and Mcbeth's tragedie at 16p. the piece, 5 shils. and a groat

Upon morning drinks for sundry dayes, 6 pence

For a black muff to my wife, i j shillings

To the contribution for the prisoners amongst the Turks, a mark

For a sword belt, 22 pence

Item, payd for a cow, 34 lb. Scots.

For seing the lionness and other beasts at Kirkcaldy, 12 pence

Upon sweities to be tane to my brother George at Idington, a mark

To Samuell Borthwick for letting blood of my wife, 3 mark

Payed to the coallman, 10 lb.

QUEEN ANNE'S COMMON HABITS
Sir John Clerk of Penicuik, c. 1706

This portrait of Queen Anne could not be more unkind. Anne, who succeeded to the throne after William and Mary (her sister), and presided over the Union of Parliaments in 1707, suffered poor health from her thirties. That she went through seventeen pregnancies, yet had only one child who survived infancy (he died at the age of eleven), might partly explain the condition in which Clerk found her.

I was frequently at Kensington with him [the Duke of Queensberry], where the Queen keept her Court, and I twice saw her in her closet, to which the Duke was always admitted, being nominated Commissioner by her Majesty for representing her in the inseuing parliament of Scotland. One day I had occasion to observe the Calamities which attend humane nature even in the greatest dignities of Life. Her majesty was labouring under a fit of the Gout, and in extream pain and agony, and on this occasion every thing about her was much in the same disorder as about the meanest of her subjects. Her face, which was red and spotted, was rendered something frightful by her negligent dress, and the foot affected was tied up with a pultis and some nasty bandages. I was much affected at this sight, and the more when she had occasion to mention her people of Scotland, which she did frequently to the Duke. What are you, poor mean like Mortal, thought I, who talks in the style of a Soveraign?

A FLYING WOMAN
Robert Wodrow, c. 1712

Superstition thrived, even as the Age of Enlightenment dawned. Despite being a historian, supposedly rigorous about truth, Wodrow was as susceptible as anyone else.

I am weel assured that the Countess of Dumfreice, Stairs's daughter, was under a very odd kind of distemper, and did frequently fly from the one end of the room to the other, and from the one side of the garden to the other; whither by the effects of witchcraft upon her, or some other way, is a secret. The matter of fact is certain.

❧

A JACOBITE WIFE SPRINGS HER HUSBAND FROM THE TOWER OF LONDON

Winifred Maxwell, Countess of Nithsdale, 23 February 1716

The 1715 Jacobite Rising, following the accession of George I, was led by the disaffected Earl of Mar and had so much popular support in Scotland it ought to have succeeded. It did not, however, and before the Old Pretender had even landed in the country, events had been sealed by the Battle of Sheriffmuir on 13 November, when the inept Mar's vastly larger contingent was held at bay by the king's men. One of the defeated rebels was William Maxwell, fifth Earl of Nithsdale, who was captured at Preston and sent to the Tower of London to await execution. This was scheduled for 24 February 1716. In a letter to her sister, his wife Winifred describes how she carried out an audacious plan for his escape after learning that of all the prisoners, her husband was the one for whom there was no hope of reprieve.

I immediately left the House of Lords and hastened to the Tower, where, affecting an air of joy and satisfaction, I told all the guards I passed by, that I came to bring joyful tidings to the prisoners. I desired them to lay aside their fears, for the petition had passed the House in their favour. I then gave them some money to drink to the Lords and His Majesty, though it was but trifling; for I thought, that if I were too liberal on the occasion, they might suspect my designs, and that giving them something would gain their good humour and services for the next day, which was the eve of the execution.

The next morning I could not go to the Tower, having so many things in my hands to put in readiness; but in the evening, when all was ready, I sent for Mrs Mills, with whom I lodged, and acquainted her with my design of attempting my Lord's escape, as there was no prospect of his being pardoned; and this was the last night before the execution. I told her that I had everything in readiness, and I trusted that she would not refuse to accompany me, that my Lord might pass for her. I pressed her to come immediately as we had no time to lose. At the same time I sent for Mrs Morgan, usually known by the name of Hilton, to whose acquaintance my dear [maid] Evans had introduced me, which I looked upon as a very singular happiness. I immediately communicated my resolution to her. She was of a very tall and slender make, so I begged her to put under her own riding-hood, one that I had prepared for Mrs Mills, as she was to lend her's to my Lord, and that in coming out he might be taken for her. Mrs Mills was then with child, so that she was not only of the same height, but nearly of the same size as my Lord. When they were in the coach I never ceased talking, that they might have no leisure to reflect. Their surprise and astonishment when I first opened my design to them, had made them consent, without ever thinking of the consequences. On our arrival at the Tower, the first I introduced was Mrs Morgan; for I was only allowed to take in one at a time. She brought in the clothes that were to serve Mrs Mills, when she left her own behind her. When Mrs Morgan had taken off what she had brought for my purpose, I conducted her back to the staircase; and, in going, I begged her to send me in my maid to dress me; and that I was afraid of being too late to present my last petition that night if she did not come immediately. I despatched her safe, and went partly down stairs to meet Mrs Mills, who had the precaution to hold her handkerchief to her face, as was very natural for a woman to do when she was going to bid her last farewell to a friend on the eve of his execution. I had indeed desired her to do it, that my Lord might go out in the same manner. Her eye-brows were rather inclined to be sandy, and my Lord's were dark and very thick; however, I had prepared some paint of the colour of her's to disguise his with. I also brought an artificial head-dress of the same coloured hair as her's; and I painted his face with white and his cheeks with rouge, to hide his long beard as he had not time to shave. All this provision I had before left in the Tower.

The poor guards, whom my slight liberality the day before had endeared to me, let me go quietly with my company, and were not so strictly on watch as they usually had been; and the more so, as they were persuaded, from what I had told them the day before, that the prisoners would obtain their pardon. I made Mrs Mills take off her own hood, and put on that which I had brought for her; I then took her by the hand and led her out of my Lord's chamber; and in passing through the next room, in which there were several people, with all the concern imaginable, I said, 'My dear Mrs Catherine, go in all haste, and send me my waiting maid; she certainly cannot reflect how late it is; she forgets that I am to present a petition tonight, and, if I let slip their opportunity I am undone, for tomorrow will be too late. Hasten her as much as possible, for I shall be on thorns till she comes.'

Every body in the room, who were chiefly the guards' wives and daughters, seemed to compassionate me exceedingly, and the sentinel very officiously opened the door to me. When I had seen her out, I returned back to my Lord, and finished dressing him. I had taken care that Mrs Mills did not go out crying, as she came in, that my Lord might better pass for the Lady who came in crying and afflicted, and the more so, because he had the same dress she wore. When I had almost finished dressing my Lord in all my petticoats, excepting one, I perceived that it was growing dark, and was afraid that the light of the candles might betray us, so I resolved to set off; I went out, leading him by the hand, and he held his handkerchief to his eyes; I spoke to him in the most piteous and afflicted tone of voice bewailing bitterly the negligence of Evans who had ruined me by her delay.

Then said I, 'My dear Mrs Betty, for the love of God run quickly and bring her with you; you know my lodging, and if ever you made dispatch in your life, do it at present; I am almost distracted with this disappointment.' The guards opened the doors, and I went down stairs with him, still conjuring him to make all possible dispatch. As soon as he had cleared the door, I made him walk before me, for fear the sentinel should take notice of his walk, but I still continued to press him to make all the dispatch he possibly could.

At the bottom of the stairs, I met my dear Evans, into whose hands I confided him. I had before engaged Mr Mills to be in readiness, before the Tower, to conduct him to some place of safety, in case we succeeded. He looked upon the affair as so very improbable to succeed, that his astonishment, when he saw us, threw him into such consternation, that he was almost out of himself, which Evans perceiving, with the greatest presence of mind, without telling him any thing, lest he should mistrust them, conducted him [my husband] to some of her own friends, on whom he could rely, and so secured him, without which we should have been undone. When she had conducted him, and left him with them, she returned to find Mr Mills, who, by this time, had recovered himself from his astonishment. They went home together, and, having found a place of security, they conducted [my husband] to it.

In the mean while, as I had pretended to have sent the young lady on a message, I was obliged to return up stairs and go back to my Lord's room, in the same feigned anxiety of being too late, so that every body seemed sincerely to sympathize with my distress. When I was in the room, I talked to him, as if he had been really present, and answered my own questions in my Lord's voice, as nearly as I could imitate it. I walked up and down, as if we were conversing together, till I thought they had time enough thoroughly to clear themselves of the guards. I then thought proper to make off also.

I opened the door, and stood half in it, that those in the outward chamber might hear what I said, but held it so close, that they could not look in. I bid my Lord a formal farewell for that night, and added, that something more than usual must have happened to make Evans negligent on this important occasion, who had always been so punctual in the smallest trifles; that I saw no other remedy than to go in person; that, if the Tower were still open when I finished my business, I would return that night; but that he might be assured I would be with him as early in the morning as I could gain admittance into the Tower, and I flattered myself I should bring favourable news.

Then, before I shut the door, I pulled through the string of the latch, so that it could only be opened on the inside. I then shut it with some degree of force, that I might be sure of its being well shut. I said to the servant as I passed by, who was ignorant of the whole transaction, that he need not carry in candles to his master till my Lord sent for him, as he desired to finish some prayers first. I went down stairs, and called a coach. As there were several on the stand, I drove home to my lodgings, where poor Mr Mackenzie had been waiting to carry the petition, in case my attempt had failed. I told him there was no need of any petition, as my Lord was safe out of the Tower, and out of the hands of his enemies, as I hoped; but that I did not know where he was . . .

REGULATIONS FOR MIDWIVES

Edinburgh, St Cuthbert's parish, 12 December 1718

The strictness of this bond shows how seriously midwifery was taken. Scotland was later to lead the way in this profession, but by this early date it was already forming itself into a recognisable and accountable body, under the aegis of the authorities to whom they had to report. Less than twenty years later, the Faculty of Physicians and Surgeons of Glasgow introduced a system in which midwives were examined and licensed, which was ahead of anywhere else in Great Britain. It's worth noting that by the time this bond was signed, there were a few male midwives too, although they were controversial.

Forasmuch as there are several women in the said parish who of late have brought forth Children in Uncleanness, and tho' much pains have been taken upon them, to bring them to confess who are the fathers of their Children, yet they obstinatly refuse to give an account of them, they still alledging that they were gott with child in open fields by persons they never saw before, and there are others also who give up false fathers to their Children and other strumpets also who are guilty of Exposing their children brought forth in uncleanness. Therefore we by the Tenor herof Bind and Oblige us the said Midwives of the Westkirk parish to perform these Rules following First That at all times we

shall serve the poor in our occupation when required. Secondly that we shall
at no time whatsomever administer drugs to any woman with child without
advice of a physician, Thirdly That we shall give an Account of all unlawfull
Births which come to our knowledge within the said parish to the Ministers
or Elders of the Bounds where these births happen and that within the space
of Four hours before or after, and if it shall happen that if the mother vary
anent the child's father or we have any suspicious therof, that we shall call for
the said ministers or Elders in time of Labour, or in their absences for two
habile Witnesses in the Neighbourhood, and thoroughly examine the Mother
before child bearing in order to oblige her to give an impartiall account of the
Child's Father, and we shall neither conceal, nor concurr in concealing of
the father or mother of any child so brought forth in the said parish . . . and
that we shall faithfully discharge our duty in our offices respective and use our
utmost diligence for the safe delivery preservation & well-fare of every mother
and child which shall come under our care And so oft as we shall fail in the
performance of any of the saids Rules we bind & oblige each of us for our
selves to pay [t]he summ of Twenty pounds scots money for the use of the
poor of the said Westkirk paroch.

WELL-BRED GIRLS

Elizabeth Mure, early to mid 1700s

*Recalling the lifestyle of the middle classes and minor gentry during in her life, diarist
Elizabeth Mure describes the customs of her contemporaries. Her frustration at the way
women were treated is plain, and at one point she fulminates against the lack of contact
between the old and the young. This, she says, resulted in 'no enlargement of mind' and
produced pride, bigotry and 'want of refinement'. She added damningly that mothers
could not give much time to their children since 'Domestic affairs and amuseing her
husband was the business of a good wife.'*

Those that could afoard governesses for their Children had them; but all
they could learn them was to read English ill, and plain work. The chief
thing required was to hear them repeat Psalms and long catechisms, in which
they were employed an hour or more every day, and almost the whole day
on Sunday. If there was no governess to perform this work, it was done by
the chaplan, of which there was one in every family. No attention was given

to what we call accomplishments. Reading and writing well or even spelling
was never thought off. Musick, drawing, or French were seldom taught the
girls. They were allow'd to rune about and amuse themselves in the way they
choiced even to the age of women, at which time they were generally sent
to Edinr. for a winter or two, to lairn to dress themselves and to dance and
to see a little of the world. The world was only to be seen at Church, at
marriages, Burials, and Baptisams. These were the only public places where
the Ladys went in full dress, and as they walked the street they were seen by
every body; but it was the fashion when in undress allwise to be masked.
When in the country their employment was in color'd work, beds, Tapestry,
and other pieces of furniture; immitations of fruit and flowers, with very
little taste. If they read any it was either books of devotion or long Romances,
and sometimes both. They never eat a full meal at Table; this was thought
very undelicat, but they took care to have something before diner, that they
might behave with propriety in company. From the account given by old
people that lived in this time, we have reason to belive there was as little care
taken of the young men as of the women; excepting those that were intended
for lairned professions, who got a regular education throw schools and
Coledges. But the generallity of our Country gentlemen, and even our
Noblemen, were contented with the instruction given by the Chaplin to
their young men.

Of Marriages: The Bride and the Garter
But that the manners of the times I write of may be showen in a fuller light, I
shall give Mr. Barclays relation of the most memorable things that past in his
father's house from the begining of the centry till the 13, in which year he [i.e.,
Sir James Stewart] died.

'My brother was married (says he) at the age of twentyone; few men were
unmarried after this time of life. I myself was married by my friends at 18,
which was thought a proper Age. Sir James Stewart's marriage with President
Delrimple's second Daughter brought together a number of people related to
both familys. At the signing of the eldest Miss Delrimple's Contract the year
before there was an entire hogshead of wine drunk that night, and the number
of people at Sir James Stewart's was little less.

'The marrige was in the President's house, with as many of the relations as
it would hold. The Brides favours was all sowed on her gown from tope to
bottom and round the neck and sleeves. The moment the ceremony was
performed, the whole company run to her and pulled off the favours: in an
instant she was stripd of all of them. The next ceremony was the garter, which
the Bridegroom's man attempted to pull from her leg; but she dropt it throw

her peticot on the floor. This was a white and silver ribbon which was cut in small morsals to every one in the company. The Bride's mother came in then with a basket of favours belonging to the Bridegroom; those and the Bride's were the same with the Liverys of their familys; hers pink and white, his bleu and gold colour. All the company dined and suped togither, and had a ball in the evening. The same next day at the Advocate's. On Sunday there went from the President's house to Church three and twenty Cupple, all in high dress: Mr. Barclay then a boy led the youngest Miss Delrimple who was the last of them. They filled the lofts of the kirk from the Kings sate to the wing loft. The feasting continued every day till they had gone throw all the friends of both familys, with a ball every night.'

Of Baptisms and Cummer's Feasts

As the baptisam was another public place, he goes on to describe it thus. 'On the forth week after the Lady's delivery she is sett on her bed on a low foot-stool; the bed coverd with some neat piece of sewed work or white sattin, with three pillows at her back coverd with the same; she in full dress with a lapped head dress and a fan in her hand. Having informed her acquaintance what day she is to see Company, they all come and pay their respects to her, standing or walking a little throw the room (for there's no chairs). They drink a glass of wine and eat a bit of cake and then give place to others. Towards the end of the week all the friends were asked to what was called the Cummer's feast. This was a supper, where every gentleman brought a pint of wine to be drunk by him and his wife. The supper was a ham at the head and a pirimid of fowl at the bottom. This dish consisted of four or five ducks at bottom, hens above, partrages at tope. There was an eating posset in the midle of the table, with dryed fruits and sweet-meats at the sides. When they had finished their supper, the meat was removed, and in a moment every body flies to the sweet-meats to pocket them. Upon which a scramble insued, chairs overturned and every thing on the table; wrassalling and pulling at one another with the utmost noise. When all was quiet'd, they went to the stoups (for there was no bottles) of which the women had a good share. For tho it was a disgrace to be seen drunk, yet it was none to be a little intoxicate in good Company. A few days after this the same company was asked to the Christening, which was allwise in the Church; all in high dress; a number of them young ladys, who were call'd maiden Cummers. One of them presented the Child to the Father. After the Cerrimony they dined and supped togither, and the night often concluded with a ball.'

FORNICATION

Aberdeen Kirk Session records, 1723

The Kirk was incensed and troubled by the crime of sex outside marriage, firstly on moral grounds, but also for the hardship illegitimacy caused (and the pressure this put on the public purse). Consequently it hunted down the fathers of pregnant unwed women like bloodhounds on a scent. In cases such as this one from Aberdeen, the interrogation of mothers-to-be could be forensic, not to say intrusive and humiliating, but in this instance, the inquisitors had met their match.

21 October

Christian Tellie, whose child was born in September, confesses that she is a trilapse in fornication and names William MckGee, who she says is 'a Caithness man of no fixed residence'. The session thinks she is 'prevaricating'.

11 November

She now names Alexander Kempt, senior mason, and says she was induced to name MckGee by him, 'but now, for the ease of her conscience, she was content to tell the truth'. She says that when she told Kempt she was with child to him he first told her to go to her aunt in London, and then to name MckGee as father, 'and after that she resolved to go south and bring forth her child, & when she came to Stonehaven, she heard that the said Alexander Kempt was working at Fetteresso, & sent a boy for him, and he came . . . and said he had little money to spare, however he gave her half a crown and two shillings sterling and six pence, & told her, when she sent him word of her delivery, he would come & see her, though it were forty miles distance from this place, & would give her money from time to time, & ever since she was put in prison, he hath sent her money by her mother'.

She says he was also the father of her last child and that 'thereafter did lye carnally with her severall times', and that 'when she came to be in courtship with one George Gilchrist sometime servant to Baillie Gellie, & got a ring from him worth a guinea, he the said Alexander Kempt, upon her acquainting him with so much, diverted & diswaded her from going on with the said George Gilchrist in that matter, telling her that it was not a fit bargain for her, & bad her delay a while, until his wife, who was an aged frail woman, should die, and that then he would marry her, & that would be a better bargain for her & withall added that the said Alexander Kempt told her, that if she gave him up as the father of any of her children he had begotten with her in uncleanness with her, that he would confidently deny it before Magistrates and Ministers, & finally added, that upon her mother's signifying her displeasure in his coming so frequently about the house, when she was with the second child, & putting him to the door, he thrust the door up again & did strike both her & her mother as the people thereabout can declare when called'.

19 November

She says that when she was in prison her mother told Kempt that she would not be able to conceal his name any longer, and that he had offered to pay two pence out of every sixpence he earned if she would continue to conceal it. She gives in a list of witnesses who saw them together. Kempt appears and denies everything.

23 December

They both appear. He is told that the session is ready to hear anything he has to say and to witnesses on his behalf, but he refuses to offer anything, where-upon the session prepare to hear her witnesses and Kempt refuses to stay. Numerous witnesses depone. One, a weaver of 37, says that on King George's coronation day in 1714 they were in Christian's mother's house, and Christian and Kempt were there when Kempt's wife came and from the door and, 'in the deponent's hearing, cryed out, come out you adulterous dog & you adulterous whore, I have found you out'. Another witness, an excise officer, declares that one night about two years ago he had attempted to enter Christian's mother's house and when he finally got in he found that 'they had barriceaded the door with daills, trees and a form, and having gone and looked about him, saw Alexander Kempt lying among the peats'. He had then pursued Kempt, 'calling to him by his name Alexander Kempt, and saying Alexander this is wrong, this will make all good that is said of you, & that he the deponent pursued him so hotly that he the said Alexander Kempt losed his hat & wig'.

NURSEKEEPERS

Elizabeth Mure, early to mid 1700s

Diarist Elizabeth Mure recalls the selfless behaviour that was considered quite normal among women when friends or relatives fell ill.

Society was not yet so much enlarged as to weaken the affections of near relations. This may be easyly ascertained by every one now alive that is turned of fifty. Not only Brothers and Sisters, but Brothers and Sisters in Law, mothers in Law, and even more distant connections, would leave their own familys for ten or twelve days, and attend with the outmost care a friend in a fever or dangerous disorder. These were the Nursskeepers for the first 30 years of this centry, who by every method endeavour'd to lessen their distress, nor left them night or day till recover'd or buried. The intercourse betwixt relations and friends was kept up in another way, which was by small presents, mostly consisting of meats or drink. Any thing rare or good of its kind was in part sent to a friend whatever rank of life they were in. These presents were received with thanks, and return'd on proper occasions. Nather was strangers or people of high rank sought after in their entertainments. It was their Relations, the Friends they loved, that shared their delicacys. Those manners still remain in many places in Scotland.

LIKE AN OVERGROWN COACHMAN

Rev. Alexander Carlyle, 1733

Alexander Carlyle was minister of Inveresk Kirk near Musselburgh, renowned for his idiosyncracy (he once rode his horse naked in public). The extraordinary woman he describes here was a relative, encountered while he was touring the Borders with his father and their kinsman Mr Jardine, the minister of Lochmaben. Carlyle was thirteen at the time.

I had never seen such a virago as Lady Bridekirk, not even among the oyster-women of Prestonpans. She was like a sergeant of foot in women's clothes; or rather like an overgrown coachman of a Quaker persuasion. On our peremptory refusal to alight, she darted into the house like a hogshead down a slope, and returned instantly with a pint bottle of brandy – a Scots pint, I mean [i.e. three imperial pints] – and a stray beer-glass, into which she filled almost a bumper. After a long grace said by Mr Jardine – for it was his turn now, being the third brandy-bottle we had seen since we left Lochmaben – she emptied it to our healths, and made the gentlemen follow her example: she said she would spare me as I was so young, but ordered a maid to bring a gingerbread cake from the cupboard, a luncheon of which she put in my pocket. This lady was famous, even in the Annandale border, both at the bowl and in battle: she could drink a Scots pint of brandy with ease; and when the men grew obstreperous in their cups, she could either put them out of doors, or to bed as she found most convenient.

CAPTIVE ON ST KILDA

Rachel Erskine (née Chiesley), Lady Grange, 1738

The story of Lady Grange is operatic in its drama. The spirited and beautiful daughter of a convicted murderer, Rachel Chiesley was said to have forced James Erskine to marry her at the point of a gun. Theirs was a tempestuous marriage, which produced nine children despite Erskine's infidelities and her drinking, and eventually they agreed to live apart. It was then that her husband, the Lord Justice Clerk, appears to have grown concerned, either that she was going to expose him, possibly for his treasonous Jacobite sympathies, or simply intended to murder him. In 1732 he took the measures described below, methods even his supporters thought were extreme. Lady Grange's violent abduction eventually led to her incarceration in a stone hut on the tiny Outer Hebridean island of St Kilda, from which only those with a boat or wings could ever hope to escape. Possibly to avoid her rescue, after seven years she was moved to the island of Skye, where she died in 1745, still a prisoner. This letter was written to her cousin, Charles Erskine, the Lord Advocate, but did not reach him until 1740. As the paper was running out, her handwriting got smaller and smaller.

January 1738
Sir –
. . . upon the 22d of Jan 1732, I lodged in Margaret McLean house and a little before twelve at night Mrs McLean being [in] on the plot opened the door and there rush'd in to my room some servants of Lovals and his Couson Roderick MacLeod he is a writter to the Signet they threw me down upon the floor in a Barbarous manner I cri'd murther murther then they stopp'd my mouth I puled out the cloth and told Rod: MacLeod I knew him their hard rude hands bleed and abased my face all below my eyes they dung out some of my teeth and toere the cloth of my head and toere out some of my hair I wrestled and defend'd my self with my hands then Rod: order'd to tye down my hands and cover my face most pitifully there was no skin left on my face with a cloath and stopp'd my mouth again they had wrestl'd so long with me that it was all that I could breath, then they carry'd me down stairs as a corps at the stair-foot they had a Chair and Alexander Foster of Carsbonny in the

Chair who took me on his knee I made all the struggle I could but he held me fast in his arms my mouth being stopp'd I could not cry they carr'd me off very quickly without the Ports, when they open'd the Chair and took the cloath of my head I saw I was near to the Mutters of hill it being moonlight; I then show'd them that all the linnins about me were cover'd with blood.

They had there about 6 or 7 horses they set me on a horses' behind Mr Foster and tyed me fast with a cloath to him that I might not leope of. If I remember right it was Peter Fraser Ld Lovaels page that set me on the horse, Rod: MacLeod and Ld Lovaets tenants rode along with me and Andrew Leishman come attending Mr Foster he is a servant in Wester Pomeis he knows the names of Lovaets Ser: we rode all night it being Saturday we mett no body or day breakes they took me into a house which belongs to John MacLeod advocate a little beyond Lithgow, I saw in that house a Gardener a Ser: of Johns and a Ser: of Alex: MacLeod advocate but I'm not sure if he was his first or his second man. They keep me there all day at night I was set on a horse behind Mr Foster they rode with me to Wester Pomeis [Wester Polmaise, near Falkirk] it belongs to M Stewart and Mr Foster is his Factore he took me to the house of Pomeise thro a vault to a low room all the windows nailed up with thick board and no light in the room he was so cruel as to leave me all aloan and two doors lock'd on me, a Ser: of Ld Lov: kept the keys of my prison James Fraser, And: Leishman mention'd before is a tennant in Pomeise near thirtie years he brought what meat and drink I got and his Wife mead my bed and wash'd my linens.

I was kept so close I grew sick then And: told Mr Foster he would not have a hand in my death then I was allow'd to the court to get the Air I then saw a son and three daughter which this Wife his born to And: I told them I was Ld Grange Wife in hopes they would lett it be knowen for Mr Fos: kept a gar'ner (George Rate) and his Wife in the house that what provisions came might pass as to them he had a meal yeard and house in Stirlin, they had two sons and a daughter come often to see them I give them some thing to tell the ministers of Stirlin Hamilton and Erskine that I was a prissonr in Pomeise but all in vain. I was their near seven moneth Aug 15 Peter Fraser Ld Lov: page came and three men with him.

I had kept my bed all that day with grief and they set me on a horse behind Mr Foster I fainted dead with grief as they set me on the horse, And: Leishman rode that night's journey with me, whenever I cri'd they came to stope my mouth, they rode to the highlands with me our guide a Servant of Sir Alexander Macdonald Ronall Macdonald he since marr'd to Lady Macdonald own woman. We rode all night or day breake they took me in to a little house Mr Foster never came near me after that night, but left the charge of me to Lov: Servants I saw Rod: MacLeod at that house and a servant of his Duncan Swine since that bond apprentice to a Wright in or about Edin' Mr Foster and

Rod: MacLeod rode a partie of the way with us I not write the anguish and sorrow I was in I never read or hear'd of any Wife whatever was her crime so cruely and barbarously treatt as I have been.

Peter and James Fraser left me with the three men that came to Pomeise for me and two other came one of them belong's to Ld Lov. two days after we came to a Loch on Glangerry ground Lochnern they had a sloop waiting there for me. The master of the sloop told me he had been with Rod: MacLeod, he order'd him to take me home to his own house and keeps me till farther orders they met in Scotoss, he is uncle to this Glangerry his wife Rod: Aunt Scotass Sons the Isle Huskre [Heisker, or the Monach Isles], it belongs to Sir Alexander Macdonald and this man is the tannent, after I was some time there he thought it was a sin to keep me he said he would let me go for tho Sir Alex: should take the Isle from him he could not take his life. I sent a man for a boat and he ran away with my money. In Jun: 1734 Rod: sent for the tanant of the Isle his name Alex. Macdonald to come to the Captain of Clan Ronalds house he told him I was to be taken from him. On the 14 of Jun: John MacLeod and his Brother Normand came with their Galley to the Huskre for me they were very rud and hurt me sore.

Oh alas much have I suffer'd often my skin mead black and blew, they took me to St Kilda. John McLeod is call'd Stewart of the Island he left me in a few days, no body lives in it but the poor natives it is a viled, neasty stinking poor Isle I was in great miserie in the Husker but I am ten times worse and worse here, the Society sent a minister here I have given him a much fuller account then this and he wrat it down. You may be sure I have much more to tell then this. When this comes to you if you hear I'm alive do me justes and relieve me, I beg you make all hast but if you hear I'm dead do what you think right befor God.

I am with great Respect
your most humble servant
but unfortunat Cousen
RACHELL ERSKINE

TWO DAYS AFTER CULLODEN
Mrs Robertson of Inches, 18 April 1745

Mrs Robertson, Lady Inches, was a Whig, and no fan of the Jacobite cause, and her son was in the Duke of Cumberland's army, whose soldiers were known as the Red Coats.

She was attending her husband's funeral when the Battle of Culloden, which spelled the end of the Jacobite Rising, began.

Some time before, and at the time of the battle, Lady Inches was living with her family in Inverness, her husband being in a dying condition, who was laid in his grave just as the cannonading began upon Drummossie Moor. On Friday after the battle, April 18th, she went home to her house called the Lees, within a mile or so of the field of battle. Upon the road as she went along she saw heaps of dead bodies stript naked and lying above ground. When she came to the Lees she found sixteen dead bodies in the close, who as soon as possible she caused bury. When she came into the close some of the soldiers came about her, calling her a rebel-bitch, and swearing, that certainly she behoved to be such, or else so many of these damned villains would not have come to get shelter about her house. Then pulling her by the sleeve they desired her to come along with them, and they would show her a rare sight, which was two dead bodies lying in the close with a curtain over them. They took off the curtain, and bade her look upon the bodies, whose faces were so cut and mangled that they could not be discerned to be faces. They told her that the party who had been formerly there had cut and mangled these villains, and he'd left them in the house in their wounds; but when they themselves came there they could not endure to hear their cries and groans, and therefore had dragged them out to the close and given them a fire to warm their hinder end. 'For,' said they, 'we roasted and smoked them to death.' Lady Inches said she saw the ashes and remains of the extinguished fire.

The house of the Lees was all pillaged, the doors of the rooms and closets, the outer doors, the windows, and all the liming being broke down to pieces. The charter-chest was broke open, and the papers were scattered up and down the house; all her horses and cattle were taken away, though Inches was not in the least concerned in the affair, save only that he was a great Whig, and had a son out with the Duke of Cumberland.

When she complained to David Bruce, he told her to go through the camp and see if she could spy out any of her furniture or goods among the sogers, and if she did, the fellows should be seized upon, and she should have the satisfaction of having them hanged. But seeing she could have no reparation of damages she did not chuse to follow Mr Bruce's advice, and she declared she had never received one farthing for the losses sustained.

On the day of the battle when the chase happened, one of Inches's tenants and his son who lived at the gate of the Lees, stept out at the door to see what was the fray, and were shot by the red-coats, and fell down in one another's arms, the son dying upon the spot; but the father did not die till the Friday, the 18th, when Lady Inches went to see him, and he was then expiring. Much about the same place they came into a house where a poor beggar woman was spinning, and they shot her dead upon the spot. In a word, Lady Inches said, they were really mad; they were furious, and no check was given them in the least.

SAVING PRINCE CHARLES
Flora MacDonald, 12 July 1746

After defeat at the Battle of Culloden, Prince Charles Edward Stuart took refuge on the island of Benbecula. A bold idea of disguising him as Betty Burke, a strapping Irish maid, was hatched by the prince's companion, Captain Conn O'Neill. He was a distant relative of Flora MacDonald, whose father was Ranald MacDonald, of Milton, in Skye. Flora agreed to help, and was aided by the fact her stepfather Hugh MacDonald was in charge of the local militia and could give her a pass to the mainland without arousing suspicion. In a statement made at Applecross Bay before government officials, Flora explained what happened as she and her family aided the prince in making his escape. Under cross-examination, Flora said she would also have helped the Duke of Cumberland, had he been defeated and in need of assistance. She was briefly imprisoned for her actions in the Tower of London.

Miss Mc. Donald, Daughter in Law of Mc. Donald of Milton in Sky, being, by General Campbell's order, made Prisoner for assisting the eldest son [Prince Charles Edward Stuart] of the Pretender in his escape from South Uist, & asked to declare the Circumstances thereof, says, That about six weeks ago, she left her Father in Law's house at Armadach [Armadale] in Sky, & went South to see some friends.

Being asked, if she had any Invitation from those who persuaded her to do what she afterwards ingaged in for the young Pretender or any Body else, before she left Sky; answered in the Negative, and says that at the time of her leaving Sky, she did not know where the young Pretender was, but only heard He was Some where on the long Island: that she stay'd at (what they call) a Sheilling of her brother's, on the hills, near Ormaclait the house of Clan Ronald; and that, about the 21 of June, O Neil, or as they call him Nelson, came to where she stay'd, & proposed to her, that as he heard she was going to Sky, that the young Pretender should go With her in Woman's cloathes, as her servant which she agreed to. O Neil then went and fetched the young Pretender who was on the Hills not far off, when they settled the manner of their going.

Miss MacDonald says, that after this she went & stay'd with Lady Clan Ranold [Ronald], at her House, three days, communicated the scheme to her,

& desired that she would furnish cloathes for the young Pretender, as her own would be too little. During Miss MacDonald's stay at Ormaclait, O Neil came frequently from the young Pretender to Clan Ronald's House to inform her where he was, what stepps had been taken for their voiage, and at the same time to hasten her to get her affairs in Readiness for going off.

Miss Mac Donald says, that the 27th past, she, Lady Clan Ronald, her eldest Daughter, & one John MacLean, who had by Lady Clan Ronald's order, acted as Cook to the Pretender, during his stay on the Hills, went to a place called Whea where they expected to meet the young Pretender; but not finding him there, they went on to a Placed called Roychenish, where they found him, taking with them the women's Apparel furnished by Lady Clan Ronald, he was dressed in. Here they heard of General Campbell's being come to South Uist, & that Captain Fergussone was within a mile of them. When they got this Information, they were just going to Supper. But then went of very precipitately, & sat up all night at a Sheilling call'd Closchinisch.

Saturday, June 25th: the Cutter and Wherrier, which attended General Campbell having got from Bernera [Berneray], near the Harris, through the last side of the long island, & passing not far from them, put them again into great Fears, least anybody should land there. However, they continued there 'til about 9 at Night, when the Young Pretender, Miss Mac Donald, one MacAchran, with five men for the Boat's crew, imbarked & put to sea, Lady Clan Ronald having provided Provisions for the voyage.

The 29 about 11 in the Morning they got to Sky near Sir Alexander MacDonald's House. Here Miss Mac Donald and Mac Achran landed, leaving the young Pretender in the Boat, they went to Sir Alexander Mac Donald's House; and from thence Miss MacDonald sent for one Donald Mac Donald, who had been in the Rebellion, but had delivered up his arms some time ago. She imployed this Person to procure a Boat to carry the young Pretender to Rasay, after acquainting him with their late voyage & where she had left the young Pretender. Miss Mac Donald stay'd & dined with Lady Margaret Mac Donald, but Mac Donald & Mac Achran returned to the Boat, to inform what was done.

Miss Mac Donald being asked why Rasay was pitched upon for the young Pretender to retreat to, she answered that it was in hopes of meeting Rasay himself, with whom he was to consult for his future security.

After dinner, Miss Mac Donald set out for Portree it being resolved that they should lodge there that Night; but on the Road overtook the young Pretender & Mac Anchran [*sic*] of Kingsbury. She told them she must call at Kingsbury's House, & desired they would go there also. Here, Miss Mac Donald was taken sick, & therefore with the other two, was desired to stay all night, which they agreed to. She had a Room to herself; But the young

Pretender & Mac Achran lay in the same Room. At this time he appeared in women's Cloathes, his Face being partly concealed by a Hood or Cloak.

Being asked, if while they were at Kingsbury's House, any of the Family inquired who the disguised Person was; answers, that they did not ask; but that she observed the People of the Family whispering as if they suspected him to be some Person that desired not to be known and from the Servants she found they suspected him to be Mac Leod of Bernera, who had been in Rebellion. But, being pressed to declare what she knew or believed of Kingsbury's knowledge of his Guest, owns, that she believes, he must suspect it was the young Pretender.

The 30th of June, Miss Mac Donald set out on Horseback from Kingsbury's House for Portree, having first desired the young Pretender might put on his own cloathes somewhere on the Road to Portree, as she had observed that the other dress rather made him more suspected. Miss got to Portree about 12: at night, where she found Donald Mac Donald, who had been sent before to procure a Boat then The young Pretender & Mac Ancran [*sic*] arrived about an Hour after. Here he took some Refreshment, changed a Guinea, paid the Reckoning, took his Leave of Miss Mac Donald & went out with Donald Mac Donald, but who, after seeing him to the Boat returned. She believes he went to Rasay, but cannot tell what is become of him since.

PIPE-SMOKING

George Ridpath, 11 July 1756

The diarist George Ridpath was minister of Stitchel, a couple of miles from Kelso in Roxburghshire. He had an eye for a good anecdote, helped by his telescope. The interest in this entry is not that a woman was smoking a pipe – many well-bred women enjoyed doing so in the eighteenth century – but what she used to light it.

Tuesday, July 11th.– Read some of Keith [the historian and bishop Robert Keith] and amused a good deal of the afternoon in reconnoitring the Kelso Fair people with the telescope. Slept on the Offices. Alison Hog here in the afternoon. She had lighted her pipe with the note I gave her for the money owed her two or three weeks ago, and wanted another, which I gave her.

BRUSSELS LACE AND OTHER FASHIONS
John Ramsay, before 1745 to c. 1800

John Ramsay was a lawyer turned agriculturalist and historian, who lived on the estate of Ochtertyre in Perthshire, which he had inherited from his father. He kept copious notebooks detailing events and changing attitudes across the entire eighteenth century, relying on what he had heard from those who recalled the early days of the period, and from his own experiences of the second half. His records are so extensive only fragments have ever been published. From the pieces that follow, it's clear he had information and opinions on every aspect of social and economic life. Even the ways in which women dressed were rigorously documented.

Frugality in dress
The most rigid economy appeared in the dress and domestic expenses of the tenants [before 1745]. The clothes of the family, and even of the servants, male and female, were for the most part spun and dyed at home; and thus, though hardly anything was made for sale, the wife's thrift in a numerous household turned to excellent account, as it saved her husband from going to market for a variety of necessaries. In the last age, the most substantial farmers seldom had anything better than a coat of grey or black kelt, spun by their wives. Twice or thrice in a lifetime, perhaps, they had occasion to buy a greatcoat of English cloth, as what was homespun would not keep out rain. Harn shirts were commonly worn, though upon holidays the country beaus appeared with linen necks and sleeves. Among no set of people was female vanity ever confined within narrower limits.

Brussels lace
The milliner business was hardly known in Scotland about the beginning of this century; and though it was introduced by degrees from London, yet in 1753 there were only five or six in Edinburgh. When so very few had an interest in changing or inflaming the fashions, it is not surprising that the ladies' head-dress and other decorations should be stationary. A head-dress called *pinners* [with long flaps over the cheeks] maintained its ground an unconscionable time. It is mentioned in the 'Tatler,' and in my younger years I remember it among the ladies of this country. At that time, however, a few of them that were far advanced in life wore a dress still more antiquated, called a toy, part of which hung over the shoulders. It is still worn by some very old-fashioned tenants' wives. But even then there was one article of extravagance: people thought nothing of laying out large sums of money for Brussels

lace. It was generally a nuptial present, being regarded as one of the append-ages of wealth and fashion.

Curls and ringlets

Of old, the ladies' hair cost them little trouble or expense. As it was artlessly disposed in curls or ringlets, they themselves, or their maids, could dress it – nay, their companions sometimes assisted them. Between forty and fifty years ago, Morison the barber, who had been *valet de chambre* to Lord Perth, intro-duced the Paris style of dressing the ladies' hair.

Indecent and dangerous

In mentioning fashions of a fugitive nature connected with the spirit of the times, the scantiness and thinness of the fashionable ladies' clothing must not be omitted, in consequence of which they make no scruple of displaying those beauties which they used either to conceal or give only a glimpse of. That, however, is by no means peculiar to the present times. The rules of Queen Anne's reign were very severe upon a similar practice. And in 1753 it was no less common at Edinburgh, it being difficult to say whether the ladies' necks or legs were most exposed to the public eye. It is, however, peculiar to the last five or six years [around 1800] to find the fashion of unveiling hidden beauties, accompanied with wearing very few or scanty garments, which is no less indecent than dangerous in a changeable climate conducive to consumption. It is one of the absurd or worse than absurd fashions which originated in France, and was from thence imported into Britain by travelled ladies enamoured of novel fashions. They surely lost sight of nature and common-sense, for beauty is never so attractive as when half withdrawn.

HOW TO KILL TIME WHILE MEN DRINK AND GAMBLE

Elizabeth Mure, 1760s

The moralising and sometimes exasperated diarist and social commentator Mrs Elizabeth Mure believed modern men's bibulous habits made it exceedingly hard for women to find a husband.

[Around the 1760s] more of the English fashions took place, one of which was to dine at three, and what Company you had should be at dinner. These dinners lasted long, the weman satt for half an hour after them and retired to tea; but the men took their bottle and often remained till eight at night. The weman were all the evening by themselves, which pute a stope to that general intercourss so necessary for the improvement of both sexes. This naturally makes a run on the Public places; as the women has little amusement at home. Cut off from the company of the men, and no familie friends to occupie this void, they must tire of their mothers and elderly sosiety, and flee to the public for reliefe. They find the men there, tho leat in the evening, when they have left their bottle, and too often unfitted for every thing but their bed. In this kind of intercourss there is little chance for forming attachments. The women see the men in the worst light, and what impression they make on the men is forgot by them in the morning. These leat dinners has entirely cut off the merry suppers very much regreated by the women, while the men passe the nights in the Taverns in gaming or other amusment as their temper leads them. Cut off in a great measure from the Society of the men, its necessary the women should have some constant amusement; and as they are likewise denied friendships with one another, the Parents provides for this void as much as possible in giving them compleat Education; and what formerly begun at ten years of age, or often leater, now begines at four or five. How long its to continue the next age most determine; for its not yet fixed in this. Reading, writing, musick, drawing, Franch, Italian, Geografie, History, with all kinds of nedle work are now carefully taught the girles, that time may not lye heavie on their hand without proper society. Besides this, shopes loaded with novels and books of amusement, to kill the time.

HAPPY SUNDAYS

Lady Anne Barnard, 1760s

Anne Barnard, née Lindsay, was born in Balcarres House in Fife, to an aged bookish father and unloving mother. Her upbringing was eccentric, to say the least, as was her life as a travel writer and one of the most unusual yet well-connected ladies of her day. She spent much of her life in London, and was described by one eminent admirer as 'the best specimen Scotland ever sent to London'. For some time there was a possibility she would marry Lord Henry Dundas, so powerful a politician he was effectively ruler of Scotland. She was not keen, however, and eventually married a young army captain, Andrew Barnard, with whom she moved to the Cape of Good Hope. Long widowed, she wrote six volumes of memoir, never intended to be published, that were gloriously indiscreet. Hints of sexual abuse at Balcarres by a friend of her father's may explain why she took so long to marry, and indeed, why she did not view her childhood with rose-tinted spectacles.

There was in each week one whole day which I may call a happy one, and that was Sunday; on it, along with the man-servant and the maid, the ox and the ass, we all enjoyed the privilege derived from the fourth commandment, of 'doing no manner of work,' save getting by rote twelve verses of a psalm, which we repeated to our tutor before breakfast. We then walked to church, which was two miles distant, and listened with reverence to all we understood, and with smiles to the horrid discords with which a Presbyterian congregation assails the ears . . . We then returned to dinner, at which we all appeared, and after it received my father's Sunday bounty, viz., eleven heaps of sweetmeats of all sorts and shapes. The rest of the week was devoted to acquirements, but, alas! our house was not merely a school of acquirements, it was often a sort of little Bastile, in every closet of which was to be found a culprit, – some were sobbing and repeating verbs, others eating their bread and water – some preparing themselves to be whipped, and here and there a fat little Cupid, who, having been flogged by Venus, was enjoying a most enviable nap.

HOUSES AND HOVELS
George Robertson, c. 1765

There is a shrewd scientific mind behind tenant farmer George Robertson's careful accounts of conditions on farms and crofts. A tenant farmer, born around the middle of the century, he wrote a series of reports for the government, illuminating how people lived, and eventually published Rural Recollections: or the Progress of Improvement in Agriculture and Rural Affairs *(1829), a remarkable and detailed record. Here, he offers a vivid idea of the domestic environment in which women lived and worked.*

Biggins
These biggins were commonly arranged in one row. The dwelling-house in the middle, with the barns at one end, and the cattle-houses at the other. They were all low in the walls, and all were covered with straw, in some cases

interlaid with thin sods or turfs, to keep it together. The sit-house or dwelling consisted always of two main divisions, distinguished by the names of the but and the ben. The first was used as the kitchen and servants' apartment, where all the household assembled at meal-times, and where the female part of the family slept – that is, the daughters and the maid-servants; the second, or ben-the-house, was the master's (or the gudeman's) peculiar quarters, where he and his wife and younger children lay, and where friends or other strangers were at times entertained. The walls of this part of the steading, both but and ben, were generally raised a foot or two higher than those of the other conterminous houses. This gave room for a low story above, which served for various purposes; as a lumberroom or store-place, where stood the meal-ark and bag of groats [milled oats], and where also the gudewife kept her butter-kitt and her cheeses, her lint and her wool, her yarn and her webs.

But-the-House

[It] was the place where all the victuals were prepared; where they baked the bread, kirned the milk, washed the clothes, and ironed them; and, in addition to all, was almost continually occupied by one or other of the lasses, at the spinning-wheel. And, as if all this were not enough, it was the general rendez-vous of all the comers and gangers about the family; even the very beggars were the inmates of its most capacious fireside; and where the ever-active gudewife held the sole rule and sway, and kept every thing in order. The dimensions of this ha', in those times, was very limited, seldom exceeding sixteen feet by fourteen; this, too, was further circumscribed by the standing furniture, and by the great lum, or vent, erected over the cradle-chimney, or grate, for carrying off the smoke.

Ben-the-House

[Generally] of the same size as the other, and to a certain extent [it] was occu-pied in the same manner with plenishing of various sorts, and, above all, the napery-chest, where the thrifty gudewife had commonly a store of home-made linen, as white as the driven snaw. The flooring of this apartment was generally of deal; that of the other was usually of earth, or of beat-up clay. The windows were only one in each, and of very moderate size, not exceeding thirty inches in height, by twenty in breadth, divided into two leaves on hinges, to shut and open like a door, and used occasionally to let out the smoke, or let in the air, as might be required. The glass, of small dimension, was cut lozenge-fashion, and fixed in with thin strips of lead. The fire-place, with its vent, was constructed in the gable-wall, and furnished with an iron grate, of simple form and small in size. Even the joists that supported the upper floor were open to view; and, as every thing was well husbanded in those days, the interstices between them were all applied to some useful purpose; for by means of a few spars nailed below across them, and at such distances as seemed convenient, the whole was converted into so many shelves, for stowing away such articles as were applicable to the situation: such as, the gudeman's gun, his whip, and his spurs, his bone-headed staff, and more especially the great Bible and other books, which were all safely deposited here, and secure from the handling of the servants, or of the children. In after times, when, from the progress of refinement, this out-of-the-way repository was shut up by the lathing and plaster, it was the cause of great regret to the more elderly gudewives, who had been accustomed to this very convenient stowage, in this upper region of their buts and bens, for their dried fish, and their reestit [dried] tongues, and their black puddings, and their kebbucks [cheese] and even of their webs and their yarn. The great lum, too, contributed towards this conveniency, as in it the haddocks and the salt herrings, arranged in half-dozens on small rods, were hung up to get a flavour of the smoke; as were also the maws of the calves, for yirning [rennet] to the cheese.

Furniture Ben-the-House
The bedsteads, in general, were constructed wholly of wood, being enclosed on all sides, like unto close presses, and opening only in front, with two sliding doors. There was, however, a distinction betwixt those in the kitchen, or but-a-house, and those in the parlour, or ben-a-house: in the former they were composed of the plainest deal; in the latter they were generally ornamented with carved work. There was also a small oaken table, with carved work on its four massy legs; some wooden chairs, decorated in the same style, on their long, upright unaccommodating backs; an easy-chair, for the repose of the gudewife at bairntime [during pregnancy], or when she was nursing; and a good oaken elbow-chair for the gudeman. Besides all this, there was a plain clothes-press, set up against the wall; a three-sided cupboard, stuck up in a corner; also a chest of drawers, for the gudewife's napery; and in some cases a similar chest for the gudeman, but surmounted with a writing-desk or cabinet for depositing money or papers. There was generally a small looking glass. In one instance I met with a pair of ancient sconces, or metallic mirrors, so well burnished up as to afford a pretty clear reflection: they were each about fifteen inches long, and five inches broad; both were stuck up over the fireplace, directly above the chimney-jambs. The eight-day clock, which had very generally found its way by this time into the farm-houses, was also stationed in this apartment. But watches were not nearly so very common as they became afterwards. It was not every gudeman that had one: in carrying on

their out-doors' work, they were seldom at a loss to know the time of day by the sun. Every farm-house had a certain known point in the horizon, over which it stood at noon and at six o'clock in the evening.

Furniture But-the-House

In the kitchen, or but-a-house, there was no scarcity of plenishing, though all on the plainest style. There was an aumry, or store press, for provision; a bink [shelf], to hold cogs [wooden dishes], caps, ladles, and aprons; a rack, or press of spars, for displaying the pewter plates and stoneware of various fabrics, from Dutch delft to the brown, earthen, thick basin, variegated with yellow strips; a babret, or bakeboard, with its fluted roller, for forming and pressing out the oat-cakes; a flat, iron girdle, for firing, and a heater, for toasting them; a salt-backet, which was made and used in the form of a stool, and was the warmest birth about the house, as it was always set down close by the chimly; also spit and raxes, goosing-irons, etc., etc. Besides all these, there were the never-wanting spinning-wheels, and the check-reel. The more ancient distaff, or spindle and rock, with the hand-reel, had both, ere this time, gone almost into desuetude. I recollect only to have seen the former but once. It was in the hands of a decent-looking cottar-wife, whirling it away at her own door, in a warm, sunshiney day, having a string of lammer (amber) beads about her neck – an ornamental piece of finery, as rare now as the distaff itself.

Keeking Glasses

In this but-a-house, or kitchen, there was no allowed looking-glass; but the servant-lasses had a substitute for it, in a full pail of water, brought to the light in a clear day, in which the reflection was as distinct as in any mirror. They some-times had a small Dutch keeking-glass, about the size of a playing-card, concealed in their chests, at which they took a stolen glance before going to church.

BEGIN THE WORLD AGAIN

Flora MacDonald, 1772

The heroine of the Jacobite Rebellion, Flora MacDonald married an army captain, Allan MacDonald, in 1750, with whom she had five sons and two daughters. At this period, before the mass emigration of crofters cleared from the land, even those of their social standing found it difficult to make a living from their estates. Like so many before and since, especially from the Highlands and Islands, they decided to move to America, to North Carolina. Flora's letter, to John Mackenzie of Delvine, is written from Kingsburgh in Skye, shortly before their departure. During the American War of Independence, she was obliged to go into hiding while the family lands and property were destroyed, and her husband, who fought as a Loyalist, was taken prisoner for two years. On her way home to Scotland, she refused to go below deck when the ship was attacked by pirates, and was wounded. Her husband later joined her back in Scotland, since, again like others, their attempt at emigration was not a success.

To John Mackenzie of Delvine, concerning the Macdonalds' imminent emigration to America,
12 August 1772
Dear Sir

This goes by my Son Johnie who thank God tho I am missfortunat in othere respects is happy in his haveing so good a freind as you are to take him under his protection, he seemed when here to be a good natured bidable Boy, without any kind of Vice; make of him what you please and may the Blessing of the almighty attend you alongs with him which is all the retourn I am able to make for your many and repeated freindships shown to me and this family; of which there will soon be no rememberanc in this poor miserable Island, the best of its inhabitance are making ready to follow theire freinds to america, while they have any thing to bring them; and among the rest we are to go, especially as we cannot promise ourselves but poverty and oppression, haveing last Spring and this time two years lost almost our whole Stock of Cattle and horseis, we lost within there three years, three hundred and twenty seven heads, so that we have hardly what will pay our Creditors which we are to let them have and begin the world again, a newe, in a othere Corner of it. Allen was to write you but he is not well with a pain in his Side this ten days past Sir I beg of you if you see any thing amiss in the Boys condut to let me know of it as some Children will stand in awe of ther parents more then any body Else, I am with my respects to you and Mrs McKenzie, Sir with esteem your most obedient humbe Servant

Flora McDonald

DR SAMUEL JOHNSON MAKES AN IMPRESSION
Lady Anne Barnard, 1773

Lady Barnard clearly enjoyed putting down her impressions of the fêted Samuel Johnson. He was on his famous tour with James Boswell when she met him at a concert and dinner organised by Sir Alexander Dick at Prestonfield House in Edinburgh. In those days she was still Lady Anne Lindsay. Boswell recorded that Johnson was greatly amused by her quickness of wit, and would often ask him, 'Boswell, what is it that the Young Lady of Quality said of me at Sir Alexander Dick's?'

The figure of the doctor is a mountain of deformity and disgust, without any point about him being crooked. His colour is sallow, his motions paralytic . . . his manner self-sufficient, his sentences pronounced to be repeated. He was silent for the first hour and a half, till he had fed the animal part, which he conducted nastily. That over, he assumed a more 'questionable shape'. Someone asked him if he had seen the fine new house of Lord Findlater at Banff? Boswell replied hastily that the Doctor never looked at new houses . . . old castles, lakes, mountains and inhabitants pleased him better. On this the Doctor quoted the reply that a French Compte had made the preceding summer to a question of that sort – that he had not left France to go to Scotland to see a fine house.

The company laugh'd at the jest, as people do who are in the hopes of getting more. Now for rousing the Lion (thought I) and in a quiet way I said that the most remarkable part of that speech in my opinion was that it had been made by a Frenchman. The Doctor squinted at me thro' the curls of his bushy wig and, playing with a knife awkwardly flourishing in his hand, opened on the subject of French politesse.

Having now stirred the beast, who was evidently disposed to be sulky, I wished to give him a little flattery to quiet him. He told us that the old Countess of Eglinton always called him 'Son' as he was born the year after she was married. 'No,' said Boswell, 'the year before, Sir.' 'Had that been the case,' said Johnson, 'she would have had little to boast of.' 'Would not the Son have excused the Sin, Doctor?' said I.

The dose took. He became excessively agreeable & entertaining (and I saw Boswell steal to the window to put down the Jeu de mot in his commonplace book).

UPSKIRTING

Edward Topham, 1774

A young English visitor to Edinburgh, later to become a journalist, Topham wrote enthusiastically to his friends about what he found. Unlike many, he does not seem to have disliked the capital's reputation as 'the windy city'.

No women understand better the rules of decorum, nor are they rivalled by the French in the talent of agreeable conversation, for which they seem to be better calculated as well from their superior knowledge of the world as from their extensive acquaintance with books and literature.

At other mites the winds, instead of rushing down with impetuousity, whirl about in eddies. The chief scene where these winds exert their influence is the New Bridge. It is far from unentertaining for a man to pass over this bridge on a tempestuous day. In walking over it this morning I had the pleasure of adjusting a lady's petticoats, which had been blown almost entirely over her head, and which prevented her disengaging herself from the situation she was in.

FAR–SIGHTED MRS SOMERVILLE

Thomas Somerville, 1780s

Mrs Martha Somerville was the aunt of the brilliant mathematician Mary Somerville, who was born in her house near Jedburgh. Martha's husband, a minister, wrote a memoir of their times, from which this vignette comes. Many guessed who the author of the Waverley novels was long before Scott confessed, but since this was a fairly open secret, Mrs Somerville's perception of his abilities was much more precocious. Mary Somerville, arguably an even greater genius, later married Martha and Thomas's son William, who was her second and much-loved husband.

She was endowed with an uncommon share of good sense, and with refined taste, which she had cultivated all her life, and found a source of constant enjoyment. It was an instance of her penetration which may be worth specifying, that she very early discerned the rising genius of Mr. Walter Scott, and was among the first to predict his future celebrity. While he was yet young, just emerging from boyhood, he occasionally visited me when making excursions into the Border districts in prosecution of those antiquarian researches for which he always shewed an instinctive predilection; and he used to entertain us with his conversation on the subject of the old traditions of the neighbourhood, repeating with an astonishing readiness of memory, many of the ballads he had picked up, and which are now published in the Border Minstrelsy. My wife always said she was confident he would soon make a brilliant figure as a man of letters. She survived to derive exquisite gratification from the perusal of the Lay of the Last Minstrel and Marmion.

THE PROBLEM WITH HOOPS

Robert Chambers, late 18th century

By the time Robert Chambers – co-founder of the famous dictionary publishers – was writing, ladies' fashions were less extreme, though also less spectacular. The period he writes of had clearly been relayed to him by those who recalled – indeed, could never forget – the lengths to which women of quality felt obliged to go to remain à la mode. The side hoops, or panniers, of the mid to late eighteenth century originated among the Spanish royalty, but became highly popular when they were adopted at Louis XIV's court. It is said that in this period, women took up three times as much space as men.

There were different species of hoops, being of various shapes and uses. The pocket-hoop, worn in the morning, was a pair of small panniers such as one sees on an ass. The bell-hoop was a sort of petticoat, shaped like a bell, and made with cane or rope for frame-work. This was not quite full dress. The full-sized evening hoop was so monstrous that people saw one half of it enter the room before its wearer. This was very inconvenient in the Old Town, where doorways and closes were narrow. In going down a close or a turnpike stair, ladies tilted them up and carried them under their arms. In case of this happening, there was a show-petticoat below, and such care was taken of appearances that even the garters were worn fine, being either embroidered or having gold and silver fringes and tassels. Ladies in walking generally carried the skirt of the gown over the arm and exhibited the petticoat: but when they entered a room they always came sailing in, with the train sweeping full and majestically behind them.

EXCELLENT SCOTCH OLD LADIES

Lord Henry Cockburn, late 18th century

An eminent judge, and equally talented memoirist, Lord Cockburn was in awe of some of the older women he had once known.

Mrs Rocheid of Inverleith

Nobody could sit down like the lady of Inverleith. She would sail in like a ship from Tashish, gorgeous in velvet or rustling in silk, and done up in all the accompaniments of fan, earrings and finger-rings, falling sleeves, scent-bottle, embroidered bag, hoops, and train – all superb, yet all in purest taste; and managing all this heavy rigging with as much ease as a full-blown swan does its plumage, she would take possession of the centre of a huge sofa, and at the same moment, without the slightest visible exertion, would cover the whole of it with her bravery, the graceful folds seeming to lay themselves over it like summer waves.

Old Lady Don

The venerable faded beauty, the white well-coiled hair, the soft hand sparkling with old brilliant rings, the kind heart, the affectionate manner, the honest gentle voice, and the mild eye. [Living in George Square] she was about the last person in Edinburgh who kept a private Sedan-chair. Hers stood in the lobby, and was as handsome and comfortable as silk, velvet and gilding could make it. And when she wished to use it, two well-known respectable chair-men, enveloped in her livery cloaks, were the envy of their brethren. She and Mrs Rocheid both sat in the Tron Church, and well do I remember how I used to form one of the cluster that always took its station to see these beautiful relics emerge from the coach and the chair.

A singular race of excellent Scotch old ladies. They were a delightful set; strong handed, warm hearted, and high spirited; the first of their temper not always latent; merry even in solitude; very resolute; indifferent about the moods and habits of the modern world . . . Their prominent qualities of sense, humour, affection, and spirit were embodied in curious outsides, for they all dressed, and spoke, and did, exactly as they chose.

It is remarkable that though all these female Nestors were not merely decorous in matters of religion, but really pious, they would all have been deemed irreligious now. Gay hearted and utterly devoid of any tincture of fanaticism, the very freedom and cheerfulness of their conversation and views on sacred subjects would have excited the horror of those who give the tone of these matters at present.

HATS LIKE BALLOONS
The Lounger, *1785*

In addition to hoops, women embellished themselves with marvellous millinery. As so often, they took their lead from Paris. There the craze for ballooning was sparked by the Italian aeronaut Vicenzo Lunardi, who in 1784 flew twenty-four miles in a hydrogen balloon (with a cat, a dog and a caged pigeon). His extraordinary feat resulted in balloon-shaped skirts, hats and bonnets (600mm high, and worn by all classes, even washer-women), but also buckles, muffs and snuffers. This fad quickly reached Scotland and is captured by an anonymous columnist in The Lounger, *after an evening with his friend 'Colonel Caustic'. As well as laughing at polite society, this Edinburgh periodical is best-known for a review by Henry Mackenzie, which coined the phrase 'heaven-taught ploughman' of Robert Burns. Burns was also struck by the fashion known as the Lunardi Bonnet, which is given a mention in his poem, 'To a Louse', which creature made its home in his heroine's headgear.*

On one side of the Colonel sat a lady with a Lunardi hat; before him was placed one with a feathered headdress. Lunardi and the Feathers talked and nodded to one another about an appointment at a milliner's next morning. I sat quite behind as is my custom, and betook myself to meditation. The Colonel was not quite so patient; he tried to see the stage, and got a flying fizzy now and then, but in the last attempt got such a whisk from Miss Feathers on one cheek, and such a poke from the wires of Miss Lunardi on t'other, that he was fain to give up the matter of seeing; as to hearing, it was out of the question.

'I hope, Colonel, you have been well entertained,' said the mistress of the box at the end of the act. 'Wonderfully,' said the Colonel. 'In your ladyship's box one is quite independent of the players.' He made a sign to me: I opened the box door and stood waiting for his coming with me. 'Where are you going, Colonel?' said the lady, as he stepped over the last bench. 'To the play, madam,' said he, bowing and shutting the door . . . [and heading for the pit].

CLARINDA STRUGGLES WITH HER CONSCIENCE
Agnes Maclehose, 24 January 1788

The poet Robert Burns's roving eye was famous, but he appears to have found favour with Mrs Agnes Maclehose by appearing at first to have no interest in anything beyond intellectual discussion. For reasons of discretion, in their year-long correspondence the pair refer to each other as Clarinda and Sylvander which, like most pet names, appear ludicrous as soon as exposed to public view. Agnes was a respectable but unhappily married woman, long separated from her husband at the time of their liaison, and clearly guilt-ridden at the direction in which their friendship was turning, as this letter shows. She was one of Burns's most famous muses – he was thinking of her when he wrote 'Ae Fond Kiss' – but when Sir Walter Scott met her many years later, he considered her 'charmless and devout'.

Thursday, Forenoon,
24 January, 1788

Sylvander, the moment I waked this morning, I received a summons from Conscience to appear at the Bar of Reason. While I trembled before this sacred throne, I beheld a succession of figures pass before me in awful brightness! Religion, clad in a robe of light, stalked majestically along, her hair dishevelled, and in her hand the Scriptures of Truth, held open at these words – 'If you love me, keep my commandments.' Reputation followed: her eyes darted indignation, while she waved a beautiful wreath of laurel, intermixed with flowers, gathered by Modesty in the Bower of Peace. Consideration held her bright mirror close to my eyes, and made me start at my own image! Love alone appeared as counsel in my behalf. She was adorned with a veil, borrowed from Friendship, which hid her defects, and set off her beauties to advantage. She had no plea to offer, but that of being the sister of Friendship, and the offspring of Charity. But Reason refused to listen to her defence, because she brought no certificate from the Temple of Hymen! While I trembled before her, Reason addressed me in the following manner: 'Return to my paths, which alone are peace; shut your heart against the fascinating intrusion of the passions; take Consideration for your guide, and you will soon arrive at the Bower of Tranquillity.'

Sylvander, to drop my metaphor, I am neither well nor happy today: my heart reproaches me for last night. If you wish Clarinda to regain her peace, determine against everything but what the strictest delicacy warrants.

I do not blame you, but myself. I must not see you on Saturday, unless I find I can depend on myself acting otherwise. Delicacy, you know, it was which won me to you at once; take care you do not loosen the dearest, most sacred tie that unites us? Remember Clarinda's present and eternal happiness depends upon her adherence to Virtue. Happy Sylvander! that can be attached to Heaven and Clarinda together. Alas! I feel I cannot serve two masters. God pity me!

CONVICT SHIP

John Nicol, 1789

Born in Currie, near Edinburgh, the sailor John Nicol recounted his tales in 1822. The story below comes from the voyage of the Lady Julian, *which was bound for Botany Bay from London, with 245 female convicts on board. Women represented around a fifth of those sent to Australia, and would have been found guilty of petty crimes, since more serious acts, such as major theft and murder, were punishable by death. Prostitution also was not a transportable offence, but those who wanted protection would form relationships with male convicts or sailors. In this way, Nicol became involved with one of the women, who bore him a child. He later returned to Australia to find her, but she had fled to India.*

One, a Scottish girl, broke her heart and died in the River. She was buried at Dartford. Four were pardoned, on account of His Majesty's recovery. The poor young Scottish girl I have never yet got out of my mind; she was young and beautiful, even in the convict dress and her eyes red with weeping. She never spoke to any of the other women, or came on deck. She was constantly seen sitting in the same corner, from morning to night: even the time of meals roused her not. My heart bled for her: she was a countrywoman in misfortune. I offered her consolation, but her hopes and her heart had sunk. When I spoke she heard me not, or only answered with sighs and tears; if I spoke of Scotland she would wring her hands and sob till I thought her heart would burst. I endeavoured to get her sad story from her lips, but she was silent as the grave to which she hastened. I lent her my Bible to comfort her, but she read it not; she laid it on her lap after kissing it, and only bedewed it with her tears. At length she sunk into the grave, of no disease but a broken heart. After her death we had only two Scotswomen on board.

AN ABUSED WIFE

Mary Eleanor Lyon Bowes, Countess of Strathmore, 1793

The dreadful marriage of Mary Eleanor Lyon Bowes, from whom Queen Elizabeth II is descended, is shocking in its misery. A fun-loving, reckless English heiress, Mary married the Earl of Strathmore and Kinghorne, whose handsome looks soon lost their allure as they discovered they had little in common and he continued to see other women. Mary had friends of her own, and began an affair with a Scottish merchant called George Gray, who later sued her for breach of contract, after she broke her promise to marry him. Their liaison began before her husband's death, but afterwards she was tricked into marrying an Anglo-Irish adventurer, Andrew Robinson Stoney, who turned into a brute, beating and intimidating her. A sadistic man, he insisted she write an account of every misdemeanour she had committed. This journal is enlightening not only for the first properly documented case of domestic abuse, but for the insight it offers into abortion, of which Mary had at least four, as well as attitudes to infidelity and duty. At one point, Mary writes that when her friend's husband Mr Stephens was away, she advised Mrs Stephens 'to take a vomit, thinking she was with child; as I had taken a ridiculous notion into my head, that having children, made a man like his wife less.'

In this manner we went on till Lord S. [Strathmore, her first husband] returned to town, and he [her friend George Gray] went to Bath, agreeing not to correspond till I wrote to tell him he might return, which I did in a month's time, when Lord S. went away, but did not see him for some days, I cannot recollect how many, but once in that month he came up to town, and contrived to convey me a note, letting me know that his impatience had made him disobey my orders, and come up to town without a summons, just to see me for an hour or two. He therefore begged I would meet him at Lever's, as by accident, which I did, and he returned directly to Bath, where he staid till I wrote to him to return. The weather being extremely severe the day before he went to Bath, and I having just met him very early in Saint James's Park, my shoes extremely wet, and bottom of my petticoats, and I not having leisure to change them for some time after I came home, I caught a slow fever, and cut myself dreadfully by falling on the ice; so that I was ill when I went to Lever's, where I encreased [*sic*] my complaints; and just after Lord S. went away, I fell into an ague, in my face, from which I suffered for near a month, half of every twenty-four hours such torments . . . : my head swelled so, yet without easing my pain, that I was blind, and even spoke with pain. In this miserable condition, Mr G. visited me every evening unknown, as I thought by all but George, who let him in, and unsuspected by all but Mrs Parish, who sometimes remonstrated, but very gently, and I turned it off with a laugh or joke: at first, she thought it only flirtation, and then she said nothing . . .

I omitted to mention, in its proper place, that I told Mr. Gray he had my friendship and esteem; that my heart had long been in possession of another, from whom I had determined to withdraw it, but had done it so short a time, that I should think it an injury against the friendship and confidence he was entitled to, if I concealed this circumstance from him: also, that I had been so unhappy in matrimony, that I was determined never to engage myself indissolubly, though I would most faithfully, if, on these conditions, he would be satisfied with my affection, he should have it entire if Lord S. died; that if he recovered, he must give me up; and that during my husband's life, he must decline all thoughts of me. To all this with reluctance, and finding me peremptory, he consented, and gave me his promise, which he strictly kept till I was just recovered, when I found he expected to be rewarded, for the very great attentions (by writing to me all day, and sitting by me all evening) which he constantly paid during my confinement: and one unfortunate evening I was off my guard, and ever after that (the middle of February) I lived occasionally with him as his wife; and from that time, till my connection with you, I declare, I never had a thought of any other man.

I was once with child by him, before I heard of Lord S.'s death, which I did not till the 6th of April; but was so frightened and unhappy at it, that I prevailed on him to bring me a quack medicine he had heard of for miscarriage, but never tried it: it was of a copperas [sic] substance, by the taste and look; he gave it me very reluctantly, as he said he did not know but it might be poison; however, I would have it.

All the time of my connection with Mr. Gray, precautions were taken; but an instant's neglect always destroyed them all: indeed, sometimes, even when I thought an accident scarce possible . . .

I have now punctually, minutely, and most entirely given you a full account of every thing I ever did, said, or thought, that was wrong.

I have, under my own hand, furnished you with a perpetual fund for unkindness, and even good excuse for bad usage; but you are my husband – I obey you, and if you continue to distrust, abuse, and think of me as you have hitherto done, Providence must and will decide which of us two is most to blame.

I know, according to your promise, you will never again repeat past grievances; but if you think of them I shall suffer as much and more from the unkindness, your brooding silently over them will constantly create; for indeed I fear you are of an unforgiving, and in this respect, unforgetting temper; else you could not, for so many months together, have behaved so uniformly cruel to one whose whole wish and study was to please you.

If you think my sincerity and unreserved confession of my faults may entitle me to ask a favour, let me beg your promise to burn these papers, at least, that you will destroy them when I die, that I may not stand condemned and disgraced, under my own hand, to posterity . . .

A black inky kind of medicine (which I have mentioned before) occasioned two of my miscarriages: the third, after trying the black medicine without effect, was occasioned by a vomit of emetic; eating much pepper, and drinking a wine-glass of brandy. I am ashamed to say, I tried all these things the fourth time, without the smallest effect.

I do assure you, that no man ever took the smallest liberty with me (Lord S., yourself, and Mr G. excepted) except three or four times that Mr. Stephens kissed me, under one pretence or other; and once or twice that Mr. G. S. as we were standing by the fire-side, put his arm round my waist . . .

You saw a bit of these papers last night, when you came into my dressing-room, though I begged you would not look, and was angry at my minute news, and telling you such trifles: if I had done otherwise (besides my oath) might you not with justice, and would you not have said, I ordered you to be exact, minute, and scrupulous; so as to declare every thought that you had; were not these your own words? And how did you know what I should esteem trifling? Therefore, my dearest, you should excuse this minute news, and whatever manner I may mention the facts in, so they be but facts!

God bless you, and forgive me all my sins and faults . . . May I never feel happiness in this world, or the world to come; and may my children meet every hour of their lives unparalleled misery, if I have, either directly or indirectly, told one or more falsehoods in these narratives; or if I have kept any thing a secret . . .

❦

ROBERT BURNS'S WIFE REMEMBERS
Jean Armour, 1780s and 1790s

'Long-suffering' is inadequate to describe Robert Burns's lover and eventual wife. Known as 'The Belle of Mauchline', Jean Armour's relationship with the rough and lusty farmer was unacceptable to her genteel family, and she had borne him five children (four were twins, of whom one died) before they kicked her out, and the pair were

officially wed. Her brilliant and volatile husband's infidelities must have been painful, yet she took in one of his illegitimate children to raise as her own. Clearly the love between them was strong, and her forbearance suggests not that she was cowed and help-less, but rather that her affection never dimmed. There is little by Jean in the archives, and she is usually glimpsed either in Burns's poems or letters. Here, however, is her description of the household when Burns was at home, recorded years after Burns's death by biographer John McDiarmid. It is followed by the memories of Jessy Lawers, whose father and brother were in the Excise service at the same time as Burns. And finally, there is Burns's last letter to his wife, written shortly before he died. She was to give birth to their ninth child on the day of his funeral, one week later.

Jean Armour

The family breakfasted at nine. If he lay long in bed awake he was always read-ing. At all his meals he had a book beside him on the table. He did his work in the forenoon, and was seldom engaged professionally in the evening. He dined at two o'clock when he dines at home; was fond of plain things, and hated tarts, pies, and puddings. When at home in the evening he employed his time in writing and reading, with the children playing about him. Their prattle never disturbed him in the least . . .

Jessy Lawers

He was always anxious that his wife should be well and neatly dressed, and did his utmost to counteract any tendency to carelessness – which she sometimes excused by alleging the duties of a nurse and mother – not only by gentle remonstrance, but by buying her the best clothes he could afford. He rarely omitted to get for her any little novelty in female dress. She was, for instance, one of the first persons in Dumfries to wear a dress of gingham – stuff which was at its first introduction rather costly, and used almost exclusively by the well-to-do.

ROBERT BURNS'S LAST LETTER TO JEAN

14 July 1796

My dearest Love
I delayed writing until I could tell you what effect sea-bathing was likely to produce. It would be injustice to deny that it has eased my pains, and, I think, has strengthened me; but my appetite is still extremely bad. No flesh nor fish

can I swallow; porridge and milk are the only things I can taste. I am very happy to hear, by Miss Jess Lewars, that you are all well. My very best and kindest compliments to her, and to all the children. I will see you on Sunday.

Your affectionate husband
R.B.

❦

THE FIRST FEMALE BENEFIT SOCIETY
Eliza Fletcher, March 1798

By the time Eliza Fletcher and her friends set up the Edinburgh New Town Female Friendly Society, there was rising interest in politics among women, especially of their class. Blue stockings were generally laughed at and dismissed, and even though there were increasing numbers of literary ladies to add a fresh perspective to dinner table talk, their opinions were still viewed as exotic rather than profound. Mrs Fletcher, the wife of a most liberal-minded lawyer, was one who led the way, her friendship with Lord Cockburn (despite his reservations about bookish women) and Lord Brougham helping her win influence. Her great friend Anne Grant described her friend's household as 'for many years the centre of attraction to everything that is elegant or enlightened about town'. This extract comes from her fascinating autobiography, written between 1838 and 1844, which shows simultaneously her growing political awareness and her close family attachments. Years later one of her daughters remembered her work in creating asylums for women, and in helping a prostitute find a better and far happier life. The Female Benefit Society lasted almost half a century. Its aim was 'to be composed of two classes: those females in the higher ranks who chuse to subscribe a small sum annually in aid of the funds, but to receive no benefit . . . and servants and married women of good character' who, when they fell on hard times, would be able to call on financial support.

It was in March, 1798, that I prevailed on several ladies of my acquaintance to join me in the institution of a Female Benefit Society in Edinburgh, and after much difficulty and opposition this club was established for the relief of maid-servants and other poor women in sickness. Such institutions among men had long been in operation in Scotland, but this was the first Female Benefit Society attempted, and as all innovations at that time were looked upon with suspicion, and especially where ladies suspected of democratic principles were concerned, this poor 'sick club' was vehemently opposed by the constituted authorities – namely, the Deputy Sheriff and the Magistrates, when these were legally applied to, to sanction the rules of the Society. I mention this to mark the spirit of the time at that period in Edinburgh, both as regards politics, and with regard to the condition of women. For ladies to take any share, especially a leading share, in the management of a public institution, was considered so novel and extraordinary a proceeding as ought not to be countenanced.

AN ABERDEEN BREAKFAST

Rev. Donald Sage, early 1800s

Donald Sage, a son of the manse who was born in Kildonan in 1789, and became a Free Church minister, is most famous for his recollections of the Highland Clearances, which he witnessed. Here, as a student at the College of Aberdeen, he revisits the habits of his landlord's daughter, who clearly had all the makings of a fine Caledonian land-lady in her own right.

To give us a more than ordinary treat tea was prepared for breakfast, a luxury almost unknown in these hyperborean regions. Gordon's second daughter Anne, who then had the management of her father's house, would insist on preparing it. She put about a pound of tea into a tolerably large-sized pot, with nearly a gallon of 'burn' water, and seasoned the whole as she would any other stew, with a reasonable proportion of butter, pepper, and salt! When served up at the breakfast table, however, the sauce only was administered, the leaves being reserved for future decoctions.

THE FARMER'S WIFE

Ian Niall, 1800s

A novelist and memoirist, born in Old Kilpatrick, near Glasgow, in 1916, Ian Niall's paternal family were tenant farmers in the Machars of Wigtownshire. His first three books appeared under his own name, John McNeillie. His history of the farming way of life, Speed the Plough, *includes a vivid chapter on the role of the farmer's wife, whom he called Mrs Giles, in the previous century. He was well ahead of his generation in appreciating the work that women did. As he wrote, 'If the running of a farm depended on patriarchal influence it also depended upon a long tradition of matri-archal control from one generation to another. A man might know from his father what field to plant and what crop to grow in it. A woman knew how to prepare for tomorrow and tomorrow.'*

To cope with all she had to do Mrs Giles rose before cockcrow and spent the first half-hour of her working day coaxing life into the fire once again. Once she had it lit she was off on what was little less than a positive marathon of cookery, especially at harvest time, or when corn was being threshed.

It began with breakfast for milkers and horsemen, the setting of a porridge pot to boil, frying eggs in an iron frying pan along with salt bacon and scones perhaps, but there were other things to do between times, hens to let out, calves to feed as well as pigs. Never for more than a minute could she or any member of the family stand to admire the sunrise. No one dared dream of leisure. The sunrise itself began to waste the day, climbing the sky. Leisure was for grass-hoppers and the gentry who cantered across paddocks, jumping fences for fun, or chasing a fox that could have been brought to his proper end with a charge of shot from a muzzle-loader. There never was a more taken-for-granted, hard-working woman than this one, or a woman upon whom a family was more dependent. When she had done her outside chores, and long before noon, she would be found sitting peeling as much as half a stone of potatoes, preparing rabbits for a stew, or setting up her baking board to make bread or scones. The family simply demolished her work. Carters and ploughmen came hungry from the field and greedily supped the broth she had made, drank the buttermilk, swallowed the buttered potatoes and salt beef she set before them and reached for her oatcakes and cheese. For her there was really no tomorrow even although she did all she could to lay up stores against it. When the invaders went clumping back to the field or the rickyard she scrubbed her flagged floor, scoured her heavy black iron pots and sighed for the coming of evening, not so that she could doze by the fire or read a romance, but find time to work on her patchwork quilt or the sampler asking God to bless this house!

While the most brilliant inventors were busy inventing things to make a man's life easier they found little time to think of ways of making his wife's work less arduous. It is true that after listening to the more articulate gentle-woman they had given her a coffee grinder and a knife cleaner, both items to delight the domestics employed in the country house, but farmers' wives were not great coffee-makers and weren't looking for mere gadgets. It was the iron-founder who gave her the kitchen range, that great lump of iron to fill the big open fireplace. The range really came into its own when coal became available at distribution points handy to the rural community; the range had broad hobs. It had an oven on one side and a waterboiler on the other that might be filled from the well or the pump outside; boiling water could be had at the turning of the brass tap although the boiler might crack and deliver a rather rusty fluid with an iron sediment. The range pleased the woman who had worked for so long with a primitive cooking fire. She stood before it like a high priestess at an altar. Regularly she had to get down on her knees before it – to burnish and polish its steels with black-lead applied with a boot-brush. If she neglected her devotions her guilt would be plain for everyone to see . . .

The farm kitchen's furniture varied little from one part of the country to another. Wooden settles and forms had always been popular, furniture might be of scrubbed deal or well-worn oak. The grandfather clock stood by the wall, a wallclock wagged on the wall, an American clock became a prized timekeeper. Armchairs tended to have horsehair stuffing that made them less comfortable to the uncovered leg or arm . . .

The bedroom had been modernized to some extent by the busy men of Birmingham who gave the family its first iron beds to replace the sort of four-posters Elizabethans had slept in. The iron bed was trimmed and decorated with brass, solid brass knobs and rails that added to its great weight. Its great heavy iron casting made the bed almost as immovable as the four-poster until someone discovered a way of welding the frame. The iron bed, its advertisers claimed, was insect free! They didn't expand upon this. It had to be. Woodworm had never been found in iron. Perhaps the real claim was that the bedbug didn't like the ironmongery upon which the mattress was laid. The farmer's wife who polished her warming pan and her candlesticks was pleased to find that the brass of the iron bed was lacquered and didn't need to be burnished or rubbed up. The bed was a delight to the eye at a time when ornamentation in everything was the fashion. It still needed to be made, however, and bed-making was no small task when the mattress was stuffed with feathers. It took two women to make a feather bed, but who thought of this when no one studied women's work, except to cut their pay if they happened to be working on a loom? The feather bed had to be turned, and pounded into shape once this was done. Making it was a sort of wrestling match even if it contained nothing but the down of ducks and geese. Each year, at Christmas and Michaelmas when fowl were plucked for the market, feather beds would be changed or refilled. The feathers of duck were used for pillows as well as in the mattress, but no hen feathers were ever used for these are of too coarse a fibre and have much harder quills. There was another tick-filling material used by farmers – chaff – which was stored in a chaff house below the threshing floor or the floor of the granary. A chaff bed was always much cooler to sleep in than a feather bed, and much healthier on this account. It could be changed more often and it was easier to make. The man who slept in a feather bed was always slow to rise. He slept deeply. His senses left him, and he never heard the clock chime the hour, or so his master said . . .

Before a young woman married a farmer she did well to know how to deal with a pig. This involved salting its hams. It also required her to know how to make brawn from its head, use its blood and intestines to make sausage and black puddings, to render its fat and store the lard, to smoke its whole side, minus the head, in the chimney, having lit a fire with oak chippings and sawdust. When she cured the ham she would spend an hour or two every day rubbing in a mixture of ordinary brine and saltpetre with perhaps a little brown sugar, some molasses or honey, depending upon her mother's recipe. When she helped to pluck and dress scores of Michaelmas and Christmas fowl she might trim the combs of the cockerels and blanch them for stewing, or cut out the tongues of her ducks and geese. These she would stew and flavour with essence of ham and a few herbs. It took fifty tongues to make a small dish! The essential thing in all this was frugality and frugality was inborn in women, particularly countrywomen.

THE GUNNER'S WIFE

John Nicol, March 1801

During the seemingly never-ending Napoleonic Wars, John Nicol was aboard the Goliah *during the bloody Battle of Abukir (Abu Qir), near the Nile delta. In this engagement, the British landed and began to drive back the French, at a cost of more than 700 British troops. His unenviable post was in the magazine beside the gunner. Women, it seems, played a key role in the conflict, even though they never fired a shot.*

Any information we got was from the boys and women who carried the powder. The women behaved as well as the men, and got a present for their bravery from the Grand Signior. When the French admiral's ship blew up, the *Goliah* got such a shake we thought the after part of her had blown up, until the boys told us what it was. In the heat of the action, a shot came right into the magazine, but did no harm, as the carpenter plugged it up. I was much indebted to the gunner's wife, who gave her husband and me a drink of wine every now and then, which lessened our fatigue much. There were some of the women wounded, and one woman belonging to Leith died of her wounds, and was buried on a small island in the Bay. One woman bore a son in the heat of the action. She belonged to Edinburgh.

A CHURCH SERVICE IN THE HIGHLANDS
Elizabeth Grant, 1809

The well-travelled author of The Memoirs of a Highland Lady *wrote this journal only for her family's eyes, and it was not published until after her death. One can see why.*

The minister gave out the psalm; he put a very small dirty volume up to one eye, for he was near-sighted, and read as many lines of the old version of the rhythmical paraphrase (we may call it) of the Psalms of David as he thought fit, drawling them out in a sort of sing-song. He stooped over the pulpit to hand his little book to the precentor, who then rose and calling out aloud the tune – 'St. George's tune', 'Auld Aberdeen', 'Hondred an' fifteen', etc. – began himself a recitative of the first line on the key-note, then taken up and repeated by the congregation; line by line, he continued in the same fashion, thus doubling the length of the exercise, for really to some it was no play – serious severe screaming quite beyond the natural pitch of the voice, a wandering search after the air by many who never caught it, a flourish of difficult execution and plenty of the tremolo lately come into fashion. The dogs seized this occasion to bark (for they always came to the kirk with the family), and the babies to cry. When the minister could bear the din no longer he popped up again, again leaned over, touched the precentor's head, and instantly all sound ceased.

MISS BAILLIE SEES TOO MUCH
Elizabeth Grant, 1809

A country house could feel like a hotel when guests were demanding, and the house-maids had a hard time. A similar situation to the faux pas *below was encountered some years ago by a renowned journalist who entered his room at the Balmoral Hotel, to hear splashing in the bathroom. On opening the door, he came face to face — the rest was concealed by bubbles — with a famous writer. Her novels suggest she would not have been fazed in the slightest.*

The Cummings of Altyre were always up in our country and an Irish Mr. Macklin, a clever little, flighty, ugly man, who played the flute divinely, and wore out the patience of the laundry-maids by the number of shirts he put on per day; for we washed for all our guests, there was no one in all Rothiemurchus competent to earn a penny in this way. He was a 'very clean gentleman,' and took a bath twice a day, not in the river, but in a tub — a tub brought up from the wash-house, for in those days the chamber apparatus for ablutions was quite on the modern French scale. Well, Miss Baillie coming upstairs to dress for dinner, opened the door to the left instead of the door to the right, and came full upon short, fat, black Mr. Macklin in his tub! Such a commotion! we heard it in our schoolroom. Miss Baillie would not appear at dinner. Mr. Macklin, who was full of fun, would stay upstairs if she did; she insisted on his immediate departure, he insisted on their swearing eternal friendship. Such a hubbub was never in a house before. 'If she'd been a young girl, one would a'most forgive her nonsense,' said Mrs. Bird, the nurse. 'If she had had common sense,' said Miss Ramsay, 'she would have shut the door and held her tongue, and no one would have been the wiser.'

A CHILD'S VIEW
Marjory Fleming, 1809–10

For the last eighteen months of her life, Marjory Fleming kept a diary, an educative act encouraged by grown-ups. At this time Marjory, born in Kirkcaldy in 1803, was being brought up in Edinburgh, and tutored by her cousin Isabella Keith. That she was reading Ann Radcliffe's gothic romance The Mysteries of Udolpho, *which was among the best-selling novels by female authors in this period, shows how avidly women's fiction was sought out. Marjory died at home, shortly before her ninth birthday, not long after telling her cousin that 'we are surrounded by measles at present on every side', although the cause of her death was more likely meningitis. Her admirers included Robert Louis Stevenson, who wrote: 'Marjory Fleming was possibly — no, I take back possibly — she was one of the noblest works of God.'*

The day of my existence here has been delightful and enchanting. On Saturday I expected no less than three well-made Bucks the names of whom is here advertized: Mr Geo Crakey and Wm Keith and Jn Keith the first is the funniest of everyone of them. Mr Crakey and I walked to Crakyhall hand in hand in Innocence and matitation sweet thinking on the kind love which flows in our tender-hearted mind which is overflowing with majestick pleasure. Nobody was ever so polite to me in the hole state of my existence. Mr Crakey you must know is a great Buck and pretty good looking.

I confess that I have been more like a little young Devil than a creature for when Isabella went up the stairs to teach me religion and my multiplication and to be good and all my other lessons I stamped with my feet and threw my new hat which she made on the ground and was sulky and was dreadfully passionate but she never whiped me . . .

Today I pronounced a word which should never come out of a ladys lips it was that I called John a Impudent Bitch and Isabella afterwards told me that I should never say it even in a joke but she kindly forgave me because I said that I would not do it again I will tell you what I think made me in so bad a humour is I got 1 or 2 cups of that bad bad sina tea to Day.

This is Saturday and I am very glad of it because I have play half of the day and I get money too – but alas I owe Isabella 4 pence; for I am finned 2 pence whenever I bite my nails. Isa is teaching me to make Simecolings nots of interrigations peorids and commas etc. As this is Sunday I will meditate uppon senciable and Religious subjects first I should be very thankful I am not a beggar as many are.

It is melancholy to think that I have so many talents and many there are that have not had the attention paid to them that I have and yet they contrive to be better than me.

Now am I quite happy for I am going tomorrow to a delightfull place Braehead by name belonging to Mr Craford where there is ducks cocks hens bubbyjocks 2 dogs 2 cats and swine; which is delightful . . .

I am going to tell you that in all my life I never behaved so ill for when Isa bid me go out of the room I would not go and when Isa came to the room I threw my book at her in a dreadful passion and she did not lick me but said go into room and pray and I did it . . .

My religion is greatly falling off because I dont pray with so much attention when I am saying my prayers and my character is lost among the Braehead people I hope I will be religious agoin but as for regaining my character I despare for it . . .

I should like to go and see the curosities in London but I should be affraid of the robbers for that country is greatly infested with them at Edinburgh their is not so many of them . . .

At Braehead I lay at the foot of the bed becase Isabella says I disturbed her repose at night by continial figiting and kicking but I was very continialy at work reading the Arabin nights entertainments which I could not have done had I slept at the top. I am reading the Mysteries of adolpho and am much interested in the fate of poor poor Emily.

THE STRATHNAVER CLEARANCE

Rev. Donald Sage, 1814

The beautiful glen of Strathnaver in the far north of Scotland was among the most savage sites of the Highland Clearances, as the Countess of Sutherland – and later other land-owners – cleared people off the land to make way for more profitable sheep. The idea appears originally to have been the Countess's, Elizabeth Gordon, who wrote that, on touring her land with her husband in 1807, 'he is seized as much as I am with the rage of improvements, and we both turn our attention with the greatest of energy to turnips'. In 1809, her husband, who later became the Duke of Sutherland, employed a factor to evict his tenants. Patrick Sellar, a lawyer, went down in legend for his cruelty, although for lack of evidence he was exonerated of culpable homicide for setting light to a croft in Strathnaver with a woman still inside. The area had been settled since Neolithic times, but in the space of a few years it became desolate. This account by the Minister of Grummore, who had left his post a few days earlier, explains why even now the memory of these events is bitter.

The middle of the week brought on the day of the Strathnaver Clearance. It was a Tuesday. At an early hour of that day, Mr. Sellar, accompanied by the Fiscal, and escorted by a strong body of constables, sheriff-officers and others, commenced work at Grummore, the first inhabited township to the west of the Achness district. Their plan of operations was to clear the cottages of their inmates, giving them about half-an-hour to pack up and carry off their furniture, and then set the cottages on fire. To this plan they ruthlessly adhered, without the slightest regard to any obstacle that might arise while carrying it into execution.

At Grumbeg lived a soldier's widow, Henny Munro. She had followed her husband in all his campaigns, marches and battles, in Sicily and in Spain. Whether his death was on the field of battle, or the result of fever or fatigue, I forget, but his faithful helpmeet attended him to his last hour, and, when his spirit fled, closed his eyes, and followed his remains to their last resting-place. After his death she returned to Grumbeg, the place of her nativity, and, as she was utterly destitute of any means of support, she was affectionately received by her friends, who built her a small cottage and gave her a cow and grass for it. The din of arms, orders and counter-orders from head-quarters, marchings and counter-marchings and pitched battles, retreats and advances, were the leading and nearly unceasing subjects of her winter evening conversations. She was a joyous, cheery old creature; so inoffensive, moreover, and so contented, and brimful of good-will that all who got acquainted with old Henny Munro could only desire to do her a good turn, were it merely for the warm and hearty expressions of gratitude with which it was received. Surely the factor and his followers did personally not know old Henny, or they could not have treated her as they did. After the cottages at Grummore were emptied of their inmates, and roofs and rafters had been lighted up into one red blaze, Mr. Sellar and his iron-hearted attendants approached the residence of the soldier's widow. Henny stood up to plead for her furniture – the coarsest and most valueless that well could be, but still her earthly all. She first asked that, as her neighbours were so occupied with their own furniture, hers might be allowed to remain till they should be free to remove it for her. This request was curtly refused. She then besought them to allow a shepherd, who was present and offered his services for that purpose, to remove the furniture to his own residence on the opposite shore of the loch, to remain there till she could carry it away. This also was refused, and she was told, with an oath, that if she did not take her trumpery off within half-an-hour it would be burned. The poor widow had only to task the remains of her bodily strength, and address herself to the work of dragging her chests, beds, presses, and stools out at the door, and placing them at the gable of her cottage. No sooner was her task accomplished than the torch was applied, the widow's hut, built of very combustible material, speedily ignited, and there rose up rapidly, first a dense cloud of smoke, and soon thereafter a bright red flame. The wind unfortunately blew in the direction of the furniture, and the flame, lighting upon it, speedily reduced it to ashes.

WATERLOO BLUE

Elizabeth Grant, 1816

The Duke of Wellington's defeat of Napoleon at Waterloo, in June 1815, after twenty years of conflict, had the nation rejoicing, though not everything about it was welcome.

We were inundated this whole winter with a deluge of a dull ugly colour called Waterloo blue, copied from the dye used in Flanders for the calico of which the peasantry made their smock-frocks or blouses. Everything new was 'Waterloo,' not unreasonably, it had been such a victory, such an event, after so many years of exhausting suffering; and as a surname to hats, coats, trousers, instruments, furniture, it was very well – a fair way of trying to perpetuate tranquillity; but to deluge us with that vile indigo, so unbecoming even to the fairest! It was really a punishment; none of us were sufficiently patriotic to deform ourselves by wearing it.

EDINBURGH WELCOMES KING GEORGE IV
Mrs Fletcher, 1822

Excitement about George IV's visit ignited the capital. Sir Walter Scott's role in organising the visit is well recorded, as is the eye-watering scarlet tartan outfit the king elected to wear with pink hose. To judge by Mrs Fletcher's response, he cannot have appeared as outlandish to his contemporaries as later commentators have suggested.

When we returned to Edinburgh, in the summer of 1822, the whole community there, rich and poor, were agog in expectation of a visit from George the Fourth. He appeared there in August; and if he had been the wisest, bravest, and most patriotic of kings that ever wore a crown, he could not have been received with more loyal devotion than was shown him by the good town of Edinburgh. My sons were both called upon to get up their military duties and accoutrements, for the occasion of the public entry into Edinburgh from Leith. I went with my three daughters to a window above Trotter's shop in Princes Street, to see the royal cavalcade come down St. Andrew Street to cross the Calton Hill to Holyrood. It was certainly a most imposing and gorgeous sight; but it was not the gilded coach or the fat gentleman within it which made it an affecting one: it was the vast multitude assembled – some said a hundred thousand people – animated by one feeling of national pride and pleasure in testifying their loyalty to their Sovereign. Sir Walter Scott had so admirably arranged the reception, that the poorest and humblest of his subjects had an opportunity afforded them of bowing to their King.

FLIRTING WITHOUT A LICENCE

Lord Henry Cockburn, early to mid 19th century

Cockburn was a master recorder of social life. That he was a stickler for good behaviour makes his memoirs more rather than less fascinating and informative.

Here were the last remains of the ball-room discipline of the preceding age. Martinet dowagers and venerable beaux acted as masters and mistresses of ceremonies, and made all the preliminary arrangements. No couple could dance unless each party was provided with a ticket prescribing the precise place, in the precise dance. If there was no ticket, the gentleman, or the lady, was dealt with as an intruder, and turned out of the dance. If the ticket had marked upon it – say for a country dance, the figures 3.5; this meant that the holder was to place himself in the 3d dance, and 5th from the top; and if he was anywhere else, he was set right, or excluded. And the partner's ticket must correspond. Woe on the poor girl who with ticket 2.7, was found opposite a youth marked 5.9! It was flirting without a licence, and looked very ill, and would probably be reported by the ticket director of that dance to the mother. Of course parties, or parents, who wished to secure dancing for themselves or those they had charge of, provided themselves with correct and corresponding vouchers before the ball day arrived. This could only be accomplished through a director; and the election of a pope sometimes required less jobbing. When parties chose to take their chance, they might do so; but still, though only obtained in the room, the written permission was necessary; and such a thing as a compact to dance, by a couple without official authority, would have been an outrage that could scarcely be contemplated. Tea was sipped in side-rooms; and he was a careless beau who did not present his partner with an orange at the end of each dance; and the oranges and the tea, like everything else, were under exact and positive regulations.

❧

EXPERIMENTING ON A CHILD
Elizabeth Storie, 1822

Born in Tradeston, Glasgow, in 1818, Elizabeth Storie's horrific account of her treatment by a doctor who used her as a guinea pig is not easy to read. Despite what happened, she lived to become a dressmaker and seamstress, though only able to drink through a hole surgeons made in her jaw. As an adult, Storie took her abuser to court, unsuccessfully. She wrote her autobiography, she said, 'having a strong impression that injustice is often done to the poor, and more especially to the women of that class'. Her conclusion was bleak. Trust in God, she urged anyone in a similar position, because 'vain is the help of man'.

When four years and four months old, I was seized with a complaint common to childhood, called nettle-rush and which is generally completely removed by the use of a little gentle medicine. But, alas for me! under it I fell a victim to the unskilful treatment practised upon me by one whom the Medical Faculty entitled to call himself Surgeon. My father, John Storie, was on intimate terms of friendship with Robert Falconer, weaver, who lived in the same street, and whose son, William, had lately become Surgeon. Dr Falconer, as this son was called, was in the habit of frequently visiting my father's house, and during this early illness of mine, he came in one day while my mother was in the act of giving me sulphur and senna. He asked my mother what was the matter with Elizabeth, (meaning me) and what it was she was giving to me. She told him what she thought ailed me, and the remedy she was using, but he replied that that was no medicine for nettle-rush, but that he would send up a few powders that would do me good. Accordingly his brother Archibald brought some, two of which were given to me that day. I have a distinct recollection that they tasted like chalk.

On visiting me the next day, Dr Falconer ordered two more of the powders to be given to me, which was accordingly done. The day following he found me rather feverish, and took a bottle containing calomel out of his pocket, emptied some of it into a spoon, mixed it with water, and kept my hands down till I swallowed it. Like most children, I disliked medicine. The dose he gave to me tasted like the powders, and was of the same greyish white colour. I was ordered a warm bath and cold water to allay my thirst which was great. Dr F. called on the next day, still inquiring if there was any smell, and gave me another powder. On the fifth morning after his first visit he found me very feverish and restless. He gave me another spoonful from the bottle, and again ordered the hot bath. The same evening he called, and I was still more restless and uncomfortable. He did not make any change in his mode of treatment, though the prescriptions he had ordered seemed only to have increased the feverishness and restlessness of my complaint. He ordered two or three of the powders to be given to me daily – the hot baths to be continued – and cold water to drink as before. This treatment was continued for three weeks I think – I continuing in the feverish and restless condition I have described. The smell was by this time very bad, and my head began to swell to a great extent, and saliva to flow in large quantities from my mouth. Dr Falconer ordered me, while in this state, to be taken out of bed and carried round the house in the open air – the snow lying five feet deep on the ground at the time. The salivation continued – my mouth and gums began to mortify, and all my face to become black. My parents began to get seriously alarmed about me – and while they and some of the neighbours were one day standing round my bed and talking of my distressing condition, Dr Falconer came in. After looking at me he ordered me to be lifted out of bed, and asked for a basin. My sister took me on her knee. I did not know what he was going to do, but a sensation of great fear came over me.

While I was sitting on my sister's knee I saw the doctor pour a yellowish liquor from a bottle he had brought with him into a white basin. This was afterwards proved to be aquafortis. He then filled a syringe with this fluid. He asked John Campbell, a person who was in the house at the time, to assist him by holding my hands. He agreed to do so, and while doing this Dr Falconer discharged the contents of the syringe into my mouth. The agony I suffered from this cruel operation was so dreadful that I did not know what I was doing, and I believe I kicked the doctor in the face with such force as to cause him to fall backwards. He, however, in a few minutes afterwards repeated the operation. Part of my tongue fell off – all my teeth and part of my jaw-bone gave way. The pain I suffered was indescribable; but although I was in such agony, the doctor, irritated at some remarks from John Campbell about apparent neglect, went away in a passion and left me without prescribing anything to alleviate the intensity of the pain I was enduring. Some of the neighbours, more humane, ran to the Brewery, Buchan Street, Gorbals, and brought some porter barm which was made into a poultice with carrots and applied to my face. My mouth was soaked with barm sponge all night. I felt considerable relief from these applications. Dr Falconer called as usual next morning, and expressed surprise that I was alive. My father and mother were very anxious to call in another medical man, but Dr Falconer would not hear of it. However they afterwards sent for Dr Smeal, who, as soon as he saw me, told them that I was 'ruined for life by the excessive use of mercury' and stated that the medical man who prescribed it must have known the effect of such treatment. My mother told him that I had got a great many powders, but she was not aware they contained mercury, otherwise her child would never have got them. He asked the name of the doctor who was attending me. My mother told him. He said, before going away, 'Your daughter may survive for two or three days, but not longer.'

My parents were deeply grieved to hear this, and anxious to see what further medical advice could do, they called in Dr Litster, who only confirmed Dr Smeal's opinion. Dr Litster called next day and examined the powders, and found that they contained two ordinary doses of mercury in each. He sent for Dr Falconer, and they held a consultation together, the result of which was that Dr Falconer said he would follow the same course of treatment to-morrow. Dr Litster told him he would be doing what he knew to be wrong. They then parted. Dr Falconer called again in the evening. He came up to me and said, 'Poor thing, she is far through; however there is a powder I would like to give to her, which is a certain cure;' but neither my father nor mother gave him any answer. The doctor's father came in that evening also, as he had been in the habit of doing during my illness. He mentioned to my father that his son was particularly anxious that I should get the valuable powder he had been speaking about, as it would do Elizabeth so much good. My father did not consent to give it to me, but said he would think of it. Next morning Dr Falconer sent up the powder by his brother, with directions how to give it. The powder was never given to me, though Dr Falconer was under the impression that I had got it. He called in the evening, and observing a jug standing by the fire, he lifted it and asked what it contained. My mother told him it was apple-tea. He said, 'Very good, give her as much of it as she likes to drink, but no other medicine. Poor thing, she will not survive long – there will be a change for the worse in the night, however; Dr Crawford and I will call in the morning.' Dr Crawford was Dr Falconer's partner. As my end was expected to be so near, many of the neighbours, as well as our own family, sat up with me that night. I grew no worse, though suffering almost unbearable agony. One of the neighbours, Mrs M'Arthur, occupied herself while sitting up in making what was intended to be my shroud. Mrs Angus crimped the border of the cap I was to have been attired in.

Morning came, and I was still in the land of the living, and the place of hope. The powder which was professedly to have done me so much good, having never been given to me, no change for the better or worse was perceptible. The doctor's inadvertent remark, 'there will be a change for the worse during the night,' seems rather to indicate that evil and not good was the expected result of the valuable powder he had sent to me. There was death in the powder, and he knew it. No wonder, then, at the astonishment of Dr Falconer and his companion in guilt, when they saw that life still animated the body they expected to find rigid in death. No wonder that they exclaimed, 'She is proof of shot,' when the powder they intended for me was afterwards found to contain as much arsenic as would have killed seven persons!

A PUBLISHER CONGRATULATES HIS AUTHOR
William Blackwood, 1824

Susan Ferrier was a publishing sensation, her novel Marriage *(1818) becoming a best-seller. These were followed by* The Inheritance *and* Destiny, *each of which enhanced her reputation in Britain and abroad. She is almost unread today, which is a pity since her subject was the awakening of female consciousness, described with many jibes against conventional notions of what women ought to be thinking and doing. As this letter shows, her publisher William Blackwood seemed keen to keep up her spirits, perhaps hoping it would inspire her to even greater heights. In an earlier letter he quoted Sir Walter Scott's opinion of* Marriage. *He tells her Scott said, 'you had the rare talent of making your conclusion even better than your commencement, "for," said this worthy and veracious person, "Mr. Blackwood, if ever I were to write a novel, I would like to write the two first volumes and leave anybody to write the third that liked."'*

Madam, – On Saturday I lent in confidence to a very clever person, upon whose discretion I can rely, the two volumes of 'The Inheritance.' This morning I got them back with the following note:

'My dear Sir, – I am truly delighted with "The Inheritance." I do not find as yet any one character quite equal to "Dr. Redgill" – except perhaps the good-natured old tumbled [troubled] maiden – but as a novel it is a hundred miles above "Marriage." It reminds me of Miss Austen's very best things in every page, and if the third volume be like these, no fear of success triumphant. Yours &c.'

I could not resist sending you this, and I hope you will be pleased with it, and drive on to your conclusion with full confidence in your own powers.

I am, madam, yours respectfully,
Blackwood.

CELESTIAL MECHANICS

Mary Somerville, c. 1829

Mary Somerville was an exceptional woman, whose intellectual curiosity overcame poor schooling and social stigma, and made her one of the most celebrated figures of her day. The daughter of a naval captain, she was brought up in straitened circumstances in Burntisland, though well connected through her mother. She was largely self taught, with a little help from her brother's tutor. Her first marriage ended in her husband's death, which, for posterity, might have been a blessing since she later wrote that 'He had a very low opinion of the capacity of my sex, and had neither knowledge of, nor interest in, science of any kind.' With her two sons, she returned from London to Scotland, where her work was encouraged by James Playfair and David Brewster, among others. Her second marriage, in 1812, to her cousin William Somerville, who was a hospital inspector, was a much better match. When her extraordinary mathematical abilities became known, Lord Brougham, on behalf of the Society for the Diffusion of Useful Knowledge, wrote to her husband to suggest she translate the French mathematician Laplace's Mécanique Céleste. *Brougham believed that if Mrs Somerville did not undertake this, 'none else can'. She, however, thought mere translation insufficient, and instead decided to turn algebra 'into plain English', thereby introducing Britain to a form of maths then virtually unknown. Its title was* The Mechanism of the Heavens. *In her very readable autobiography, she recalls the request that led to her international acclaim. Half a century later, Somerville College, Oxford was named in her honour.*

The letter surprised me beyond expression. I thought Lord Brougham must have been mistaken with regard to my acquirements, and naturally concluded that my self-acquired knowledge was so far inferior to that of the men who had been educated in our universities that it would be the height of presumption to attempt to write on such a subject, or indeed on any other. A few days after this Lord Brougham came to Chelsea himself, and Somerville joined with him in urging me at least to make the attempt. I said, 'Lord Brougham, you must be aware that the work in question never can be popularised, since the student must at least know something of the differential and integral calculi, and as a preliminary step I should have to prove various problems in physical mechanics and astronomy. Beside, Laplace never gives diagrams or figures, because they are not necessary to persons versed in the calculus, but they would be indispensable in a work such as you wish me to write. I am afraid I am incapable of such a task; but as you both wish it so much, I shall do my very best upon condition of secrecy, and that if I fail the manuscript shall be put into the fire.' Thus suddenly and unexpectedly the whole character and course of my future life was changed.

I rose early and made such arrangements with regard to my children and family affairs that I had time to write afterwards; not, however, without many interruptions. A man can always command his time under the plea of business, a woman is not allowed any such excuse. At Chelsea I was always supposed to be at home, and as my friends and acquaintances came so far out of their way on purpose to see me, it would have been unkind and ungenerous not to receive them. Nevertheless, I was sometimes annoyed when in the midst of a difficult problem some one would enter and say, 'I have come to spend a few hours with you.' However, I learnt by habit to leave a subject and resume it again at once, like putting a mark in a book I might be reading; this was the more necessary as there was no fire-place in my little room, and I had to write in the drawing-room in winter. Frequently I hid my papers as soon as the bell announced a visitor, lest anyone should discover my secret.

SIR WALTER SCOTT'S ANXIOUS DAUGHTER
Anne Scott, c. 1830

It was often the lot — or the choice — of daughters not to marry but to look after their parents as they aged. Anne Scott's affection for her father was genuine, but there are hints in her correspondence, as here to novelist Susan Ferrier, that the position could take its toll.

Sunday morning: Abbotsford.
My dear Miss Ferrier,— I am so very, very sorry I have been so long in answering your kind enquiries; but indeed I did write immediately after your second kind note, but my letter slumbered in papa's desk about a fortnight, and it looked so old, even in appearance, that I did not like to send it, and more days passed on as I have been hurried about people coming and not coming. In short, I would have a thousand of good reasons were I to tell them to you all, but I shall spare you the nine hundred and ninety-eight. Papa is indeed quite well; I never saw him better in spite of reform and east wind; and he really does take great care in regard to diet and exercise. His spirits are as good as possible, and, without having many people staying here, we have had one or two of his old friends, which, I think, does him much good to see. I am now getting quite

well myself, and, except on a cold day, have no return of sore throat; but I mean to take great care, and not put myself under a country doctor's hands again with their horrid pills and potions, as I am sure Dr. Clarkson had nearly killed me with camomile . . . I must now, my dear Miss Ferrier, conclude, as we are just going to walk with the cows abroad in the meadows – very pretty and pastoral . . . I hope, my dear Miss Ferrier, you do not suffer so much from your eyes. I do hope you will come here – I am so sure the country would do you good; and indeed we would have so little light at night, and you would, I hope, feel as much at home here as you could do anywhere else. But I will not trouble you with more about the matter, as I am sure you will come to us whenever you can . . . Ever believe me, dear Miss Ferrier,

Yours very affectionately, A. Scott.

❦

THE WELL-DRESSED THIEF
Anderston Case Book, 1832

Contrary to popular belief, in the nineteenth century almost as many women were convicted for crime as men. Ten years before this particular case, for instance, Glasgow's tolbooth and bridewell prisons held 200 male criminals and 151 female. Figures for those transported show even closer parity. When women appeared in court, as here, their acts often betray the desperation of those in dire want and – in the depths of winter – bitter cold.

Saturday the 14th Jany. 1832
Complains the Procurator Fiscal agt.
Ann Finlayson, Wife of David Niven, Labourer, residing in Partick, who was brought to the office this morning at a quarter to eight o'clock, charged with entering the dwelling house of Robert Nicol, residing in Kidston's land, Main Street, and while therein wickedly and feloniously breaking open a lockfast chest, and theftuously stealing and carrying away therefrom, about eight pound weight of Oat Meal, the property or in the lawful possession of the said Robert Nicol. She is also farther charged with having, on or about the seventh day of November last, feloniously entered the dwelling house of Robert Jaffray residing in Kirkwood's land, Main Street, and theftuously stealing and carrying away therefrom one blue and white printed Gown, one Cotton Damask Shawl, one black Cloth Vest, one pair of Shoes, and other

articles, the property or in the lawful possession of the said Robert Jaffray. The Gown and Shawl were found on her person when apprehended.

Witnesses: Mrs Jaffray, Mrs Currie, Anderson Nicol, Sergt. McLean

MATERNITY HOSPITAL RULES AND REGULATIONS
Glasgow Lying-In Hospital and Dispensary, 1834

The rules for the newly founded Glasgow Lying-In Hospital and Dispensary in the Old Grammar School in Greyfriars Wynd show the scope of its ambitions. The institution quickly expanded, and moved first to St Andrews Square and then, in 1860, to Rottenrow, from which it soon took its name. It quickly became a byword for medical excellence. Today it is officially the Glasgow Royal Maternity Hospital. The judgemental tone of the regulations was intended to reassure the hospital's benefactors that moral standards would be high, but in practice help was offered to all. Indeed, the destitute were sought out, married or not, and no questions asked. In 1836, for instance, its second annual report described the situation of one patient when found by a policeman, who brought her to the hospital: 'She was confined in an apartment lately used as a coal cellar, with the damp rising to a height of four feet. There was no fireplace, no bed or mattress.'

5. That this Institution may not in any degree tend to the encouragement of improvidence, none shall be admitted but those who are married and are really destitute, being unable to pay for medical attendance, and otherwise proper objects to be admitted to the benefit of this Asylum. These conditions shall be expressly vouched in the printed forms that shall be issued for the recommending of patients.

6. To poor women, who may wish to be attended in delivery at their own houses, that attendance shall be furnished to them upon leaving their addresses at the Hospital, along with a certificate from an Elder, District Surgeon, or other respectable person cognisant of the case, stating that the applicant is unable to pay for medical attendance.

7. At a stated hour, two days every week, Advice shall be given on Female Complaints, and the Diseases of Children, to all who may apply at the Hospital for that purpose, a part of economy which is expected to afford much relief to the applicants, & to contribute greatly to improvements in this very important part of Professional Knowledge.

9. The domestic arrangements of the Hospital, hiring servants, making markets, and similar duties, shall be under the management of a Matron chosen by the Directors, she being a person of unexceptionable character, qualified by education and practice as a Midwife. It shall be her duty also to superintend the ordinary cases of delivery in the Hospital, to call or summon the several classes of students entitled to be present at these cases, and to take care that every thing be done according to the rules of improved midwifery, and that rigid propriety and decorum be observed by every person in the Hospital. It would be proper that no more than four pupils should be at once in attendance on any ordinary case, and that after delivery the management of the case should devolve chiefly on the Matron, the students being admitted only at the ordinary hour of visiting along with the domestic Medical Superintendant.

A SCHOOLMISTRESS'S TRAGIC TALE

Janet Kemp, 1838–40

The publication in 1892 of a memoir called Aunt Janet's Legacy *won a devoted readership, and led to a clamour to know about the author. She was Mrs James Kemp, who was widowed in 1836, and for a time ran a school in Dalkeith. Before that, she had started her teaching career in a school for children of the millworkers on the Esk Mills in Penicuik. One awful incident so affected her that she described it in a letter to a friend in Edinburgh, who sent it to* The Witness *newspaper, whose editor was the geologist Hugh Miller. Here it is, filled with Victorian piety yet also redolent of an age when children had to grow up fast.*

It was on the 10th of October 1838 that R—— entered my schoolroom, with his daughter Eliza in one hand, and her younger brother Hugh in the other. He told me that he had brought his little boy to my school; and as he went off with Eliza, I could not help looking after her, and wishing from my heart that she also had remained. In a few minutes, however, he returned, and said 'I have brought back my little girl. She has besought me with tears to allow her to attend your school; they are motherless children, and I cannot bear to hear them cry.'

A few weeks passed by without anything particular occurring. Eliza was one of my best readers, naturally sprightly, and a good singer. She was regular in her attendance, and always came very clean, although her father's only housekeeper.

I am told that her management of household affairs was quite wonderful for one of her age. One day, when I observed her sad, and inquired what was the matter, she burst into tears, and told me that her brother had used a bad word. She had entreated him to pray for forgiveness, which he refused to do, and she looked in my face most tenderly, saying, 'Oh, ma'am, I am afraid he will go to hell.'

In the beginning of March 1839, she came to me, looking very happy, and said, 'Mistress, I have got a halfpenny to buy a roll for my dinner, but I wish rather to put it in the mission-box.' I told her that God did not require so much at her hand – that I only wished her to bring the halfpence which she used to waste. She added, 'Please, ma'am, put it in; I am so sorry for the poor children who have no teacher, no minister, no Bible, and who do not know how to pray to God.' As I took the little, or rather the great sacrifice, I felt ashamed of myself for I had never made such a one. She continued to bring her halfpenny every day, and when I tried to dissuade her, she would look so sweetly in my face, and tell me she would run and get a potato from her grandmother. In the course of the following month, another little girl brought me a halfpenny and said, 'Please, ma'am, take this to help to get light for the poor children who live in darkness.' Before I had time to reply, Eliza said, 'Margaret, the children in Africa have the sun as well as we – it is the darkness of the heart.'

Soon after this, Eliza's father was seized with inflammation in the eyes, which appeared to distress her sorely. She often told me what a good father he had been, and that she was afraid lest he should die; and when I tried to comfort her, by telling her that God is a father to the fatherless, and that he would care for her and her little brother, she still looked sad, and said, 'Oh, my dear Mistress, if my father dies, will you take me and Hughie? and we will work for you when you grow old.' So much tenderness combined with grace was indeed a lovely sight . . .

My reader may ask, Were there no traits of our fallen nature in this child? Did she never behave amiss? I must confess that in many respects she was much like the other children; still with all her faults, there was something more than nature – grace had been at work.

I must now come to the last day she was in school, Sabbath, 19th January, 1840. Every one observed her on that day to be unusually attentive, and that her eye never wandered from me for one moment. I remarked it myself, and thought she was afraid I did not love her as I had done.

On the Monday following, Eliza was left at home to prepare the dinner, while her aunt was at the mill. In putting the pan of potatoes on the fire, her pinafore caught the flames, and before any one came to her assistance she was burnt in a dreadful manner. It was about one o'clock when they came to tell me the sad news. On entering the room I saw the form of a child standing in the bed, and heard from it a well-known voice – 'Mistress, do you know me? I'm a' burned. I have no mother, and my father is far away. O, this is dreadful suffering!' I took her in my arms, and said, 'It is, my lamb; but you know who suffered more.' 'O, yes;' she exclaimed, 'my Saviour; I know I am dying; but I am not afraid to die. There is no fire in heaven, that happy place.' I said 'are you glad, my dear, that you have been taught to know and love your Saviour?' She said, 'O, yes! if I had not known and loved my Saviour, I must have gone to hell, where I could never have got a drop of water to cool my tongue. But though this fire burns my body, it cannot hurt my soul; and I cannot go to hell, because I love God, and He loves me.'

She repeated several of her hymns – in particular, 'How sweet the name of Jesus sounds,' and 'Here, we suffer grief and pain.' I asked her if she was able in the midst of her own sufferings to think of her Saviour's. 'O, yes,' she said; 'I will soon see Him; and he will not have a crown of thorns on His head.' Her sufferings were extreme, and it was only for a short time that she could speak. She said, 'O, Mistress, Heaven must be a happy, happy place! You told us on the first Sabbath of the year, that it was possible some of us would die before the year was over. You said you did not know which you could best spare, but God knew which to take. I must die first! but I am not afraid. How sweet is that hymn – "But if some one of us should die!"' She said, 'Oh, let me see my own brother Hughie!' I took him in my arms to the side of her bed, when she said, 'Oh, Hughie, keep from the fire, say your prayers, and do not learn bad words, or you will go to a bad place.'

She asked me to lie down beside her, which I did. She bore her sufferings with great patience; and they must have been very great. The flesh was quite burnt off her hands – I saw the bare bones, yet she murmured not. She showed great affection for her friends, asked if they had all come, and often cried out for her dear father, who was then at work in another part of the country. When I asked her if she would like the minister to pray with her, she told me he was not at home, and bade me pray myself. I asked her if she wished to get better. She looked at me half surprised, and said, 'Oh, I cannot get better; pray that I may go to Heaven, that happy place.' I felt my whole soul drawn out in behalf of the little sufferer. She lay perfectly quiet, and listening to every word; and when I had done, she said, 'Thank you, ma'am; will you kiss me? I know you love me; do not cry; it will not make me better. We will meet in Heaven, that happy place.'

At about half-past ten the same evening she breathed her soul into the hands of her Redeemer. My heart was filled with gratitude to God for his mercy in releasing her so soon. Eliza R—— died on 20th January 1840, aged nine years.

❦

SERVANT TROUBLE

Jane Welsh Carlyle, 1840

Arguably the finest writer from Victorian Scotland, Jane Welsh Carlyle was the wife of the historian Thomas Carlyle. Theirs was a turbulent marriage, partly because of their personalities – Jane could be sharp and argumentative, Thomas dour, stubborn and thoughtless – but the tensions in their household make for fascinating reading. A gifted letter-writer, Jane kept a running commentary throughout her married life on domestic, political and personal matters. Here, she is writing to her mother-in-law.

To Mrs Carlyle at Scotsbrig
5 Cheyne Row, Chelsea/ Autumn 1840
Dear Mother,
At present I have got a rather heavy burden on my shoulders, the guarding of a human being from the perdition of strong liquors. My poor little Helen has been gradually getting more and more into the habit of tippling – until, some fortnight ago, she rushed down into a fit of the most decided drunkenness that I ever happened to witness. Figure the head of the Mystic School and a delicate female like myself up till after three in the morning, trying to get the maddened creature to bed; not daring to leave her at large for fear she should set fire to the house or cut her own throat. Finally, we got her bolted into the back kitchen, in a corner of which she had established herself all coiled up and fuffing like a young tiger about to make a spring, or like the Bride of Lammermoor (if you ever read that profane book).

Next day she looked black with shame and despair; and the day following, overcome by her tears and promises and self-upbraidings, I forgave her again, very much to my own surprise. About half an hour after this forgiveness had been accorded I called to her to make me some batter – it was long of coming – and I rang the bell – no answer. I went down to the kitchen to see the meaning of all this delay – and the meaning was very clear; my penitent was lying on the floor, dead-drunk, spread out like the three legs of Man [The Isle of Man], with a chair upset beside her, and in the midst of a perfect chaos of dirty dishes and fragments of broken crockery; the whole scene was a lively epitome of a place that shall be nameless. And this happened at ten in the morning! All that day she remained lying on the floor insensible, or occasionally sitting up like a little bundle of dirt, executing a sort of whinner; We could not imagine how she came to be so long of sobering, but it turned out she had a whole bottle of whiskey hidden within reach, to which she crawled till it was finished throughout the day.

After this, of course, I was determined that she should leave. My friends here set to work with all zeal to find me a servant – and a very promising young woman came to stay with me until a permanent character should turn up. This last scene 'transpired' on the Wednesday; on the Monday she was to sail for Kirkcaldy. All the intervening days, I held out against her pale face, her tears, her despair – but I suffered terribly for I am really much attached to the poor wretch who has no fault under heaven but this one. On the Sunday night I called her up to pay her her wages and to inquire into her future prospects. Her future prospects! it was enough to break any body's heart to hear how she talked of them. It was all over for her on this earth, plainly, if I drove her away from me who alone have any influence with her. Beside me she would struggle – away from me she saw no possibility of resisting what she had come to regard as her Fate. You may guess the sequel – I forgave her a third time, and a last time . . .

Affectionately yours,

Jane W. Carlyle

TESTIMONY OF COAL WORKERS

Janet Cumming, Janet Allen, Jane Johnson, Isabel Hogg, Jane Peacock Wilson, Katharine Logan, Helen Read and Margaret Watson, 1840

The Children's Employment Commission of 1840 was one of the most shocking documents of its time. Its inspectors, who had been sent to investigate whether the provisions of a series of factory acts limiting the working hours of apprentices and children were being implemented, decided also to examine conditions in the mines. In mining towns, baby girls were disparagingly described as 'a hutch of dross', while boys were 'a hutch of coal'. Even so, girls and women were enormously useful in the mines, partly because of their willingness to crawl into the most uncomfortable areas without complaint. The foreman at Ormiston colliery was reported as saying: 'In fact women always did the lifting or heavy part of the work and neither they nor the children were treated like human beings where they are employed. Females submit to work in places where no man or even lad could be got to labour in; they work in bad roads, up to their knees in water, their posture almost double. They are below till the last hour of pregnancy. They have swelled ankles and haunches and are prematurely brought to the grave or, what is worse, to a lingering existence.'

Although the Commission's focus was the conditions of children, the report unexpectedly threw up voices of women as well as girls. When it was published, with illustrations, the public was so horrified that a law was passed making it illegal for women and children to go down the pits. This heightened the misery of those women for whom the pit was their only source of income. To evade the law, some disguised themselves as men; their co-workers turned a blind eye. Here are a few of the comments the Commission recorded.

Janet Cumming, 11, coal bearer: 'I gang with the women at five and come up at five at night; work all night on Fridays and come away at twelve in the day. The roof is very low; I have to bend my back and legs and the water is frequently up to the calves of my legs. Have no liking for the work. Father makes me like it.'

Janet Allen, 8, who pushed tubs: 'It is sair, sair wark, would like to be playing about better.'

Jane Johnson: 'I was seven and half years of age when my uncle yoked me to the pit as father and mother were both dead. I could carry two hundredweights when fifteen but now feel the weakness upon me from the strains. I have been married ten years and had four children, have usually wrought till one or two days of birth. Many women get injured in back and legs and I was crushed by a stone some time since and forced to lose one of my fingers.'

Isabel Hogg, 53, retired coal bearer 'Been married thirty seven years; it was the practice to marry early, when the coals were all carried on women's backs, men needed us. I have four daughters married and all work below till they bear their bairns. One is very badly now from working while pregnant, which brought on a miscarriage from which she is not expected to recover. Collier people suffer much more than others – my guid man died nine years since with bad breath, he lingered some years but was entirely off work eleven years before he died.'

Jane Peacock Watson, 40, coal bearer: 'I have wrought in the bowels of the earth thirty three years; have been married twenty three years and had nine children; six are alive, three died of typhus a few years since, have had two dead born, think they were so from oppressive work; a vast women have dead births . . . I have always been obliged to work below till forced to go home to bear the bairn, so have all the other women. We return as soon as we are able, never longer than ten or twelve days, many less if we are needed.'

Katharine Logan, 16, coal carrier, who was put in a harness: 'drawing backward with face to tubs. The ropes and chains go under pit clothes, it is o'er sair work, especially when we crawl.'

Helen Read, 16, '[I work] from five in the morning till six at night and carry two hundredweight on my back. I dinna like the work but think I'm fit for no other. Many accidents happen below ground, I've met with two serious ones myself. Two years ago the pit closed on thirteen of us and we were two days without food and light. Nearly one day we were up to our chins in water. At last we picked our way to an old shaft and were heard by people working above.'

Margaret Watson, 16: 'We often have bad air, had some a short time since and lost brother by it. He sunk down and I tried to draw him out but the air stopped my breath and I was forced to gang.'

MARRIAGE

Jane Welsh Carlyle, 1843

Even before she married Thomas Carlyle, Jane knew she was not in for an easy time. This cryptic letter to her cousin explains why she accepted his proposal nearly twenty years earlier. It hides a wealth of feeling, at which one can perhaps guess.

To Jeannie Welsh
10 January 1843
. . . in virtue of his being the least unlikable man in the place, I let him dance attendance on my young person, till I came to need him – all the same as my slippers to go to a ball in, or my bonnet to go out to walk. When I finally agreed to marry him, I cried excessively and felt excessively shocked – but if I had then said no he would have left me – and how could I dispense with what was equivalent to my slippers or bonnet? Oh if I might write my own biography from beginning to end – without reservation or false colouring – it would be an invaluable document for my countrywomen in more than one particular – but 'decency forbids'!

THE SEX TRADE

William Logan, 1843

A leading light in the Scottish Temperance Movement, William Logan was appalled at the degradation and poverty he found across the country, at least some of it attributable to drink. He wrote several works on the escalating problem of prostitution, as found in London, Leeds, Rochdale and 'especially in the City of Glasgow', and seems to have been a tender-hearted man. After the death of his four-year-old daughter Sophie, he wrote Words of Comfort for Parents of Bereaved Little Children, *proving that high rates of child mortality did not diminish a parent's pain. This grim statistical account of the sex trade in Glasgow was published in a pamphlet that was so eye-opening, it quickly sold out.*

Number of houses of ill-fame	450
Average number of prostitutes (four in each house)	1800
Number of bullies or 'fancy men'	1350
Number of mistresses of said houses	450
Total living on prostitution	3600
Number of visits of men to each house weekly	80
Making weekly visits to the 450 houses	36000
The girls receive, on an average, from each visitor 1/-	
making the sum weekly, of	£1800
Robberies (2/6 from each visitor is a low average)	4500
Average sum spent on drink, 2/- by each visitor	3600
Total for prostitution weekly	£9900
Do. do. annually	£5148000

Number of girls who die annually (six years being their average
life-time) three hundred!

Mistresses are all old harlots – seldom make money – and are, in general, very ignorant. Several who keep first-class houses in Glasgow cannot sign their names. In each of the houses they claim half of what the girls receive in presents and charge high for board: £1 weekly in first-class houses; and 14s in second houses. The girls have also to pay for the loan of dresses, &c., and when they have money, which is seldom, it is spent on drink, fruit, trinkets, shows, low musicians, &c. In first-class brothels it is quite common for the girls to receive from £1 to £5 from visitors.

I have stated that 2s are spent on drink on an average by each visitor, but the fact is, only one-half of that sum is spent while he is present. The mistress receives the money, and pretends to go or send out for the intoxicating liquor, (except where public-houses are regular brothels,) and it is an understood law, that she retains one-half of the sum for what they call in England 'wack brass,' and in Scotland 'the good-will of the house.' Drinking is also very common in first and second-class houses. Some mistresses send out for it, and others sell it in the house at a great profit; but regular visitors are aware of this, and generally cause it to be brought in. It is not long since several gentlemen drove up to a first-class house in my district, in a carriage and four horses; they had along with them a basket filled with bottles.

MARITAL HARMONY RESTORED
Jane Welsh Carlyle, 1846

To Thomas Carlyle's ordinary flaws was added a much more serious problem. In 1843 he began a close friendship with Lady Harriet Baring, who gathered clever men about her like a flower attracting bees. An unashamed flirt, and adored by her husband, she held prestigious soirées and weekend parties in London and at her country houses, one of which – Addiscombe, near Croyden – Carlyle once referred to as a 'Shrine'. Despite Jane's obvious distress at the pleasure he took in Lady Harriet's company, he continued to visit and correspond with her. For years Jane was in torment, though whether the relationship was anything more than an infatuation was never clear.

To Thomas Carlyle at Chelsea
Seaforth/ 14 July 1846
Oh! my dear Husband

Fortune has played me such a cruel trick this day! – but it is all right now! and I do not even feel any resentment against fortune for the suffocating misery of the last two hours. I know always, when I seem to you most exacting, that whatever happens to me is nothing like so bad as I deserve – But you shall hear all how it was – . . .

– None for me the postmistress averred! – not a line from you on my birthday . . . I did not burst out crying – did not faint – did not do anything absurd, so far as I know – but I walked back again without speaking a word, and with such a tumult of wretchedness in my heart as you who know me can conceive – And then I shut myself in my own room to fancy everything that was most tormenting – Were you finally so out of patience with me that you had resolved to write to me no more at all? – had you gone to Addiscombe and found no leisure there to remember my existence? Were you taken ill so ill that you *could* not write? That last idea made me mad to get off to the railway, and back to London – Oh mercy what a two hours I had of it! – And just when I was at my wits end, I heard Julia crying out thro the house – 'Mrs Carlyle Mrs Carlyle! Are you there? here is a letter for you!'

And so there was after all! – the postmistress had overlooked it – and given it to Robert when he went afterwards not knowing that we had been. I wonder what love-letter was ever received with such thankfulness! – Oh my dear I am not fit for living in the World with this organisation – I am as much broken to pieces by that little accident as if I had come thro an attack of Cholera or Typhus fever – I cannot even steady my hand to write decently. But I felt an irresistible need of thanking you by return of post – Yes I have kissed the dear little card case – and now I will lie down a while, and try to get some sleep – at least to quieten myself – will try to believe – oh why can I not believe it once for all – that with all my faults and follies I am 'dearer to you than any earthly creature' . . .

Your own
J.C.

THE FACTORY GIRL

Ellen Johnston, late 1840s–60s

There is an off-putting self-congratulatory tone to much of Ellen Johnston's writing, yet the story she tells is compelling. Few factory workers, especially women, ever recorded their lives and travails. Fewer still, of any background, alluded to sexual abuse, which nearly drove Ellen to suicide.

About two months after my mother's marriage my stepfather having got work in a factory in Bishop Street, Anderston, they removed to North Street . . . My stepfather could not bear to see me longer basking in the sunshine of freedom, and therefore took me into the factory where he worked to learn power-loom weaving when about eleven years of age, from which time I became a factory girl; but no language can paint the suffering which I afterwards endured from my tormentor.

Before I was thirteen years of age I had read many of Sir Walter Scott's novels, and fancied I was a heroine of the modern style. I was a self-taught scholar, gifted with a considerable amount of natural knowledge for one of my years, for I had only been nine months at school when I could read the English language and Scottish dialect with almost any classic scholar; I had also read 'Wilson's Tales of the Border,' so that by reading so many love adventures my brain was fired with wild imaginations, and therefore resolved to bear with my own fate, and in the end gain a great victory.

By this time my mother had removed from Anderston to a shop in Tradeston, and my stepfather and myself worked in West Street Factory. When one morning early, in the month of June, I absconded from their house as the fox flies from the hunters' hounds, to the Paisley Canal, into which I was about submerging myself to end my sufferings and sorrow, when I thought I heard like the voice of him I had fixed my girlish love upon. I started and paused for a few moments, and the love of young life again prevailed over that of self-destruction, and I fled from the scene as the half-past five morning factory bells were ringing, towards the house of a poor woman in Rose Street, Hutchesontown, where, after giving her my beautiful earrings to pawn, I was made welcome, and on Monday morning following got work in Brown & M'Nee's factory, Commercial Road. I did not, however, remain long in my new lodgings, for on the Tuesday evening, while threading my way among the crowd at the shows, near the foot of Saltmarket, and busy dreaming of the time when I would be an actress, I was laid hold of by my mother's eldest brother, who, after questioning me as to where I had been, and what I was doing, without receiving any satisfaction to his interrogations, compelled me to go with him to my mother, who first questioned me as to the cause of absconding, and then beat me till I felt as if my brain were on fire; but still I kept the secret in my own bosom . . . However, I consented to stay again with my mother for a time, and resolved to avoid my tormentor as much as possible.

Dear reader, I will now bring you to my sixteenth year, when I was in the bloom of fair young maidenhood. Permit me, however, to state that during the three previous years of my life, over a part of which I am drawing a veil, I had run away five times from my tormentor, and during one of those elopements spent about six weeks in Airdrie, wandering often by Carron or Calder's beautiful winding banks. Oh! could I then have seen the glorious gems that have sprung up for me on those banks, and heard the poetic strains that have since been sung in my praise, what a balm they would have been to my bleeding heart, as I wandered around the old Priestrig Pit and listened to its engine thundering the water up from its lowest depth. For days I have wandered the fields between Moodies-burn and Clifton Hill, wooing my sorry muse . . . had it not been for the bright Star of Hope which lingered near me and encouraged me onward, beyond doubt I would have been a suicide.

Dear reader, should your curiosity have been awakened to ask in what form fate had then so hardly dealt with the hapless 'Factory Girl,' this is my answer:— I was falsely accused by those who knew me as a fallen woman, while I was as innocent of the charge as the unborn babe. Oh! how hard to be blamed when the heart is spotless and the conscience clear.

While struggling under those misrepresentations, my first love also deserted me, but another soon after offered me his heart – without the form of legal protection – and in a thoughtless moment I accepted him as my friend and protector. I did not, however, feel inclined to die when I could no longer conceal what the world falsely calls a woman's shame. No, on the other hand, I never loved life more dearly and longed for the hour when I would have something to love me – and my wish was realised by becoming the mother of a lovely daughter on the 14th of September, 1852. No doubt every feeling mother thinks her own child lovely, but mine was surpassing so . . .

As my circumstances in life changed, I placed my daughter under my mother's care when duty called me forth to turn the poetic gift that nature had given me to a useful and profitable account, for which purpose I commenced with vigorous zeal to write my poetical pieces, and sent them to the weekly newspapers for insertion, until I became extensively known and popular . . . but as my fame spread my health began to fail, so that I could not work any longer in a factory.

My stepfather was unable longer to work, and my mother was also rendered a suffering object; my child was then but an infant under three years of age, and I, who had been the only support of the family, was informed by my medical adviser that, unless I took a change of air, I would not live three months.

Many sleepless nights did I pass, thinking what to try to bring relief to the afflicted household – although I did not consider myself in duty bound to struggle against the stern realities of nature, and sacrifice my own young life for those whose sympathies for me had been long seared and withered. Yet I could not, unmoved, look on the pale face of poverty, for their means were entirely exhausted, without hope to lean upon. Neither could I longer continue in the factory without certain death to myself, and I had never learned anything else.

Under those conflicting conditions and feelings, one night as I lay in bed, almost in despair, I prayed fervently that some idea how to act would be revealed to me, when suddenly I remembered that I had a piece of poetry entitled 'An Address to Napier's Dockyard, Lancefield, Finnieston,' which a young man had written for me in imitation of copperplate engraving, and that piece I addressed to Robert Napier, Esq., Shandon, Gareloch-head, who was then in Paris, where it was forwarded to him. Having written to my employer for my character, which was satisfactory, Mr Napier sent me a note to call at a certain office in Oswald Street, Glasgow, and draw as much money as would set me up in some small business, to see if my health would revive. According to the good old gentleman's instructions, I went as directed, and sought L.10, which was freely given to me; and I believe had I asked double the amount I would have readily received it.

My mother had been an invalid for several years, and, to add to her sorrow, a letter had come from her supposed dead husband, my father, in America, after an absence of twenty years, inquiring for his wife and child; on learning their fate he became maddened with remorse, and, according to report, drank a death-draught from a cup in his own hand; and my mother, after becoming aware of the mystery of my life, closed her weary pilgrimage on earth on 25th May, 1861. Thus I was left without a friend, and disappointed of a future promised home and pleasure which I was not destined to enjoy.

CHOLERA

James Maxwell Adams, 1847–48

Sanitation, or the lack of it, was the scourge of the Victorians in rural areas as well as cities. Five years before this account, the Chadwick Report was published, outlining the atrocious living conditions in which the poor lived. In urban districts levels of disease were dreadful, in part because their cause was still unknown and even the most basic hygiene was lacking. Doctor James Maxwell Adams had a close working knowledge of such maladies, his practice being the thirteenth medical district of Glasgow, the warren of slums around George Square, the High Street and Argyle Street. He estimated that around 14,000 people lived in this quarter, in cramped, filthy conditions. Nobody could have remained in doubt that propinquity, squalor and malnutrition contributed to the spread of such disease. Strangely, though, Adams does not explain or hypothesise why all the cases he refers to here were of women.

Cholera first appeared in the district on 9th December 1848, in the ground flat of a building in 22 Shuttle Street. The patient, a female aged fifty-six, was of occasionally intemperate habits, and her previous general health was not good. She had not been in communication with any infected district or locality so far as could be ascertained. She was immediately conveyed to hospital, where she died on the following day. I immediately got the house lime-washed, and the straw-bed on which she had lain destroyed, but the inmates would not consent to removal.

The next case occurred in the same house. A female child, aged two years became affected on 12th December with bilious diarrhoea, which was followed on the 17th by all the symptoms of cholera. She died on the following day.

The third case occurred in 51 Shuttle Street, being on the opposite side of the street, and at a distance of about thirty yards from the last locality. The patient, a female aged twenty-six, was of irregular habits, of infirm intellect, and subject to occasional attacks of dysenteric diarrhoea. She resided in the top story of the tenement: and for a few days prior to December 18th, had been very little out of doors, and had not, so far as I could ascertain, been in communication with the sick. I had her conveyed to hospital, where she died on the following day.

The fourth case occurred in the same house with the preceding. The patient, a female, aged fifty-three, of irregular habits, and average good health, became affected with bilious diarrhoea on December 23, and, on the following day, with all the best marked symptoms of the malignant disease. She recovered after a somewhat protracted convalescence.

The fifth case occurred in 34 Shuttle Street, in the top flat of a building closely adjoining that in which the first case occurred. There is no direct communication between the buildings. The patient was a healthy temperate female, aged eighteen. She had slight diarrhoea on December 24, and next morning, soon after breakfast, she was seized with vomiting, speedily followed with purging and cramps. I had her immediately sent to hospital, where she died, soon after admission.

Up to this date, there had occurred, in all, of cholera and diarrhoea, only seven cases, all within a circle of a few yards, and at the extreme north-east corner of the district; but within the next three days, I was called to twenty cases in various parts of the district, and of this number, eleven were malignant cholera.

A MISSIONARY'S MOTHER-IN-LAW PROTESTS
Mary Moffat, April 1851

Mary Moffat, the mother of Mary Livingstone, was as full of Christian zeal as her son-in-law David Livingstone, soon to be a world-famous explorer. In fact, he had been inspired to follow a religious calling after hearing her own missionary husband, Robert Moffat, preach. Despite her disapproval of the match, Mrs Moffat's plain, stoical Midlands daughter made the best of wives for Livingstone, never complaining, bearing children in alarmingly isolated conditions, and following him into danger without a blink. It's no wonder he called Mary his 'rib'. But when Livingstone's exploration began to overtake his proselytising work, Mrs Moffat tried to put her foot down.

Before you left the Kuruman I did all I dared to do to broach the subject of your intended journey, and thus bring on a candid discussion, more especially with regard to Mary's accompanying you with these dear children. But seeing how averse you and Father were to speak about it, and the hope that you would never be guilty of such temerity (after the dangers they escaped last year), I too timidly shrunk from what I ought to have had the courage to do. Mary had told me all along that should she be pregnant you would not take her, but let her come out here after you were fairly off. Though I suspected at the end that she began to falter in this resolution, still I hoped it would never take place, i.e. her going with you, and looked and longed for things transporting to prevent it. But to my dismay I now get a letter, in which she writes, 'I must again wend my weary way into the far Interior, perhaps to be confined in the field?' O Livingstone, what do you mean? Was it not enough that you lost one lovely babe, and scarcely saved the others, while the mother came home threatened with Paralysis? And will you again expose her & them in those sickly regions on an exploring expedition? All the world would condemn the cruelty of the thing to say nothing of the indecorousness of it. A pregnant woman with three little children trailing about with a company of the other sex, through the wilds of Africa, among savage men and beasts! Had you found a place to which you wished to go and commence missionary operations, the case would be altered. Not one word would I say, were it to the mountains of the moon. But to go with an exploring party, the thing is preposterous.

I remain yours in great perturbation.
M Moffat

Mrs Moffat's fears proved well founded. On one awful occasion the couple and their children spent four days alone in the Kalahari desert with no water, before their team returned to them on the fifth day. Livingstone later wrote:

This was a bitterly anxious night; and the next morning, the less there was of water, the more thirsty the little rogues became. The idea of them perishing before our eyes was terrible; it would have been a relief to have been reproached with the entire cause of the catastrophe, but not one syllable of upbraiding was uttered by their mother, though the tearful eye told the agony within.

By the time Livingstone was better known for his expeditions than his evangelism, Mary returned to Scotland and then England, there miserably to await his return from the interior. After an especially long separation, she wrote the following poem for his arrival, in December 1856. It shows optimism was another of her qualities. As was a vein of romance which possibly only her husband ever saw. By 1858 she was back in Africa, and pregnant again.

A hundred thousand welcomes, and it's time for you to come
From the far land of the foreigner, to your country and your home.
Oh, long as we were parted, ever since you went away,
I never passed an easy night, or knew an easy day.

Do you think I would reproach you with the sorrows that I bore?
Since the sorrow is all over now I have you here once more,
And there's nothing but the gladness and the love within my heart,
And hope so sweet and certain that never again we'll part.

A hundred thousand welcomes! How my heart is gushing o'er
With the love and joy and wonder just to see your face once more.
How did I live without you all those long long years of woe?
It seems as if t'would kill me to be parted from you now.

You'll never part me darling, there's a promise in your eye;
I may tend you while I'm living, you will watch me when I die.
And if death but kindly lead me to the blessed home on high,
What a hundred thousand welcomes will await you in the sky!

LETTER TO A DOOMED YOUTH

Madeleine Smith, 3 July 1856

Written eight months before she is thought to have poisoned him, this letter from the middle-class Glaswegian Madeleine Smith to her lover Pierre Emile L'Angelier, an apprentice gardener, shows her excitable, dramatic and possibly erratic personality. When she became engaged to a wealthy suitor, William Harper Monnich, thereby crushing Emile's long-held expectations, she asked him to return her letters. Knowing they were incriminating, he tried to blackmail her into marrying him. All her pleading would not budge him, and not long afterwards, he was found dead. Madeleine's letters, discovered in the dead man's room, and her purchase of arsenic in the weeks before his death, led to her trial in 1857. It caused a sensation. Many refused to believe a well-brought-up young woman could have killed a man in such a sinister and premeditated fashion. Others were transfixed by the scandalous revelations of premarital sex. The charges were found not proven, that peculiarly Scottish verdict which lies between Guilty and Not Guilty. Smith went on to marry twice, have two children, and live a quiet life in England and New York until her death in 1928.

Helensburgh
Wednesday Night
My own ever beloved Emile
I trust to Heaven you got home safe – I was not heard by anyone – So I am safe – Were you dearest any the worse of being out in the night air – Emile perhaps I did wrong in taking you into my room – but are you not my own husband – It can be no sin dearest – But I wont do it again – I was so glad to see you darling – would I could be ever with you to keep you company – You stayed so short I got nothing said to you – I had thought of so many things to ask you about – But I hope love your next visit will be longer – Emile my husband I have been thinking of all you said to me last night – Now in the first place – I promise you I shall safe as much of my pin money as I can – I shall put it to many useful things – I shall spend the money I safe on things I shall require when I am your wife. Will this please you – In the second place – I shall not go about as of old with B/- I shall go out before the afternoon – And in the next place – I shall not go to any Public Balls without getting your consent – will this please you my dear little husband – I shall try and do all I can to please you and keep your mind free and do be happy – And darling if you continue to love me I shall please you in many things – Emile if you go away and go into the French army – you know you

will never return to Scotland – and of course I am your wife and I can never be the wife of any other one – So my mind is made up if you go – I shall go where no one shall see me more – I shall be dead to the World. But dearest love I trust we shall get on so that you wont go. I shall behave well for your dear sake – Yes My own My sweet Emile I shall make you happy. You shall some day I hope say you have a faithful and loving wife, And my prayer shall be that you shall never regret taking me for your wife – One of my annoyances is that I may not suit you – or that I am not half good enough to be your wife – Emile I often think we do not [know] each other much that is – we do not know the temper or character of each other – We have never seen each other but under peculiar circumstances so we shall have all that to study after our marriage. But I dont think dear love it shall be difficult to do – What do you say pet . . .

I shall now say Good Night – It is later than when you left me last night – Adieu my love my good dear husband – I adore you more and more each time I see you – You were looking in my eyes very very well last night – I forgot to tell you last night that I have had great pain in getting my <u>first Wisdom tooth</u>. So after I get them all you will expect something like wisdom from me. Adium sweet love my fond embrace – A dear sweet Kiss from your devoted and your truly loving your affectionate wife your own dearest true

Mini

I NURSED MY HUSBAND NIGHT AND DAY

Margaret Oliphant, 1859

Mrs Oliphant, the name by which she wrote, was a prolific novelist from Wallyford in East Lothian. She might not have written so much had it not been for the early loss of her artist husband, Frank, which left her to provide for her three children (of six) who survived. Unlike many middle-class women, she had the means to earn a living, but the prospect of having to do so must have been daunting. Before Frank's death, they had travelled to Italy in the vain hope it would cure his tuberculosis. Many years later, she revisited those dark days when, heavily pregnant, she had to prepare for the worst.

The Noccioli lived in the upper floor of his big old square house, with a wonderful view from the windows, and partially frescoed walls, scarcely any furniture, and a supper-table gleaming under the three clear flames of the Roman lamp, and the melons on the table, which Monsignor ate, I remember, with pepper and salt. But Frank grew very ill here. He became altogether unable to eat anything, not comparatively but absolutely; and the awful sensation of watching this, trying with every faculty to find something he could eat, and always failing, makes me shiver even now . . . We got an Italian doctor there, who was quite cheerful, as I believe is their way when nothing can be done, and spoke of our return next year, which gave me a little confidence. On the 1st of October we went back to Rome, to an apartment we had got in the Noccioli's house in the Babuino, where he got worse and worse. We had Dr Small, who brought a famous French doctor, and they told me there was no hope: it was better to tell me *franchement*, the Frenchman said, and that word *franchement* always, even now, gives me a thrill when I read it. They told me, or I imagined they told me in my confused state, that they had told him, and I went back to him not trying to command my tears; but found they had not told him, and that it was I in my misery who was taking him the news. I remember he said after a while, 'Well, if it is so, that is no reason why we should be miserable.' In my condition of health I was terrified that I might be disabled from attending my Frank to the last. Whether I took myself, or the doctor gave me, a dose of laudanum, I don't remember; but I recollect very well the sudden floating into ease of body and the dazed condition of mind, – a kind of exaltation, as if I were walking upon air, for I could not sleep in the circumstances nor try to sleep. I thought then that this was the saving of me. I nursed my husband night and day, neither resting nor eating, sometimes swallowing a sandwich when I came out of his room for a moment, sometimes dozing for a little when he slept – reading to him often in the middle of the night to try to get him to sleep. And when I came out of the room and sat down in the next and got the relief of crying a little, my bonnie boy came up and stood at my knee and pulled down my head to him, and smiled all over his beaming little face, – smiled though the child wanted to cry too, but would not – not quite three years old. When his father was dead I remember him sitting in his bed in the next room singing 'Oh that will be joyful, when we meet to part no more,' which was the favourite child's hymn of the moment. Frank died quite conscious, kissing me when his lips were already cold, and quite, quite free from anxiety, though he left me with two helpless children and one unborn, and very little money, and no friends but the Macphersons, who were as good to me as brother and sister; but had no power to help beyond that, if anything could be beyond that. Everybody was very kind. Mr Blackett wrote offering to come out to me, to bring me home; and John Blackwood wrote bidding me draw upon him for whatever money I wanted.

I had sent for Effie M., my husband's niece, to come out to me, sending money for her journey; but her mother arrived some time after Frank's death, his sister, Mrs Murdoch – a kind but useless woman, who was no good to me, and yet was a great deal of good as a sort of background and backbone to our helpless little party, – for I was young still, thirty-one, and never self-confident. And there we waited six weeks till my baby was born – he as fair and sweet and healthful as if everything had been well with us. My big Jane was my stand-by, and took the child from the funny Italian-Irish nurse, Madame Margherita, who attended and cheered me with her jolly ways, and brought me back, she and the baby together, to life. By degrees, so wonderful are human things, there came to be a degree of comfort, even cheerfulness; the children being always bright, – Maggie and Cyril the sweetest pair, and my bonnie rosy baby. While I write, October 5, 1894, he, the last, is lying in his coffin in the room next to me – I have been trying to pray by the side of that last bed – and he looks more beautiful than ever he did in his life, in a sort of noble manhood, like, so very like, my infant of nearly thirty-five years ago. All gone, all gone, and no light to come to this sorrow any more! When my Cecco was two months old we came home – Mrs Murdoch and Jane and the three children and I – travelling expensively as was my way, though heaven knows our position was poor enough.

When I thus began the world anew I had for all my fortune about £1000 of debt, a small insurance of, I think, £200 on Frank's life, our furniture laid up in a warehouse, and my own faculties, such as they were, to make our living and pay off our burdens by.

COOK'S HOT TEMPER

Janet Story, 1860s

Janet Story (née Maughan) was born in 1828 in Bombay, the daughter of a captain in the East India Company. She had written six novels before marrying the Rev. Robert Story in 1863, and moving to his parish of Rosneath in Argyll and Bute. Twenty years later they moved to Glasgow, where he had been appointed to a university job. After her husband's death in 1907, she wrote two lively memoirs, from which this recollection comes. By no means all domestic servants caused trouble, but as this story suggests, when they had a troublesome personality they could take over a household.

We had an admirable cook, Betty by name; but unluckily her temper was as hot as her very superior curry; and between her and the housemaid was a feud of long standing, which every now and then developed extra energy. On this occasion the outburst had been unusually bad; the wretched housemaid had been dragged across the kitchen by her thick coil of hair, and stretched across the table, while the cook brandished over her a large carving knife, and threatened her in a manner that rendered the poor creature almost unconscious: the prompt intervention of the parlourmaid, who chanced to enter at the moment, being believed by her and by the victim to have just averted a bloody murder.

It was out of the question to put up with conduct like this, so I summoned the culprit to my presence, and informed her, that much as I regretted parting with her, she must go. She was very contrite, and very unwilling to leave our service, but the fact of the carving knife would not be overlooked; it was an enormity of which no respectable cook ought to have been capable. Poor Betty had to depart, bag and baggage, greatly regretted by us all. The housemaid feeling aggrieved by some remarks which I addressed to her, left also; and a friend of mine, a Mrs. Sprot engaged them both to go to her.

Not long after she had taken up her duties, Mr. Sprot, hearing from his wife that what she considered too large fires were being burnt in the kitchen, and that the cook paid no attention to her remonstrances, went downstairs one day to have a look for himself. The fire was large, and he began to venture on some observations, when he was promptly accosted by Betty seizing in her hand a large kitchen towel and flapping it violently on the table, exclaiming in a furious tone, 'Oot o' ma kitchen! Oot o' ma kitchen! I'll hae nae spyin' maisters here!' while her attitude and manner were so menacing that the much alarmed gentleman lost no time in retiring from the lower regions, with the loud refrain of 'Oot o' ma kitchen,' and the heavy flop of the cloth sounding stridently in his ears. No more remonstrances were attempted, but Betty and her boxes made a second and speedy exodus.

A RIGHT-MINDED WOMAN

The Ardrossan and Saltcoats Herald, *14 May 1864*

There is something of Dickens's Betsey Trotwood in the character of redoubtable Betsy Miller, who was determined not to be felled by circumstances. In so doing, she carved a most unusual career for herself as a shipmaster and one she evidently loved, since she was still sailing at the age of seventy.

At Quay Street, Saltcoats, on the 12th Instant, Miss Betsy Miller, aged 71 Years
The demise on Thursday last of Miss Betsy Miller, at the advanced age of 71 years, ought not to be passed unnoticed by a local journal. Her name has been mentioned, if we mistake not, in the House of Commons, and a leading Review has quoted her life and labours as illustrative of what a right-minded, an earnest, and indefatigable woman can do in order to discharge a debt and earn an honourable maintenance.

After some ten months illness she is numbered with the departed, but her memory, her deeds, and her example, will live and be spoken of long after the generation, who knew her personally, will have passed away.

Miss Miller was a daughter of the late Mr W. Miller, for a long time a Shipowner and Wood-Merchant in Saltcoats. In her younger years she acted as a clerk and 'ship's husband' to her father, and when business affairs took an unfavourable turn, with a resolution which might truly be called heroic, she took the command of an old brig, 'The Clitus', and became 'sailing-master'.

So successful was her career as a 'shipmaster' that she was enabled to pay off a debt of £700, which her father's estate owed to creditors, maintain herself in comfort, and bring up two sisters left dependent upon her.

The Clitus traded between Ardrossan and the coast of Ireland, particularly the ports of Belfast, Dublin and Cork, for more than thirty years. She transacted all the business connected with freight cargo and ships stores, engaged the crew, and directed the ship's course through all weathers.

Such labours could only be undertaken from a high sense of duty. Where other women would have succumbed to necessity, and sunk into penury, their father's name dishonoured by leaving obligations undischarged, and orphan sisters cast upon the parish, or the charity of friends, she boldly grappled with her difficulties, adopted a vocation suited only for the sterner sex, and redeemed honour, secured a competence, performed a noble sisterly duty, and in her humble sphere, gained a name honourably mentioned both in her own country and in the states of America.

We cannot recommend women to become 'ship-masters' but Miss Miller has at least shown what an earnest woman is capable of doing.

GIVING BIRTH ON THE STREET
Board of City of Edinburgh Poorhouse, March 1866

Horror and shame at the conditions in which the poor and helpless lived was growing by the middle of the century, when the numbers of paupers was rising in step with the advance of industrialisation. This tragic case highlighted how especially vulnerable pregnant women were. That the poorhouse where Ann Burns lived offered no assistance when her time came was an indictment of the entire system.

The Committee took into consideration the letter from the House Governor of the City of Edinburgh Poorhouse transmitting copies of the House Committee's meeting of 18th April relative to the case of Ann Burns, who on her way on foot during a cold winter night from the Poorhouse to a maternity Hospital had been delivered of a child in the street and had subsequently died at that Hospital.

In answer to the Board's enquiries what measures have been taken to prevent the occurrence of such a lamentable event in future the House Committee seem to consider it enough to inform this Board that the House Governor is instructed in all cases in future to obtain a medical certificate before parties are sent to the Maternity Hospital. The minute does not state what it is that the medical certificate is to certify, neither does it state in what manner the pauper is to be conveyed to the Hospital should she be sent there, nor what arrangements have been made for her proper accommodation in the Poorhouse if she should not be sent to the Hospital. In short a matter that has been the subject of judicial investigation raises a question as to the humanity with which the inmates subject to the control of the House Committee are treated would seem from the terms of its minute to be disposed of by that Committee in a manner indicating a want of due consideration which the Board could not have anticipated and which they hope is more apparent than real.

The Board must again call upon the House Committee to inform them in a more intelligible and specific form what measures have been taken to prevent the recurrence of any such lamentable event in future.

A ROOM OF ONE'S OWN

Margaret Oliphant, 1866–88

Mrs Oliphant was one of the most popular novelists of her day, and made a living for her fatherless family by her writing. Yet even she, like almost every other female author before her, had trouble being taken seriously and finding the necessary space and peace in which to work.

My study, all the study I have ever attained to, is the little second draw-ing-room where all the (feminine) life of the house goes on; and I don't think I have ever had two hours undisturbed (except at night, when everybody is in bed) during my whole literary life. Miss Austen, I believe, wrote in the same way, and very much for the same reason; but at her period the natural flow of life took another form. The family were half ashamed to have it known that she was not just a young lady like the others, doing her embroi-dery. Mine were quite pleased to magnify me, and to be proud of my work, but always with a hidden sense that it was an admirable joke, and no idea that any special facilities or retirement was necessary. My mother, I believe, would have felt her pride and rapture much checked, almost humiliated, if she had conceived that I stood in need of any artificial aids of that or any other description. That would at once have made the work unnatural to her eyes, and also to mine. I think the first time I ever secluded myself for my work was years after it had become my profession and sole dependence – when I was living after my widowhood in a relation's house, and withdrew with my book and my inkstand from the family drawing-room out of a little conscious ill-temper which made me feel guilty, notwithstanding that the retirement was so very justifiable!

LEWD PRACTICES

Board of Inveresk Poorhouse, 1868

The bijou village of Inveresk on the outskirts of Musselburgh housed Inveresk Combination Poorhouse. Like other such establishments, it was intended as a place of last resort for those too aged, infirm or constitutionally incapable of making a living. Such was the stigma of the poorhouse, however, that many preferred quite literally to die in a ditch. For the respectable elderly, especially, it was a terrifying prospect, and they did all they could to avoid it. This report records an unusual experiment in which young girls were allowed to live among the adults. The results were alarming, as documented here, and the trial came swiftly to an end. The word Combination would be struck out of the poorhouse's title, though not soon enough for the well-being of the children involved.

The documents respecting apprehension of David Gunn an inmate of the Poorhouse, on a charge of lewd practices towards one or more of the girls, inmates of the house . . . were again submitted. The Board are of opinion that those documents disclose the most unfortunate instance of mismanagement that has been brought to their notice with reference to any poorhouse in Scotland. The House Committee knowing that a considerable number of the inmates both male and female were of bad character and vicious habits not only failed to punish their delinquencies when brought to its notice by the House Governor – but at the same time failed to provide reasonable care and protection for the female children whom, at their own urgent request, the Parishes had been permitted to receive into the House. It is much to be regretted that the feelings of benevolence which led the Committee to refrain from punishing drunkenness and other breaches of discipline and decorum, should not have led them to incur the expense of providing a suitable paid nurse for the female children, after the bad character of the pauper in whose immediate charge those children were left, had been brought to the notice of the Committee not only verbally but in writing by the House Governor. The consequences of threatening the vicious with indulgence and withholding adequate protection from the innocent have now been made apparent and the Board cannot doubt that it must be the desire of the House Committee to abandon a system which has led to results so painful.

❧

O PIONEER!

Susan Allison, 1869 and 1879

When she was fifteen, Susan Moir's family headed for British Columbia, hoping to make untold wealth. As she later wrote, 'In 1860 there was great talk in England of the Fraser River and its gold bearing sands. It had taken the place of California in the minds of English people. I say English people because I was living in London at that time. I am Scotch and I feel sure that my countrymen were there mining while we Londoners were talking about it.' Eight years after reaching British Columbia she married a cattle rancher and miner, John Fall Allison, with whom she settled in a log cabin he had built on Lake Okanaga. In the space of twenty-three years, Susan Allison bore fourteen children, all of whom lived. Like many pioneer wives, she had to rely on her own wits to survive. The only white woman in the area, she learned not just to speak the language of the tribes around her, but to cook, to lead a cattle drive, and handle rattlesnakes, disease and daunting winters. She also ran her husband's fur-trading post. Throughout she proved indomitable but droll. Below are two memorable events she recalled in her upbeat memoir, in which she confessed: 'I had learned that even if you are terrified it is best not to show it, then you get the credit for being fear-less – I certainly was not.'

August 1869

As my husband had business in Westminster that August I thought I would take the trip with him. The baby was now a month old [born two months prematurely] and I got one of the women to make me a birchbark basket to pack him in. It was a very comfortable little nest and my husband said he would carry it himself. As we needed only take one pack horse with a tent and food for three days we thought we could make the journey without help. We were told that there were fires on the road when we started. My husband thought the fires might not be bad though the air was full of smoke. When we made the 'Nine Miles' it grew unpleasantly thick. As we neared Powder Camp we found the trees were blazing on both sides of us. My husband handed me the baby to carry and went on leading the pack horse. Poor pony he did not like the fire and had to be dragged along the road. My husband wanted to turn back but I, not knowing what was ahead, said 'go on' and we pushed on until it became clearer. Near Skagit we met a man on horseback who stopped to speak to us. He said 'turn back while you can, no one can get through that fire, the Skagit is boiling.' But as the smoke and fire behind us looked far worse, we told him we would try it, and that he had better hurry if he wanted to get through. So we parted. He had not exaggerated. When we got to the Skagit we found the timber on both sides of the creek (which here is smaller) on fire. The rocks were red hot and the water was boiling or at any rate it seemed like it. We dared not stop but hurried on thinking to get out of it. When we reached the cedars Pony and the other two horses had to be blinded [blind-folded]. The whole forest seemed to be on fire [and] the heat was almost unbearable. The smoke was suffocating and we kept a blanket wrapped around little Edgar's basket. To add to our misery a huge cedar crashed across the trail. I held the three horses and baby while my husband tore the bark from some of the cedars lying near and made a bridge on to the top of the cedars over one side and down on the other, then led Nelly and Pony over this bridge with the third horse. The bridge caught fire and his leg was badly burned, but we did get over, and a little farther we got beyond the fire. We were afraid to camp but too exhausted to go farther that night. We left our dangerous camp early next morning and reached Lake House where we camped and took our ease and rested till next day.

Nearly ten years later, she faced another ordeal, which disturbed her a great deal more.

Winter, 1878

That winter the lake partially froze. Solid ice bridged it at the head and the narrows. The Indians took advantage of the open water to pass over to the Mission every day or two, but as Spring advanced ice down at Penticton receded from both banks and a solid cake of ice of several miles in length broke off forming a huge floating island which drifted up and down the lake with the wind and current.

On the morning of which I write there was a large open streak of water between [our home] Sunnyside and the Mission, with the ice island becalmed just below our harbour. Everything was so still, mountains and trees reflected in the lake, perfect, unbroken. We had had no mail for nearly two months and my husband wanted outside news so he thought he would take the boat over and return immediately. Edgar, then nearly ten years old, took the tiller and as there was no breeze to sail, my husband rowed across. I watched the boat as long as I could and then went about my work, watching through the window to see the lake. About noon I saw the boat, sail up, coming home. There was quite a strong wind – she was just flying – but to my horror I saw the ice island flying too – and if she was not quick enough the boat would be crushed between the cakes of ice. I ran to the children, told them I was going to meet their father and that they must stay in the house till my return.

Then I ran down to a cliff above the lake which was now in a terrible tumult. The ice [was] closing in on the poor little boat, which seemed on wings. The passage had narrowed to a few yards and, as I watched in horror, to a few feet. Then with a dreadful crash the two cakes came together sending a formation of ice and water up to the sky – but the boat I could not see, only rough lumps of ice piled over the cake that was largest. As I watched two black dots seemed to emerge from the debris and come towards Sunnyside. As they got closer I saw that they were each carrying something long. They came nearer. It was Edgar and his father each carrying an oar. The ice they were on was rapidly breaking up and they jumped from block to block. They got nearer and I saw a more solid mass upon which they could walk, but between it and shore there was a long lane of water which ran dark and deep. Looking above me I saw an Indian riding madly along the road and recognised Sher-man-i-shoot [Chiru-man-choot]. I tried to beckon and called but he took no notice, then when I looked again at the ice I could see neither Edgar nor his father. They might have rounded the bend but it did not seem possible. My courage failed. I tried to retrace my steps – I was on a deer trail – it seemed too narrow and my feet too big. I turned off the trail up a ravine. I hardly knew where I went, then I threw myself on the ground – I don't think for very long. I struggled on to another trail above the lake, which was now seething in tempestuous fury, and was watching the water when I felt a hand on my shoulder. It was my husband. 'Edgar?' I asked, 'With Chiru-man-choot.' The Indian, seeing their danger, had galloped to their rescue, and finding a deep lane of water between the shore and the ice, had pushed a dead tree into the lake, got astride of it, and paddling with his hands, reached the ice and made them come on board his improvised boat which they all paddled back.

HIGHLAND TRAGEDY

Queen Victoria, June 1872

The love felt by Queen Victoria for her home at Balmoral was never disguised. Bought for her by her husband Albert in 1852, and rebuilt on a new site, it became a refuge after his death. It was here the queen grew close to her Highland ghillie John Brown, who was a great support, and 'her heart's best treasure'. The queen's diaries of her visits to the Highlands were affectionate, and show her appreciation of the country and its people, and how at home she felt among them. The entries below are rather more eventful than her normal jottings, which generally recorded carriage rides, walks and picnics. They show that despite her eminence, Victoria could be deeply touched by other people's afflictions.

Tuesday, June 11, 1872

Brown came in soon after four o'clock, saying he had been down at the water-side, for a child had fallen into the water, and the whole district was out to try and recover it – but it must be drowned long before this time. I was dreadfully shocked. It was the child of a man named Rattray, who lives at Cairn-na-Craig, just above where the new wood-merchant has built a house, and quite close to the keeper Abercrombie's house, not far from Monaltrie Farmhouse in the street. At a little before five, set off in the waggonette with Beatrice and Janie Ely, and drove along the north side of the river. We stopped a little way beyond Tynebaich, and saw the people wandering along the riverside. Two women told us that two children had fallen in (how terrible!), and that one 'had been gotten – the little een' (as the people pronounce 'one'), but not the eldest. They were searching everywhere. While we were there, the old grandmother, Catenach by name, who lives at Scutter Hold, came running along in a great state of distress. She is Rattray's mother. We drove on a little way, and then turned round.

We heard from the people that the two boys, one of ten or eleven and the other only three, were at Monaltrie Burn which comes down close to the farmhouse and below Mrs. Patterson's shop, passing under a little bridge and running into the Dee. This burn is generally very low and small, but had risen to a great height – the Dee itself being tremendously high – not a stone to be seen. The little child fell in while the eldest was fishing; the other jumped in after him, trying to save his little brother; and before any one could come out to save them (though the screams of Abercrombie's children, who were with them, were heard) they were carried away and swept by the violence of the current into the Dee, and carried along. Too dreadful! It seems, from what I heard coming back, that the poor mother was away from home, having gone to see her own mother who was dying, and that she purposely kept this eldest boy back from school to watch the little one.

We drove back and up to Mrs. Grant's, where we took tea, and then walked up along the riverside, and heard that nothing had been found and that the boat had gone back; but as we approached nearer to the castle we saw people on the banks and rocks with sticks searching: amongst them was the poor father – a sad and piteous sight – crying and looking so anxiously for his poor child's body.

Drove up to the Bush to warn Mrs. William Brown never to let dear little Albert run about alone, or near to the burn, of the danger of which she was quite aware. She said her husband, William, had started off early at three this morning. Some people went down to Abergeldie and as far as the Girnoch to search, and others were up and below the castle.

No word of the poor child being found. All were to start early to search.

Thursday, June 13
At half-past ten drove out in the waggonette with Beatrice and Janie Ely, and drove beyond Mrs. Patterson's 'shoppie' a little way, and turned up to the right off the road behind the wood-merchant's new cottage, and got out just below Abercrombie the keeper's house, and walked a few paces on to the small cottage called Cairn-na-Craig, at the foot of Craig Noerdie, in a lively position, sheltered under the hill, yet high, and was received by the old grandmother; and then we went in, and on a table in the kitchen covered with a sheet, which they lifted up, lay the poor sweet innocent 'bairnie', only three years old, a fine plump child, and looking just as though it slept, with quite a pink colour, and very little scratched in its last clothes – with its little hands joined – a most touching sight. I let Beatrice see it, and was glad she should see death for the first time in so touching and pleasing a form.

Then the poor mother came in, calm and quiet, though she cried a little at first when I took her hand and said how much I felt for her, and how dreadful it was. She checked herself, and said, with that great resignation and trust which it is so edifying to witness, and which you see so strongly here, 'We must try to bear it; we must trust to the Almighty.'

The poor little thing was called Sandy. She herself is a thin, pale, dark, very good, and respectable-looking woman. She has one boy and two girls left, and the eldest and youngest are taken.

They were playing at the burnside, but some way above the road, where there is a small bridge. As we were leaving I gave her something, and she was quite overcome, and blessed me for it.

We walked down again, and then drove back, and walked at once past the stables to the riverside, where, on both sides, every one was assembled, four in the boat . . . And all with sticks, and up and down they went, searching under every stone. They had been up to the boat pool and back, but nothing appeared. I remained watching till one o'clock, feeling unable to tear myself away from this terrible sight. The poor father was on our side, William Brown amongst the others on the other side. I sat on the bank with Janie Ely for some time (Beatrice having gone in earlier than I), Grant as well as Brown standing near me. When they came to that very deep pool, where twenty-two years ago a man was nearly drowned when they were leistering for salmon, they held a piece of red cloth on a pole over the water, which enabled them to see down to the bottom. But all in vain. The river, though lower, was still very high.

At four took a short drive in the single pony carriage with Janie Ely, and back before five. Saw and talked to the school-master, Mr. Lubyanka, a very nice little man, and he said that this poor child, Jemmie, the eldest, was such a good, clever boy. Every one shows so much feeling and kindness. It is quite beautiful to see the way in which every one turned out to help to find this poor child, from the first thing in the morning till the last at night – which, during these long days, was very hard work – and all seemed to feel the calamity deeply. We heard by telegraph during dinner that the poor boy's body had been found on an island opposite Pannanich, below Ballater, and that steps would be taken at once to recover it.

Saturday, June 15
After luncheon, at a quarter to three, drove with the two children up as far as the West Lodge, and then just descried the sad funeral procession slowly and sadly wending its way along the road; so we drove back again, catching glimpses of it as we went along, and drove on a little way beyond the bridge, when, seeing the first people not far off, we turned and drove back, stopping close to the bridge, and here we waited to see them pass. There were about thirty people, I should say, including the poor father, Jemmie and Willie Brown, Francie's brother, Alick Leys, Farmer Patterson, etc. The poor father walked in front of one of the coffins; both covered with white, and so small. It was a very sad sight.

HOW TO BE A DOMESTIC GODDESS
Margaret MacKirdy Black, c. 1880

The founder and principal of the West End School of Cookery in Glasgow (1878–1903), Margaret MacKirdy Black had a Free Church upbringing, echoes of which can be heard in her best-selling guide, Household Cookery and Laundry Work. *She began her career in teaching after her husband was drowned, in 1874, in the River Kelvin. The extracts below come from her wide-ranging manual, whose insights, such as the efficacy of turnips for curing a chest complaint, led to sales of around 200,000 copies. Its popularity vindicated her belief that: 'A great deal more of a country's prosperity depends upon comfortable homes than philosophers might be willing to acknowledge'* . . .

The home is the nursery of the present and future inhabitants of a country, and the care of the home devolves generally upon woman; and by the manner in which she performs her most important duties, not only the present comfort, but it may be the future destinies of the inmates may be influenced, if not moulded. Whatever other duties a woman may have, she must either manage her house herself or devolve the care of it upon some other woman; consequently all women should be carefully trained for this their occupation.

Parents would never think of setting a young man up in business unless he had been trained, probably by a long apprenticeship; and yet it has been practically decided by many people that a young woman instinctively knows all about housekeeping: that she can cook without being taught, and can manage a house, and instruct servants without ever having studied the subject of domestic management; that if she has received a liberal education and some knowledge of needlework, everything else necessary to set her up as the mistress of a house comes naturally.

Good mothers do and have always done great things in training their daughters, but many girls have not that advantage; and even mothers may see the necessity of their best instructions being supplemented.

Domestic economy

Rooms in use should be brushed out daily with a short brush, and a dust-pan held in front of it. A hard brush is very wasteful for carpets, and brushing the dust out of the room into the hall or lobby sends it flying into corners, and causes much additional work. Afterwards the room ought to be carefully dusted with a clean, well-shaken duster. Once a week each room should have a thorough cleaning in every corner.

Bedrooms require great attention as to cleanliness and ventilation, otherwise injury to health is the consequence. The fresh pure air inhaled is carried by the blood all over the body, and in its journey gathers up the impurity or waste of the body, and brings it back to the heart, from whence it goes to the lungs, and is sent out of the body by the breath exhaled. This breath is poisonous, and has often caused death; if persons must be in such a close space that no fresh air can be admitted, they are poisoned very quickly by the impure air they exhale. This impure air is much lighter than pure air and ascends to the roof of a room first. The simplest way to ventilate a room is to have the window open a little at the top to allow the impure air to escape, the space will then be filled with pure air, which will rush in under doors, at keyholes, and every available opening. A fire in a bedroom in sickness keeps the atmosphere of the room warm, though the window be slightly open at the top and also ventilates the room by the current of fresh air that fire draws to it.

Bedroom carpets ought to be so easily lifted that they may be frequently shaken and the floor washed. Bedsteads ought to be drawn aside one a week, and the floor swept and washed underneath; the blankets taken off, and the bed left for an hour, before being made, to cool and air.

Every corner of the house ought to get a thorough turn over once a week, and a good housekeeper will so manage that a portion is done every day, and thus no one is incommoded, and the household machinery works smoothly.

Model washing
The day before the washing, look out all the articles that require to be washed, and arrange them in lots; mend what requires to be mended, and soak what should be soaked. Mix hot water and soap, in the proportion of a quarter of an inch from a bar of soap to a gallon of water, and a full dessert-spoonful of washing powder. (The soap is better to be melted beforehand.) Into this put body linen, shirts, and linen collars to soak all night. The bed linen may be soaked in cold water, or just put aside to dry, waiting till its turn comes; the laces and fine muslins tied up by themselves; and the window blinds and curtains put in cold water, to draw out the smoke that has gathered on them.

Begin work early on the washing day. The best part of the day is the forenoon, and an hour gained in the morning is worth two later in the day. The first thing to do is to light the boiler-fire, and have plenty of hot water; add some of it to the soaked clothes. Wash them out carefully, removing all stains. The soaking will have rendered hard rubbing almost unnecessary. Put them in a second tub with warm water, and wash again, always beginning with the finest articles. Then have a tub with plenty of cold water in it; drop them into this, and let them lie in it a short time

These instructions continue ad infinitum for linen, laces and muslin, flannels, table-linen, stockings, coloured dresses, etc.

Sick-room cookery

Sick nursing is even more essentially women's work than housekeeping, and requires knowledge, combined with tenderness and care, a feeling heart, and skilful hands.

The food of the sick should be varied as much as possible, and prepared in the very best manner that materials will admit of. Beef tea particularly requires skilful preparation, as life and returning health often depend upon it.

Nice toast or grated bread may be used with beef tea, as well as other things of the same kind. It may also be coloured a little brown with either ketchup or Harvey sauce to make it look appetising, as what commends itself to the eye is usually more easily digested than what is taken unwillingly, or is repulsive in appearance; at the same time it should be remembered that the body is nourished not by what is eaten, but by what is digested.

ORPHANS IN THE SNOW

Report of Parochial Board Sub-Committee, and other witnesses, 1889

The Parish Council fostered out the large, orphaned Hunter family to Charles and Mary Croucher, a couple who lived near Newtyle in Angus. Doubtless the authorities thought they were doing their best for them, but as the following accounts show, this was not the case. These testimonies were gathered by a concerned minister, the Rev. Wilson, who was unconvinced by the Parochial Board's own investigation into accusations of child neglect. As the different parties give their side of the story, it is like being in a courtroom. What emerges vividly is the harsh treatment of these vulnerable children, among them a girl with a learning disability, by a foster mother who connived with her abusive husband in making money from them.

Report of Parochial Board Sub-Committee on visiting foster home:
The building is a cottage of one storey, with southern exposure, and having in front and on the west a considerable quantity of vacant ground, where, the Committee were informed, the children along with other children of the village are in the habit of amusing themselves. Entering off the kitchen there is a clean and snug apartment containing an enclosed bed, in which three of

the orphan children sleep, namely: Alexander (aged 5 and 10 months), Euphemia, and Nelly. This arrangement it was explained had been adopted because these children – especially the eldest one, who is weak-minded – are inclined to dirty habits, rendering it necessary for Mrs Croucher to lift them during the night. The bedding was sufficient, and both bed and bedding were clean and in good order.

The large room at the west end of the lobby is a spacious apartment. The floor, of wood, is carpeted, and the window, which admits abundance of light, is draped with muslin curtain. Two iron bedsteads, each 6 feet by 4 feet, are placed close to each other and on end against the north wall. They are provided with chaff mattresses, and the clothing was both abundant and clean. One of the beds is occupied by two little girls of the orphan family, and the other bed by three of Croucher's own children, the eldest of whom, a girl, is twelve years; and the youngest, a boy, five years of age.

The Committee were satisfied with all they had seen and examined. The whole house is free from damp and thoroughly comfortable. The Committee were particular in examining the beds and bedding, and in ascertaining how the children are fed, clothed, and generally cared for, and they were unable to find any appearance whatever of their being neglected or ill-treated.

Statement of Mary Croucher, aged 40

One Sunday evening last winter, when it was dark, one of the children – Elizabeth Hunter, aged nine years – in going for milk slipped on the ice on the door step of my house and fell, hurting her right elbow. We did not think that there was anything wrong with her, but I sent for my neighbour Miss Anderson, and asked her advice as to whether she thought there was anything the matter with the girl's arm. We discovered nothing wrong. However I rubbed the elbow with vinegar. Two or three days after this I noticed that when the girl lifted her arm it appeared to be stiff. I then poulticed the elbow two or three times, and also frequently rubbed it with vinegar. As the treatment brought about no improvement, I asked Dr Mills, Newtyle, to come and see the girl. Her elbow was beginning to get yellow and I sent for him.

Statement of Charles Croucher

Neither I nor my wife ever beat the children unmercifully. Occasionally they, as well as my own children, need correction, but they are treated in every respect the same as my own children, and with the utmost regard for their comfort and welfare. Never on any occasion were the children required to search dunghills for bones or rags.

Statement of Constable William Shephard

I said to him [Rev. Inglis] that I did not think they were proper Guardians for the children. I formed this opinion from the appearance of the children, who seemed to be thin and ill-clad. I have seen Mr Croucher two or three times under the influence of liquor, and once I would have said he was drunk.

Statement of Mrs Walker, neighbour and wife of gamekeeper

About a fortnight after the orphan children came to the Crouchers I saw Croucher's boy striking one of the orphans – Jeannie – with a stick on the brow. The child was not chastised by his mother for what he did which I thought was improper. On one occasion, while passing Croucher's house, I heard a child crying inside, and on looking through the window I saw Mrs Croucher whipping one of the orphan children on the buttocks with a leather strap. I do not know the cause for which the child was chastised, but she chastised it more severely than I chastised my children. On another occasion, about twenty minutes to ten o'clock a.m. on a week-day, I saw the eldest orphan girl at Croucher's door washing herself and crying. Mrs Croucher came out of the house and addressing the girl, said 'Blackguard, come on.' The girl dried her face with a towel and hurried into the house, and as she was going in at the door, Mrs Croucher, who was standing there with a strap in her hand, struck the girl with it across her bare shoulders. I have heard Mrs Croucher swearing nearly every day; it seemed to be a general practice with her. I saw Croucher drunk once.

Written and signed statement of Rev. Inglis

I was amazed to learn that five children were placed under the care of a woman who had five children of her own, the youngest of whom was eight months old; and under the guardianship of a man who had been but recently convicted of cruelty to animals. I know the house well. It was, when occupied by farm servants, a two-roomed house, with a closet off the kitchen for sticks, coals, and lumber – a very common arrangement in farm servants' houses. That a man and a woman with ten children should be located under such conditions was scandalous. In my opinion it was simply a business set up for making a living off the children . . . On sanitary grounds alone such a house was totally inadequate for such a number of people. As for sanitary arrangements, there were simply none.

When Constable Gibson called my attention to the treatment of two of the children whom he had observed in an open shed at all times of the day and night, and kept outside of the door in the most severe wintry weather, I could hardly credit such a statement. I went, however, to the place as he requested me, and I found the children shivering with cold, poverty-stricken, and neglected. On one occasion I met three of the children at the foot of the Kirkton farm road, returning from Dronley Woods with bundles of fire-wood. This was in mid-winter. They were thinly clad, and blue with cold, and one of them – the youngest of the three – was crying. I asked them who sent them out to gather sticks in such weather, and they said 'Mrs Croucher'. From their answers to my questions I understood they dared not return to the house without their bundles. It appeared to me to be shocking cruelty to send such children to gather firewood in such severe weather. During the severe snow storm in the month of February I had occasion to return home by the Knowe Head Road; it was quite dark and the road was blocked with snow, and it was snowing heavily. When I was working my way with difficulty around the wreaths and through the drift, to my astonishment I heard children crying and appealing for help. I asked them who they were, and what they were doing there on such a night. I found them to be two of the orphan children. They told me they had been sent for milk, and had lost their way in the storm and darkness. They were in a most pitiable condition from cold and exposure. They had become bewildered among the wreaths and with blinding drift. One of the children, somewhat weak mentally, appeared quite stupefied. I got them out of the wreaths, and took them to the village. I considered it a down-right shame and disgrace that two helpless children, one of whom was weak in mind, should have been sent away nearly a mile for milk on such a night, and through such a storm. I never, in all my experience, witnessed a worse case of cruelty to children than I did that night.

Written and signed statement of J. M. Gibson, former policeman
I may say that I had occasion to visit Alexander Walker, who was then game-keeper on Auchterhouse estate, and lived next door to the Croucher's, several times a week during the evenings in the winter season, and there was scarcely a night that I visited Walker's, be it good or bad weather, but what these children were standing at Croucher's door with the door shut against them, say between six and ten o'clock pm. I do not think Croucher a fit and proper person to be a guardian for the children, owing to their being kept standing at the door in the cold on the bitter cold nights.

NEWHAVEN FISHWIVES

Janet Story, 1890s

Memoirist Janet Story must have lived for a spell in Edinburgh, where these remarkable hawkers made an impression. Heavy physical work was frequently undertaken by women in the fishing community, who would sometimes walk miles over the old herring roads across the hills with creels on their heads. As Story indicates, it did nothing to diminish their spirits.

In consequence probably of the convenient multiplicity and the excellence of the Edinburgh fish shops, the once familiar and picturesque figure of the Newhaven fishwife is becoming less evident in our streets; and this fact is greatly to be regretted. They were a hardworking and industrious class of women, a great assistance to their equally hardworking husbands, and most surely an interest and a pleasure to all who looked on their sonsy faces and fascinating costume, with the wide sleeve showing their strong round arms, and the snowy cap that often surmounted a weather-beaten but still handsome countenance.

A certain number of them preferred carrying their fish about with them and calling at the different houses, sending the cry of 'Caller haddies' before them to announce their coming. Fearful and wonderful scenes took place on these occasions, especially if the cook was inexperienced and did not understand how to cope with the lady of the fish baskets. A price was invariably demanded far and away beyond reason, and much above what the fish woman intended to take; so the haggling was lengthy and excited, and might frequently be heard half way down a street: the cook being at first addressed as 'Ma lamb' and 'Ma lady,' while later, when a tough antagonist had been encountered, it descended to 'Od wumman!' and 'Ye limmer!' I never heard anything stronger in the way of remonstrance: I never heard a fishwife swear. They seldom quitted a house without selling their fish: they had a very persuading way with them, and few could resist it.

❦

STAYS AND PARASOLS

Catherine Carswell, 1890s

When it came to dressing as a grown-up, journalist and novelist Catherine Carswell discovered that it was one thing to talk revolt, another to put it into practice.

When we were verging on our teens, my sister and I, in scorn of young ladies, vowed to each other (1) that we would never wear 'real stays with bones in them', and (2) that we should never carry a parasol. We did not keep our vows. At eighteen I wore the same garments as at eight – except that they were longer and the top petticoat was a divided affair, white camisole above and frilled silk or stout mohair as to skirt. The straight padded band of our stays became confining and stiff with steel fronts. The neckbands of the dresses were fortified with whalebones and the lined bodices also. The skirt, also lined, and reaching to the ground in front and at the back, had braid all round inside the hem which came constantly unstitched as it caught in the wearer's heel. Our hair was rolled up over a pad on top, to which pad a hat was precariously pinned and a veil adjusted. Gloves were a necessity, and usually an umbrella or parasol. With one hand, while out walking, the back of the skirt had to be held clear of the pavement in such a manner as just to show an edge of petti-coat but no stocking or ankle. This involved many backward and downward glances. The other hand was usually occupied in grasping the hat brim and frantically adjusting the veil – both subject to the least breath of wind. The umbrella or parasol being on the hat arm it was hard to assume an uncon-cerned smile. At fifteen or so I had more or less reorganised my costume, discarding much below and removing neckbands above, and at all times in the country or by the sea we went about anyhow, often in trousers or jerseys. But when my skirts grew long and I was corsetted, I succumbed for a time to overpowering convention.

MARY SLESSOR'S BABIES

Mary Kingsley, 1893

Dundee mill-girl turned missionary Mary Slessor is in a class of her own for courage and determination. When she first reached Calabar in Nigeria in 1876 the barbaric treatment of the local tribes towards their own people, and especially newborn twins, was horrifying. She knew what she had to do, writing home that 'I am going to a new tribe up-country, a fierce, cruel people, and every one tells me that they will kill me. But I don't fear any hurt – only to combat their savage customs will require courage and firmness on my part.' Somehow, Slessor managed not only to survive as a single, unprotected woman, but to gain the tribespeople's respect. Her particular mission was to change attitudes towards twins, who were killed at birth. Her house filled with abandoned babies, many of whom she adopted, and she set up missions for the care of orphaned and ill children. Her ideas gradually gained ground, but the health and welfare of the infants she took in continued to distress her, as two late diary entries from 1911 show: 'Baby Mbiatbet died and buried in lower garden. Gave so little trouble, and fought so for life. Jaundiced as I never saw a baby. White of eyes quite green for days. Could not remove it.' 'Me Mbim died this morning, . . . Could not take his milk, but tried to when I begged him. Very hard to say Amen.' The account below is by the English travel writer Mary Kingsley. She arrived in Ekenge, in Okoyong, where Slessor was based for many years, in the middle of dramatic events. A beautiful young woman called Iye was a slave whose owner's attitude towards her changed completely when she gave birth to twins.

She [the new mother] was subjected to torrents of virulent abuse, her things were torn from her, her English China basins, possessions she valued most highly, were smashed, her clothes were torn, and she was driven out as an unclean thing. Had it not been for the fear of incurring Miss Slessor's anger, she would, at this point have been killed with her children, and the bodies thrown into the bush. As it was, she was hounded out of the village. The rest of her possessions were jammed into an empty gin–case and cast to her. No one would touch her. Miss Slessor had heard of the twins' arrival, and had started off, barefooted and bareheaded, at that pace she can do down a bush path. By the time she had gone four miles she met the procession, the woman coming to her, and all the rest of the village yelling and howling behind her. On the top of her head was the gin–case, into which the children had been stuffed, on the top of them the woman's big brass skillet, and on the top of that her two market calabashes. Needless to say, on arriving Miss Slessor took charge of affairs, relieving the unfortunate, weak, staggering woman from her load and carrying it herself, for no one else would touch it, or anything belonging to those awful twin things, and they started back together to Miss Slessor's house in the forest-clearing . . .

I arrived in the middle of this affair for my first meeting with Miss Slessor, and things at Okoyong were rather crowded, one way and another, that afternoon. All the attention one of the children wanted – the boy, for there were a boy and a girl – was burying, for the people who had crammed them into the box had utterly smashed the child's head. The other child was alive, and is still a member of that household of rescued children, all of whom owe their lives to Miss Slessor.

The natives would not touch it, and only approached it after some days, and then only when it was helped by Miss Slessor or me. If either of us wanted to do or get something, and we handed over the bundle to one of the house children to hold, there was a stampede of men and women off the verandah, out of the yard, and over the fence, if need be, that was exceedingly comic, but most convincing as to the reality of the terror and horror in which they held the thing. Even its own mother could not be trusted with the child; she would have killed it. She never betrayed the slightest desire to have it with her, and after a few days' nursing and feeding up she was anxious to go back to her mistress, who, being an enlightened woman, was willing to have her if she came without the child.

The surviving infant, Susie, was widely loved, especially by Mary Slessor, but when she was fourteen months old, following an accident in which she was burned by boiling water, she died.

DEATH OF A BELOVED SON

Mrs Margaret Isabella Balfour Stevenson, 1894

Robert Louis Stevenson must have inherited his wanderlust from his mother. Leaving Edinburgh and sailing around the world for a new life in Samoa with her son and his wife Fanny, Margaret Stevenson made as little fuss as if she were taking a train to North Berwick. She settled unfazed into the tropical climate, with its devastating storms and sometimes startling customs, perhaps happy simply to be near her ailing son. RLS's tuberculosis was by this stage advanced, but for much of the time he appeared to be well, and certainly happy. The end, when it came, was swift. Fanny wrote to a friend, 'That very day he had said to me "the thought of dying in bed is horrible to me; I want to die like a clean human being on my feet. I want to die in my clothes, to fall just as I stand." He did. It was only at the very end, for the last few breaths, that we laid him down.'

Vailima, December 4, 1894

How am I to tell you the terrible news that my beloved son was suddenly called home last evening. At six o'clock he was well, hungry for dinner, and helping Fanny to make a Mayonnaise sauce; when suddenly he put both hands to his head and said, 'Oh, what a pain!' and then added, 'Do I look strange?' Fanny said no, not wishing to alarm him, and helped him into the hall, where she put him into the nearest easy-chair. She called for us to come, and I was there in a minute; but he was unconscious before I reached his side, and remained so for two hours, till at ten minutes past 8 p.m. all was over.

Lloyd went for help at once, and got two doctors wonderfully quickly – one from the Wallaroo and the other, Dr. F——, from Apia; but we had already done all that was possible, and they could suggest nothing more. Before the end came we brought a bed into the hall, and he was lifted on to it. When all was over his boys gathered about him, and the chiefs from Tanugamanono arrived with fine mats which they laid over the bed; it was very touching when they came in bowing, and saying 'Talofa, Tusitala'; and then, after kissing him and sitting a while in silence, they bowed again, and saying 'Tofa, Tusitala,' went out. After that our Roman Catholic boys asked if they might 'make a church,' and they chanted prayers and hymns for a long time, very sweetly . . . We had sent for Mr. C——, who stayed with us till all was over, and made the necessary arrangements for us; Louis wished to be buried on the top of Vaea Mountain, and before six this morning forty men arrived with axes to cut a path up and dig the grave. Some of Mataafa's chiefs came this morning; one wept bitterly, saying, 'Mataafa is gone, and Tusitala is gone, and we have none left.'

Lying in state, 4th Dec., 1894

They have just gone up the mountain now. The letters must be posted to-night, and I scarcely know what I am writing. None of us has realised yet what has happened, and we shall only feel it all the more as days go by. I feel desolate indeed, and don't know what I shall do.

December 9

I must tell you a very strange thing that occurred just before his death. For a day or two Fanny had been telling us that she knew – that she felt – something dreadful was going to happen to someone we cared for; as she put it, to one of our friends. On Monday she was very low about it, and upset, and dear Lou tried hard to cheer her. He read aloud to her the chapter of his book that he had just finished, played a game or two of Patience to induce her to look on, and I fancy it was as much for her sake as his own that the Mayonnaise sauce was begun upon. And, strangely enough, both of them had agreed that it could not be to either of them that the dreadful thing was to happen! Thus far, and no further, can our intuitions, our second sight, go.

COMBINATIONS

Naomi Mitchison, c. 1900

Naomi Mitchison, a fine novelist and writer, was noted for daring to write about things polite people didn't discuss, such as sex, rape and abortion. To that list can be added combinations.

But could Edinburgh in winter have been quite as cold as I remember it outside? Perhaps our clothes were inadequate, though I had a muff on a string and of course gaiters with a row of horrible pinching buttons. Most ladies had muffs and fur necklets for winter, often with an animal's head on one end; these replaced the summer 'boas' of short ostrich feathers, white or dyed, but these were garden-party wear and of little practical merit. Next to us we all wore woollen combinations, thick in winter, thinner and short-sleeved in summer. One had clean ones on Sundays. The difficulty was that the edges round the slit at the bottom tended to get a bit sticky and scratchy. Over these one wore serge knickers, buttoning below the knee, but these had linings which could be changed more often. Men and boys had thick woollen vests and long pants in an unattractive 'natural wool' colour. Combinations went on during all my young life until the early twenties when I cast them off in favour of longish chemises of fine linen or printed silk – and of course I mean real silk – man-made fibres were still rather nasty. But I expect my mother's generation stuck to their ladies' combinations until the end.

BLACK HOUSE

Alexandra Stewart, c. 1902

The daughter of a shoemaker and Gaelic scholar, Alexandra Stewart was born in 1896 and brought up at Woodend in Glen Lyon in Perthshire, with seven sisters and a brother. When she was a young child, the traditional black house – low, thatched with turf, with only a hole for a chimney – was almost a thing of the past, though it would survive longer in the Western Isles. These cosy dwellings looked romantic, but this reminiscence suggests they were anything but.

Old Lizzie Lothian lived in the only black house I can remember seeing in the Glen. The house was at Invervar, not far from the present school and three or four miles from Woodend, and quite near the roadside. The house was indeed black inside and out, and Lizzie with it from years of smoke. The chimney was a hole in the roof with a large canopy coming down over the fire to draw the smoke up. The fire itself was placed on large stone slabs at floor level. There was an iron swey placed somewhere in the centre of the canopy with a hook suspended to hang a pot or kettle for cooking. The walls were of unworked stone and the roof of thatch; they say that a dozen pairs of hands making light work could put up a black house in a day. There were two rooms, one the sleeping quarters and the other the living space where Lizzie moved about in the perpetual stinging smoke of a wood fire to the sound of her clucking and cackling hens. They were housed in a corner of the roof with an opening where they went in and out as they pleased. There was no sanitation; her water supply came from a tap which she shared with a few neighbours.

Lizzie was old but had kept her faculties and had a good knowledge of the use of herbs. When she was young she used to supervise the collection of lichen used in dyeing the wool for spinning. She had a taste for the 'barley bree' and could always get a neighbour to fetch a wee spot on the grounds that it was for medicinal purposes. She also knew her Bible well and could quote long passages from memory.

She had a direct link with the battle of Culloden, for she remembered talking to her grandfather who had fought there on Prince Charlie's side. He was lucky to escape from the slaughter when the Government artillery wrecked the Jacobite formations and the Redcoats went in with bayonets. He and my father's great-grandfather, Alan Stewart, owed their lives to the hillman's advantage on foot over a lowland pursuer on horseback. They dodged through a bog where the cavalrymen could not follow and made their way back to the

Glen by many miles of devious hill paths. They were plain folk back among their own, and no one was looking for them.

Lizzie was very interested in the Free Church and during the upheaval in 1900 my father had to go in and report on his way home. After evening meetings we often went with him to Lizzie's house. We were a bit in awe of her as we used to think her like a witch – and seeing an old-fashioned broomstick by the fire we were sure she must be. She was a kindly old soul and we were always treated to a piece of black bun that she kept in a tin. We thanked her and said we would eat it on the way home but I am afraid the birds of the air got it as it reeked of smoke.

FORCE-FEEDING SUFFRAGETTES

Medical officers of Perth and Barlinnie prisons, 1909

By the early twentieth century, suffragette activity in Scotland, which had been gathering pace since the 1870s, was causing headaches for the authorities. The problem was how best to handle the women they had imprisoned. This letter to the Prison Commissioners for Scotland gives a glimpse of what protesters were prepared to endure for their cause. In 1909, in Edinburgh, Ethel Moorehead became the first suffragette to be force-fed in Scotland. It was Perth prison, however, that became notorious for this practice, so much so that a notice was pinned outside ahead of a royal visit, saying 'Welcome to your majesty's torture chamber in Perth Prison'. Despite the horrors of jail, suffragette activism reached its peak in 1913. There was an almost daily tally of criminal acts, from arson at Ayr and Perth racecourses, acid poured into letterboxes, an attempt to smash the windows of the king's car, an ambush on the Prime Minister at Lossiemouth Golf Course, and intimidating Winston Churchill into hiding in a shed. According to one historian, by 1905 Scotland was 'punching above its weight' in the campaign for votes. A political ceasefire was called during the First World War, and in 1918 women – though only those over the age of thirty – were finally given the vote, partly in recognition of what they had done during the war.

1909, 15 November
Prison Commissioners,
The Secretary for Scotland asks for full information as to the conduct of the operation of artificial feeding. This information has been fully supplied in the Reports of the Medical Officers of Perth and Barlinnie Prisons, and their

experience as well as that of Medical Officers of Asylums and other institutions may be epitomized as follows: –

There are three methods in use; (1) by means of a feeding cup; (2) by means of an oesophageal catheter, and (3) by means of a nasal tube.

Feeding by means of a feeding cup consists of introducing the mouthpiece of the feeding-cup between the teeth and pouring the contents into the patient's mouth. For prisoners who offer resistance it is a method attended with considerable risk of injury.

For feeding by means of an oesophageal catheter, it is necessary that the movements of the patient be carefully and fully controlled, and for that purpose five assistants may be required. The ordinary method of controlling the patient is to put the patient into bed; one assistant sits on the bed at the pillow end and steadies the patient's body with his or her knees and steadies the patient's head by pressing the head against his or her chest; an assistant is required to control each of the patient's limbs. The patient being under control, the medical officer inserts a gag into the mouth and leaves the subsequent charge of the gag to another assistant. The medical officer then introduces the catheter, previously smeared with oil or Castile Soap into the upper part of the gullet and then the involuntary contractions of the gullet carry the end down into the patient's stomach. A risk in this method of feeding is the introduction of the catheter into the windpipe instead of into the gullet, but this is an exceedingly rare accident and the effects of the accident can be obviated by observation after the introduction, for if the catheter happens to be in the windpipe respiratory movements of air would take place through the catheter, while if the catheter be in the gullet and stomach there are no such respiratory movements. The medical officer being satisfied that the catheter is properly in the stomach, connects the catheter with the feeding funnel, and then introduces a small quantity of warm water, which is a further precaution against introduction into the windpipe; when he observes that the water enters the stomach, he gradually introduces the food, which generally consists of a thin custard or a strained mixture of milk and eggs, or broth. After administering the food, the medical officer passes a little more warm water through the catheter, he then pinches the catheter to prevent entrance of the food into it at the stomach end and withdraws it in that condition. The operation should be completed in from two to three minutes. It may produce discomfort but is not painful.

(3) For feeding by means of the nasal tube, similar control to the above is necessary and the proceedings are generally the same excepting that the tube, which is smaller in calibre than an oesophageal catheter, is introduced through the nose. The advantage of this method over that of the oesophageal catheter

is that the gag can be dispensed with, but it is slower in operation on account of the narrowness of the tube, and it is not entirely free from inconvenience of the tube accidentally entering the windpipe.

It appears to me that feeding by means of a cup is altogether unsuited for prisoners who purposely resist artificial feeding, as by it considerable damage might be done to the prisoner's mouth.

In regard to oesophageal feeding, it is attended with the objections inseparable from the forcible insertion of a gag, whereby the opportunities for resistance on the part of the prisoner are increased and may result in accidents such as the breaking of teeth and the production of superficial wounds of the mouth with bleeding. Its chief advantage is that a somewhat shorter period of time is required for the passage of food than is the case with nose-feeding, but the difference is immaterial.

Nose feeding is not attended with any of these drawbacks or slight risks, and its easy application is only rarely interfered with by an exceptional narrowing of the nose passages.

I am, accordingly, of the opinion that when artificial feeding is adopted the nasal method should be preferred . . .

The Secretary for Scotland also raises the question of how long it is safe for a prisoner to remain without food. Deprivation of food, while liquids are being freely drunk, may be continued for many days in healthy and normal persons, without immediate danger to life. It commences, however, to be detrimental to health in a few days, when the individuals are weakly and untrained for deprivation, and this is especially so in women of high-strung nervous susceptibilities. In the latter, also, the chances of deterioration in health would be increased if, when strength had already been lost by deprivation of food, they were subjected to the emotional incidents inseparable from mental and physical resistance to artificial feeding.

I am therefore of the opinion that artificial feeding should always be employed from forty-eight to sixty hours after food has last been taken and in women of weakly constitution nearer forty-eight than sixty hours.

It would be advisable to convey definite instructions to this effect to the officials of H.M. Prisons.

Thomas R. Fraser

VOTES FOR WOMEN – DANGEROUS

Greenock Telegraph, *December 1909*

There were only around 100 militant suffragettes in the country by 1909, but thousands took a more peaceful route, such as writing to the newspapers. This correspondence highlights what women were up against when they encountered males with an antediluvian outlook.

Gourock, 17th Dec.

Sir, The president of the 'Men's League for opposing Women's Suffrage' overlooks the primary motive in the pro-suffrage movement, viz., that these women who pay taxes and have the same qualifications as men voters ought to have a Parliamentary vote. All other statements as to 'women's opinions being represented under the present system' and 'that their interests are regarded' and 'the majority of women do not wish to vote' are beside the point. How this granting of votes to tax paying women would lead to universal suffrage for adults I leave to Lord Cromer to explain. It has not yet led to universal suffrage in the case of men.

I am, yours faithfully,
Jus Suffragii

Greenock, 20th Dec.

Sir, – 'Jus Suffragii' has gone far off the track. She – for clearly that writer is not only a woman but also one of those book-taught, swell-headed women with a smattering of Latin and other worthless learning they mistake for education – treats us to all that tiresome nonsense about people who pay taxes being of right entitled to a Parliamentary vote. No sane person who knows anything of the subject could make a statement of the kind. The basis of franchise in manhood is householding – not mere payment of taxes – so that the argument is hollow as a blown egg! (Obviously no woman can ever possess manhood!) Surely that ends the matter.

Women already have the local vote, and they do not appreciate the privilege, nor is it to any extent worth speaking of. Nevertheless, they have thus a voice in the management of the parish pump, and that is enough for them. I am not an old man, but in my time I have met many scores of sensible, intelligent women, though never yet have I met one who was fit for the Parliamentary franchise. They say there is only one [such] woman in the country, and that is

Mrs. Bernard Shaw. I take leave to doubt even her fitness. When a markedly virile nation such as Germany gives its women the vote it will be time enough for us to think about it. Meanwhile such a step would not be safe!

I am, yours faithfully,

Z

❦

WAR BEGINS

Annie S. Swan, July 1914

Novelist Annie Swan wrote over 200 works of romantic fiction. A devout Christian, she was a champion of good causes, among them women's suffrage. Born in Gorebridge, she was married to a doctor, and at the time of which she is writing, lived between Hertfordshire and Kinghorn. Her son had been killed four years earlier in a shooting accident. Here, she describes the start of the conflict.

The last week in July I had travelled with the household [to Kinghorn] by train, leaving the Doctor and Effie to come by road in a new car he had just given her. It was a Studebaker, a dashing little two-seater, painted a lovely blue. She was one of the first women motorists to be seen about the Hertfordshire lanes, and was very proud of her new treasure. Little did we anticipate the ultimate fate of our pretty blue Judy, nor how she would return to her base a shattered hulk, covered with the wounds of war.

They were on the road on August the fourth, and had some adventures, also much trouble about petrol, the entire supply of which was at once commandeered by the Government. The whole country was immediately thrown into an incredible state of panic, in which many foolish and unnecessary things were done.

They were late in arriving and considered themselves lucky to have got through with the car, as the authorities were seizing everything in the way of motor vehicles, sometimes causing the bereft serious inconvenience. Never, surely, did a country go into war so utterly unprepared.

We often laughed afterwards at the haste with which Effie drove her new possession up to Glassmount [in Kinghorn], where some friends offered to hide it in the barn. It was covered entirely over with hay and straw, until the panic had somewhat subsided. I don't remember that we had any qualms about this wicked deed. What use, anyway, would a girl's dainty toy be in the war zone? Later on, however, it did its bit.

Kinghorn was one of the most unpleasant of the Home Bases to live in during the war. It had become – after we built our house – one of the most important defences of the Forth. Its proximity to the Forth Bridge and the Naval Base at Rosyth made it of the first importance. Greatly to our regret, year by year the defences were strengthened, barbed wire appeared everywhere, and bigger and better guns were installed on terrifying emplacements. The biggest of all was not more than two hundred yards from our house, the chief gunner's cottage intervening in the space between.

The close proximity of the Fort entirely destroyed the amenity of our property, and when the guns were fired for practice our windows were regularly shattered. For that there was no compensation.

Immediately the war broke out, Kinghorn became a lively centre of military activity. Barriers were erected across the road just outside our front gate, in order to prevent any unauthorised persons from approaching the Fort. Sentries were posted there night and day, and there was no respite from the challenge:

'Halt! Who goes there? Advance one, and be recognised!'

The panicky atmosphere of these first weeks was indescribable. The bogey was German invasion, which was reported to be imminent, sometimes actually to have materialised, at every vulnerable spot along the coast. Trenches were dug and manned by night and day, vigilant watch kept everywhere, explicit instructions handed out to the civilians as to their procedure when the enemy actually arrived.

The whole of life was transformed into something grim and sinister. Our cellars were commandeered for the Red Cross stores, so that they would be quickly available when the fighting began. It was, of course, necessary to keep vigilant watch over the narrow channel leading to the Forth Bridge, which the enemy were anxious to blow up, in order to block the outlet for the Fleet at the Rosyth Base.

All the little islands we so loved and had often picnicked on became armed camps; the sea, a menacing highway on which anything might happen. The scares were continuous and exciting. One day it was reported that the Germans had actually effected a landing at Largo Bay . . .

One day there arrived at our gate a small military contingent with a quantity of boards and tools to deal therewith, informing me that their instructions were to board up the bathroom window, as it overlooked the Fort. My husband arrived on the scene and made short work of them, ordering them off, as he had no intention whatever of allowing his bathroom window to be boarded up. They departed meekly, though evidently surprised. Of course we knew the matter could not end there, so after consulting together, he made a happy suggestion that we should invite the Military Governor and his aide-de-camp to become guests in our house. We knew they had not got comfortable quarters, as there was no good hotel in the place. The invitation was duly conveyed and gladly accepted, and we heard no more about boarding up the bathroom window.

They were delightful guests and gave me a certain sense of security, though I never got used to the telephone bell from the Fort ringing suddenly in the middle of the night, or men rushing along the paved passage to the front door, opening it – for it was never allowed to be locked – and dashing up to the Governor's room. Then we would hear a hurried colloquy, and presently the Governor and his aide dashing down the stairs. Of course we never heard anything about the scares. Our job was to endure. I remember one day Major Baker Kerr, the aide, who was rather amused at my nervous fears, showed me a German paper in which it was quite seriously reported that Kinghorn Fort had been destroyed and Edinburgh bombarded. That was the sort of stuff the German public was fed on. I suppose they needed it to keep up their blind faith in their military and naval strength . . .

Of course I was anxious to get out to France, and it was not long before the opportunity came through the Y.M.C.A., for whom I had already done much work in the home camps, also at the munition factories.

I was allowed to take Effie with me, though the censorship of unauthorised visitors to France was strictly enforced, the authorities being determined that there should be no repetition of the plague of useless women of whom Kitchener complained during the Boer War. Effie's proficiency in the French language paved the way, and soon we were on our way from Southampton to Havre, the longer sea-route being considered rather safer than the much-menaced Channel passage . . .

It was chiefly at Havre that the constantly reinforced army was sifted and partly trained, and the camp at Honfleur was a sight to see.

I started in to work at once, speaking in the huts every night. It was a message of gratitude and encouragement from the women at home I was charged with, as well as the burden of deeper things, and how joyfully they received it! For these young recruits were all Crusaders still, eager and undismayed, because convinced of the righteousness of their cause. The little services were good, but for me the best part of the work was the 'for-gathering' at the close, when we talked face to face, they telling me all about their homes, showing me pictures of their mothers, wives, bairns, sweethearts, and sisters. I took down sheaves of addresses and did my best to write to all their dear ones when I got home, but as time went on, the task became gargantuan, and had to be abandoned.

. . . One day the Superintendent asked me whether I would go and speak to the men in a concentration camp some way outside the town. Not having the faintest idea what a concentration camp was, I said cheerfully: 'Of course

I will!' When he came to fetch me from our lodging, I thought he looked rather oddly at Effie, then said: 'Oh, well, we can leave her in the car.'

I sat in front with him, and on the way he enlightened me about the nature of the concentration camp, where over a thousand men and lads were segregated from their comrades, having contracted venereal disease. It was a great shock to me, and I could not imagine what I could find to say to them. However, having put my hand to the plough, there was no turning back, but it was a poignant moment when I, a woman, alone, faced them on that sunny hillside to offer them my message. It is marvellous how one is helped in such moments of stress. I have never known it to fail. I found words, beholding in them the menfolk of praying and anxious women at home. But it shook me a little. It was my first introduction to one of the minor horrors of war . . .

We ended our marvellous pilgrimage at Etaples where we spent a week. Once a quaint old fishing village, familiar and beloved of artists, it had become one of the most stupendous bases of the war. The camps covered miles of the sand-dunes, hospitals, already full, had been built, canteens established – everything necessary for handling vast bodies of troops under all circumstances.

Effie said suddenly one day: 'Mother, I'm stopping here.'

I was not surprised. I had watched the way in which the whole new world was gripping her. I explained that we should have to go home first and interview Lady Bessborough, the head of the Bureau responsible for sending out women workers to the Y.M.C.A.

Effie was under the prescribed age, but her expert knowledge of French, and the fact that she was willing to take her car with her, disposed of all the objections.

In a week or two she crossed the Channel again, in full working kit, to remain there, except for short leaves, for the 'duration.' When the Armistice was signed, she went to Cologne with the Army of Occupation, and was absent from us for over four years.

WORKING AT THE PITHEAD

Margaret Davie, c. 1914

What a difference a century makes. Women and children no longer worked down the pits, but a young woman like Margaret Davie, from Prestonpans, doing a physically demanding job at the mine, could take pride and pleasure in her work. She left school at fourteen, and her mother wanted her to go into service, as she had done, but Margaret quickly realised that was not for her. Instead, she followed her miner father's example and made for the pithead. With so many young men in the armed services, Prestongrange's managers were doubtless grateful to have such a reliable and eager employee.

Ma mother she wis wantin' money. She wanted money. Ah got 2s.6d. for the tattie week. Onywey, ah dug up half a sovereign this day in the earth. And here when ah seen it ah says, 'Oh!' Ah didnae ken what it wis. Ah'd never seen yin before. It wis shinin' braw on the black earth ahead o' us. And of course the man that wis gafferin' us wanted it and some o' the weemen said, 'Oh, if ye gie him that ah'll tell yer mother!' And here when ah gave ma mother it, oh, she wis that pleased. Oh, ah wis goin' tae get a'thing. Ah, but here, on the Tuesday ah says tae her, 'Mother, what am ah gettin' off the half-sovereign ah fund?' She says, 'What?!' Of course, cheek again, ah says, 'What am ah gettin' off the half-sovereign ah fund?' She says, 'Say that again!' And of course, it wis that way – airms akimbo. Ye kent it when it wis that way. She says, 'Ye got a pair o' stoackins six weeks ago.' So that wis that.

So efter that ah went on the pitheid at Prestongrange. Ah got a job through the brickwork, where ah yaised tae gether the coal in the mornins, and then it was up tae the pitheid. But ah'll tell ye, ah enjoyed it. Ah never shirked ma job, ken what ah mean. Ah wis strong enough tae dae it. And ah wis the youngest there. There were four o' us and ah wis the youngest o' the four lassies. Ah wid be sixteen then, goin' on seventeen.

. . . Well, on the pitheid there were what ye cry the windin' engine. Well, that ta'en the cage up and doon. Well, in the mornin' men went doon until six o'clock, tae the horn blew. And then efter that it wis coal came up. Well, the men went doon and went tae their different jobs and that. But there wis yin man he went doon about fower o'clock in the mornin' and of course he wis the only man there. He wis the ostler. He had tae go doon fur tae feed horses, ye ken, the pownies that wis workin'. He had tae clean them and feed them and get them ready for the fellaes comin' doon. And yin fellaw wid, ken, maybe take a carrot for his powny. They yeaised tae be guid tae their pownies, ken, the fellaes. But we never got near the cage or anything.

Then the coal came up, ken, maybe twa hutches. And then the coal went roond like that on wee rails and they came tae what ye cry the justicemen. And say yin hutch wis ower heavy, or he thought it wis ower heavy, that wid go doon a certain rail tae the end and that wis cowped up for tae take the stanes oot o' it. See, this wis somebody tryin' it on.

Well, we wrocht the tumblers on the pitheid. There were three tumblers, what ye cried tumblers. See, they had sets o' rails side by side and underneath there were hutches. That's what them put the coal intae tae come up. Then there were bogies, which wis a bigger size again but they never left the pit. They did a' the grund work on the pit. And then there were the waggons, but that wis the railway.

Well, the railway, the big waggons, there were a man wi' yin airm, Dod Shaw they cried him, ticketed them. He did a' the ticketin'. Ah think Dod Shaw got his accident no' in Prestongrange, some other pit. But onyway when you put the certain tumblers the hutch went in and you stepped on it and turned it, and a' the coal fell doon at the other end. Ye pit the hutch away oot the road – another yin comin', ye see. And ye'd tae keep this tumbler goin'. And the waggons underneath wis catchin' the coal. And then some o' it was overweight and that had tae gaun doon on tae the tables. They'd tae gaun doon another bit, because there were laddies on the tables pickin' the stanes out o' thir coal.

And then efter that there were yin wi' what they cried redd. White rock went intae a tumbler jist there, jist at the side where it came oot o'. And then there were a big long scaffold for the redd, and the redd wis taken up frae the bing and it wis put ower the bing. Well, this wis where we used tae get the coal in the mornin' for the hoose. Well, ah had a horse tae drive for, oh, over a year. Ah wis on this long, long scaffold masel'. Ah, ah wis seventeen past then. So ah wis on the tumblers first and then ah wis put on tae the horse.

Ma wages when ah started first on the pit heid wis nineteen shillins. Ah got a shillin' for somethin': it wis eighteen shillins for wir pey, but ah had nineteen shillins. Ken, ye jist got your pey line and ye had tae gaun doon tae the office and get your pey, and that wis that. Mind ye, it didnae gaun very far nineteen shillins, but it was a big improvement on what ah'd had before.

That wis still durin' the First War, of course. And me startin' at six o'clock in the mornin; ah got hame for ma breakfast aboot quarter tae nine, ye see. Then ah came back up tae the pitheid at ten o'clock. Well, by that time the post wis roond the doors and then ye wid hear, 'So-and-so's been wounded, so-and-so's been killed,' ken. Well of course, they were a' waitin' on ye at the pitheid comin' in: 'What news did ye get? Did ye get news about this yin, get news aboot that yin?' That wis a daily event, the postman comin' roond. They were a' wantin' tae ken a' what the news o' the Pans wis.

RENT STRIKES

Grace Kennedy, 1915

While men were away at war, landlords in Glasgow took advantage of their absence to raise rents. Even if householders protested, with thousands flocking to work at the ship yards and in munitions, there would always be someone willing to take their place. These cynical opportunists were unprepared, however, for the collective anger of wives and daughters on the home front. Already enraged by landlords' neglect of their properties, they went on strike, refusing to pay rent from April to November 1915. Operating in shifts to prevent evictions, women would harass the eviction officers by throwing flour at them, or in one case pulling down his trousers. A full-blown demonstration in November, of women and shipyard and engineering workers, so alarmed the authorities that striking tenants who had been arrested were released. Led by Mary Barbour, from Govan, who was one of the city's first female councillors, this revolt eventually resulted in the Rent Restriction Act in December 1915. As a result rents were fixed at pre-war levels until the end of the war, and for six months thereafter. Women like Grace Kennedy who took part in the protest were known as Mary Barbour's Army.

During the war years there was people getting put out of their homes because they couldn't pay their rent. A lot of their men were in the Forces and at that time the soldiers' allowance was a shilling a day and they got half pay. The rent courts were full of people. And then there was what they called enrolments, re-enrolments and other re-enrolments. Sometimes the sheriff said you had to pay seven shillings. If you couldn't pay five shillings a week rent how on earth could you pay seven shillings a week?

Well, the women got together and we decided that not one soldier's wife would be put out of her home. And guided by Baillie Mary Barbour, who was a plodder and who did tremendous work – we picketed these homes. They barricaded themselves up and we picketed the homes.

They couldn't put anybody out between sunset and sunrise. The picket had to be between sunrise and sunset. Then after that you could go home. Then you put the food up to the people who were barricaded in their houses.

Then later on there was the Rent Strike. The landlords decided to put the rent up and they did get a 47½ per cent increase, which was supposed to be for repairs. Then we had nine months of a Rent Strike. Well, quite a lot got into difficulties through the Rent Strike – financial difficulties . . . Some of us saved our rent and had then to pay a certain amount and pay the arrears. But then the Rent Restriction Act was brought in and I think it was due to the work of Baillie Mary Barbour particularly and the women that the Rent Restriction Act was brought into being.

John Heenan was a great man in the Rent Strike and I think he was on the Clyde Workers' Committee at that time. But he attended the rent courts. He was a councillor for a period and he was chairman of the Trades Council and of the City Labour Party.

I mind being on duty one day and I threw a pail of water over a gentleman that I thought was a sheriff officer. He came round the corner and it was in Drive Road, Govan, and we were picketing this day. We were determined that this woman wouldn't be put out of her home. But the gentleman turned out to be John Heenan. He had been at a funeral and he had on a bowler hat.

. . . I used to go up to the rent courts, just more or less as a spectator. Sometimes I was allowed to speak on behalf of tenants. In fact, you didn't get speaking. They just said, 'Do you owe this rent?' The tenants said, 'Yes.' 'We'll say seven shillings a week.' If it was five shillings a week then it was seven shillings. How on earth could you pay two shillings more? It became so bad that Lloyd George came to the city and I have a memory of going up to some meeting and I think we bawled him out.

THE LADY TRAM DRIVER HAS ARRIVED

People's Journal, *December 1915*

The shortage of male labour in the war years offered unexpected opportunities for women. As this article in a Glasgow paper shows, they were able – slowly – to overcome prejudice about their ability to do what was previously considered men's work. Lest it seems the battle has been won, however, there are still areas where old taboos prevail. Even today, the number of female pilots, for instance, is extremely low, the job still being seen as a male profession.

A few weeks ago, when the experiment of trying women tram drivers was mooted in Glasgow, the general public decided that the new departure would only end in failure. Women were constitutionally unfit for such an onerous post, they argued, and the majority of the tramway employees were of the same way of thinking. But now the lady tram driver has arrived. At the beginning of the week five motor women put in a full day's work on the front platform, and there were no complaints.

During the busiest part of one day I journeyed from St. Vincent Street to Newlands on a car driven by Miss Mary Campbell of Newlands Depot. The vehicular and passenger traffic was heavy; the hour was between five and six, when the light was bad; and the rails were none too reliable owing to a slight drizzle of rain.

Down Union Street the car was guided safely; through the maze of traffic at Argyle Street, the young motorwoman forged ahead: Glasgow Bridge was taken at full power, as the gong sounded a warning note to a zig-zagging carter in front; the policeman on points duty on the south side of the Bridge held up no restraining hand and, with another thump at the gong, we sparked merrily on.

'By Jove, that driver of ours can handle a car,' remarked a passenger, unaware that a lady was the guiding and controlling factor.

'My experience as a lady tram driver,' repeated Miss Campbell, a most prepossessing young lady, whose rosy cheeks testified eloquently to the healthiness of the open-air life. 'Well, I've scarcely had time to collect any yet. The first thing I did was to go to the window to see what state the rails were in. Thank goodness, it was raining, for although a wet rail is apt to make hand-braking a heavy task, still the magnetic emergency brake acts admirably on a clean, if wet rail.

'The first day was quiet, but the second was a big difference. I began at eight o'clock, and although the rails were still good, yet it was very cold. On the afternoon, when the traffic began to get heavy, I got my first fright, although it was scarcely a fright either. I was just passing a funeral when one of the horses stumbled and swung the carriage round on to the track right in front of me. I immediately applied the emergency brake, and stopped dead. Somehow I had been expecting such an occurrence.

'We get it drummed into us at the school to be always on the look-out for these little nerve trials, and I felt quite proud of my quick stop. Then a motor came flashing out of a side street as I was advancing at a pretty fair speed. I had to look lively again. But, thank goodness, I managed to check the speed of the car in time.

'The youngsters constitute our greatest worry, however. They will be clinging on to a heavy vehicle and invisible to any one going in the opposite direction and they will dart out unthinkingly in front of you. It means that every instant a tram driver must be on the alert, and there is no time for day dreaming.'

'How about keeping time, Miss Campbell? Do you experience any difficulty in running to a schedule?'

'Not so far. You see a lot depends upon the conductor. A good man or woman behind will get the passengers on and off expeditiously and I must say that I am fortunate in that respect. I have one of the best and most experienced conductors in the service.'

'One more question, Miss Campbell. What answer would you make to the people who still declare that women will never make efficient tram drivers?'

'They are too premature. The fact that there are five of us in Glasgow seems sufficient reply. They can't say that we were favoured with the best of climatic conditions. Our preliminary practice was undergone in frost, fog and on rails of the greasiest description. We entered on our test in midwinter; the worst period of the year, and speaking candidly I don't consider the task beyond women folks. I prefer driving to conducting; there may be occasions when dilatory carters make me wish that my command of the King's English could be more forceful and still be lady like, but taking it all over, it is a grand life. Out in the open air, with no one to bother you as long as the work is going on and the wheels revolving to time. Yes, I think we'll manage all right.'

COOKING FOR ELSIE INGLIS'S RUSSIAN UNIT
Mary Lee Milne, 1916

When Elsie Inglis offered her services as a surgeon to the Royal Army medical corps at the start of the First World War, she was dismissed with the words, 'my good lady, go home and sit still'. That day was the inspiration for Inglis's remarkable Scottish Women's Hospitals movement, whereby field hospitals, staffed by women under her management, were set up at the front lines, first in France, and then further east. It took determination even to train as a woman doctor in the late nineteenth century – Inglis was the generation to benefit from Sophia Jex-Blake's pioneering degree – so a military officer's snub was not going to put her off. The most difficult of her postings was the Russian unit that served the Serb Division on the Russo-Rumanian Front, in 1916–17. With her staff of seventy-five women (thirteen Scots, five Irish, three Welsh, fifty English) she worked in such demanding conditions – including a period of imprisonment – that only hours after returning to Britain from Archangel, in November 1917, she died. The courage and good cheer of the women she worked with was staggering, but clearly she inspired intense loyalty. Mary Lee Milne, the unit's hard-pressed cook, was a forty-three-year-old widow from Selkirk, and one of only six women who stayed with Inglis for the duration of this posting. She recorded what she witnessed in diaries and in film, some of it taken at great personal risk. Here she recalls just a handful of the hair-raising moments she experienced. Unsurprisingly, her obituary in the Hawick News *in 1948 described her as 'a woman of great individuality and force of character'.*

Hospital A, Medgidia
Saturday 4 October, 1916

This has been a terribly exciting day. I went out with Bell to get meat, and whilst we were on the way the railway was bombed. We had just left it when the first fell. Then they came thick and fast all round us – it was a terrible feeling, watching where the next would come. We drove for our lives along a road which was turned into pandemonium – horses and men flying, hay carts over-turned, horses lying dead. We picked up one man and took him with us – he had nine holes in his back. The enemy was just over us all the time – quite awful. Bell was wonderful. She pacified the frightened men, told them to lie down, held terrified horses, and kept us all from feeling upset. I was not really afraid, but I just wanted to get back to William [her brother]. I felt I didn't want to be killed, and it was just as likely to be me as anyone here. However, we got back to the hospital with the wounded man, and for the moment the enemy has gone off. But at lunch time they came back in double the number, and shelled the town afresh. They hovered over our camp for over an hour; then at tea time they were back again – guns firing and shells flying through the air . . . For the moment we are all safe, but how long will it last?

Motor party Caramurat to Hirsova
Monday 23 October, 1916

As we came to a river with a quite impassable bridge, the drivers both refused to attempt it in the dark. They were also perfectly exhausted, having driven all day through retreating multitudes, and were sadly in need of rest. So it was decided that we should just camp where we were by the roadside. When Dr Kostic, who was with Dr Inglis in the car, heard the decision, he was in a great state of excitement. He said it was dangerous: it was impossible. If we would not cross the river in the dark we must go back a little way and find a village. We could not sleep out of doors in October. He said, 'I cannot ask any of my men to stay with you. They would not do it. The enemy is too near, and I cannot ask them.' He said, 'Excuse, excuse' so often, we all laughed, and assured him we would come to no harm, and could very well look after ourselves. We would start at daybreak, and soon overtake them. So, seeing that we were not to be shaken in our reso-lution to camp for the night where we were, he very unwillingly left us, writing the name of the place for which we were bound, and handing it to Dr Inglis.

After he had left us, a Serbian soldier who had worked in the kitchen at Medgidia came up and announced in very American English that he was going to stay with us: he didn't care for 'them Bulgars'. I was especially delighted with this, as it was my job to get a fire and a meal ready. Dr Inglis herself had a most extraordinary way of getting things, and she paid us all the compliment of thinking we had the same power. But when she announced after we had decided on the patch of ground where we would have our fire, 'And now, cook, let us have a good meal – we are all ravenous,' it rather staggered me for the moment. We had been retreating for two days, and had been unable to get anything. I knew I still had the remains of a roast of pork from which we had lunched before leaving Medgidia – if it had not been taken out of the ambulance in the meantime. So with trembling I looked into the basket where I had put it; and not only was it there, but a loaf of bread had been added to it, which was to have formed the lunch for Dr Inglis and the drivers, but they never had an opportunity to stop . . . So with triumph I produced these . . . and soon we were all sitting round the fire waiting for the water to boil for our tea, and a more delightful, merry meal could not be imagined. We all told our experiences of the day, and Dr Inglis said, 'But this is best of all: it is just like a fairy tale.' And so it was; for when we looked up, there were groups of soldiers holding their horses, standing motionless, staring at us; we saw them only through wood-smoke. The fire had attracted them, and they had come to see what it could mean. Seeing nine women laughing and chatting, alone and within earshot of the guns, was more than they could understand. They did not speak, but went quietly away as they had come.

THE RUSSIAN FRONT LINE

Elsie Inglis, January 1917

These official reports by Elsie Inglis barely hint at the dreadful situation in which the staff, but particularly the soldiers, found themselves.

Hospital A Galatz
Report 1–3 January 1917
The wounded were pouring through Galatz at the rate of about one thousand a day, and we got nothing but bad cases at our hospital. Dr Potter has a story

that she gave orders for any cases that could walk to come down to the dressing room, and a few minutes afterwards the door was burst open and a man crawled in on all fours. That was the nearest we could get to a walking case!

The night we opened we got 109 cases. We bathed and dressed them all, and began operating the next afternoon at one o'clock, and then went on without a break until five o'clock the next morning. We owe a debt of gratitude to Mr Scott, Surgeon to the British Armoured Car Corps, who met one of the girls and asked whether he could be of any use. I sent back a message at once that we should be most grateful, and he worked with us without a break until we evacuated. He is a first-class surgeon, and it was a great thing to have him there. The cases stayed in a very short time, and we evacuated again down to the barges going to Reni, the hospital filling up, and more than filling up each time.

Hospital A Reni
Elsie Inglis, 24 January 1917
Fortunately we have solved the question of the wood supply, thanks to the kindness of the commandant of the 'Expedition' at Reni. It took about three days to solve this question of meat, and water. Reni itself is quite a small place, and it is only its geographical position that gives it importance now. The Expedition has made practically a new village for itself on the docks. There was no Intendance [*sic*], where one usually gets supplies, and if it had not been for Captain Yermakov, who is head of the Expedition, who is an old and tried friend of ours, I don't know what we should have done.

However, the doctor in charge of the Evacuation Hospital (a kind of clearing station) at the railway, was bent on our staying, and things gradually cleared up. We were very amused, however – the day we promised to have the hospital ready, when everybody was hard at it putting things into shape, and the wood and water problem was only being temporarily solved by the kindness of individual officers who lent us water-carts and gave us wood, two officers of the 30th Cossacks arrived on the scene with an invitation to a concert! and the 'premier line' seven versts off, and the guns booming all the time! I accepted conditionally on there being no wounded, and at 7 that evening, the majority of the unit off duty, with Dr Corbett in charge, went off to the concert, which ended in a dance, and they got back at 1 a.m. just as the first batch of wounded arrived. They [the 30th Cossacks] invited us to another one the next week too.

Those first days we did not know how long the hospital would remain at Reni. Our own guns were firing from the hill above us and we saw Galatz on fire. Our orders were to stay until ordered to go by the doctor in charge of the Evacuation and then to go to Benderi.

The hospital at Reni is being run with Russian Red Cross money, and a clerk has been attached to us – Captain Bergmann, who is very useful in many ways, besides accounts. The Russian sister has left. She was a nice little thing, but not very strong and knew nothing about keeping accounts. She helped us a great deal, however, as she knew personally such numbers of Russian officers. All her brothers are in the army. She met a colonel she knew in Galatz and got us enough wood for a week, and at Reni she got us a sheep a day out of another acquaintance, until the meat problem was solved.

Hospital A Reni
Elsie Inglis, 4 March 1917
(Following a visit by the head sanitary inspector of the army)
It was indeed a thorough inspection. The men's pyjama suits were taken off and searched for lice; the sheets were turned up, and the mattresses beaten to see if they were dusty; the food was tasted and the orderlies' rooms raided. The report eventually ran that the patients were very clean, well cared for medically, and well nursed; but that the condition of the orderlies was disgraceful. This report is absolutely true. But the condition of the orderlies shall no longer remain 'disgraceful'. I am afraid I rather thought they were not my business, as Captain Bergmann always said he was in charge of the orderlies. But during his inspection the Chief of the Medical Staff suddenly turned to me and asked, 'Do you hold yourself responsible for the condition of the orderlies?' I answered, 'Yes, and next time you come you will not find a single louse,' at which he was very delighted and amused.

MARRIED LOVE

Marie Stopes, 1918

Marie Stopes was born in Edinburgh, her mother's home city, in 1880, and returned to be educated for a few years at St George's School for Girls, before studying botany and geology at University College, London. She was a ground-breaking scientist, but made her name for posterity with her frank and controversial book, Married Love, *published in 1918. In this she advocated birth control, a theme she elaborated on in later works. In 1921, with her second husband, she established the first birth control clinic in Britain, in London. As the following extract shows, while the country was being convulsed by the Great War and its aftermath, Stopes was turning her thoughts to sex. It was probably the best thing she could have done. This passage picks up after her ruminations on the beauty of classical statues such as the Venus of Milo.*

A young man or woman perfectly naked cannot be tawdry. The fripperies, the jagged curves and inharmonious lines and colours of the so-called 'adornments' are surmounted, and the naked figure stepping from their scattered pile is seen in its utter simplicity . . . It is therefore not surprising that one of the innumerable sweet impulses of love should be to reveal, each to each, this treasure of living beauty. To give each other the right to enter and enjoy the sight which most of all sights in the world draws and satisfies the artist's eyes.

This impulse, however, is, on the part of the woman, swayed by two at least of the natural results of her rhythmic tides. For some time during each month, age-long tradition that she is 'unclean', coupled with her obvious requirements, have made her withdraw herself from even her husband's gaze. But, on the other hand, there regularly come times when her body is raised to a higher point of loveliness than usual by the rounding and extra fullness of the breasts . . . Partly or wholly unconscious of the brilliance and full perfection of her beauty, she yet delights in its gentle promptings to reveal itself to her lover's eyes when he adores. This innocent, this goddess-like self-confidence retreats when the natural ebb of her vitality returns.

How fortunate for man when these sweet changes in his lover are not coerced into uniformity! For man has still so much of the ancient hunter in his blood that beauty which is always at hand and ever upon its pedestal must inevitably attract him far less than the elusive and changing charms of rhythmic life. In the highly evolved and cultivated woman, who has wisdom enough not to restrict, but to give full play to the great rhythms of her being, man's polygamous instinct can be satisfied and charmed by the ever-changing aspects of herself which naturally come uppermost. And one of her natural phases is at times to retreat, to experience a profound sex indifference, and passionately to resent any encroachment on her solitude.

This is something woman too often forgets. She has been so thoroughly 'domesticated' by man that she feels too readily that after marriage she is all his. And by her very docility to his perpetual demands, she destroys for him the elation, the palpitating thrills and surprises, of the chase.

In the rather trivial terms of our sordid modern life, it works out in many marriages somewhat as follows: The married pair share a bedroom, and so it comes about that the two are together not only at the times of delight and interest in each other, but during some of the unlovely and even ridiculous proceedings of the toilet. Now it may enchant a man once – perhaps even twice – or at long intervals – to watch his goddess screw her hair up into a tight and unbecoming knot and soap her ears. But it is inherently too unlovely a proceeding to retain indefinite enchantment. To see a beautiful woman floating in the deep, clear water of her bath – that may enchant for ever, for it is so lovely, but the unbeautiful trivialities essential to the daily toilet tend only to blur the picture and to dull the interest and attention that should be bestowed on the body of the loved one. Hence, ultimately, everyday association in the commonplace daily necessities tends to reduce the keen pleasure each takes in the other. And hence, inevitably and tragically, though stealthily and unperceived, to reduce the keenness of stimulation the pair exert on each other, and thus to lower their intensity of the consummation of the sex act, and hence to lower its physiological value.

In short, the overcoming of her personal modesty, which is generally looked on as an essential result in marriage where the woman becomes wholly the man's, has generated among our women a tradition that before their husbands they can perform any and all of the details of personal and domestic duties. Correspondingly, they allow the man to be neglectful of preserving some reticence before them. This mutual possession of the lower and more elementary experiences of life has been, in innumerable marriages, a factor in destroying the mutual possession of life's higher and more poetic charms.

And woman's beauty wanes too often more through neglect than through age. The man, with the radiant picture of his bride blurred by the daily less lovely aspects, may cease to remind her by acts of courtship that her body is precious. But many men by whom each aspect of their wives is noted, are often hurt by women's stupidity or neglect of herself. Women lose their grace of motion by relying on artificial bones and stiffenings, and clog their movements with heavy and absurdly fashioned garments. They forget how immeasurably they can control not only their clothed appearance but the very structure of their bodies by the things they eat and do, by the very thoughts they think.

A wise man once said that a woman deserved no credit for her beauty at sixteen, but beauty at sixty was her own soul's doing.

In this respect I am inclined to think that man suffers more than woman. For man is still essentially the hunter, the one who experiences the desires and thrills of the chase, and dreams ever of coming unawares upon Diana in the woodlands. On the other hand, the married woman, having once yielded all, tends to remain passively in the man's companionship.

Though it may appear trivial . . . I think that, in the interests of husbands, an important piece of advice to wives is: Be always escaping. Escape the lower, the trivial, the sordid. So far as possible (and this is far more possible than appears at first, and requires only a little care and rearrangement in the habits of the household) ensure that you allow your husband to come upon you only when there is delight in the meeting. Whenever finances allow, the husband and wife should have separate bedrooms. No soul can grow to its full stature without spells of solitude. A married woman's body and soul should be essentially her own, and that can only be so if she has an inviolable retreat. But at the same time the custom of having separate rooms should not mean, as it often does, that the husband only comes to his wife's room when he has some demand to make upon her. Nothing is more calculated to inhibit all desire for union in a sensitive wife than the knowledge of what her husband wants when he comes, however lovingly, to her side. Every night, unless something prevents, there should be the tender companionship and whispered intimacies which are, to many people, only possible in the dark. The 'good-night' should be a time of delightful forgetting of the outward scars of the years, and a warm, tender, perhaps playful exchange of confidences . . . When this custom is maintained it overcomes the objection some people make to separate rooms as a source of estrangements.

IOLAIRE WIDOW ASKS FOR HELP

Kate Morrison, 1919

The sinking of the Iolaire *on 1 January 1919 was one of the cruellest tragedies of the First World War. When the severely overloaded aged steam yacht set sail from the Kyle of Lochalsh to Stornoway, carrying soldiers returning from the war, there were far too few life jackets for the number on board. In stormy conditions, the* Iolaire *hit rocks within yards of the shore at Stornoway, and over 200 men drowned. At least 181 were from Lewis and Harris, and the devastation this brought to the islands can only be imagined. Countless widows and fatherless children suddenly faced hardship. Perhaps to deflect criticism of the mistakes that led to the sinking, a fund was quickly established to help the dead soldiers' families. The average relief awarded was £7 to £9 10s a year. This letter from Kate Morrison, whose husband John was one of the victims, was typical. She had eight children to feed, and her claim was upheld.*

Sir,
I beg to apply for a grant from the Iolaire Disaster Fund. My husband, John Morrison, was drowned in the Iolaire Disaster. He was at the time in the Royal Naval Reserve. Before the war he was a fisherman.

My family numbers nine persons, including myself. Their ages vary from 18 years to 1 year. I myself have been under medical treatment by Dr MacKenzie for the last three years, and for the past eight months have been practically confined to bed. Am thus quite unable to do any housework. The result of this is that my two eldest daughters, aged 18 and 16 respectively, have to be always at home to look after the house & the younger children.

We have a small croft but owing to our having to pay for the ploughing and other heavy work done on it, it is a great expense. In the same way our peat-cutting costs a considerable amount, owing to there being no man at home to look after it. In fact I have had to borrow money for the working of the croft and peat-cutting this year. While my husband was in the navy we were receiving the sum of 52/6 per week but lately this had been reduced to 43/4 by the ministry of pensions. My two eldest daughters who are both over 16 are deemed to be capable of supporting themselves and are not allowed anything, altho' as I have pointed out owing to the state of my health & the claims of my young family they are both needed at home and are thus unable to go out to work for themselves.

Dr MacKenzie will, I'm sure, give information of my ill-health if such is thought necessary. Rev. R MacKenzie will also give any other information necessary in support of my statements. I shd. be obliged by your bringing my case before the Trustees as soon as possible.

Yours faithfully

Mrs John Morrison

KEPT IN THE DARK

Fiona McFarlane, early to mid 1900s

Fiona McFarlane, a Labour councillor from Glasgow, was born into a family where the men drank heavily. This affected her view of men, and she later divorced her own heavy-drinking husband. Her mother, however, was not perfect either. In neglecting to pass on any form of sex education she was typical of an easily embarrassed and repressed generation, and a nation that preferred never to talk about body or mind. The results, as in Fiona's case, could be profoundly upsetting.

I was born in the Royal Maternity Hospital in Glasgow in Rotten Row, and the reason I was born there was because my mother couldn't afford to get the doctor in, and up there they could take her in for ten days for a pound. I was the fourth of five children and my father had a reasonable job in India Tyres, but he was a typical Scot, thought his money was his own, and he would only give my mother literally the pocket money whilst he drank the rest. The first two boys were twins. My mother and father had both been in the hotel line. They were very snobbish about it, they only worked in hydros, they only worked at the very best. Marvellous tips in the hydro. We went there for a season at a time.

My mother only married my father because she was getting on. She'd not had any education at all. Her father had been a terrible drunk and her mother had died when she was quite young and they had all been brought up in homes, all in individual homes. You know how they split up the families. They took her family of four and they put them all in separate orphanages and they did not see each other again until they left the orphanages when they were adults, about sixteen or seventeen. My grandfather really was a wild drunken man, and my uncles and my aunt can tell her. My mother thought the world of her father, she thought there was nobody like her daddy, but none of the family even ever associated with him – she was the only one, she took him in when he was an old man – because they could remember their mother lying on a mattress on the floor delivering her baby, and him coming in drunk and taking her by the hair, you know, and giving her a beating up because his food wasn't ready. Anyway she died of blood poisoning about two weeks after the last child was born, and his very respectable – he only had one sister – very respectable sister came. She had a boarding house and took the baby away and gave her a very good education. My mother and her younger sister Jenny were put in homes . . .

She got married intending to start a boarding house of her own. As my mother says, they got the boarding house, but non-paying guests – five children and my father – as it turned out. I think my mother's sexual attitude might have been to blame a wee bit too, because she was so afraid of it that she wouldn't have any sex, and I think any time she did have, she became pregnant, you know. She didn't know anything about birth control and she says that if in those days she had gone to the doctor they'd have chased her – because she didn't have enough money. The working classes weren't supposed to know anything about birth control or abortion and how to prevent these.

In my family there were two boys, twins, and then my sister fourteen months later, and then three years later my younger sister. And they agreed between them that that would be the last. Well I think there was never any sexual relations from the time that my sister was born, my mother will tell you this. I never knew my mother and father to even sleep in the same bedroom. They just never slept together.

It's like when I had my periods. I had no idea what this was. I woke up one morning and blood was streaming from me – and I was screaming through to my mother in the kitchen. Nothing was sore, I felt nothing, but I thought there must be something wrong with all this blood about. All my mother said was, 'Stop that nonsense, that's you coming a woman now,' and that was it. I never associated anything I heard with me. You know it was quite a frightening experience. I stayed off school. I think that was the only time I ever stayed off school. And then she didn't bother explaining that this would happen regularly, and this happened later. I couldn't understand it. I thought there must be something wrong with me and I didn't tell her. I managed somehow by, you know, washing all underwear. I was thirteen, washing my own underwear. I managed to keep it going. I don't know how I managed – I must have used rags or something to ward it off. About a year later she took me to the doctor. She didn't say what it was until I was in – and I was so embarrassed – and I sat down and she said I had had a period on my thirteenth birthday and I had nothing since, you know – and all this time I had been hiding it from her, so afraid in case there was something wrong with me.

A MARKED WOMAN

Mary Brooksbank, c. 1922 or 1923

Born in Aberdeen in 1897, in what she described as 'one of the worst slums in the city', Mary Brooksbank (née Soutar) became a fervent Communist, and served three sentences in prison as a result. This was something of a family tradition, her father being an ardent trade unionist. She was also a gifted songwriter, best known for 'Oh, Dear Me' (putting the words to the tune of 'The Jute Mill Song'). After her family moved south, she started in a jute mill in Dundee when she was almost fourteen, and for the rest of her life agitated for better conditions for workers. In an interview with Hamish Henderson in 1968 she recalled: 'My mother put me into service for a period; tried to make me genteel you know. She gave me a lovely outfit but it didna suit me; it was the worst thing she could have did because I saw right away the contrast between their homes and ours, you know, thon's o' the gentry and ours.' She was expelled from the Communist Party after expressing her condemnation of Stalin's inhumane policies. Michael Marra and Rod Paterson wrote a song in her honour, called 'The Bawbee Birlin'. Here, she describes life in a mill shortly after the First World War.

The life of the women workers of Dundee, right up to the thirties, was, to put it bluntly, a living hell of hard work and poverty. It was a common sight to see women, after a long 10-hour day in the mill, running to the steam wash-houses with the family washing. They worked up to the last few days before having their bairns . . . Infant and maternal mortality in Dundee was the highest in the country, worse even than Lancashire. Children of 12 were given badges enabling them to sell papers in the street. Even the police had their Bootless Bairns Fund, for bootless bairns were a common enough sight in those days. So were low wages, unemployment, profiteering in food, lack of proper medical attention, bad housing conditions, and, of course, the ever-prevalent ignorance, superstition and fear.

The women in particular had much to be afraid of. Fear of losing their jobs, fear of losing their health, fear of losing their bairns, fear of offending, even unwittingly, gaffers, priests, factors, and all those whom they had been taught were placed by God in authority over them.

Unemployment continued to grow. How could it be otherwise? The imposition of the Versailles Treaty on a defeated Germany virtually made slaves of the German people, compelling them to produce the goods which we had formerly made. The British and American industrialists reaped a rich harvest by way of reparations but had to subsidise their own unemployed wage slaves. In the meantime, mass demonstrations were taking place. One in particular comes to mind. It was during the first Armistice Day, that day when two minutes' silence is held in memory of our 'glorious dead'. Yes, 'these bundles of bloody rags', mentioned by Churchill. With our banners of protest mentioning the numbers of unemployed, the homeless, the widowed and orphaned, we marched. One of our unemployed ex-servicemen had a banner depicting a soldier rising, looking up at these numbers, and saying, 'If this is what I fought for, thank Christ I'm dead!'

A local minister, the Rev. Harcourt Davidson (noted for his drinking habits), stopped our demonstration, then the police, who had been waiting, commenced arresting our leaders. We were charged with breach of the peace. I got 40 days' imprisonment, Jock Thomson, our chairman, got 60 days, and some 20 others got fines and lesser sentences. Every day we spent in gaol there were mass demonstrations outside. We could hear the people singing and shouting to cheer us up . . .

I was soon to learn that original thinking, like original sin, brought its own punishment. I found that, because of my activities, I could not get a job, and if I did, I could not keep it long.

I recall a great rally held in the Caird Hall, and sponsored by all the religious denominations in the city, against Bolshevism. One of the posters, a gigantic affair, showed a worker being led blindfold into a chasm. Over the brink was a black cloud labelled 'Communism'. Evidently plenty of money was behind this political rally, for there was no mistaking its purpose, hidden under the cloak of religion. No sooner did the chairman start to speak than there were interruptions from all over the hall. During a lull, I asked the chairman why the reverend gentlemen had made no protest at the mass slaughter between 1914 and 1918? I was immediately seized and hustled out to a waiting van.

Next day in court I pleaded guilty. The sheriff, Malcolm, asked why I had protested the previous evening. I pointed out that this had been advertised as a religious meeting, but was in fact political. He agreed, saying, 'International politics, Mrs Brooksbank!' He then fined me three guineas.

I soon realised that I was becoming a 'marked' woman. Once, while addressing a meeting outside the High School gate, in answer to a question I said that until the working class took possession of the —— means of production and became rulers of the country, we would always have unemployment, so long as we had production for profit. That night I was taken from my home by the police and kept in custody without being informed with what I was being charged.

Our organisation got a solicitor, a young man called Carmichael, a partner of Grafton Lawson. Next day I was told that I was charged with sedition. I was taken downstairs into a room where a sheriff's clerk read a long rigmarole. Then I was taken into court. Carmichael came over and in a very paternal tone of voice asked me to plead guilty. He told me that it would go hard with me if I didn't, as sedition was a very serious offence.

He said he was sorry to see me mixed up with all these riff-raff, I was very young, etc., etc. I asked him if he was being paid to represent me, or my accusers, whereupon he became very annoyed. When the Court proceedings opened, I promptly pleaded 'Not Guilty!' Carmichael addressed the sheriff, saying that this young woman had received a poor education and did not realise the seriousness of what she was saying. I interrupted, asking if I could enter the witness box. The sheriff replied, 'Certainly'.

I said I admitted that what I said was only what a former Labour Prime Minister had once said, but in different terms. I protested that I was not asking the 500 or so people at the meeting to take over the administration of the country. Came the verdict: 'Not Proven!'

❦

THE NIGHT WASHING

Molly Weir, early 1920s

A dynamo of energy and humour, Molly Weir was a diminutive actress in TV series such as Magwitch *and* Rentaghost. *She will forever be remembered for her vigorous promotion of the household cleaner,* Flash. *The domestic drudgery involved in keeping a working-class home and family clean and fed was a form of unpaid hard manual labour. As this recollection of doing the laundry suggests, Weir of all people appreciated products that lightened the load.*

There was never the same fierce competition to use the wash-house at night as there was in the daytime. Some of the night washers were younger women, daughters of those too old to do their washing during the day. They had the time, those elderly mothers, but not the strength, so the daughters had to tackle the household washing when they'd finished their day's work in shop or factory. Other women preferred to do their washing in the evenings for their own private reasons. My mother tut-tutted over this, for she felt washings ought properly to be done during the day when there was some chance of clothes being hung out in the fresh air and the wind, to dry, and acquire a fine fresh smell. Grannie would purse her lips and shake her head at the thought of pulleys in the kitchen, laden with steaming clothes, flapping in folks' faces as they moved back and forward to get the kettle from the range or put some coal on the fire. 'I don't like a house fu' o' wet cloots,' she'd say. 'It canna be good for thae lassies efter being' oot at their work a' day.' . . .

Far from sharing my mother's condemnation of the night washers, I used passionately to hope I could coax her to become one of them. There was a theatrical air about the whole scene which made a great appeal to me. The ordinary grey-stone wash-house of the daytime was transformed, as though at the wave of a magical wand, and I couldn't imagine that I had ever played shops on its window ledge, or jumped from its roof on to the wall which divided the back courts.

Guttering candles, stuck in the necks of bottles and ranged along the window-sill, provided the only illumination in what now seemed a vast cavern. Mysterious shadows flickered in the far corners, and the foaming suds in the tubs took on a romantic radiance. When the lid of the huge brick boiler was raised to see how the 'white things' were progressing (the 'white things' was our name for all the household linen), swirling steam filled the wash-house, the candles spat and flickered through illuminated clouds, and the scene became fearsome as pictures of hell. The washerwoman bending over her tub changed from her everyday self too. Hair curled round her ears with the damp, cheeks flushed with the heat and the work, and her eyes glowed in the candle-light, and she revealed a beauty I'd never noticed before.

Like animals attracted by the light, other women would drift from their tenements into the back court, and pause at the wash-house door. 'Are you nearly done noo?' was the usual greeting. The patient figure at the tubs, or 'bines' as we called them, would pause from her vigorous rubbing of the soiled clothes against the wash-board, charmed to be the centre of interest for once, and say cheerfully, 'Just aboot half-way through. I've juist the dungarees to dae, and then the white things will be ready for "sihnin" oot.' I once asked my teacher how to spell this word 'sihnin' which we used when we meant rinsing, but she'd never heard of it, for she was from the north, so I just had to make a guess at the spelling and hope it was right.

At the word 'dungarees' the women would groan in sympathy. Washing dungarees was a job they all hated, and as ours was a Railway district, most husbands or brothers or sons worked with dirty machinery, and came home with grease-laden dungarees, so this was a task they all had to face. Our tene-ment women all had raw fingers from using the slimy black soap and soda which was the only way they knew for ridding the filthy overalls of their accumulated grease and workshop dirt.

The women's eyes would lazily follow the washer's movements as she scrubbed and rinsed, and put clothes through the wringer ready for the house pulleys, or maybe for the ropes next morning, if the next woman using the wash-house could be coaxed to let her put out a rope for a couple of hours before her own were ready to be hung out. But the ropes were only put outside if it promised to be a fine day, and the women were expert weather forecasters, for everybody detested getting their nicely wrung clothes wet again. The ultimate in disaster was reached when the weight of sodden clothes on the ropes was too much for the supporting clothes pole, and the whole lot came crashing among the dirt of the back court, and had to be taken in and rinsed through all over again.

I loved when the white things were judged to be ready, for then came the scene I liked best of all. The heavy boiler lid was lifted off, and leaned care-fully against the back wall of the wash-house. Clouds of steam rushed everywhere. Up the chimney, out of the open door, into every corner. The washer, a long pole held in both hands, bent over the seething mass in the boiler, fished out a load, expertly twirling the steaming clothes to keep them safely balanced, and then ran with the laden pole across to the tub of clean water. Quickly and neatly a twist of the pole shot the clothes into the rinsing water. Back and forth she went, her figure ghost-like in the rushing steam, until the boiler was empty. I longed to be allowed to help in this exciting operation, but met with scandalized refusal. 'Do you want to burn yoursel' to the bone?' the washerwoman would say in answer to my coaxing. 'You'll have this job to dae soon enough, hen, then you'll no' be so pleased. Run away hame to your bed, or I'll tell your grannie on you!' But the women were more amused than angry at my interest in their activities, and they made sure I went nowhere near the steam.

When this final rinsing stage was reached the watching women lingering at the doors couldn't resist a bit of advice, especially if the washer was a younger unmarried woman. As the tub filled, they'd say, 'Take oot the plug, hen, and let the clean water run through the claes. You'll get rid o' a' the soap faur quicker that way.' Or, 'Jessie, you're just squeezin' the soap into them again – you'll hae' tae gi'e them another water. You're putting them through the wringer too soon.'

They were all experts. This was their world. And the young washer-woman would listen to them all, glad of their company and their advice, for it was a great source of pride to have someone say, 'Aye, she hangs out a lovely washing.' And the most disparaging thing a tenement woman could say of another's wash-house efforts were the damning words, 'She's hangin' oot her grey things!'

A THRASHING

Maggie Fuller, 1920s

When ill-health prevented the head of the house from earning a wage, life could be hard for everyone. Girls were expected to help at home, and also find paying work. Education, it goes without saying, was a luxury they could not afford.

My father had an accident at the Leith Docks, they took a kidney away. He had just one kidney and he had a wound. My mother – I used to stand and help her, you know – she put her hand all in it to clean it, it was never closed, you see. He was an invalid for about two years. He wasn't a very good man after that, poor fellow. That's where his friends should have come and helped him that he helped. I had a sister, she is older than I am but not as strong as I was. I got left with most of the work, and she wouldn't even run and go and get a book for him. You know, he was an awful great reader eventually, he was a clever enough man – he was an army man by the way.

I got away from school early. I got an exemption because my mother needed me, because she had to scrub the school. I left school at thirteen and a half and I had to go to night school to make up for it. The reason I got away was because I had to take a young child with me to school. There were no nurseries or you couldn't get them in at all and my father couldn't do anything. So I started to work at six o'clock in the morning at a Co-operative Store Bakery, and I'd come home early in the day to prepare meals for the kids that came home and to wash the stair if it was my mother's turn at the stair. One thing I never did was washing. My mother lifted big heavy pots on to a great black grate, because she only had cold water, and you'd help her, but she did all the main washing. One night, och, I had a rough time with the kids, and I couldn't cope with them by the time I came home. You're young, you're fourteen, what can you do? There had been a right fight and I was a bit late with the tea and we always had somebody looking out the window for mum coming home because she was so tired. My mother was scrubbing for the school; we used to look for her and somebody would say 'Here she's coming' and you ran to make the tea. Well this night there was only a wee drop of tea in the pot – I forgot that – and it stood up on this big high mantlepiece, and one of the kids came up against me and I just dropped this tea and it all went over the floor. And by then she was up and into the house and she nearly killed me for that, somebody pulled her off, she was choking the life out of me. Mind, I don't hold it against her, as I say, you've no idea what it was like with all these ruddy kids.

A SEXUAL HARASSER MEETS HIS MATCH
Ann Flynn, 1923

This young woman emerged unscathed from her first encounter with a sex pest. She inherited her spirit from her mother who, as a member of the Co-operative Women's Guild, was one of the organisers of Glasgow's Rent Strikes in 1915. She would use Ann and her sister as 'her little aides' and it was perhaps this formative experience of seeing their mother refusing to be oppressed or patronised that made her so effortlessly able to stand up for herself.

I left school in Glasgow in 1923 when I was fifteen. So I wrote after jobs and I got replies. I had a fancy for this one – Financier. Well, I would sure like to be in finance, high finance if possible – making a big joke about it with the family. My mother said nothing.

So I went for an interview. It was St Vincent Street, that's where it was, on the corner. And I went up and interviewed and I thought what a nice old man, he was lovely, I liked him. He had such golden grey hair and, of course, I always had an eye for beauty. I thought, oh, he's an awful nice looking old man. And he had a daughter and she was very big and handsome. He was a kind father. And I said I would like to come, yes. And he said, 'You've a very nice way of writing in a stylish hand. Would you like to take the job?' he said. 'Well, yes.' I was quite flattered, you know, being engaged then and there.

When I turned up to start work I thought it was very odd and I had no idea about things like promissory notes. Those were hard times and yet I'm getting all the gen: 'You do that and you pay so much interest.' And then I went home after the end of the second week and I explained to my mother. She said, 'Well, if you had asked, you see, you could have been told. He's a money lender and what is more he's probably Jewish.' I said, 'Well, I don't know what he is but he's a very nice man.' . . . And my mother just looked at me and said nothing. But I thought to myself, 'Well, right enough.'

I didn't stay long, I think maybe six months at the most. I quite liked it in a kind of way, because of the fascination with the sort of people that came in. And I had there my first encounter with someone trying to play me up sexwise. My first encounter was with one of my nice boss's friends. And I remember removing his hand from me and looking up at him and saying, 'Do you see these teeth?' (and I had very good gnashers then) 'See these teeth? If you so much as lay a finger on me I shall bite right through till the blood drips out of you.' And the man drew back and he looked at me with such surprise, because I had done it very dramatically. I didn't go home and tell my mother. I was very satisfied I knew how to sort people who took liberties or even tried to take liberties.

FICTIONAL SEX

Annie S. Swan, 1926

Previously the darling of romantic women's fiction, Annie S. Swan had a rude awak-
ening when she wrote The Pendulum. *For some readers' taste she had gone too far in*
her attempt at realism. There was still deeply ingrained prudery over discussing or even
acknowledging sexual experience, as D. H. Lawrence was to discover a couple of years
later to his cost when he wrote Lady Chatterley's Lover, *despite its tenderness – an*
aspect missing, one suspects, in many women's sex lives.

After the war, the late Sir Ernest Hodder Williams [her publisher], who had
great respect for my work, kept on urging me to write a story dealing with the
effect of the war on family life. I did not particularly want to write such a
book, and told him so. I had seen so much of war's deadly aftermath, had been
behind the scenes in so many tragic, broken lives, that, as I told him, it could
not be a pleasant book, that is, if it held the mirror up to life, even in only a
minor and guarded degree.

However, he brought so much pressure to bear that I wrote the book. Most
of it is true, though of course it was necessary to camouflage, even to mini-
mise, the actual happenings. It was quite well received. Some reviewers
applauded the courage they did not expect from a person like me, and the
book sold to the extent, I believe, of about 10,000 copies.

But its effect on my usual public was very curious, in some respects disas-
trous. I had always been regarded as a 'safe' writer, whose books could be put
into the hands of young persons without any fear of deleterious consequences
to the readers. Obviously, such a reputation, though comforting in parts, had
its acute limitations for the purveyor of 'safe' fiction. It means that the facts of
life must not be faced, but ignored or covered up so that they are unsuspected.
I deplore and loathe the exploitation of sex, which is the outstanding feature
of modern fiction. I do not call that facing the facts in decent, sober fashion,
but mere pandering to some of the baser instincts of humanity. Sex is not only
the most powerful factor in human relationships, but, kept in its proper place,
adds to the joy and fulfilment of life. But its proper place, in my humble opinion, is neither in the front window nor on the housetops. Moreover, it is not
all of life. There are thousands in whose lives sex plays so small a part as to be
almost negligible. To parade it as the only motif or inspiration is not only bad
art, but absolutely untrue to life.

In *The Pendulum* I told a plain tale of the temptations and difficulties which assailed ordinary and sheltered people in the war years. I was glancing through it the other day, and marvelled that such innocuous stuff should have shocked anybody or raised a flutter in the dovecotes. But it did. It more than shocked; it alarmed my public, and they were not slow in expressing their strong disapproval. One minister's wife told me quite gravely, and with considerable unction, that she was one of a little coterie who had met together to pray that I might be restored to the right way.

Another told me that, on the Leith to London boat, a group of women had met in the saloon to discuss the book, and the finding was, 'She has let us down.'

I don't believe I have ever been restored to confidence or favour in these circles. But it does not keep me awake at night.

A COUNTRY SCHOOL

Alexandra Stewart, 1920s–30s

After her upbringing in Glen Lyon, Alexandra Stewart trained in Dundee during the war, and spent several years teaching in so-called 'side schools'. These were informal classes, intended to offer education to children at minimal cost, and with as little disruption as possible to the work they had to do at home, and on the land. She lodged during the week with the farmer Mr Campbell and his wife. As well as evoking the atmosphere in which she taught, this episode captures the sense of entitlement with which landowners abused women who caught their eye.

The side school depended on humble buildings and modest pay. The teachers were paid £2 a week with board and expenses paid for books, jotters and pencils. Invermearan at the head of the Glen beside Loch Lyon was where I did most of my side school teaching. It was about 20 miles from Woodend, and I cycled there every Sunday evening, with the return trip on Friday evening. Side schools did not run to travelling expenses.

There were days when I didn't have much time for the view – including the ones when the mist closed in so that there was little to be seen. Once I was tipped into the ditch by a young spark in a touring car out for a spin with a lady friend. They drove on laughing; perhaps it didn't occur to them that I might have been hurt. I met that driver several times afterwards over many years, but I don't suppose he remembered the incident for long.

Sometimes I reached Invermearan wet through after well over two hours on the journey, but I never felt sorry for myself when I was back with my little charges, who often arrived cold and wet of a morning after a long walk through driving rain or over boggy moorland. Loch Lyon is in the west of Scotland and has several times as much rain as Strathtay. Bridge of Balgie is due north of Glasgow and Invermearan is nearer the head of Loch Etive than it is to Fortingall itself. The high peaks catch the rain clouds that sweep in over Argyll from the Atlantic.

Fortunately the school board provided plenty of coal, and the schoolhouse was entirely in my charge. This meant I had to clean it and light the fires, the only heating, but it also allowed me to provide the children with what I believed they needed, so far as I could. The first thing was to set them down by the fire with a cup of hot cocoa and a piece of bread and jam. At that time the shepherds were paid only at six-monthly intervals, and it was poor enough pay when it came. It was impossible for them to feed and clothe their families satisfactorily, especially for bad weather. I had a word with Mr McNaughton, a member of the school board. He realised there was real hardship and persuaded the authority to provide some warm coats and stout footgear for the poor bairns.

It was a pleasure to teach the children all that I could. They were biddable little things and had the natural good manners of people in country places (at least in the country places I know). Some were slow to learn but one or two were very bright and all excelled at something. One little girl who was backward at her lessons turned out to be an excellent needlewoman. Indeed, part of the delight of a little school was the chance to find what was best for each child. The youngest of these pupils, just a wee laddie of five when I left the school, came to see me more than half a century later, still with happy memories of his first teacher.

Although the workers on the estate were strictly forbidden to kill a deer for themselves, Mr Campbell would sometimes do so. There was a long view of the road down the Glen and he would keep a weather-eye open for the factor. One day he came hastily into the schoolhouse and asked for the key to my coalshed. He had a couple of deer ready for cutting up and he had just seen the factor on the way to the farm. As the landlord's representative, the factor could pry into any shed, room or cupboard on the farm, but he had no right to do so in the schoolhouse, which belonged to the authority.

The carcases were duly locked up and I kept the key in my pocket till the danger was over. I had no qualms about it, for I knew that Mr Campbell would share the venison round families who often went hungry.

When the people were allowed so little, the factor often had to be flinty-hearted if he wanted to keep his job, or at least he always had the argument that he had no choice. The proprietors and their families were often remote from the facts of day-to-day life on their estates. As a result it might be the factor who was regarded as the hard hand and often, no doubt, was.

At least the factor knew who people were. Sometimes it seemed as if the laird and the laird's guests, like the young man who dumped me in the ditch, did not even see them as more than part of the furniture.

Traditional obligations based on the clan system had long since died . . . In the Glen by my time the rights of property were absolute. The road was hard for anyone who crossed the laird or his officials, and if the laird wanted something he took it, even if he was thereby punishing someone who had done nothing wrong.

Stewart Menzies when he was laird of Chesthill was a notorious lecher. There is one story about him on the way to Rannoch on horseback when he met a handsome young lassie on the hill road. The old rake dismounted and began to flirt.

'And what's your name, my lass?' he inquired.

She told him.

'Your mother is not Mrs So-and-so?'

'Yes, sir, she is.'

Chesthill was on to his horse and away. The girl was his own illegitimate daughter, one of many.

BRINGING BURNS OUT OF THE MIST

Catherine Carswell, 1929

A writer who remains famous for her glowing review of D. H. Lawrence's sexually explicit novel The Rainbow, *for which she lost her job, Carswell was also fearless in tackling the myth of Robert Burns, who was revered as a hallowed genius with whom no fault could be found, despite his rackety personal life and frequently dubious attitudes and behaviour towards women. Even today anyone who dares point out his feet of clay risks the bardolators' ire. Carswell's biography, published in 1930, did precisely this. One reader sent her a silver bullet in the post, with the recommendation that she use it on herself, 'that the world might be left "a brighter cleaner and better place"'. In this letter to her great friend, the folklorist F. Marian McNeill – who later sent her gifts of haggis during the war – she sounds understandably pleased with herself.*

To F. Marian McNeill
19th July 1929

. . . Since writing to you I truly believe I have straightened out, without taking any liberties, the story of Burns over his crucial period (covering the Jean business, Highland Mary, the publication of the poems, etc.) for the first time. This simply because not one other biographer has taken the trouble to grapple afresh with the existing evidence. They have one and all followed Lockhart and L. has been in certain vital questions mistaken. He has, for instance, given an admittedly suppositious date to an undated letter upon which much turns and I'm sure after long, long pondering and re-examinations that he has dated it wrongly and so has gone astray. The interesting things are – 1. That the whole story now becomes simple, free from 'mysteries' and altogether credible and moving – where before all was question and confusion, and 2. that with all the attention Scotsmen have paid to Burns, not one has taken this amount of trouble to ponder over the evidence. I don't say my book is well written and I know it is full of faults, but if ever I get it done I shall have contributed an honourable and honest piece of research to my country, and how furious they will be to have R.B. brought out of the mist they have loved to keep about him! Well, well.

Just getting into Charing X. so adieu. Life thrills me just now but things are no easier. Why is this?

– Love from us both, Cathie.

THE HOCKEY PARTY

Christian Miller, c. 1930

Christian Miller was born in 1920 and brought up in a haunted castle in the Highlands. Its apparitions often alarmed guests, but were companionable for the family. 'When I was a little girl, the ghosts were more real to me than people', she later wrote in a memoir of her childhood that was first published in The New Yorker. *Her military father was a fierce and often harsh disciplinarian, and at times her privileged upbringing was far less enviable or healthy than that of children from far poorer households. Even so, her recollections of growing up deep in the country, and far from society, focus as much on the good times as the bad. Her mother, who was keenly aware of the loneliness suffered by young people from wealthy families in these parts, came up with a winning remedy.*

The lairds, even though they might be close friends with their tenants, did not mix with them socially, nor did they extend much of a welcome to local professional people. This resulted in an acute lack of companionship for their daughters. Whether these girls were home only for the holidays or, lessons behind them, were living permanently in the widely separated castles, they rarely saw one another, and even more rarely had the chance of meeting young men. They whiled away the dismal winter days with books or needle-work, with practising the piano or taking the dogs for walks. Almost always, they were extremely lonely. My mother saw this and, trying to think of a way that a lot of young people could be entertained without too much trouble, hit on the idea of a hockey party. Hastening off to a school outfitters', she bought several dozen hockey sticks. She then engaged the local band (one elderly lady who played the piano, accompanied by her son on the accordion), ordered in a large quantity of food, and sent out invitations. From north, south, east and west, the young men and girls converged on the castle; those who were too young to drive were brought by their family chauffeurs, who were themselves glad of an outing. The young people arrived after lunch, warmly wrapped in a good many layers of wool, and were at once sent out to the big lawn behind the castle to join whichever team had fewer players. There were no rules, no umpire, and no half-time – anybody who was exhausted simply dropped out, and rejoined his team when he felt better. Whoever arrived after all the hockey sticks had been appropriated used a golf club, a walking stick, or his foot. The scrimmage went on till dark, when everyone tumbled indoors to gorge on hot buttered scones and thick, spoon-supporting cocoa.

Then, while the servants busied themselves clearing away the tea and laying the tables for dinner, the girls and young men went upstairs, where, strictly segregated, they had baths. The spare rooms allocated to the girls were littered with discarded pullovers and muddy shoes; party dresses hung from curtain rails and cupboard doors, petticoats were flung over chairs, and a confusion of evening slippers and embroidered handbags lay jumbled on the sofas. Under the eiderdowns of the huge beds, laughing, gossiping groups of girls – supposed to be resting – hugged their knees and chattered as if in the space of a couple of hours they had to exchange every single thought that had ever passed through their heads.

At seven o'clock, the dressing gong boomed, and an hour later everyone was gathered in the dining room, where extra chairs had been crammed round all the tables. In the light of the flickering candles, the faces of the fifty or sixty young people who were seated at dinner glowed with excitement. That evening there seemed no such thing as an ugly girl.

In the Big Drawing Room, my mother had fixed a looking glass behind each of the wall brackets, so that it appeared that the room was lit by a hundred candles instead of fifty. Fires blazed in the fireplaces, the long curtains were tightly drawn – shutting out the blackness of the night – the furniture was pushed against the damask-hung walls, the rugs rolled back. The pianist struck a commanding chord on the piano, while her son wrestled the first note out of his accordion.

Up and down the shining parquet we raced, Strip the Willow, the Dashing White Sergeant, eightsome reels, foursome reels, sixteensome reels, the Duke of Perth, and Petronella – nobody dreamed of sitting out a single dance. One of my ancestresses had composed a strathspey that was known by the name of the castle, and this was always included in the evening's music. At midnight, the chauffeurs were summoned from their games of whist in the servants' hall, hot soup was handed around, and sheepskin coats were thrown over evening clothes. Missing girls emerged, bright-eyed, from unexpected corners, to be followed seconds later by self-conscious young men. Addresses were scribbled on starched shirt cuffs, and promises for future meetings exchanged. Half-frozen engines spluttered in the courtyard, car doors slammed, and red tail-lights vanished down the drive.

❧

BLIN' DRIFT ON THE CAIRNGORMS
Nan Shepherd, 1928–33

A poet, novelist and lecturer at Aberdeen Training Centre for Teachers, Nan Shepherd came alive when she was in the mountains. Ignoring any suggestion that these challenging heights were primarily a man's world, she would sleep outdoors, and wander at all times of day, night and year. Never marrying, and believed to have suffered a life-long unrequited love for a friend's husband, she poured her passion into her love of the wilds. The Living Mountain, written during the Second World War but not published until 1977, was nature writing of a sort then unknown: personal, poetic and spiritual. Posthumously, it made her one of the most popular writers in the genre.

Blizzard is the most deadly condition of these hills. It is wind that is to be feared, even more than snow itself. Of the lives that have been lost in the Cairngorms while I have been frequenting them (there have been about a dozen, excepting those who have perished in plane crashes) four were lost in blizzard. Three fell from the rock – one of these a girl. One was betrayed by the ice-hard condition of a patch of snow in May, and slipped. All these were young. Two older men have gone out, and disappeared. The body of one of these was discovered two years later.

Of the four who were caught in blizzard, two died on 2 January 1928, and two on the same date in 1933. The former two spent their last night in the then disused cottage where I have since passed some of the happiest times of my life. Old Sandy Mackenzie the stalker, still alive then, in the other small house on the croft, warned the boys against the blizzard. As I sit with Mrs Mackenzie, now, by the open fireplace, with a gale howling in the chimney and rattling the iron roof ('this tin-can of a place', she calls it), and watch her wrinkled hands build the fir-roots for a blaze, she tells me of the wind that was in it. I listen to the smashing of this later gale, which has blown all night. 'If you had been getting up and going away the house would have been following you,' she says, knowing my habit of sleeping by the door and prowling at all sorts of hours. And remembering how I crept down into my bag last night, I picture those two boys lying on the floor in the empty house, with the roof rattling and the icy wind finding every chink. Not that they had cared. They asked for nothing but a roof. 'And salt – they asked for salt.' Strange symbolic need of a couple of boys who were to find no hospitality again on earth. Her old bleared eyes look into the distance. She says, 'the snow would be freezing before it would be on your cheek'. John, the son, found the second body in March, in a snow drift that he and his West Highland terrier had passed many times. 'But that morning,' he told me, 'she was scraping.' 'You will not be finding a thing but in the place where it will be,' says the old woman. She had fetched the bellows and blown the logs into a flame. 'Sandy used to say, *The fire is the finest flower of them all*, when he would be coming in from the hill.' She makes the tea. But she has brought the storm in to our fireside, and it stays there through the night.

The other two boys went over Cairn Gorm in the kind of miraculous midwinter weather that sometimes occurs, and slept the night at the Shelter Stone beside Loch Avon. They were local boys. In the July of that year, on a very fine Sunday when we had gone out at dawn and had an empty hill all morning to ourselves, we saw with amazement a stream of people come up the hill the easy way from Glenmore and pass down to the Shelter Stone. We counted a hundred persons on the hill. They had come to see the place where the two boys slept and to read their high-spirited and happy report in the book that lies in its waterproof cover beneath the huge balanced boulder that has sheltered so many sleepers. That they would not reach home when they set out that morning after writing it, they could not dream. One of them was an experienced hill walker. But they reckoned without the wind. The schoolmistress of the tiny school at Dorback, which lies under Cairn

Gorm on the Abernethy side, told me, of that wind, that her crippled sister, crossing the open space of the playground, was blown from her feet. And five miles from Glenmore and safety, crawling down Coire Cas on hands and knees, the boys could fight the wind no further. It was days later till they found them; and one of the men who was at the finding described to me their abraded knees and knuckles. The elder of the two was still crawling, on hands and knees, then they found him fast in the drift. *So quick bright things come to confusion.* They committed, I suppose, an error of judgment, but I cannot judge them. For it is a risk we must all take when we accept individual responsibility for ourselves on the mountain, and until we have done that, we do not begin to know it.

MILL WORK

Betty Stewart, 1930s

The jute- and flax-spinning mill in Blairgowrie in which Betty Stewart worked was in full production in these days, other than during water shortages. Some workers stayed only a short while, tempted away by Smedley's cannery nearby, or the booming hotel business. Some quickly returned, and others came back now and again, treating it as seasonal work. This unsentimental memory shows just how dangerous the workplace could be before health and safety got into its stride.

The mill at Blairgowrie when ah worked there wis very dusty, oh, terrible. They wouldnae work in it the day withoot a mask. There wis nae dust extractors or anything . . . The conditions were, oh, terrible. Well, put it this way: ah've got a bad chist and ah had arthritis – ah've had it for twenty year. But when they had me in the hospital they did a' the tests. And ah've got like what the miners have – ken, the miners have got silicosis. Well, ah've got flax stoor at the fit o' my lungs that'll never clear up. That wis due tae the work in the mill. Ah couldnae go and sue them. That's what the doctor said, 'How can ye no' get . . . ?' And when ah telt him ah worked in a flax mill, he says, 'Well, flax stoor's finer than jute, because jute's a' threads. But flax is very, very fine dust.' Ah was always healthy as a girl. Ah was, but no' now. Oh, ah mean, ah smoked, well, ah could go through twenty at the week-end a day. Put it this way, aboot five packets did me a' seven days – about fifteen a day, somethin' like that. Oh, ah smoked frae the age o' fourteen or fifteen.

Ye were allowed time oot in the mill tae smoke. Ye jist got a couple o' minutes. Somebody wid haud your frame on for ye. They cried her the orrie woman. Oh, the orrie woman wis kept busy a' day, lettin' them go tae the toilet or for a smoke. She wis kept busy a' day. Ah mean, she had eighty machines tae let awa' and some o' the lassies that wis shiftin' bobbins and that. When you wanted tae go oot she wid come and haud on for ye, rather than stop the machine she wid watch your machine. That wis her job. Well, she was relievin' aboot forty folk a' day.

There were nae protective masks or clothin' or anythin' in the mill at Blairgowrie. Ye used tae get the hoover and hoover the dust . . .

It wis a terrific fire hazard as well. You would jist need one spark and it wid have . . . The mills used to have wee flash fires at times, oh, often. And it jist went like lightnin' frae one end tae the other. The fine dust! Well, . . . we had belts on the machines, and when ah worked on the four automatic machines ah remember one o' them – it was my frame – it burst in the middle and it went that way. And ah remember seein' the belt goin'. And ye ken what it reminded me of? A propeller goin' on fire, an aeroplane propeller. Ah jist lifted ma coat and ran like hell!

Oh, we didnae have fire drill or anything. There wis no fire drill at all. There wis nae fire engine attached tae the mill. They jist had buckets o' water! Ah mean, when ye look back things were primitive. We had no special clothin' in the mill. Oh, ye had tae have your hair tied up. It wasnae official. But if you got your hair caught in you lost it. Well, ye cannae see ma middle finger for arthritis now but it was broke, well, no' broken, it wis jist knocked that much tae bits it went oot o' shape! Ah mean, ye'd tae stop machinery that wis goin' at mair than fifty mile an hoor wi' your hand. Ye had a rubber – but ye got that yaised tae it ye never wore the rubber.

Injuries werenae really common in the mills. Ah remember one. He wis older than me. He lost an airm. He got it caught in the machinery. We cried him Winger Willie. Ah mean, it didnae bother him. But he still worked. Ah seen a lassie gettin' her hair pulled in and that but, ah mean, once ye got it oot it was a' right. Ah've seen a finger squashed. But ah've never seen anybody loss a limb. Ah've had ma claes pulled in. Oh, ye get a fright. The machinery wasnae really guarded, no' really, well, the motors were, the teeth.

❦

MAKING ENDS MEET

Anonymous, 1930s

This trauchled Aberdonian's account of the years in which her husband was in and out of work give an indication of how severe the struggle to survive was for many families. Her story was published in the Aberdeen Free Press, *but whether it resulted in greater compassion and understanding among the authorities is not known.*

Most of the people along the street were unemployed, looking for jobs. When the snow came on they used to queue the whole night to try to get a job in the snow. They got 10d an hour and Alec'd work as long as they would let him. They never got home through the day and they got 6d for a pie and a cup of tea. There was dozens of men queued up all night and the foreman came out and said, 'You, and you, and you.' Frozen with cold they'd stand – and yet they'd say the unemployed was lazy.

Then Lady Cowdray at Dunecht House started a scheme. She had hundreds of acres of estates and she wanted these great stone walls built round every bit. The men had to live in bothies on the estate and they'd to keep their wives and families in Aberdeen besides that – and she was paying 10d an hour. She got some single ones, but the married men couldn't do it – and then they were called lazy because they didn't take the work. They'd to have 2 pairs of good dungarees and 2 pairs of boots. How could they afford it?

There was so many unemployed in the town. The Broo was only giving 21/- for the four of us. The Board of Health said it wasn't enough to keep you alive and that the Councils would have to help the unemployed themselves. They started a scheme to build the golf course at Hazlehead and you would get seven and six more on your dole for working three days a week. So of course they all did that. The Hazlehead golf course was built with sweat and tears. They were soaking up to their oxters with the peaty boggy ground. His feet was frozen. He used to come home exhausted. My brother gave him an old bike. We used it for years.

He got a job in Gibb's granite yard in King Street. He took awful bouts of malaria fever because he'd been in Egypt in the war. He used to shake all over. This day he took ill at his work and he came home. Next morning he got his books sent to him and when he went to sign on at the Unemployment Exchange they said he wasn't entitled to any money because he'd left his job without cause. Well, you can never beat authority. They sent him to the Parish, and the Parish gave him a chit for 14/- to get food, but no money.

We'd no money for rent or anything like that. Oh they were hard. He got that for 3 weeks and then he'd to go before a Board. They discovered he hadn't left this job without cause so they gave him the back money, but we'd to pay back what we got from the Parish. But that was the finish of the granite yard. There was always someone ready to take your place. They used to undercut one another – take it for a few shillings less. They'd have cut one another's throats for a job. But my husband wouldn't do that – he was determined he would never take a job at less than anybody else.

My father took a job as a jobbing gardener when Col. Davidson died, but he wasn't doing very much. He gave Alex a few weeks when he was busy one time and paid him better than anybody else. He gave him £2 a week. Then in 1937 Alec got into the gasworks, after trying for years and years. And he was only there a few weeks. He'd ulcers of the stomach for years and he got word to go into hospital. You got 18/- insurance money when you were ill, and they hardly paid it till you was back to your work again. After a fortnight I hardly had any money. I went to the hospital and Sister came to me as I was leaving and she says, 'You must bring a big tin of cocoa for Mr Watt tonight when you come in. The doctor's ordered cocoa.' You had to bring in all your extras and cocoa was an extra. They never got an egg unless you took it in. I hadn't a penny to buy a smattering of cocoa, so Alec says to me, 'Go to the Parish when you're going home.' I went in fear and trembling to the Parish. The clerk at the desk would hardly listen to me. He said, 'Go to the insurance offices and kick up a row there about your money,' and slammed down the hatch in my face. I sat down in a chair in the corner and cried. I didn't know what to do. And this man come along and he says, 'What's wrong?' He took me into the office and gave me tea. He rang up the Britannic offices and gave them a right telling off about leaving people starving. And he gave me 35/- right into my hand. He says, 'When your husband comes out of hospital, come in and we'll give you extras for him.' Well, they sent me 2 pints of milk every day, and they made his money up to 35/- a week the time he was off ill. That was the only kindness we ever had from anybody.

❦

SEX — DAMNED THING
Maggie Fuller, 1930s

This interviewee, who had had a really tough upbringing and a very harsh mother, opened up in a way many more cossetted or contented women never would.

I think in all the times in my life I could count how many times ever I've got anything out of sex, now that's God's truth. I hate the ruddy thing, I'll be very frank with you. I think it is a disgusting horrible thing, I really do, aha. I didn't use to feel like that, I just did it, but I never got anything, except with my second son, and an odd time since – not now, mind . . . damned thing. But no, I could count all the times . . . I never had anything before it, I can assure you, but I knew when I was having – well, if that was what it was I had – a beautiful . . . I knew that was nice when I had my second son.

I'd rather do without it, it's been left like that, you know what I mean. My husband is older than me, and this is where I think sometimes . . . mind I don't know if it's right or wrong . . . as regards a stable man, you'll not get better. I've been allowed to do exactly what I like, but as regards sex, it's no use – if I hadn't been a kind of stable person I am sure I'd have gone off my ruddy head. You know I'd rather not have it, all that carry on, you know. It's maybe me that's cold, I don't know, I never talked about it – too late in life to talk about it now.

EDINBURGH WOMEN IN THEIR PRIME
Muriel Spark, 1931

The Prime of Miss Jean Brodie *might be a novel, but the charismatic Miss Brodie, a teacher at an Edinburgh girls' school, captured aspects of spinsters Muriel Spark recalled from her childhood. This generation of free-thinking women, whose chances of marriage and family had been ruined by the war, brought a touch of glamour and pizzazz to an often drab and narrow-minded city.*

It is not to be supposed that Miss Brodie was unique at this point of her prime; nor that (since such things are relative) she was in any way off her head. She was alone, merely, in that she taught in a school like Marcia Blaine's.

There were legions of her kind during the nineteen-thirties, women from the age of thirty and upward, who crowded their war-bereaved spinsterhood with voyages of discovery into new ideas and energetic practices in art or social welfare, education or religion. The progressive spinsters of Edinburgh did not teach in schools, especially in schools of traditional character like Marcia Blaine's School for Girls. It was in this that Miss Brodie was, as the rest of the staff spinsterhood put it, a trifle out of place. But she was not out of place amongst her own kind, the vigorous daughters of dead or enfeebled merchants, of ministers of religion, University professors, doctors, big warehouse owners of the past, or the owners of fisheries who had endowed these daughters with shrewd wits, high-coloured cheeks, constitutions like horses, logical educations, hearty spirits and private means. They could be seen leaning over the democratic counters of Edinburgh grocers' shops arguing with the Manager at three in the afternoon on every subject from the authenticity of the Scriptures to the question what the word 'guaranteed' on a jam-jar really meant. They went to lectures, tried living on honey and nuts, took lessons in German and then went walking in Germany; they bought caravans and went off with them into the hills among the lochs; they played the guitar, they supported all the new little theatre companies; they took lodgings in the slums and, distributing pots of paint, taught their neighbours the arts of simple interior decoration; they preached the inventions of Marie Stopes; they attended the meetings of the Oxford Group and put Spiritualism to their hawk-eyed test. Some assisted in the Scottish Nationalist Movement; others, like Miss Brodie, called themselves Europeans and Edinburgh a European capital, the city of Hume and Boswell.

STORMING STIRLING CASTLE

Glasgow Herald, *27 June 1932*

Four years before this mischievous adventure, Wendy Wood, an artist and writer, had been one of the founders of the National Party of Scotland – later renamed the Scottish National Party. An Englishwoman filled with patriotic pride in her adopted country, she was an idiosyncratic and mischievous figure from whom more staid nationalists were – perhaps rightly – keen to keep their distance. In later years she was on several occasions briefly imprisoned for her activities. This report from the Glasgow Herald *strikes the right tone, with nobody alarmed or offended except the stuffed shirts of the party's officials.*

Afterwards, novelist Eric Linklater claimed she had flushed the Union Jack down the castle toilets, for which she sued for libel and won an out-of-court settlement of a farthing.

A remarkable exploit was carried through by a party of young men and women attending the demonstration held in the King's Park, Stirling, on Saturday afternoon to commemorate the 618th anniversary of the Battle of Bannockburn. One of the speakers at the demonstration was Miss Wendy Wood, Edinburgh. Miss Wood was permitted to address the audience in the King's Park from the National Party's platform, although it was explained that she was not one of the official speakers.

In the course of a fiery speech she drew attention to the fact that the Union Jack was flying from the ramparts of Stirling Castle, the relief of which was one of the objects of King Edward when he marched into Scotland in 1314 and was defeated by Bruce on the Field of Bannockburn.

'Are we going to allow that flag to fly there on such a day!' Miss Wood demanded. 'Who will volunteer to take it down?'

The suggestion was evidently regarded at the time as nothing more than a rhetorical outburst. It was received with laughter and some applause by the crowd, and one lady rose up and protested against the sentiments expressed by Miss Wood. At the close of the demonstration, however, the idea was revived, and over 100 young men and women decided to support Miss Wood in her bold project.

The success of the enterprise was probably due to the fact that the Argyll and Sutherland Highlanders, for whom the Castle now serves as a depot, were holding their annual sports in a field some distance away, and consequently there were only a few soldiers on duty at the Castle.

At the gate, however, one of the guides on duty made a demand for the payment of the charge of 6d per head imposed upon visitors to the town when they desire to enter the Castle. The request, it is stated, was treated with merriment, and the 'invaders' pushed on past the astonished official and made for the flag tower. What followed was described by a member of the party.

'Several men in the party pulled down the Union Jack while "Scots wha ha'e"' was sung,' he said. 'By this time, the guards, who had been attracted by the unusual commotion, appeared on the scene and tried to put a stop to the proceedings. But there were only four soldiers to over 100 Nationalists, and the Scottish standard was fixed to the line and run up to the top of the flagpole, amid cheers.

'There were threats that the party would be incarcerated in the guard-room, although the soldiers did not attempt to put the idea into execution. Having achieved their object, the party marched off in order. The parting shot fired by the soldiers as the Nationalists left the Castle was that the police would get them.'

It is understood, however, that although the party concerned in the incident remained in the town for some time, no action was taken by the authorities.

The Scottish Standard remained on the Castle flagstaff for only a few minutes, the soldiers replacing the Union Jack whenever the Nationalists had departed.

Dr Stewart Black, convener of the Press Committee of the National Party of Scotland, in a statement made yesterday, said – 'No importance must be attached to this piece of cheap sensationalism, which was the entirely unauthorised action of a few irresponsible individuals who hold no office in the National Party of Scotland. The policy of that party is one of complete loyalty to the British Commonwealth of Nations, whose symbol is the telegram despatched from the Bannockburn gathering to His Majesty the King.'

The telegram despatched by the executive of the party to the King was as follows: –

The National Party of Scotland, assembled on the Field of Bannockburn, send loyal greetings to the King of Scots, descendant of the Bruce and honoured Sovereign of the British Commonwealth of Nations.

GREYHOUNDS FOR BREAKFAST, DINNER AND TEA
Cicely Hamilton, mid 1930s

Suffragist, feminist, writer and actress, Cicely Hamilton (her real name was Hammill) was raised in England, although her father was a captain in the Gordon Highlanders at the time of her birth. When she was young, her mother disappeared, and she later suspected she had been put in an asylum. Famous for such earnest-sounding plays and books as How the Vote was Won, *and* Marriage as a Trade, *she had a quick sense of humour, which enlivens her accounts of her life, and her travels. She was clearly astonished at discovering a well-appointed hostel for women of advanced years, since this easily overlooked group was not usually so thoughtfully catered for.*

There is one Glasgow housing scheme which is surely ideal in the matter of providing both interest and amusement for its inmates; and that, strange to say, is a building – a hostel – in the Carntyne district which provides cheap lodgement for women, and elderly women at that. I say it in no spirit of feminist acrimony, but simply as a fact that inquiry will verify, that it is not usual to consider the interest and amusement of elderly females until the needs, in that direction, of (a) males and (b) children and young persons have been satisfied in every particular. Hence my astonishment at this Carntyne hostel which, as I have said, is an ideal residence for ladies of the pension age; supplying them, for the sum of five shillings a week, with a self-contained flatlet where cooking and cleaning can be done to the best advantage, as hot water is on tap night and day. In addition, at the end of a passage, a communal bath and a communal washhouse is at the service of every half-dozen inmates; I was told, however, that these particular facilities were not much sought after – having plenty of hot water ready to hand, the old ladies prefer, as a general rule, to scrub both themselves and their garments on their private premises.

Considered as lodgings at five shillings a week, the flatlets are more than good value; but, in addition to the benefits already enumerated, they have an advantage peculiar to themselves which must rouse the envy of municipal tenants with domiciles less fortunately situated. All the windows in that hostel – thirty-four in number – look out upon a greyhound racing track; so that free, gratis, and for nothing those happy old ladies have a comprehensive view of proceedings for which others have to plank down their shillings. And this sporting prospect enjoyed from the windows is not only an interest in itself – it brings other interests into the lives of the hostel's occupants. The racing season means frequent visits from their children and grandchildren – who, but for the dogs, might be tempted to neglect their elderly relatives . . . I cannot help suspecting that this advantageous residence was allotted in error to old ladies; the officials responsible being unaware of the amenities which might have been placed at the disposal of (a) masculine or (b) juvenile Glaswegians.

THE FAMISHED PROSTITUTE

Ralph Glasser, 1935

Ralph Glasser was born in the Jewish quarter of the Gorbals in Glasgow between the First and Second World Wars, and began work in a garment factory at the age of fourteen. After years of studying at night he won a scholarship to Oxford University. He went on to become a psychologist, economist and notable memoirist. This is a record of a conversation he had with a fellow factory worker as they walked home one night through the Saltmarket, a particularly poverty-stricken and ill-lit district renowned as the haunt of prostitutes. The young woman he describes was like countless others of her background, obliged to find a way of making extra money when times were hard. As in other cities, she and her kind were a nightly reminder of deprivation and desperation.

We were walking home from the factory late one night, about ten o'clock, the streets stilled. Something in his [Alec's] mood suggested he wanted a cue to talk.

I said: 'Have you ever had one of them?'

'Aye, a few times,' he replied in assumed indifference, 'when ah've been hard up for ma hole. That wis where ah had ma first hoor, when ah was aboo' fifteen. Ah wis jist this minute thinkin' aboo' 'er! In fact, she comes tae mind many a time. She wis ma first proper fuck!' He fell silent. 'But that's no' the reason. She was, ah don't know how tae put i'. She wis warm an' understandin' an', well, she was genuine. She wanted me tae be happy! She made me feel ah wisnae jist *anybody*. Ah'll never ferrget it. Never. A wee thin-faced lassie wi' red hair, verry pale, shiverin' in the cauld wi' a thin coat an' skirt on. A guid bi' older than me she was, aboo' twenty-five. An' wi' a weddin' ring on.'

He pushed his lips out: 'It wis one payday, an' it was snowin' an' cauld, an' ah wis comin' away frae the workshop late at night dog tired an' for some reason ah don't remember ah wis gaun hame through the Saltmarket an' no' thinkin' aboo' anythin'. An' suddenly there was this lassie beside me an' caught haud o' ma hand sayin': "C'mon ah'll show ye somethin' wonderful!" An' she pulled me intae a big dark archway an' before ah knew anythin' she'd put ma haun' up 'er skirt – Jesus I can feel it this minute – an' she'd got haud o' me an' a couldnae stop masel'! Christ was ah ashamed! Bu' she said, quiet an' soft: "Never yew mind. Ah'll wait. An' ye'll be fine wi' me in a wee while." And she held me tight, an' kissed me as if she really meant i'. An' efter a minute she shivered and said: "Ah'm sae cauld! Ah'm tha' hungry. Will ye gie me a sixpenny piece an' ah'll go an' ge' a bag o' fish an' chips?"

He snorted. 'If a hoor said that tae me the noo ah widnae trust her tae come back! Bu' ah wis ony a boy. An' she'd been sae warm and gentle wi' me. She looked sae peaked ah wanted 'er tae have somethin' tae eat. Ah gave her a whole shillin'. Ah'd have tae tell ma mither ah'd lost it on ma way hame. In a way that wis true! She took tha' shillin' in baith 'er hauns it could've been a gold sovereign! An' she said: "Yew jist wait here an' rest yersel'. Ah'll be back in a wee minute."

'An' ah wis left standin' there all flustered an' lonely an' wonderin' whit was happenin' tae me. Ah felt ah wis seein' this wurrld fer the verry furrst time. Aye, seein' a lo' o' things fer the furrst time. Ah thought of 'er walkin' aboo' hungry in tha' God forsaken place, through piles o' rubbish an' horse shit dirty white wi' the snow left lyin'. A' the emptiness an' loneliness. And the bitter cauld that had driven a' the ither hoors hame. An' her sae desperate. Grabbin' hold of a boy tae ge' a shillin' aff of, for a bag o' fish an' chips an' pennies fer the gas an' the price o' a pint o' milk! An' *her* bein' nothin' tae me, and *me* bein' nothin' tae her. An' the next minute ah thought: "No. That's wrong! I' *is* somethin'! If it wis nothin' ah wouldnae be carin' at a'! It's *got* tae mean somethin'!" Ah started shiverin', standin' there under the arch, the freezin' cauld creepin' up ma legs frae the pavement. Ah wanted tae feel 'er warm body pressin' against me again, an' 'er gentleness, sayin' nothin', jist *bein'* there wi' me. An then ah started wonderin' if it wid be different fuckin' her than blockin' ma sister.'

I should not have been shocked but I was, and I must have shown it, or at least that I was surprised, perhaps by the slightest shift in my step or a questioning turn of the head, for he looked at me in astonishment.

'Yours've done it wi' yew surely?'

I shook my head, not sure what words would fit.

'Come on!' he said, disbelieving, 'Yewr sisters must've shown ye whit's what? Ah'll lay ye odds o' a hundred tae one ye'll no' find a feller, who's go' an older sister, who's no' been intae 'er – aye many, many times, sleepin' in the same bed night efter night! Hiv ye really no' done i'? Ah'll no' tell on ye mind!'

'No. It really is true.' I searched for a bland excuse. 'Maybe it was because they were so much older than me.'

Most Gorbals parents, trying to instil the standard prohibitions, fought against impossible odds. Girls and boys were not even supposed to undress in each other's presence after a certain age, but in most families they had to share bedrooms and as often as not beds, and so the rules were dead letters . . .

Alex paused for only a moment: 'Aye, ah see whit ye mean. Maybe that's it.' He dismissed it. 'Anyway, *ma* sister went at i' wi me fer years. She used tae play wi' ma prick in oor bed even before ah'd go' any hair on me; an' after ah grew ma bush an' started comin', she go' me tae take 'er maidenhied.'

The memory jolted him: 'Christ tha' was a night an' a half! Wonderin' whit tae do aboot the big bloodstain in the bed. Though at first when she saw it she was sae overjoyed – no, ah mean light-hieded like she was drunk. Ah couldnae understand it . . .

'Well, anyway, in the end we decided she'd pretend she'd had a freak early monthly! An' ah'm no' sure tae this day if ma mither believed 'er! Still an' a', nothin' wis said. Efter tha' she go' me tae block 'er over an' over again, nearly every night sometimes! But it was never a proper fuck 'cos she never let me come inside 'er. She always knew when ah wis goin' tae come an' pulled me oo' jist before. Well, she stopped a' tha' when ah wis aboo' sixteen. Ah've go' an idea that Father Millan, seein' ah was gettin' tae be a big lad, had a quiet word wi' 'er one day in Confession, an' tellt 'er it was bad for her immortal soul! An' mine too. How 'e knew, well, ye can guess. Them priests! Aye, them priests. They're on tae everythin' that's goin' on. Too bliddy much.'

I wondered if he was about to branch off into that familiar pastime, scurrilous talk about priests and female parishioners. Not this time. The encounter in the Saltmarket long ago, shining within him over all the years, needed to have its say.

'Anyway, as ah wis sayin', ah stood there under the arch freezin'. It was snowin' again. There wisnae a soul aboo'. Every single hoor must a' given i' up that night. An' ah did begin tae wonder if she'd come back. An' then ah heard the quick steps muffled in the snow, an' ah smelt the chips an' vinegar, an' the next minute she was pressin' against me there in the dark.. Shiverin' an' movin' against me tae get the warmth. An' d'ye know? She'd waited till she was back wi' me afore she started to eat any! Ah could tell she wis real hungry 'cos she ate them fish an' chips as if she hadnae had anythin' tae eat fer days. Ah hadnae the herrt tae take a chip frae the bag. Bu' after she'd had most of i', she stood there leanin' close an' put chips in ma mouth on a' a time till the bag was finished . . .'

We walked on for several minutes in silence and I thought he would reveal no more. He needed to, but couldn't.

At last he did, quietly, sombrely: 'Well, as she'd said, ah' was fine wi' her in the end. She showed me many things. Aye, many things. An' then she came! She really did. A lo' o' hoors jist pretend tae come so's tae make ye feel great. Aye an' tae make ye think they're enterin' into the spirit o' things an' no jist standin' there thinkin' aboo' the gas meter! Anyway ah'd never felt anythin' like i'. I' made me feel – ah don't know how tae say it – i' made ma herrt feel full tae burstin' an' then she went very quiet an' hung on tae me all limp an' said: "Haud me up dear ah cannae stand."'

It had all been said sadly . . . He might have been pouring out his heart for a long lost love. His silence could have been of mourning, for the lost bounty of innocence and revelation . . .

'Did you see her again?' I asked.

'Whit did ye say?'

He had fallen into reverie once more.

'Did you ever see that hoor again?'

'See her? Ah wish ah could've stayed wi' 'er fir ever!' The words rushed out. He stopped and looked at me, in wonder at himself . . .

'Ah never fucked 'er again if that's whit ye mean. Bu' ah've seen 'er plenty o' times. She's lived a' the time in the next close tae us! Married wi' two kids. Her man's on the booze and knocks 'er aboo' regular. He's given 'er that many black eyes she cannae see tae wurrk. She used tae be a button hole hand. *They always ge' bad sight, bu' gettin' a' them black eyes as well must've buggered up 'er sight good and proper!* She cannae see tae thread the needle any more. Come tae think of i', if 'er eyes'd been be'er she'd 'ave recognised me in the dark that night afore she'd got hold o' me. An' maybe left me alane? Anyway, bein' hungry an' cauld, whit can ye say? She needed that shillin'.'

THE SPANISH CIVIL WAR OBSERVED

Katharine Stewart-Murray, Duchess of Atholl, 1936

The first Scottish woman MP, Katharine Stewart-Murray won Kinross and West Perthshire for the Scottish Unionist Party in 1923. Nervous at facing the hustings, she later wrote of one ordeal that: 'I thought I had answered all the heckling and, being late for my next meeting, hurriedly left the platform. But when I had got halfway down the hall, I heard a stentorian "No, we're no done wi' ye yet", and crestfallen, had to retrace my steps and submit to further questions.' She was a trained musician, with a strong social conscience, and was among the earlier members of Parliament to denounce Hitler's fascist views, as well as decrying Mussolini and the abuse of people's rights in the Soviet Union. When the Spanish Civil War broke out, she was keen to visit. For her support for the Republicans, she was called a Communist, and an anarchist, and dubbed the Red Duchess. This account of that trip is taken from her autobiography – one of many books she wrote – which, despite the eventful times in which she lived, is surprisingly bland. A sentence such as 'In September we were invited to Balmoral, and Bardie managed to get in some stalking . . .' is typical. Bardie was her husband, the Duke of Atholl, whose seat was Blair Castle.

Late autumn, 1936
Not long after my return to London from Eastern Europe, Ellen Wilkinson, who was keenly interested in Spain, asked me if I would consider a short visit there to see what was going on. She was going herself, as were Eleanor Rathbone and Dame Rachel Crowdie, whom I had met on a Red Cross Committee. We went by train to Toulouse, whence I took my first trip by plane to Barcelona, and in Barcelona we were warmly received at the beautiful old Generaladid by Señor Companys, President of Catalonia.

The seat of the Spanish Government had by then been moved and our Minister there, Mr. Ogilvie Forbes, was a former officer in the Scottish Horse.

We found him both friendly and on good terms with the Spanish authorities, and we were soon presented to the President, Señor Azana. Azana was apparently friendly, but rather annoyed at some recent interference by British ships with ships bringing supplies to the Spanish ports.

At Valencia the first thing we saw was one of the schools for refugee children, which showed clearly the interest in education taken by the Republican Government. Next came a visit to a prison for political prisoners, until lately occupied by the present President and Prime Minister.

The prison consisted of a large well-lit building with a central hall from which radiated staircases to various galleries. Outside these there was a good-sized gravelled recreation ground in which some fifty men were standing about, looking well clothed and fed. We were allowed to call out for men who could speak French or English, and any who could do so were hastily pushed forward. In reply to our questions they said that little was wrong with the food, and that letters and gifts from friends were received regularly. The only complaint made to us was that no visitors had been allowed for a month.

In another prison we visited, two hundred Italian prisoners-of-war, Mussolini's so-called 'Volunteers', were confined. We were allowed to talk to them freely and we asked them how they came to be here. Several replied that they had thought they were being taken to one of the Italian colonies. Others had come with their own officers, as a regiment. When we asked them how they were being treated, several ran off to fetch samples of the bread they were getting, which they obviously found satisfactory. They looked well cared for, and happy to be out of the fighting . . .

Naturally our party was pressed to visit Madrid, then under siege by Franco, and we agreed to go there for a night. The country through which we drove seemed barren and poor – almost African – and the occasional houses along it were primitive. The city itself was amazing in its calm courage. It looked almost normal. The shops were open and the streets were full of people. Yet none of it was more than a mile or two from the front line, and the people who were going about their business so casually might at any moment be struck down by a sudden shell-burst.

As it happened, the day we spent in Madrid there was what was described as a heavy bombardment by the insurgents' artillery. A shell hit the official centre just before our party visited it. Another shell exploded at the entrance of the hotel basement where we were lunching, killing three people and wounding five. Three shells fell in the central square; one of them blew a bootblack to pieces, while the client whose shoes he was cleaning escaped unscathed.

A Republican officer took us to a point near the University City from which we could see the fighting going on in the lovely green park of the Casa del Campo. Government batteries were shelling Garabitas Hill, on which we could see the shells bursting, while nearer by, insurgent trench mortar bombs were falling on the Government lines in the University City. Yet on the lake in the Casa del Campo, a militiaman in a bathing dress was calmly paddling a canoe, apparently quite indifferent to what was going on around him.

In the city, I visited the house of the Duke of Alba, which had been badly damaged, obviously by bombs: I was shown a lovely bathroom with a huge round hole in the ceiling. Yet Franco's supporters were making out that the house had been sacked by the 'Reds'. All of us were received by the Government Commander-in-chief, General Miaja. He spoke to us quite bluntly. The authorities much appreciated our presence in Madrid, he said, but if democracy in Spain were to survive, it needed concrete help rather than sympathy.

FISH GUTTERS

Cicely Hamilton, 1937

A founder member of the Women Writers' Suffrage League, whose members included Ivy Compton-Burnett and Olive Schreiner, Cicely Hamilton had a keen eye for the work and conditions of other women. Here, observing one of the least glamorous jobs in the country, she nevertheless finds people who take pride and satisfaction in their work.

On the quay at Wick I once watched consignments of herring (destined for Germany and the Soviet Union) being gutted and packed in their barrels; the gutters – girls and women – getting through their work with the amazing slickness that comes of long practice therein. Three of them, working together, make up what is called a crew; one of the two packs the fish into a barrel after the other two have gutted them, a feat which they accomplish at a truly astonishing pace. The skilled rate, I believe, is about two seconds per herring – thirty a minute; and as they finish with their herring they fling it over their shoulder into one of the baskets standing behind them – always the right basket for its size – whence the third member of the crew removes it to pack in her barrel. As is well known, these girls, in the wake of the fishing-fleet, move along the coast from port to port; and those many among them who have their homes in the Western Isles must get through a considerable amount of migration before they finish up the season in one of the English coast towns. Their earnings, as a matter of course, vary with the luck of the season; the Fishery

Report for 1935 gives their average earnings for the three 'fishings' of the year – the Scottish winter and summer and the East Anglian autumn – as £3, £15, and £16 respectively; £34 in all.

Not a high wage when the hardship of the work is considered, but £7 higher than the average of 1934. In addition, their travelling expenses are paid and they receive, on engagement, an extra payment, known as 'arles', or earnest-money, as token of work for the season.

Working-clothes adapted to the use of the trade and the comfort of the wearer usually have a touch of the picturesque about them, and the working-kit of the gutters and packers, as I saw it at Wick, was no exception to the rule. Details varied according to personal taste, but a typical get-up was sweater, knee-skirt, protected by an oilskin apron, long rubber boots, and a handkerchief tied round the head. In some cases an ordinary waterproof overall – the kind that is worn for housework – was substituted for the oilskin apron. The day when I watched them at their gutting and packing the season was midsummer and the sun was a glare on the quay; but when the sun is in, and the wind is out, the gutting and packing of fish must be a bitter job. Still, if you are bred to it, probably a healthy one, judging by the looks of the rubber-booted lassies whom I saw stride away from the quay to the streets when midday gave them their half-hour's respite for a meal.

TEASHOPS

Cicely Hamilton, 1937

Where better to watch womankind than an Edinburgh teashop? The elegant Cicely Hamilton would have blended in well as she observed.

The Edinburgh teashop is an establishment of a very different type from its opposite number in London – which caters mainly for a class accustomed to mass-produced food and appreciative rather than resentful of clatter and rush in its surroundings. In Edinburgh, on the other hand, the typical teashop atmosphere is more leisured, more decorous; it is true that on one occasion recently I found myself distressingly adjacent to a saxophone but that misfortune was due to the fact that, arriving late at a crowded hour, the only vacant table was in the room afflicted with jazz. In the matter of cakes the tea-room is a place hard to beat; harder still in the matter of edibles accompanied by butter – oat-cakes and every sort of scone; as the discerning customer will note with thankfulness, its dainties at present suggest not the factory but the oven. The larger establishments let off rooms for meetings; women's associations which, in England, would meet in an hotel or restaurant, in Edinburgh will meet in a teashop. On one or two occasions, when visiting the city, I have been asked to 'say a few words' there.

It is possible that what may be termed the higher rank of the Scottish teashop, as compared with the English, is due to the traditional barring of women from places where alcohol is consumed. By that it must not be understood that the teashop is not patronized by men – on the contrary they form a considerable proportion of its customers; but it was not primarily for their service that it came into being. Everywhere, as women took to business – and as suburbs grew and their women travelled citywards for shopping – there came into existence the teashop, for provision of cheap meals unaccompanied by alcohol; but whereas in England the growth of the teashop was followed before long by an expansion of the restaurant which does serve alcohol, and which nowadays, by its fixed-price lunches, caters largely for the woman shopper, such expansion still lags in Scotland. Save in hotel dining-rooms and a few restaurants in the larger cities, the places where alcohol is obtainable are not frequented by women; and that fact must be, in part at least, accountable for the character and development of the tea-room.

HEALTH, HUSBANDS AND HOUSEKEEPING
Margery Spring Rice, 1938

A social reformer, and founder member of the National Birth Control Association, Marjery Spring Rice was concerned, like many, about the impact of the depression years on the working classes. Aware that real voices spoke louder than cold statistics she travelled Britain interviewing daughters, wives and mothers from all corners. Her areas of interest covered income, standards of living, diet, attitudes to marriage, children, and their own welfare. Below are the responses of some of the Scots she met.

Mrs. MacN. of Glasgow, lives in one room and kitchen. She says it has no drawbacks. 'I take everything as it comes, and the only difficulty is when baby is restless.' Her husband is an unemployed carter, and she gets £2 unemployment money and 10/- from one boy (aged 16) who is working. Out of this £2

10s. 0d. she pays 9/– rent. She is 37 and has had 14 pregnancies, which include four children who have died and two miscarriages; there are therefore eight living children; five boys and three girls, living at home; the eldest girl of 18 is married and 'living in her own home'. She is 'never ill unless with children, and that passed off comfortably'. She gets up at 6 and goes to bed at 10. Her leisure consists of '15 minutes round the block with baby till he goes to sleep; 15 minutes for messages at 2 p.m. Club gymnasium on Tuesday, 45 minutes, and sewing class Thursday one hour or so'. Porridge and milk and vegetable soups are regular items of diet. The visitor who saw her says 'This woman has absolutely no complaints about accommodation, health or lack of funds. She plans her time very methodically and manages to feed herself and her family sufficiently well to maintain health.' The Scots are truly a wonderful people . . .

And there is Mrs. P. of Glasgow, (Glasgow seems to abound in buoyant, intelligent, and infinitely energetic women!) whose indomitable spirit is shown in every answer. She is 46, and has had five children born alive, one miscarriage and one still-birth. Two children have died. The family live in a tenement house, in one room and a kitchen for which she pays 9/– out of a total allowance of 40/–. (Her husband pays for clothing for the family in addition to this.) Under the drawbacks of her house she says 'Outside lavatory (used by six families). Public house at close which is objectionable owing to disgusting habits of men and bad language. House too small; no difficulties otherwise, except smell of beer worst in summer.' Three of her children (she does not mention whether the two dead ones are included in this) have been in the T.B. hospital for six months, and a convalescent home for six months; these also attended T.B. Dispensary regularly. One boy has been operated on for appendicitis. She is a very good mother, (in spite of this rather alarming evidence to the contrary); she attends regularly V.A.D. and Public Health classes; holds a certificate for First Aid and Home Nursing, and got second prize in 'care of children'! As to her own state of health, she says that she feels quite well and fit except for hernia (umbilical), caused by child-bearing. She has had one operation for this five years ago, and is waiting for another. She had a Caesarian section also five years ago (this was her youngest child, who has T.B.), and she has been sterilised. She broke her ankle a short while ago, but that is all right now; she apologised for speaking of the hernia to the visitor as a complaint, and has had no holiday whatever for nine years . . .

Husbands

Mrs. D. of Glasgow is 36. She has ten children, all living at home, and all under 15. In addition she has had one miscarriage. For three years she has suffered from spinal trouble, the cause of which has not been medically diagnosed, but Mrs. D. says it is 'caused probably by worry about the children, and about husband's unemployment'. She is taking phospherine and the doctor wants her 'to go to hospital for a womb operation' as she had post-natal trouble after the still-birth ten years ago (since when she has had six children). She finds her work very hard as she has to sit down very often, – and her eldest daughters (twins of 15) are able to help her a certain amount, – but they go out to work. They get the breakfast, so that she need not get up till ten-o'clock. Mrs. D. does not drink water as it gives her a pain, but she drinks a lot of tea. Her diet is fair. She lives in a Council flat of four rooms, for which she pays 9/6 rent out of £2 4s. od. total income. The Health Visitor writes 'Mrs. D. is very much crippled with her trouble, and according to the doctor it is due to constant worry. Each new arrival was a cause for fresh anxiety. Husband also causes worry owing to gambling habits, or inattention to home. He lost good employment through his inattention to business (and has now been unemployed for several years). Mrs. D. is considered incurable. She refuses to go into hospital as she worries about the children at home. She is an excellent mother.'

Housekeeping and diet

Mrs. T. lives in three rooms on the first floor of a tenement house in Arbroath; 25 people use the W.C. She is 32 and has five children, a boy of 7 and four girls of 14, 8, 3 years and a baby of 14 months. Her husband is unemployed and she cleans offices every morning, her total housekeeping is 36/9. Her chief trouble is lack of water laid on to her rooms, it has to be carried from the washing house. She suffers from headaches.

Out of the 36/9 housekeeping the regular weekly payments are:–

	s.	d.
Rent . . .	5	6
Coal . . .	3	4
Gas . . .	3	0
	11	10

so that there is 24/11 left for food and clothing for the family of seven.

Mrs. T. gives the following family menus: –

Breakfast:	Porridge, Tea, rolls
Dinner:	Soup (Broth, potato, lentil, etc.) Potatoes
Tea:	Bread and butter, an egg if cheap
Supper:	Tea or cocoa, bread and butter, jam

The Health Visitor says the house is 'very clean and tidy'. The husband was in hospital for two years as the result of a neglected accident when on farm work and he has now lost a leg due to this accident. The income is derived from parish relief 20/–, half of her husband's insurance 8/9, (he keeps the other half), and her own wage for cleaning offices 8/–.

When the second and third child were born, (now aged 8 and 7) Mrs. T. was in bed three days for her confinement. The district nurse attended her. For the youngest child she was in bed for ten days. Since then she has been much troubled with a festering breast.

OPERATION PIED PIPER

The Bulletin, *2 September 1939*

Two days before war was declared, Operation Pied Piper began, in which three million British children were evacuated from areas under threat of bombardment. In Scotland, around 170,000 children from Glasgow, Edinburgh, Dundee and the naval ports of Rosyth and Clydebank were packed onto trains, and expected to bring a change of underwear, nightwear, toothbrush, tin cup and enough food to last for a day. Many came from such poverty they had almost none of these items. And while the picture painted by The Bulletin *is of smiling stoicism, for some it was a dreadful experience. Children from the Gallowgate who found themselves, for instance, in rural Perthshire, were terrified by bees and insects. Where they came from there wasn't even a garden. 'Mister, they coos are eating all your grass', they would tell the farmer. One child fled onto the roof of the house where he was billeted, certain they were trying to drown him, when they'd only been running him a bath. As one schoolteacher accompanying her class from the slums of Camlachie later recalled, 'it was the best of times and the worst of times'. For mothers, sending their children off to be cared for by strangers meant a heart-rending struggle between doing what they thought was best while never wanting to let them out of their sight. As* The Bulletin *records, some preferred to trust their own instinct rather than the authorities.*

At the schools where evacuation did not begin until late in the forenoon there was something like a rush on the trains. Many of the children had obviously got together their belongings in a very short time. The persons least affected by the partings were the children themselves. Most of them were happy and gay, as if they were going away on a picnic. A postman, leaning over a railway bridge to watch them getting into a train that would take them to the peace of the moors, remarked – 'After all, they don't know what they're being sent away to avoid. And it will be best if the authorities can manage to keep them from ever knowing.'

There was no hitch, no congestion and little or no hindrance to citizens going about their business. Arrangements worked, in the words of an official, 'like clockwork'. But at Strathaven, Lanarkshire, where only a little over 500 evacuees turned up out of 1,600 scheduled for the town, a 'revolt' broke out among a large number of mothers, when they learned from billeting officers that individual families could not be accommodated in one house, but must split. Some of the mothers had as many as seven and eight children – some were toddlers and others were still being carried in arms. They came from the Kinning Park district of Glasgow, and had been up as early as five o' clock in the morning.

At the Town Hall, one of the four receiving centres, harassed billeting officers endeavoured to persuade the mothers there was no alternative but to allow some of their children to be taken to other homes. 'We won't leave our children. We'll take them back to Glasgow rather than be separated from them. They will cry their eyes out if they are taken from us', chorused a number of flushed and excited mothers.

After waiting five hours, two mothers decided to take the law into their own hands. They walked out of the Town Hall with nine children between them, determined to get back to Glasgow. As they wandered through the town, a Strathaven resident stopped them and learned of their plight. He took them into a restaurant and ordered a meal for the two families. The two mothers broke down and wept, and after they had finished their meal and rested, they boarded a bus for Glasgow.

Realising that it was impossible for everyone to be accommodated in the same house, other mothers of large families ultimately gave in to the billeting officer and by the early evening everyone was satisfactorily billeted. No difficulty was experienced in billeting unaccompanied children but residents in some houses scheduled to accommodate as many as six or eight persons definitely refused to take the children if the mother was with them.

Glasgow's evacuation organisation was brilliantly successful. Special trains to carry the departing children slid alongside the station platforms and left again with their loads only a few minutes later. The trains were leaving in some cases only a quarter of an hour after the leaders of the children's procession reached the station entrance. The railway staff handled the evacuation with less trouble than an ordinary holiday rush would have caused.

Mothers of Glasgow, standing outside city schools or walking with the evacuation processions to the stations, watched red-eyed with tears but bravely quiet, struggling to hide their feelings as their children disappeared behind the station barriers to the waiting trains. 'See you soon' was all that most of them said.

LIGHTS GOING OUT ALL OVER EUROPE
Marion Crawford, September 1939

Governess to the princesses Elizabeth and Margaret, Marion Crawford was a graduate from Moray House Training College in Edinburgh, who fell into the job by accident. After her long and dedicated service to the House of Windsor – out of loyalty she delayed marrying for sixteen years – she made the dreadful mistake, in 1950, two years after retiring, of publishing an affectionate memoir. The royal family never forgave her. She was banished from court, and from her grace and favour home, and never spoken to again. Thereafter, the royals referred to acts of treachery or indiscretion as 'doing a Crawfie'. Although Crawford's picture of life behind the scenes is entirely uncritical, it is a valuable record of a most private – and unforgiving – family. On 3 September, 1939, Crawford was recalled from her summer vacation, as the king and queen had to hurry back to London from Balmoral. She starts by describing the usual procession north for the family's holiday, which this year would be very different. In retrospect, she recognised that 1939 marked 'the end of an epoch' for the royals.

They went up on the private train from King's Cross Station to Ballater. This train consists of luggage vans, waggons to take the royal cars, and three sleeping- and dining-coaches for the children and their parents . . .

The Queen has a bedroom and a small sitting-room; the King has a bedroom and shares the Queen's sitting-room. The children shared a sleeping-car with Alah [Clara Knight, the princesses' nanny] and Bobo, the nursemaid, who had a small compartment curtained off. This business of going to bed in the train was always a very exciting one.

The journey took in all about fourteen hours, as the royal train did not allow speed to interfere with comfort. At Ballater the party was met by cars and did the remaining nine miles or so by road. The children's ponies were sent on ahead by ordinary horse-box. Their endless dogs, including the Queen's bad-tempered Dookie, went with them. Little they dreamed how long it would be before they saw London again.

War was declared on September the third. I was still on my holiday when I got a telegram asking if I could come as soon as possible to Birkhall. I collected my things and caught my train for Birkhall, wondering what was going to happen.

It was a gloomy journey. All about Aberdeen station anxious knots of people stood talking. The blackout had started and already shed its gloom over half the country. The station lights had all gone out, and darkened trains were already taking off the young men. When I arrived at Birkhall I found the King and Queen had already gone south in great haste the night before. The Honourable Mrs Geoffrey Bowlby, the Queen's lady-in-waiting, had stayed for two or three days until such time as I could get there. The two little girls and Alah were waiting for me. They were anxious and very apprehensive about their parents.

'Why had Mummie and Papa to go back, Crawfie? Do you think the Germans will come and get them?' Margaret asked me.

I remember assuring her heartily that there wasn't the slightest chance of it. I have wondered since why it was that I felt so absolutely confident, but I did. Lilibet was very calm and helpful as usual and at once ranged herself on the side of law and order.

'I don't think people should talk about battles and things in front of Margaret,' she said. 'We don't want to upset her.'

The King and Queen telephoned through to us every night at six o'clock. The children waited anxiously for the telephone bell to ring. Then there would be a mad rush. The Queen always had a word with me first. I think they felt it very keenly that at this distressing time the family had to be separated. Both the Queen and the King were most anxious that the children should be kept as far as possible away from it all.

'Stick to the usual programme as far as you can, Crawfie. We don't know what is coming, of course, but carry on as long as possible, just as usual.'

Up there among the moors and heather it was easy to do this. The heather was coming out, and the moors all about us were wine-red and beautiful. The River Muick rippled merrily through the gardens just as usual in those lovely autumn days, while Poland was being over-run and 'lights were going out all over Europe'.

Up here in the Highlands all was peace. The curlews called. The grouse raised its familiar old cry, 'Go back, go back', unharried for once by the guns which were all employed elsewhere.

There was now no Mummie and Papa to visit in the early morning, so they both came to me very punctually at half-past nine. We worked until eleven o'clock, then had our usual break, coffee and biscuits for me, orange juice and biscuits for the little girls. Then we used to catch George, the pony, and saddle him and go for a brisk walk, the children taking it in turns to ride . . .

I read the newspapers to the children after tea, trying as far as possible to give them some idea of what was happening without too many horrible details. Hitler seemed to be marching all over the place, and I remember Lilibet saying anxiously:

'Oh dear, Crawfie, I hope he won't come over here.'

I said I considered it unlikely, but if he did so, no doubt he would be dealt with. We read of sirens sounding in London, and I tried to explain what they were.

We had just been reading *At a Solemn Musick*, by Milton, in which the line appears, 'Blest pair of sirens, pledges of heaven's joy', and I had some difficulty in making them realize the idea wasn't quite the same, and this was a new kind of siren entirely unblessed. We all laughed a great deal about it.

One night over the wireless we suddenly got the horrible news that brought us slap up against reality. A grave voice regretfully announced the sinking of the battleship *Royal Oak*. We were continually studying *Jane's Fighting Ships*, and the little girls took a personal interest in every one of them. Lilibet jumped horrified from her chair, her eyes blazing with anger. I can still hear her little voice:

'Crawfie, it can't be! All those nice sailors.'

As the situation worsened it was no longer possible to keep things from them. Sometimes tuning in on the radio in the evening we would come all unawares on 'Lord Haw Haw', the infamous Irishman, William Joyce. Most of his efforts were greeted by the two little girls with peals of laughter, but some-times when he was more than usually offensive the children would throw books and cushions at the wireless so violently I had to turn it off. There was something oddly arresting about that dreadful voice. Some evenings up in Scotland it was almost impossible to get away from it. Wherever you tuned in, there he was.

❦

STILLBIRTH

Naomi Mitchison, 4–7 July 1940

Novelist Naomi Mitchison had an open marriage with her husband, the barrister Gilbert Mitchison, but as a strong advocate of contraception, she was careful to make sure she only ever bore children fathered by him. She did, however, look forward to a time when women could have children 'by several chosen fathers uncensured'. During the Second World War she was part of the Mass Observation project, in which diaries of life on the home front were scrupulously kept. Mitchison wrote hers from 1 September 1939 until 10 August 1945, the day after the second atomic bomb was dropped by the Americans on Nagasaki. As this entry suggests, there was one event she would rather not have had to record, certainly not when it was so raw. The baby she lost was called Clemency.

I had better get this over. The induction began to work about 1.30 on the 4th; by 3.15 I had vomited, etc, had a very severe shivering fit, and was beginning to have very adequate first stage pains. I was however very glad it had started. By 6 they were quite severe, and shortly afterwards I asked for some kind of dope. I had scopolamine and morphine, on the strict understanding that these would have no effect on the baby. After a quarter of an hour I got drowsy, had another injection, and all but the worst pains got clouded over. I think I had another later, but my time sense is uncertain, and I remember little until two or three violent pains, which appeared to me to be second stage; I said that the head was breaking through and I wanted some chloroform at once. I was right and the final stage was over in a few minutes, before Dr Cameron had arrived, even. I awoke to hear them say I had a lovely little girl; I said that was right, that was what I wanted. I asked several times, was she all right. They said yes, and I think I thought so, as they had worked on her for some time and thought she was breathing all right; I just saw her and kissed her. The rest of the night – it was then after 2 o'ck, I lay, uncomfortable but happy, mostly listening to her small noises, but thinking they were not very loud. In the morning I was still rather persistent to know what they thought of her; they said she was not very strong, but no more; I thought she was no worse than Val as a tiny. Then they said she should be bathed to get her to cry and fill her lungs, and brought her through. Ruth came in, and Val. Nurse bathed her close to me. I thought she looked cyanosed, but hoped it was a matter of establishing breathing properly. I watched her in the bath, and touched her soft hands; she had a pretty shaped head and a lot of dark hair, but seemed very weak and never opened her eyes.

I was a little worried, but not much; I said to put up the flag, so they hoisted the Red Flag for her.

They said she should not come to me but must stay warm all day; I was rather sad about it, but began reading Agnes Mure MacKenzie's history of Scotland; my throat still a little sore from the chloroform. I was very thirsty. I had got to the chapter on the Bruce when the Nurse came in saying Baby's not so well. It sounded pretty ominous; she and Dr Hunter were in the other room. Rosemary came to me; I asked her to look in; she said, She's not responding. I sat up, trying to make up my mind to something which still seemed not quite inevitable. By this time Denny and Val had started for Tarbert to meet Dick. Then Dr Hunter came in and I knew.

The septum of the heart had not closed properly. It would not have made any difference if she had been ten days later at full term. If she had lived it could not have been for more than a few months or years of a very wretched kind of existence. It was just one of those things which do happen. It was excessively hard to face. No one was to blame. Nothing could at any point have been done.

Dr Hunter was extremely nice to me. I did to some extent break down, although realising all sorts of logical things. It was a pretty complete crash at the moment and one could not fix on to anything else. I said to take the flag down, and asked Dr Hunter to tell Dick. I said I would like one of the boats to take her out to sea. It was no use my seeing her again, my poor sweet . . .

. . . The silly thing is that I realise perfectly that much worse things are happening at this moment to thousands of people (and indeed have done so for a long time), but one cannot generalise as simply as that. I at least cannot change pain into love. And all the little things hurt, hurt, hurt, and there is nothing to be done. Nor is it fair to speak about them to others; nor indeed, would the others understand one's minding so much. But she was part of me, and wanted, all these months, and warm, and one said what a nuisance, but lovingly, and now the whole thing is ended: the love has no object. I had dreamt so often of the sweet warmth and weight of a baby at my breasts and now my bound breasts ache. If I get at all drowsy I begin to expect someone to bring the baby in, and that's hell. One has to keep awake.

❧

LAND GIRLS

Mona McLeod, 1940

The Women's Land Army, formed during the First World War, was reactivated in June 1939. By 1941, over 20,000 women had volunteered to join, to bring more land into agricultural use and make the country more self-sufficient. Late in 1941 conscription was brought in, and the following year a timber corps was established. At its peak, over 80,000 women were employed in the WLA. The work was hard, and could involve handling horses, mending tractors and killing vermin such as foxes, rats, rabbits and moles (one pair of women killed 12,000 rats in a single year). The basic wage was 28 shillings a week, 10 shillings less than the male average, and 14 shillings were deducted for board and keep. Initially there were no holidays, but after a Land Girls' Charter was drawn up in 1943, they were allowed a week's holiday, and the minimum rate of pay was increased. These two young women, both volunteers, recalled their experiences as part of the crucial war effort. Mona McLeod worked on a farm in Kircudbrightshire.

My grandmother and my two younger sisters and I were evacuated to a cottage in the Yorkshire Dales, and shortly after Dunkirk my father came out to see us and he said, 'Mona, I want to speak to you.' So I said, 'Yes Daddy'. He called me into his study: when he did this it usually meant we were in trouble. On this occasion, however, he said, 'I believe as I always have done in the importance of the higher education of women', and I said, 'Yes, Daddy', and he said, 'but I think we ought to concentrate on winning the War'. So I said, 'Yes, Daddy'. He said, 'So I've arranged that you could join the Women's Land Army [WLA] . . . I had arranged that you should go to the University Farm (this was Leeds University), but I've discovered that the RAF has got camps all round the farm, so I don't think it would be a very good idea. So I spoke to the farm manager's wife (who happened to have been my Guide Captain) and she has spoken to her father, who's a farmer in Galloway, so I've arranged that you should go and work for Mr Armstrong' – and a fortnight later I found myself either making hay, or if it rained, as it often did, cutting thistles. An extraordinary thing is, it was years after before I thought what an extraordinary situation, where my father had decided what I should do without asking me.

I felt quite excited about it. I had been to the farm in Galloway when I was a Girl Guide in 1938. Our Guide Captain, the daughter of the farmer, had taken us there, so I did know the family.

[My uniform consisted of] short-sleeved shirts, one jumper, one pair of ill-fitting breeches, three pairs of woollen knee-length stockings, one pair of leather boots and a pair of wellie boots, two pairs of dungarees, one short cotton coat, one raincoat, one hat, one tie and badge. Items of uniform could be replaced annually if they were worn out. After about three years we got a very nice coat, well-cut but impossible to work in. For any girl working out of doors in all weathers, the uniform was grossly inadequate. Women in the armed services had protective clothing; we did not. In my first winter I had chilblains on my ears, hands, knees and feet. The turnips I had to pull and shaw were often covered in ice; if you did wear gloves they were rapidly soaked. Wearing my brother's cast-off tweed jacket or battle-dress top and the gloves, waterproof leggings, woollen long-johns and clogs which I had to buy, I discovered in my second winter that it was possible to keep warm in all but the hardest conditions. The clogs were a wonderful discovery. When lined with straw which had been heated over the boiler in the dairy, they kept your feet warm and dry all day.

Una A. Stewart (née Marshall), 1942

A daughter of the manse, who had gained entrance to university, Una knew she would be conscripted, and chose the land army over joining the uniformed services. She was reported in a local newspaper as being taken aback at the 'dirt and bad language' she encountered on a farm near Arbroath, but had no trouble settling in.

The farmer and his wife were pretty old. He was crippled with rheumatism. She was bitter because she had two sons who had fearful stammers of the mouth-gaping type. If you guessed what they were trying to say, it helped.

We drew up in the close at the back entrance to the house – no one uses the front door of a farmhouse. As we got out of the car, the byre door in the steading opened a little and three young men looked out to see the new Land Girl; the two farmer's sons, Douglas and Ian and Henry Edward Murray Stewart – the foreman, horseman and my future husband.

That night Kate – the Land Girl who was leaving, the farmer's sons, Ed and I gathered round the kitchen range and Ed produced his button accordion. The farmer's wife produced a large bar of Cadbury's chocolate which I hadn't seen since before the War. We had four squares each. Ed put his on the side of the range where I watched it begin to melt as we sang songs of the day. I was too shy to point it out to him and I was relieved when he spotted it before it was too late. About nine, the party broke up and we headed for the back door to see Ed off, opened it and discovered it was snow to the top! We dug him out and he set off home across the fields, because the road was up to the top of the telegraph poles in drifts. And so to bed.

Next morning a call came at quarter past four. I got up, put on my dressing gown, and set off across a huge expanse of polished linoleum (there was a lambskin rug at the bedside) to find my slippers, and, wash-bag and candle in my hand, made my way downstairs to the bathroom. The door consisted of two halves lengthways, with a bolt top and bottom. As I opened the right-hand side, somebody opened the back door and the draught crashed the door in my face and blew out the candle. As I stood in stygian blackness, the kitchen door opened and I was given another candle with the sharp remark, 'we don't bother with all that, Miss Marshall'! A freezing cold splash wakened me completely and it was out to the byre in double-quick time to make the acquaintance of thirty-odd cows and rather surly cattleman. I quickly cottoned on to washing udders and clamping on milking machines. Kate was very help-ful and showed me how to pull the dung into the grip, put in fresh straw and sluice down the cement centre walkway. In for breakfast. The farmer's wife had made a huge pot of porridge. The farmer, Kate and I had some with fresh milk. Very nice, but what happened to the rest? Was it for lunch? Or for tea? A row of bowls in the scullery (where we washed up cans and machines) was filled. Cold porridge for lunch and tea? My fears were dispelled at lunch time – a plate of soup with potatoes cooked in it and a bit of boiling beef.

She later learned the row of porridge bowls was for the dogs.

A DAY IN THE LIFE OF . . .

Irena Hurny, 1941

After Russia and Germany invaded Poland in September 1939, there was debate about which side treated the country more harshly. By the time the pact between the two powers came to an end, in June 1941, the Soviets had taken around half a million Polish nation-als prisoner. Shortly before her sixteenth birthday, Irena Hurny and her mother, who were living in Warsaw, were arrested, believed to be from a family of nationalists and counter-revolutionaries, and therefore 'enemies of the people'. In the early months, Irena was frequently interrogated about her father's and brother's activities. At this point she did not know that her brother was already dead, and she mistakenly thought she could hear him screaming under torture, in one of the prisons where she was kept. Soon separated from her mother, who was sentenced to eight years in a labour camp, she spent years in prisons and camps. Estimates of the numbers killed under occupation and incarceration by the

USSR in this period range from 150,000 to 500,000. Finally reunited with her mother, Irena made her way to Scotland, where she settled for the rest of her life. This description comes from the time when she learned that she and all the inmates of a young offenders' camp at Starodub, in southern Russia, near Ukraine, were to be transferred to Siberia. It was a journey from which many did not return.

So all of us were taken to the station, put into these cattle trucks again as usual, and the journey started. The five of us Polish girls who had been in isolation at Starodub were put in a separate corner in the train. The others were not allowed to talk to us. We were in a rather dodgy situation. Of course, in our truck there was just a tiny window with bars and it was almost impossible to look through the window because the stronger girls were sitting there and wouldn't let any other body near it. At least there was some fresh air coming through it.

I remember the stations where the children used to come to beg for bread from us prisoners on the train. I heard the same story from other people on their way to Siberia. So, I mean, it must have been a pretty bad situation in the country altogether.

Eventually, however, they got us to Barnaul, in Siberia. We were put into the ordinary labour camp. [It] was absolutely terrible.

We were in wooden barracks. The most awful thing was bugs which were living in the sort of moss between the big trunks of trees of which the barracks were built. It was tree trunks, not planks, because in Siberia they were needed to give some sort of protection, otherwise the prisoners would freeze to death. But at night the bugs in the moss between these tree trunk walls were practically eating people alive. There were huge bugs and small brown flat ones. When you killed them – a horrible smell. Well, we couldn't sleep because we were being eaten alive. Whenever you put your hand down then lifted it there were hundreds of bugs. It was terrible. Lice seem to be frightfully subtle creatures compared with those bugs.

Our work at Barnaul consisted of going out in the morning to a little pond, full of water and mud and straw. For fourteen hours a day we had to go round this pond, stamping with our feet, so that later on they could make some kind of straw bricks. They built houses in Siberia out of these bricks. It was terrible work. It was September by then and there were already frosty mornings – pretty cold. And starvation really started then. We got some sort of watery soup once a day and a tiny bit of bread, which was almost always running with water. Somebody later on explained to us that according to the law they had to give us so much bread in weight. So of course they put water on it to make it heavier.

The camp officials kept telling us, 'You are going soon to be free, according to the amnesty for Polish citizens you are going to be free.' Well, on the 22nd of September 1941 we were set free. I was left for a few hours longer. I suppose they just wanted to frighten me, to tell me to keep quiet or whatever!

Then we were sent to a sewing factory in the town of Barnaul which was making uniforms for the Red Army. Our Polish group was given a tiny little cottage on the river Ob to live in. We had no fuel, we had no bedding we had no pots and pans not even a cup or a spoon to our names. We just huddled together and slept like that there on the floor.

In the mornings we went to the factory. We usually had some sort of dinner, well, soup and our ration of bread in the factory. And then the winter set in. It was a terrible winter, that winter of 1941–42. It was absolutely awful. All winters in that part of the world are very, very severe. I remember we had over minus 50 degrees centigrade at Barnaul. Luckily, Barnaul was very much inland and very dry. Otherwise I don't know who would have survived the winters.

We had no clothing, we were in rags. I remember I went with my friend, another outspoken girl, to the man who was the main executive of that factory. He was the only man I ever saw in that factory. All men otherwise were in the army. We said to this executive: 'We are going to freeze to death. We have no fuel in that little cottage where we are living. And we must have some clothing.' So eventually they provided us with some clothing. Actually, it was a wonderful thing – a quilted anorak, and we were also given quilted shoes with sort of rubber soles. That made us relatively warm. But of course whenever you went outside it was so cold that your eyelashes froze. Your breath froze around your mouth – it was like Scott of the Antarctic.

And there was not a single drop of milk. There was no milk. I remember once going out of the camp in Barnaul and there was some sort of market going on. And I thought, 'My goodness! Not that we had any money to buy things. And I saw slabs of a frozen sort of bluish white thing. It was milk. It was frozen stiff. You just chopped it. But of course we couldn't afford that at all . . .

We were near to breaking down, I suppose, each of us. Well, I stayed at Barnaul until January 1942. I was pretty ill there. I think it was just the climate. I didn't know what was wrong with me but all my joints were swollen. It may have been arthritis or rheumatic fever. I could hardly walk. But I was sent from Poland the address of my cousin . . . And she wrote to me: 'Irena, please come to me if you can.' So I went to the director of that factory in Barnaul and said how I would like to go to my cousin. So I got the permission and I got the railway tickets.

That was the most fascinating journey I ever made in my life. I boarded the train in Barnaul and went to Novosibirsk. Novosibirsk station was very, very beautiful. It was marble and bronze and all the rest of it. But all the floors of that station were covered by people in rags and starving. The contrast was terrible.

From Novosibirsk station I had to go westwards to Petropavlovsk and then change to Karabanda, down south again, and then to a station called Kokchetav. But nobody knew at Novosibirsk when the train to the west was going to come. So I just sat there at Novosibirsk station. I had managed to save a little slice each day of my bread ration and had dried them and I had these rusks with me. Knowing that I was going on that journey I managed. And that's the way I survived. I was sitting waiting six days in that station at Novosibirsk, afraid to fall asleep. Well, I'm sure I was dozing off – but always I was listening. People would say, 'The train to Petropavlovsk is coming.' Eventually, after six days, the train came.

Again it was not really a passenger train – it was just the usual cattle or goods trucks. But I got in there, into one of the trucks. I remember there was a little fire in the middle of it. That was January, the end of January, so it was frightfully cold. I just dropped off and slept, I don't know for how long.

Eventually somebody dragged me to the fire in the middle of the truck. I had been sitting against the metal wall of the truck and my legs were practically frozen. However, an elderly man helped me. Later on I learned that he and his family were Germans, Soviet Germans. There used to be a German Republic in the Soviet Union, somewhere near the Volga. Of course, when the war with Germany started in the summer of 1941 they were thrown out – deported. Nobody wanted them anywhere. I believe they were just sort of travelling all the time through Siberia and Kazakhstan and elsewhere, trying to find a place that the Soviet authorities would let them stay. I don't really know what happened to these people. But I was very grateful to that old German in the truck. He had obviously noticed that I was freezing and in danger and he helped me.

Then suddenly, in the middle of the great white nowhere the train to Petropavlovsk stopped. The railway officials said, 'This train doesn't go any further. But there is a train along the line and hopefully you will find a place in it.' So everybody rushed along the line toward the other train. The snow was chin high. Nobody on that other train wanted to open the door to us. And the train was full anyway. So that was a very grim situation. I don't know how many people were left stranded there and died of cold.

But we all ran along that train and knocked at one carriage, then another carriage. Suddenly in one carriage when I knocked I heard somebody saying in broken Russian, 'Sorry, you can't come in here. Here are only Polish men going to join the army in Kuibyshev.' 'My goodness!', I said. So I started shouting in Polish: 'Surely you will let me in? I'm Polish!' Of course, they opened the door then and dragged me in.

They were young Polish men, well, most of them were young. Some seemed to me – then seventeen – frightfully old: about forty, probably! So I stayed with them and, oh, I felt so safe. For the first time I felt safe.

SALES ASSISTANT

Anonymous, 1940s

A department store was a microcosm of wider society, with its rigid hierarchy and snob-beries. This was never more the case than in Edinburgh, the capital of class distinctions.

I remember my mother making me stay on at school till I was about 15. Her ambition was for me to work in an office but I never wanted to work in an office. I went to Binn's, it was Maule's then, at the West End.

We thought we were frightfully posh yet we got a lot less pay than in a factory. There was a thing which you could call class distinction. There was the 1st Sales (Assistant), the 2nd Sales, the 3rd Sales and, when you started, you would be the 4th Sales. If a woman came in and the 1st Sales wasn't busy she got the sale, and if another woman came in, well the 2nd Sales got that. Sometimes you never got a sale because by the time it came round to the 4th there weren't enough customers in the department.

I remember I was promoted just before I was married, up to 1st Sales, and oh dear – we had a different canteen. There was one for the bosses, one for the 4th, 3rd and 2nd Sales, and 1st Sales went to another canteen. Mind there was just an urn and it was just that one lot sat on benches and another lot sat on chairs but that was real distinction. I wasn't conscious of class distinction but of being a bit better than a 4th Sales. I think I got 10/- and the supposed encouragement of a 1d. in the £1.00 commission.

I remember the buyer always wore a long black dress, made of crepe, right down to the floor. We all had to wear black dresses – you were lucky if you had two.

The buyer we had was the most terrible woman. You weren't allowed to stop for a second. You had to clean out, or dust tops of cupboards, or fold all the stuff in the glass drawers, whether or not they'd been done the day before, rather than stand about. She was like an eagle ready to pounce and we all had to 'watch out here's the boss'. So it wasn't a very nice atmosphere but I liked the work. We got a Saturday half day like all the shops in Princes Street. We worked 9–6 or 9–7 on the other days.

❧

GROWING OLD

Catherine Carswell, 1940s

The writer Catherine Carswell had no illusions about growing old, but seems to have applauded the spirit of those women who raged against the dying of the light, in the form of hair dye and make-up.

Women, being more physically conscious, are more apt to square their behaviour with appearance, even while they may endeavour – being the less vain sex – to resort to artificial aids. But few old women who paint and dye are under any real delusion as to the result, which is mainly intended to cheer them for their loss and to bear about an impression of gaiety rather than of gloom.

❧

ADVICE TO SONS

Maggie Fuller, 1940s–50s

This mother of sons was a little unusual in being so frank with them, and so supportive of their imaginary girlfriends.

I never got a girl so I don't know what would have happened. The way the world is they don't have a chance, unless they are very strong-willed. No matter how much bringing-up you give them. I am glad I didn't really. I said to my sons, 'Well, do you know?' I said, 'You's have lamb and sheep.' And they said, 'Now Mother, if it's sex you're on about, we know all about it!' I used to say to them, 'Well mind, if you ever put a girl in the family way, and you don't take her after spoiling her, you'll have the decency to come and tell me and I'll see she's all right.' I always said that to them, I did always and I would always, because I think it's a shame. I don't see why a girl should be left like that, I truthfully don't. It's a damned disgrace. I don't see why a boy should spoil a girl and get off scot-free, I don't honestly, and I used to say that to ours. I remember because I'd say, 'It'll come back on you, if I ever hear about it. Don't shut the door on them, for,' I said, 'it's a shame.'

GENTEEL WAR-WORK

Catherine Carswell, 1943

As war-time dragged on, there were ways of making a little extra money that were particularly suitable for the educated middle-classes. Journalist Catherine Carswell suggests as much to her friend, F. Marian McNeill, by this time famous for her books The Silver Bough *and* The Scots Kitchen.

3rd June 1943
Dearest Flos— . . . I worry about you and the censorship (I know I couldn't stand it long). I should have thought there was any amount of domestic work in Edinb, as there is in London. What about mending? I do it professionally and could get enough to keep myself if I made a push. Household linen is all in rags and clothes need repair. The way is to go out and to charge by the hour (not less than 2/– an hour). I'm sure a cleverly worded card could be put up in clubs, ministries, etc. People in jobs simply have not time to mend. Of course it is hard on the eyes, or so I find. What about making rag dolls? I'm doing one now. Finnicky job though . . .

THE LANDLADY

Christopher Rush, 1947

Growing up in the fishing village of St Monans in the East Neuk of Fife, Christopher Rush was mesmerised by his terrifying great-great-aunt Epp. The iron fist with which she handled him is a reminder of how sternly and even alarmingly children could be treated by their elders, even as recently as this. For those of a fiercely Presbyterian bent, childcare was evidently more about instilling moral fibre than making them comfortable or happy.

Epp was our landlady at East Shore Street, for the house was not our own. She was Queen Victoria at number sixteen, well into her eighties when I knew her and dead before I was three . . .

It was Epp who began my literary education. Throned on her massive moss-green velvet armchair, all curves and buttons, she sat there in a black waterfall of lace, her skirts spilling across the floor, and thundered at me: 'The Charge of the Light Brigade'. I stood no higher than her dark silken knee, a tiny little man. Stormed at by the shot and steady shell of her wrathful cannonades, I would watch with horror the trembling of her dreadful dewlaps when her frail white fists descended on the sides of her chair, beating out the rhythms of the verse. She held the windowed sky in her spectacles and her head was lost in the clouds of her snowy white hair . . .

When I was bad and uncontrollable, and all the men in the house at sea, I was taken to Epp.

'Oh you scoundrel!' she scolded. 'You bad wild boy!'

Then she would tell me that the horned and hoofed devil had flown over the rooftops on black, scaly pinions of soot, that he was sitting on our chimney right this minute, listening to me, and would be down the lum at my next word. His mouth was full of sinners and that was why I couldn't hear him mumbling, but at the next swallow there would be room in his jaws for one more gobbet of begrimed humanity and that would be me. Didn't I hear the soot falling? Open-mouthed, I looked from her to the lurid red glow within the black grate of her fireside. Sinister scrabblings came from the awful tall blackness of the chimney, which led up to the universe, the unknown corners of God's coal-cellar. Quaking, I turned my eyes back to my torturer, her pale old face laved in flames. She spitted me on her tongue.

'You will go to hell,' she leered. 'You will be crying for a single drop of water to cool your parched mouth. Your throat will be like the desert. But

Satan will just laugh at you before he crunches you up. And not one drop of water will you get! Oh yes, my bonny man, you'll get something to cry for in hell!'

When I ran to her, screaming, she never softened.

'Go away, you bad lad! You're like every other boy that was born, picked up from the Bass Rock you were, that's where your father got you, didn't you know? Why didn't he go to the May Island, the silly kipper that he was, and bring us all back a nice wee lass instead of you, you nasty brat!' . . .

Poor Epp. Her two sons had run away from home and had died in scarlet in the war against the Zulus, leaving her naked in her age. If she never stopped blaming them through these tireless tirades of hers against the whole masculine world, perhaps it was that she kept up a kind of praise and lamentation in her wild volleys of heroic poetry, dedicated to their reproach and their renown. At any rate she was a stern Eve. She had known a sharper sting than the serpent's tooth. And the apple of life had turned to ashes in her mouth. So she bit back with venom.

But she unbent for the ceremony of the pan drop.

I was summoned to the hearth.

Taking a pan drop from a glass jar, the holy grail of her dresser, she would place it on the fender and pulverise it with the poker. She turned the fire-iron the wrong way in her hand. Its head was a burnished bronze mushroom. With this she would execute the frivolous indulgence that was the sweet, and I always feared for the precious pieces. It was placed on the whorled corner of that fender and broken between bronze and brass, smashed like a criminal on the wheel – rendered innocuous for the tender tongue of the anxiously waiting youngling. Epp waited there to the end, watching me haughtily as I sucked away the last white crumbs . . .

'Away you go now, you young rascal, that's all there is.'

She lifted the poker and shook her free fist at me. I ran from the room. I was horrified of her in those moods.

But she was my first queen and I her quaking subject. Her sceptre was the gleaming poker, her court the flickering hearth with its high-backed buttoned throne. The pan drops were the favours she dispensed . . .

For I can remember [one winter's] night when the grownups faced one another across a bare table, all of them as dumb as stones for sheer poverty, the fishing that year having proved a failure. I was up whining for food, but there was none to be had, nor a toy in the house between ceilings and floor. I roamed about the distempered walls following my gaunt hungry shadow beneath the gasmantles, glancing narrowly at the grown ones as they sat there in that grim-faced gathering that both angered and upset me. So it was

I who heard the small silver chiming at the dark brown door – so small a sound I saw that the others had not even taken their faces out of their fists. Blotting myself against the wall I moved silently to the door. I stared down in wonderment at two shining circles on the floor, two bright winter moons that lit up the linoleum.

Two half crowns.

Down to the edge of our door, where the gray daggers of the winter winds struck her between the ribs, my great queen had knelt in the lonely darkness of her empty hall. She had laid her old bones down there unseen and had pushed back our rent money that we could not afford to pay. Through the door it had come again, from the probing tips of her white ringless fingers. Epp who never said a word, though everyone knew of that tender mercy which became her in the end better than her reign of terror.

But she breathed her last, old Epp, before she could receive the thanks of her meanest vassal. Such is the breath of old queens – brief in the bitter mornings of little boys.

NATIONAL HEALTH SERVICE
Mary Brooksbank, 1948

The founding of the National Health Service in 1948 promised to transform the lives of the poor by offering swift, free treatment for their ailments. Socialist Mary Brooksbank of Dundee was not impressed by her first encounter with it. Yet, if the attitude of the doctors she encountered was typical of the old regime, one sees why this new service was so badly needed.

I will not readily forget the attitude of some of the doctors after the inauguration of the National Health Service. The doctors who attended my father and mother were Drs Buchanan, Sen., and his son.

My mother asked to be sent to hospital as she thought it was too much for me. But Dr Buchanan, Jun,. said there was no use in keeping a dog and barking themselves. That was what I was there for. I remember my mother's reply, 'Is that the way of it, well I am not going to allow the medical profession to use me to destroy her'. Dr Rorie, who attended my father, said to me he was not really ill only being bad. This to an old man of 86 who had worked hard all his days and never needed a doctor till he got old . . .

I got a job in the Eagle Jute Mill but I was not able for the work and got a line from my doctor to this effect. But the Labour Exchange would not accept this and sent me to Dr Gordon Clark of Windsor Street. My mother went with me. As I gave him the letter from the bureau he turned to my mother and said, but you are not the patient. She said no, but I'm her mother. He said to her, and how old are you. She replied I'm 72, doctor. He then said you should be shot. I saw my mother go white at the lips, but she signed to me to say nothing. So, for her sake, I held my tongue. He then turned to me and said everybody over 70 should be shot. At that I could no longer hold my tongue and said is that the Nazi philosophy doctor? He said no more but handed me a certificate freeing me from the job.

❦

A PROTESTANT GIRLHOOD

Liz Lochhead, 1947–51

Poet and dramatist Liz Lochhead's early childhood captures the turning point when post-war dreariness blossomed into something more modern and hopeful. Stafford Cripps was Chancellor of the Exchequer in Clement Attlee's Labour government and credited for the turnaround in Britain's economy. Lochhead's memory is good, because while rationing ended completely in 1954, sweets came off the proscribed list only the year before.

I was born at the bleak end of 1947. Stafford Cripps' Age of Austerity, I know now. I remember, can I really remember, or is it just mythology – Power Cuts and Sweetie Rationing?

There were a lot of us born then, most of us to parents just as recently demobbed, just as newly optimistic and no better housed than my father and mother were. We were the Bulge. I knew that then, as we advanced from Primary School to Secondary School to Higher Education with a lot of fanfare and rhetoric from the newspapers. The Bulge. A single frame from a comic book, this gigantic Easter Egg a spotted snake had swallowed in the Dandy Annual – this was how I pictured it as we were squeezed through the gullet of the Education System stretching everything to breaking point.

We lived, my mother, my father and I, in a single upstairs room in my grandparents' house. My father's side. A big between-the-wars council five-apartment. Roughcast. Pebbledash. Six in the block. In the shadow of all the steelworks, Colvilles, Anderson Boyes, the Lanarkshire – number thirteen, the Broadway, Craigneuk, Wishaw. Whenever I heard on the radio the Lullaby of Broadway I thought they were singing about us.

The place was full of adoring grown-ups all easily charmed and exploited by a smartypants toddler. There was my Gran, my Grandad, my father's youngest unmarried sister and brother – my Auntie Jinnet who was engaged and my Uncle George who was Restless. He was considering emigrating to Corby with half the workforce of Anderson Boyes. My Grandad spent a lump of every afternoon lying on the bed under the top knitted blanket in the back bedroom, often with me burrowed in between him and the wall, prattling and pulling his hair. He had been a miner before the steelworks and he had a touch, more than a touch of silicosis. His lungs weren't so good.

But he was good and loud in arguments. Round the tea-table I remember him, long before I could make head or tail of it, the arguing – especially on Sundays if the rest of the family were there, Bill and Jean who had two children and a prefab and Annie and John with my baby cousin. He had been a miner. He was a Unionist. He was angry at how his sons and daughters had come back from the Forces voting Labour. Said they'd sold old Churchill down the river. He blamed the war for a lot.

He had been a miner. He was a Unionist. In the early twenties, preying on fears aroused by the recent large influx of Irish Catholics to Glasgow and the industrial West of Scotland, the competition for jobs, the suspicions about cheap blackleg labour, the hard times a-coming, the Scottish Unionist Party successfully neatly split the working classes. I know that now. Divide And Rule. People have told me. Then I knew a father and his sons around a table. His white hair. My grandmother wheeshting and clucking. The words Catholic and Protestant. Raised voices.

He was not an Orangeman. He used to say he had nothing against anybody. He was a good churchgoer. Regular. He talked about Idolatry. And told me about Covenanters. There was a blue and white plate on the wall with a man-on-a-horse who was William of Orange. He was Dutch. Delft. They had brought it back from Holland when they had visited my Uncle Robert's Grave, my Gran and Grandad. After the war. He had been my father's second-youngest brother. He was dead. There was a picture of him in his uniform. I spent a lot of time looking at this photograph to see if there was anything different about a picture of somebody who was dead. It was easier with my Aunt Edith. She had died aged seven of measles ten years, fifteen years, a long time ago. It was possible to imagine, when I squinted at the family group with her in front, something slight and shifting and otherworldly about her sepia presence among her lumpier solid brothers and sisters. They said I'd her Eyes. My mother said nothing at the time, later up in the privacy of our own room said nothing of the sort. Mine were brown.

The room wasn't that big. There was my mother and father's big high bed. And my brown-varnished cot squashed in at the end of it. A green-top card table and chairs, big brown boxy rexine chairs. There was the radio, no, it was only a speaker really, it had one on-off switch, no tuner, it was attached to my grandparents' radio downstairs. We had to listen to whatever they listened to, when they switched it off we'd had it. We listened a lot though, plays, music-nights. Take It From Here. In April 1948 over the speaker they heard Stafford Cripps' Budget increase the price of cigarettes from two-and-four pence to three-and-four pence and my forty-a-day father looked at his sleeping or squalling four-month old daughter, said well that's that and gave up just like that, never smoked again. Another piece of family mythology.

There were few ornaments. My mother and father's engagement photo, framed. Head and shoulders, printed in monochrome then hand-tinted. Cherryblossom – brown hair, pink cheeks, carmine lips. A sweet smile each and a youthful look. And the wedding photograph. Full length. My father in his army uniform, my mother in the A.T.S. She said she could stand it, the Khaki, because she'd good colouring and anyway there just weren't the coupons. She'd had nothing else to fit her because the army food blew you up. She'd consoled herself with what the teacher had told her away back when she'd had to wear the brown fairy dress in 'Fairy-Leather-Apron' in the school concert – that brown eyes like that could bring out the beauty. She said the big excitement had been seeing if my father's leave got cancelled and the whole thing was off for the time being. It had been touch and go, she said. But she'd got a lot out of the A.T.S., enjoyed it, met all sorts. She said the main thing was not to marry too young. She recommended waiting until you were twenty-four like her. It had been the ideal age.

She talked to me a lot, did my mother. All day when my father was away at work. Bits of her life became legends. Descriptions of dance dresses, what devils they'd been she and her sisters, stories of how my Auntie Elsie, fifteen and with soot on her eye-lashes, had brazenly stolen someone's officer. She says now I was great company as a kid. She was that bit plumper again than in the wedding photograph. Seems that every time something my grandmother said rankled her (it was my father's side remember) every time she had to just swallow it all or just start a row over some domestic division, every time they'd had yet another disappointment over some house they'd been after – she'd walk me in my go-chair, chewing in her misery a whole quarter of newly unrationed sweets.

For a while we tried the other set of grandparents. I don't suppose things were much happier or easier for my mother and father. They kept putting in for houses here and there, getting nowhere.

They didn't seem quite so deadly respectable, my Gran and Grandad Forrest. For instance he swore, up to the point of 'bloody' and 'wee bugger'. He had been in the Navy in the First World War, still sang songs my grandmother tutted at. He had a terrible voice. A groaner. Tone deaf. He sang me Sad Songs – 'The Drunkard's Raggit Wean' – and laughed and tickled me when I got a lump in my throat. My mother always said what a right good storyteller he was, had a way with words, embroidered things just enough.

My grandmother said poems. Long storytelling poems. At sixteen she'd been maid to one of the Misses Reid who'd been an elocutionist. And gave lessons. My grandmother had remembered by heart every word, every inflection, every arch or pointed gesture of the voice. I grew wide-eyed at Little Orphan Annie (and the goblins will get you/too/if/you/don't/watch/out), tearful at the melodrama about the little girl searching for her dead mother (And I'se looking for heaven/but I can't find the stair).

I absolutely loved them both. But it's easy to love your grandparents.

MEASURING OUT A LIFE IN PERCOLATED COFFEE
Margaret Tait, 1950s

Orcadian filmmaker Margaret Tait trained as a doctor and served in the Royal Army Medical Corps during the Second World War. In 1950 she went to Italy to study film, which she was to make her career. On her return she set up Ancona Films in Rose Street in Edinburgh, where she also was friendly with the poets who gathered in the nearby pubs, among them Hugh MacDiarmid, Norman MacCaig, George Mackay Brown and his troubled muse, Stella Cartwright. Her method was experimental, and many of her films were short. All but three were self-funded. In the 1960s, she returned to Kirkwall. Here she describes a technique she realised she needed to work on to perfect.

I found that if I clicked the shutter then walked into the house to the kitchen, took the coffee pot out of the cupboard and filled it with water and set it down, then returned to the camera, the minute was up. In the next minute I went in, took the coffee tin from the shelf, put several spoonfuls in the appropriate part of the percolator, replaced the tin. Next minute, put the inside into the perc., set it on the stove and switched on. And so on.

Some minutes I just stood by the camera and almost *felt* the time going by, *participated* in the flowers opening. I was especially conscious of the character of the light minute by minute. Characteristics of time and lighting would bring a feeling of essentially similar atmosphere elsewhere – Orkney, Dal Lake, and so on. There was a particular feeling of identification of place with place and participation because of the exactness with which I was observing the time passing. Watching the light acutely because of my exposure for one thing.

I remember how determined I was some time in my childhood to really see the clover closing up, feeling sure that if I kept on looking I couldn't fail to see, and being disappointed because I never did but putting it down to the fact that I never had the patience to keep on watching, not perceiving how the movement could be imperceptible.

(Cf. T.S. Eliot 'I have measured out my life in coffee spoons'!)

Incidentally, the piece of film exposed was not satisfactory. I think more than once a minute would have been better.

A CROFT AT CHRISTMAS

Katharine Stewart, 1950

When Katharine Stewart and her husband Sam had a child, they decided it was time to leave Edinburgh, where they ran a small hotel. They bought a 100-acre farm in Abriachan, in the Highlands, a thousand feet above Loch Ness, and with their three-year-old daughter moved into a cottage with neither running water nor electricity. Stewart's weekly column in The Scotsman *about the crofting life was soon published as* A Croft in the Hills *(1960). There is a rose-tinted tone to much of her writing, but this perhaps reflects the joy she took in her new surroundings as much as a wilful attempt to romanticise what was undoubtedly a tough existence. Seeing the speedy erosion of the old ways of life in the Highlands, she commandeered the village hall and established a croft museum, to preserve what was soon to be lost.*

All that month winter fretted at us. There was little we could do outside but repair fences between the storms, but we carried several fallen tree-trunks down on our shoulders and cut them with a cross-cut saw. On the fine days we would work away at the chopping and splitting till the sky faded to mauve and clear shades of green and gold came up about the setting sun. Every morning, when I opened the door, I would find two out-wintered Shetland ponies waiting patiently for their bite of bread. They belonged to a distant neighbour and one day we had taken pity on them and given them some crusts. So every morning, till the spring grass came, they would be there to greet us at the door.

In the evenings we made plans and discussed endlessly the absorbing topics of sheep and cattle, hens and pigs, fertilisers and farm-machinery and crops . . .

On Christmas morning the plumber arrived to try once more to connect the pump. He had walked the two miles from the bus and was quite tired out when he reached us and amazed at the wintry conditions in our hills. In Inverness, he said, there had been promise of a reasonably mild day and he had had hopes of getting the job done. We have now come to accept this sort of thing. We leave home on a bitter winter's morning and find spring, with a flush of green in the trees, at Loch Ness-side. It's not the distance of two miles that does it but the rise of close on a thousand feet. There was little he could do, the plumber decided, so he shared our Christmas dinner and set off again to walk to the bus. At dusk we lit the candles on our little Christmas tree and played games with Helen till bed-time.

There was a party for all the children of the district in the village hall, to which we took Helen. We met her future teacher and a dozen or so lively youngsters. There were games and songs and a piper and there was tea and cakes and oranges and sweets. It was a simple little festivity but a very happy one. Everyone asked kindly how we were faring. 'It can be fearful wild here in the winter', they said, almost apologising for the climate in their hills. 'We like it', we said, and they looked at us out of their clear, shrewd eyes and I think they almost believed us. We began to feel that we nearly belonged.

On New Year's Eve we sat by the fire talking, as usual, and when midnight came we filled our glasses and slipped upstairs and pledged each other over Helen's sleeping head. We went down again and got out the black bun and some extra glasses and put fresh logs on the fire. We thought it more than likely we should have a neighbour for a first-foot. Distance would not daunt the people of Abriachan, we were sure, and the night was fine.

We sat till two o'clock, getting drowsier and drowsier. No one came and we went to bed. At about three-thirty we were dragged from the depths of sleep by what sounded like an aeroplane crashed outside the front door. We fumbled our way into heavy coats and staggered out, to find three neighbours clambering off a tractor. There was much handshaking and back-slapping. We poked the fire into a blaze and drank a toast. Later we helped them to remount and stood at the door, watching the tractor lurch off on its way to the next port of call. How the two passengers managed to keep their precarious balance, draped over the rear mudguards, will remain for ever a mystery. But we were immensely cheered by their visit and went back to bed and slept till the middle of the morning.

DAY ONE AT THE NATIONAL
LIBRARY OF SCOTLAND

Margaret Deas, 1951

The fact that Margaret didn't do well in her Highers was not the reason she didn't go to university. Young women, even if they were academically gifted, rarely saw further education as an option open to them. Educated at James Gillespie's School for Girls – later immortalised by Muriel Spark as the Marcia Blaine School for Girls – Margaret observed that the National Library was full of former pupils. Going to work in a library was a popular route for bright and bookish school leavers. Some places were more encouraging to newcomers than others, and the National Library of Scotland – in those days almost Soviet in its augustness – was never one to offer a warm welcome, whether to staff or readers. On being offered a post as a typist ('the lowest of the low'), Margaret requested a holiday before she started. Years later she could not believe her cheek.

The first day was awful; this great big place: silent, and a grandfather clock went tick-tock – Sir Walter Scott's, incidentally. There was three steps down into this great big room, and I went in and it was so quiet! But there was a young girl I recognised because she was three years above me at school. That was when the Library had the books in the Laigh Hall – all these bookcases with wire on them, a great big coal fire and old Giles, the messenger. Then these men appeared with black gowns and a white wig who had their offices in the Library along that corridor. You couldn't distinguish the National Library from the Advocates use of it. It was very 19th century.

There was a kettle, we made tea and there was Donald Brown and Bob Burnett just sitting there. Then we had to take the cups away and they said, 'We go down to the vaults, through the drill hall and then we go to L.' And I'm going, 'Vaults! Drill hall! Hell!' The wash-hand basins in the ladies' toilet was where we washed the cups. By half past eleven I'm sitting with my legs crossed; I'd just come from school, and you couldn't ask to go to the toilet in school, you had to wait. By the time I got out for lunch I was desperate. I ran along to the ladies' at the Infirmary!

❧

AN ITALIAN SCOTTISH WEDDING
Mary Contini, Edinburgh, 1952

The arrival of Italians in Scotland in the late nineteenth century revolutionised the menu, bringing fish and chips and home-made ice-cream, and opening northerners' minds to a country of delicious food and magnificent scenery and art. In the early 1920s and '30s the numbers rose as Italians from the poorest parts of the south and north-west fled in search of a better life. They integrated easily, but on the outbreak of World War Two, the internment of many as potential enemy aliens came as a shock, even though the links between Mussolini's fascisti and certain groups in Scotland were obvious. Worst of all was the sinking of the Arandora Star in 1940, whose passengers included more than 700 Italian and almost 500 German internees and eighty-six German prisoners of war, en route to internment camps in Canada. Over 800 drowned. But by the 1950s, war was over, and life improving. While the Scots-Italian community was fairly self-contained, its shops introduced Scots to more appetising fare. Alfonso Crolla was the co-founder of the first and now renowned Italian delicatessen in Scotland, Valvona & Crolla in Elm Row in Edinburgh. In an atmospheric family memoir, his grandson's wife Mary Contini vividly evokes that upbeat time. Alfonso's daughter Olivia was engaged to be married, and had been taken by her widowed mother, Maria, and sister Gloria to choose a wedding dress. Jenners in those days was considered the most upmarket department store in Edinburgh, and it took courage as well as money to enter its doors.

Maria and Gloria were waiting, perched precariously on a low sofa in the wedding salon in Jenners department store.

Miss MacDonald, the head sales manager, was displaying a beautiful couture wedding dress, fanning it out over the white Axminster carpet, gently stroking her hand down the duchess satin to indicate the luxuriousness of the fabric.

'Mrs Crolla, I'm sure this is exactly the style that will suit your daughter perfectly.'

'*Che dice*, Gloria?' What is she saying?

'She says this dress will suit Olivia. Mum, wait till you see it on.'

'There are a selection of co-ordinating bridesmaid's dresses, matching shoes and fur boleros as required.'

'*Che dice?*'

'She wants to sell us the dresses for the bridesmaids as well.' Gloria looked longingly at the fabric.

Miss MacDonald smiled as sweetly as she could at Mrs Crolla. Maria sat with her back as straight as possible, her black hat established firmly on her head and her long black coat with the mink fur collar equally firmly closed. She had an imperious-looking black handbag on her lap and an even blacker umbrella furled and planted resolutely in front of her, protecting the bag and its contents.

She was ready for action. Miss MacDonald assessed her adversary. She looked extremely warm in her winter coat ('1949, end of season sale,' she whispered to her assistant).

She cleared her throat.

'Mrs Crolla, may I take your coat for you? Can I offer you a glass of champagne?'

'*Che dice?*'

Gloria conveyed her mother's answer to Miss MacDonald. 'Just the champagne, if you don't mind.'

Miss MacDonald signalled to her assistant, who approached with a tray of Edinburgh Crystal glasses and a bottle of Moët & Chandon lodged in an elaborate silver ice bucket. Maria accepted her glass.

'Mrs Crolla, we can prepare a wedding list for your guests to choose gifts which we can deliver to your address directly.'

'*Che dice?*'

When Gloria translated for Maria, she laughed rudely out loud. '*Che* "wedding list"?'

Miss MacDonald looked a little startled. Gloria nudged her mother, 'Shh, Mum!' Mrs Crolla was well known in the Model Gown department at Jenners. This exclusive room was at the end of the grand balcony, behind imposing brown leather doors. It had been managed by Miss MacDonald for the last fifteen years. She was an immaculately dressed, tall, elaborately coiffed lady, a practised sales manager; authoritative in her assessment of her clients. With her personal team of top sales girls she showcased the new couture lines from the Paris and London fashion houses, made even more desirable every season by the impact of the beautiful young princesses, Elizabeth and Margaret, and the glamorous film stars on screen. Now that clothes rationing was ending, the department store was anticipating a boom in sales. The continual challenge for Miss MacDonald was to use every trick she could to prevent any clients walking along to the rival stores in town, R. W. Forsyth's or Patrick Thomson's. This had to be avoided at all costs.

For this reason she was astute enough to pay particular attention to the Italian women in Edinburgh and Glasgow, who were potentially good clients. She was well aware that the younger generation liked to dress well and impress each other. And, over the last few years, they had developed a habit of holding big parties: baptisms, first Communions, engagements. They kept themselves to themselves, but there seemed to be a fair enough number.

Mrs Crolla visited the department regularly, at least once a month, ostensibly to see the new fashions arriving. She was of a size and age that firmly put her 'model' looks behind her, but she looked to buy well-made black garments in a size for the larger woman. She was a shrewd purchaser and invariably bought only during the final days of the annual end-of-season sale and, notably, paid in cash.

Mrs Crolla's daughters were more promising clients. Young Miss Olivia Crolla came in often with the new Mrs Brown, a much-valued customer who embraced the new fashions with great enthusiasm.

An Italian wedding would be a great opportunity to attract the young socialites from Glasgow. They were far easier to encourage to spend money, and definitely had plenty to spend. They frequented Fraser's in Buchanan Street, which was serious competition. Miss MacDonald was aware she had to maintain a good level of service and competitiveness at all times.

Maria drank the champagne; Miss MacDonald was clever enough to keep her glass topped up. Maria couldn't really understand all this fuss for a wedding. It was a major outlay. Each one of their relations had to be invited, including those in the main Italian families in Glasgow and other cities. They had to think about their customers, keep them happy; and the church as well. There would be at least six priests at the wedding. You had to cover all angles. In all, looking at the list so far, they had over 200 guests to feed and entertain. And that wasn't counting the children and the cousins. That looked to be an additional 100 guests for the evening reception.

Maria could not help but reflect on her own wedding, all those years ago. Growing up in Italy in the tiny mountain hamlet of Fontitune, she had known Alfonso all her life. She was betrothed to him for as long as she could remember but, because he was always away, they didn't marry till she was twenty-four.

It seemed unimaginable now, but Alfonso had fought in Abyssinia, had brought her to Scotland and then fought again in another war in the north of Italy in 1914. It was tragic that he had died so young, but he had packed a lot of life into his fifty-two years . . .

Miss MacDonald noticed Mrs Crolla looking distracted. She rushed across with the champagne and topped up her glass.

'She won't be long now, Mrs Crolla. We are just getting the right shoes. Your daughter has a large foot.'

Maria looked up. She hadn't understood a word of what the lady had said. Miss MacDonald was concerned at the unhappy look on her client's face.

'Oh no, that's it. I've blown it! She's insulted that I mentioned her daughter had big feet!'

Oblivious to the concerns of Miss MacDonald, Maria drank the champagne, getting even hotter in her mink-collared coat.

Gloria popped out of the changing room. Her mother was quite flushed now.

'Mum, are you all right? We won't be long now.' Maria nodded. As young brides usually do, Olivia had lost a lot of weight and her figure was very slight. Miss MacDonald had measured her height, back, bust and waist and declared her 22-inch waist Paris model standard. She went to the changing room to check how things were progressing and opened the door with a flourish.

'She's nearly ready, Mum. Wake up.' Gloria nudged her mother. Maria had dropped off to sleep, lost in her thoughts.

Miss MacDonald held open the door of the changing room to allow Olivia to come out. Even she was impressed.

'Miss Crolla has the perfect figure; she could be on the front cover of any magazine.'

Olivia stood in front of her mother. The dress was full-length ivory duchess satin with a three-foot train. It had a Queen Anne neckline with a high collar behind her slender neck and a modest lace sleeve, narrowed elegantly to her wrist.

The ivory satin shoes gave her just enough height to carry off the gown. Olivia had longed to be married in an ivory duchess satin gown ever since she had seen the Princess Elizabeth walking down the aisle to marry Prince Philip. Standing here in front of her mother she felt as beautiful as a princess herself. When it was her turn she would walk down the aisle to marry her own Carlo, who would look even more handsome than the prince.

She looked at her reflection and twisted to see how long the train looked at the back of the dress. It extended at least halfway along the floor. The tiny white buttons down her back were each covered with lace and the edge of the train was embroidered with lace and small luminous pearls. She couldn't believe it was herself looking back from the mirror.

'Oh Mum. Isn't it just lovely? Gloria, what do you think?'

'Mrs Crolla, congratulations. It's the perfect gown for her. Just perfect.'

Miss MacDonald couldn't have selected a better gown. The ivory satin complimented Olivia's complexion, the high neckline framed her face and her dark, thick hair was an exotic mysterious contrast to the satin. Miss MacDonald was thrilled.

'These Italian girls are real beauties,' she thought, slightly envious. Then she glanced at Mrs Crolla and consoled herself. 'But their looks don't last that long!'

Maria saw Miss MacDonald look at her and knew exactly what had crossed her mind.

'*È bella*,' she admitted. '*Ma quanto costa?*' It is lovely. But how much is it? When the reply came, Maria answered with an outraged '*Che dice?!*'

Carrying a parcel of seven yards of ivory duchess satin, four bobbins of thread and a paper pattern from Patrick Thomson's, Olivia cried all the way home. Gloria felt so sorry for her sister. It had been very embarrassing when her mother, on hearing the price of the dress, had stood up, shouted something rude at Miss MacDonald and stormed out of Jenners, leaving poor Olivia in floods of tears, trying to get untangled from the dress.

A NEW WAY OF TRAVELLING

Jess Smith, 1953

Born into a family of travellers – her own mother, Jeannie, was born in a tent – Jess was the fifth of eight children, all girls, and spent her young life moving from place to place in Scotland and England, as her parents found work. She was five when her father, Charles Riley, transformed the way his family lived. Not for them the horse or wagon of bygone days. He had something more modern in mind.

After a brief spell living in an articulated wagon, Daddy purchased our new home – a 1948 Bedford bus! My bus was created in the same year as myself.

Mammy was far from happy at the thought of her proud lassies crammed like sardines in a bus. The older girls were horrified, and the wee ones were neither here nor there. Except me!

There was Baby Babsy newborn, two-year-old Renie, three-year-old Mary, then me. I was five years old and even as I write I remember well my feelings of excitement at living in a BUS.

A forever holiday. I was going home, something way deep in my young soul knew; here was my destiny, the road ahead had already been made for me by generations of travelling folks. I was about to be reborn into the old ways.

To me, my Daddy was the inventor of do-it-yourself. No matter what – building, electrics, plumbing, you name it – he could do it. Cleverest pair of hands in the whole of Scotland, I kid you not. We were living temporarily in a converted wagon at Walkers field outside Pitlochry. It was September 1953, and Mammy had just that very month given birth to my youngest sister – Barbara, her eighth child, and all girls.

I remember that day so well, the day he drove off Finab road end and onto the field with the bus, he looked so small inside it. My first memory of the inside of the bus was neat rows of seats covered with Paisley-patterned material. I watched as my Dad unbolted every seat and piled them outside, leaving an empty shell. What fun I had jumping up and down on those springy benches with the flowery purple covers.

'Mammy, it's going to look terrible, living in that thing, Daddy's lost his senses.' My oldest sister Mona had been used to living in houses; she thought of the travelling life as a way of the past, and a touch below her! . . .

'Give me over another nappy, this wind will have all the washing dry in no time,' said Mammy, ignoring her daughter's haughty remarks . . . Her turning to see me leaping high in the air on her future furniture brought a volley of curses.

'Jessie, get you off those bloody seats, your father's putting some of them back into the bus, and look at the state you've got them in with your guttery shoes! Now do something useful and play with your wee sisters.' . . .

The long seat at the back of the bus was left in place, with bolts and brackets added, allowing it to be converted into a double bed. They christened it 'the master bed', and it was the coorie doon of my parents. Next a sideboard was placed at the bottom right-hand-side of the bus. This took all dishes, pots, pans and cutlery. Our bed was placed lengthways on the left, and like the big one it had brackets fitted so it could be doubled up during the day into seating. But if ill health like measles or mumps visited then the big bed was left down. Of course in such times it became quite a squeeze to get past us. The two seats at the front were left in place, along with the one for the clippy, and as Mammy said jokingly she was the equivalent of a bus conductor she bagged this one. It was really so she could be navigator for Daddy, but we knew fine it was the seat with the best view.

❦

THE LONG JOURNEY TOWARDS MYSELF

Jo Clifford, 1954

Playwright and performer Jo Clifford was born in Stoke-on-Trent in the early 1950s, studied Spanish and Arabic at university, and earned a PhD in the dramatic works of Calderón. She was named and brought up as a boy, but knew from a very early age this was not right for her. It was only after years of making a life and raising a family in Scotland that she could act on her lifelong struggle. Here she describes the long journey towards becoming herself.

All I knew when I was a child was that the frightened bewildered boy I saw in the mirror was not me. I really doubted that perception because I could make absolutely no sense of it and did everything I could to deny it.

I was born in the nineteen fifties, and it's hard to imagine how different life was then. There was no mention of trans issues anywhere. Even words like 'transgender' did not exist. So neither my parents nor myself had any means of any kind of understanding my experience. All I knew to do was to try to keep it secret and live as if it didn't exist.

But that got harder and harder as I started to want to play with girls' toys, wanted to play and be with girls (I didn't really like being with boys) and then was sent to all-boy boarding schools. I had three brothers who were much older than me and no sisters. And then my mother died when I was 12 years old. So I grew up desperately in need of the company of women and girls.

I started to be given women's roles in school plays and it was then I found my vocation for the theatre. I also understood how much I loved dressing as a girl. How much that made me feel happy and at ease with myself. But that discovery also deepened my shame and my fear and my intense distress. I felt that inside me I carried this terrible secret that was so terrible that if anyone knew I would die of shame.

I tried to reconcile myself to the thought that I would always be alone.

When I was seventeen I began living in Scotland. I was working as a volunteer in a mental hospital in the Borders and met a psychiatrist who lent me a book called *Childhood and Society*, which mentioned the existence of Two Spirit people among the native American peoples. And for the very first time I understood that I was not alone in the world. That there had been, and perhaps even still were, societies that accepted the existence of people like me and even honoured us and gave us a place in the world.

That saved my life. That, and the fact that by then I knew I was a writer. That was something that allowed me to live in the imagination and gave a focus and an ambition and a meaning to my existence.

My vocation had been blocked by the shame I felt as an adolescent, and I spent twenty years trying to be a novelist. Which I absolutely am not. It wasn't till 1985 that I found my voice as a playwright; and I only rediscovered my vocation as a performer another twenty years after that.

And I fell in love. My partner, Sue Innes, was a writer too and we stayed together for 33 years until her untimely death from a brain tumour in 2005. She was the very first person I came out to. When we had our children we were resolved to share childcare. We literally divided the week in half, and each took one half for childcare and one half for work.

And that meant I was our daughters' father and mother and I loved that. And I wore women's clothes when I wrote and I became the female characters in my plays and the world around was opening up too. But if you asked me at that time whether I was a man, I would have said no; and I knew I wasn't a woman either, because I was living as a man, and that increasingly distressed me.

On my fiftieth birthday I came out to my friends as 'bi-gendered'. I felt it important as a man to recognise and celebrate the woman who was also inside me. I stopped buying and wearing men's clothes, though without trying to present myself as a woman.

Soon afterwards I started to have breakdowns. I began to feel with agonising intensity that I was 'in the wrong body'. Luckily, a gender specialist had begun working in the NHS in Edinburgh, and I was able to see her and begin the long process towards living as a woman.

Soon after this process began, Sue developed the symptoms of the illness that was to kill her. The horrible thing about living in a transphobic society is that it affects not just yourself but also those you love. Sue suffered as I did, and it is a sadness that she died before the issue could be fully resolved.

Once she had gone, living as a man became absolutely impossible. I was full of fear and the deepest grief; but began to present myself to the world as a woman.

Scotland in 2005 was not a welcoming place. My journeys down the street were zig zag affairs as I kept crossing the road to avoid dangerous situations – queues at bus stops, groups of teenage boys or girls, men smoking resentfully outside pubs. People would laugh in my face or shout insults or talk about me as if I wasn't there. I remember once in Glasgow two women stopping dead when they saw me and one saying 'O my god that's a man!' as if I was the most disgusting thing she had ever seen.

I kept writing. I kept taking the hormones. I tried to recover from open heart surgery. I saw the two psychiatrists that I needed to see to get permission to have gender reassignment surgery.

I had assumed at that time I needed to go through this surgery, which involves the surgical removal of all male genitalia and the creation of a vagina. It's a massively invasive operation that can have unpleasant side effects and when confronted with the reality of it I realised I didn't need to put myself through it.

All I needed was an end to the hormone warfare between the female hormones I was taking and the male hormones my body was producing. So I opted for a simple procedure called an orchidectomy and was recovered in a week.

Somehow, miraculously, that stopped the abuse.

I was a bit too preoccupied to notice this at the time, however, because I was performing a show I had written that imagines Jesus coming back to earth as a trans woman. This opened in Glasgow in 2009 to demonstrations in the street outside the theatre, and a torrent of denunciations from the tabloid press and from people all over the world.

The press mocked me as a 'sex swap playwright'. But I have never swapped sex. I have never even changed my gender. All that has happened over all the years is that I have gradually begun to accept who I am and then live this openly.

Our world only accepts the existence of 'men' or of 'women' and since I cannot live as a man I have to live as a woman. But who am I? When I was given the award of being one of the 'Ten Outstanding Women in Scotland of 2017' by the Saltire Society, many angry feminists wrote to tell me in the most insulting terms that I am a man. I know I am not a man, but whether I am 'truly a woman' absolutely does not concern me. I live as a woman, and it completely suits me. I feel comfortable in my skin.

At the time of writing this, in the spring of 2018, I have just spent the last fortnight rehearsing and performing in an art installation in the Tramway as part of the Glasgow International Art Festival. 'Dark Continent: Semiramis' was created by Tai Shani and I was one of the twelve women inhabiting her creation, which is a representation of the City of Women first conceived by Cristine de Pizan in the fourteenth century.

And of course I belonged there. In the post-patriarchal world that is slowly and painfully and convulsively being born. And that we women are creating together.

NO. I CATTERLINE

Joan Eardley, 1954 and 1958

One of the shyest students ever to attend Glasgow School of Art, Joan Eardley was also one of the finest. In her too-short career, she overcame the prejudice women artists faced, from a male-dominated profession and from society, who did not consider art a suitable occupation for females. Famous even in her lifetime for her rumpled Glasgow urchins and roaring seascapes, her work has been likened by critic Eric Newton to Goya and Turner: 'Like Turner, she paints as though the brush were an integral part of her personality that found no difficulty in expressing, in a kind of shorthand of its own devising, the way to say "cloud" or "tangle of grass" or "mop of hair".' Catterline, the name of the village near Stonehaven where she found her home, is now synonymous with her. Eardley had a long-standing love affair with Audrey Walker, whom she met in 1952, and who was married. They were close until Eardley's death from cancer in 1961, at the age of forty-two. Shortly after arriving in her cottage on the clifftops – No.1 Catterline – Eardley wrote to her.

Catterline, 1954

Dear one – It's night. And the fire is giving a great flickering light – and lamplight too – It's a great wee house. The floors are all levels at once. And the table 3 tany [tan-coloured?] boards nailed together – There's a great big bed half wood and half spring. A Grannies pot, a bucket, a basin, and that's about all, except for 3 lovely wee chairs which the old buddy next door handed to Angus [her friend and model] last time. Really beautiful wee chairs.

I wish you were here – It's a bit rough yet – but I think a few things here & there, & then I would feel that you would be safe enough – Angus has taken his chair & his cup of tea to the doorway – & is sitting looking out to darkness, & to sea.

I've pinned up your wee photo.

Are you all right – my own?

I won't be able to write very much tonight – but I wanted to speak to you a little before I go to bed – And the postman comes tomorrow at 10.30.

I think I shall paint here. This is a strange strange place. It always excites me . . .

Dear one –

Good night – I do love you –

14 February 1958

The snow has been blizzarding down nearly all day – (What you had when you were here was just nuffink!) It is piled up against the door in great drifts, & even out of drifts it is easily a foot deep. Anyway in between blizzards it has been so much just what I wanted for my painting – that stupidly I imagined I could rush out & in with my canvas – You know what a job it was setting up that canvas at the back of the house. Well I've had it 3 or 4 times to do – & undo in the teeth of the gale. I gave up after I think the 3rd time might have been the fourth – chiefly because of the length of time that I actually had in which to paint was so brief – mostly only about 1/4 hr at the most before the onset of the next blizzard . . . You really need to be tough for this game . . .

The snow will certainly lie over tomorrow – so I hope I shall get some more peaceful working times. Angus will help me out with my easel, etc., in the morning – but you see he won't be here the rest of the time. This morning he anchored my easel with a real anchor [she adds a drawing of this]. Certainly effective – in fact I have left the easel outside anchored & half buried in the snow –

❧

JEAN REDPATH WOWS NEW YORK

Robert Shelton, 15 November 1961

Folk singer Jean Redpath, from Elie in Fife, was born in 1937, studied medieval history, and left for New York in early 1961. She was to live in America for the rest of her life. In Greenwich Village she shared a flat with Bob Dylan, Jumpin' Jack Elliot, and the Greenbriar Boys. She is thought to have had a relationship with Dylan. The friends slept on an apartment floor, and of those days Redpath recalled, 'I nearly blew a gasket blowing up so many of those rubber mattresses'. With an extensive repertoire of ballads, modern folk tunes and songs by Robert Burns, she would write to folklorist Hamish Henderson, begging him to send her arrangements and recordings of specific songs. 'I'll educate these foreigners yet!' she told him. When she performed late in 1961 at Gerde's Folk City, the New York Times's *critic Robert Shelton was taking notes. His review set light to her career, so much so that years later, the* Edinburgh Evening News *wrote that to call her a folk singer was 'a bit like calling Michelangelo an Italian interior decorator'.*

The Scottish visitor is Jean Redpath, a big raw-boned, apple-cheeked, radiantly healthy girl. She is appearing at Gerde's Folk City . . . Miss Redpath would charm an audience with her repertoire alone – some 250 songs, enough to keep a ceilidh (jam session) going for days. These include luminously poetic folk ballads from plowman's shacks, moth-music with which Scots supply their own accompaniment for dancing reels and strathspeys, songs of Robert Burns, and a round of drinking, bawdy, lyric-love and children's songs . . . Her voice is a clear, rich, beautiful mezzo-soprano, sure-pitched enough to sustain unaccompanied numbers such as a seal-charmer's song . . . Although Miss Redpath has no connection with the Scottish Tourist Board she is a resolute boaster of her land, its history, customs – and music.

GANG MEMBERS

Lulu, c. 1961

One of Glasgow's more dubious claims to fame is the number and virulence of its gangs. It's a blight that gathered momentum in Victorian times, but as recently as 2006, Strathclyde Police identified over 110 gangs, spread across the city. Young women have often been drawn into these groups as girlfriends and sometimes accomplices. Pop singer Lulu (Marie McDonald McLaughlin Lawrie), then in her early teens and already making a name as a singer, did not criticise her younger brother for going around with gang members, because she recognised there was little option. The culture of violence these thugs inspired ruined many people's lives, whether they wanted to be part of it or not. As Lulu indicates, you had to be tough to survive in the districts where they roamed. Like others, she was always on her mettle.

This sense of fear and relentless tension didn't just belong to me. It was something that Glasgow seemed to instil in people. If somebody brushed against you in the playground you immediately spun around, with fists raised, ready to fight. It was a survival mechanism – an instinctive response to our environment.

My father used to say, 'If anyone starts anythin' wi' ye, make sure ye get in first. Hit them wi' everythin' yer've got and make sure they don't get up. If they do – run like fuck! It means they're tougher than you are.' This advice applied to girls as well as boys.

The streets where we lived were in between the areas controlled by the Tongs and the Monks – two of the city's notorious gangs. I knew the gangs existed but I chose to ignore them. It was more a male thing, although the Shamrocks had a lot of pretty girls in their gang.

[My brother] Billy became involved when he was about ten, but he never became firmly entrenched. One guy called Whitey, who lived around the corner from us, was with the Tongs and also the Mary Hill Fleet. Billy played football with him and he was at school with me. Whitey was only small but very tough. He normally carried a weapon, either a knife, an iron bar or an axe.

One Sunday evening Mum and Dad wanted ice cream. They sent Billy out to the shops, but on his way back he was beaten up by two guys from one of the gangs. They slapped him about and warned him he could expect worse.

Billy was in his smart suit with his wee tie. He came back with blood on his face and with his clothes creased and dishevelled. I saw him before Mum and Dad did.

'What's happened to ye?'

He wouldn't tell me.

'C'mon, Billy, tell me who did this t'ye?'

He shook his head. 'Tell me! Was it Whitey? Did he do this? It was him, wasn't it?' I was already halfway down the stairs. Billy was yelling after me, 'No, no, no.' I wouldn't listen. He tried to catch up with me. My blood was up. At that very moment Whitey happened to walk around the corner. I grabbed him by the throat and pushed him up against a wall. 'If you did this Ah'll have you,' I said.

Billy arrived. His face went white. 'It wisnae him, Marie,' he stammered. 'Let 'im go . . . please.'

Whitey had an odd grin on his face. If I had known how tough he was, I might have thought twice about taking him on, but they were all tough in those days. I also knew that Whitey had a soft spot for me.

'Here's what Ah want,' I told him. 'You go wi' Billy and find out who did this. Make sure they never touch him again. Is that clear?'

Whitey nodded.

Billy's attackers were two leaders of the Shamrocks, Burnie and Lightbody. Whitey took Billy down to Whitevale Street and told him to wait. A little later he brought Burnie and Lightbody along.

'Ah'll hold 'em doon, while you kick fuck out a them.'

'Ah cannae do that,' said Billy. 'They'll kill me.'

'Don't you worry about them,' said Whitey. 'They won't be touching anybody.'

On the streets of Glasgow, this is how problems were sorted out. I didn't look at Whitey and see a tough, axe-wielding psychopath. He was just some-body I grew up with. He was my pal. I really liked him.

❦

WHO DO YOU THINK YOU ARE?

Janice Galloway, early 1960s–70s

Novelist Janice Galloway was brought up in Saltcoats, and never allowed to forget it. Her account of becoming a writer despite the barriers she faced is a savage indictment of a repressive culture that saw signs of creativity or originality as getting above oneself. This punitive outlook blighted countless women's ambitions, and proved far deadlier than Cyril Connolly's famous opinion, aimed squarely at men, that 'There is no more sombre enemy of good art than the pram in the hall.'

When I was very wee I didn't read at all. I listened. My mother sang Elvis and Peggy Lee songs, the odd Rolling Stones hit as they appeared. These gave me a notion of how relationships between the sexes were conducted (there were no men in our house), the meaning of LURV (i.e. sexual attraction and not LOVE which was something in English war-time films that involved crying); a sprinkling of Americanisms (to help conceal/sophisticate the accent I had been born into and which my mother assured me was ignorant and common) and a basic grounding in ATTITUDE (known locally as LIP). This last, was the most useful one. In fact, the only useful one. The words to BLUE SUEDE SHOES are carved on my heart.

I was reading by the time I went to primary school. I know because I got a row for it. Reading before educationally permissible was pronounced SERIOUSLY DETRIMENTAL TO HER IN CLASS. This was true because I had to do it again their way, with JANET and JOHN and The DOG with the RED BALL. Books were read round class i.e. too slow, and you got the belt if you got carried away and keeked at the next page before you were allowed by the teacher. WHO DO YOU THINK YOU ARE? she'd roar, SOMEBODY SPECIAL? Dulling enthusiasm, or at least not showing it, became an intrinsic part of my education. This did not trouble me. I was a biddable child. Most are.

At home, I read OOR WULLIE and THE BROONS, the BEANO and BUNTY. BUNTY was best because it had girls in it. There was Wee Slavey (the maid with the heart of gold) and the Four Marys (who went to boarding school) amongst others. They had spunk. Only the former seemed a role model, however. I also read Enid Blyton Fairy Tales and Folk Tales of Many Lands, a whole set in the local library. When the Folk Tales were finished, I began fingering the Mythology Religion books on the adult shelves whereupon the librarian (Defender of Books from the inquiry of Grubby People and

Children) smacked my hands and told me I wasn't allowed those ones: I would neither like nor understand them and was only SHOWING OFF. This was another lesson in the wisdom of hiding natural enthusiasm because it sometimes annoyed people in authority. I ran errands to the same library for my nineteen-years-older sister who read six books a week and hit me (literally) if I brought back books by women authors. WOMEN CANNY WRITE, she'd say: CAN YOU NOT BLOODY LEARN? She was afraid, I think, of Romance. Other hitting offences included asking to watch A Midsummer Night's Dream, keeping a diary and, mysteriously, 'reading too much'. Words, it seemed, carried pain, traps, bombs and codes. They were also, alas, addictive. Nursing bruises, welts and the odd black eye, I blamed myself. Earlier than I learned to do the same thing with sex, I learned to look as though I wasn't doing it at all and became devious as hell . . .

Secondary school proved my sister uncannily perceptive. Women couldny write. There were none, not one, not even safely dead ones like Jane Austen, as class texts. On the plus side, they encouraged reading, largely on the grounds you could pass exams with it. You could only pass exams, though, with books from the school store, which meant the aforementioned no women and not much that was Scottish save Burns who had the added benefit of being useful for school suppers which girls might attend if they served the food. This troubled me a bit, but not oppressively. I was good at exams. I passed everything, though what to do then seemed a mystery to all, especially Head of Girls who told me I'd never get far with an accent like mine, and why I wanted to go to University was anybody's guess. Actually it was the Head of Music's idea. With treacherous speed, I fell away from books and fell in love with MUSIC because nobody had told me (not yet anyway) that women canny compose. The Head of Music became my Bodyguard and my sister and the Head of Girls couldn't say boo because he was a teacher. He taught me MOZART was pronounced MOTZART and not as spelled on the biscuit tin at home. He taught me lots of things. Through third to sixth year, I hoovered up Purcell and Byrd, Britten, Warlock and Gesualdo (my sister's example meant I wanted nothing to do with something called Romantic music, even if it was by men) and sang folk songs. These were not pop songs. They had better words and led me by a sneaky route to Opera. Opera! It was unbelievable! In my final year, the Head of Music gave me a copy of *The Prime of Miss Jean Brodie*, my first book by a living Scottish author. Read, he said. Learn. And he talked my mother, mortified in her school dinner lady overall, into letting me fill in the Uni forms. The day I left, I turned up at school in trousers and got sent home. This did not trouble me . . .

In three years of MA I read less than two Scottish authors and two women, all dead. My music list seemed not to know women or Scotland existed at all.

There were no folk songs. In my third year, I cried a lot and everyone was very nice. They let me have a year out. I was, I realised with intense embarrassment, suffering from a broken heart. I went back and finished the fastest degree they had only because someone called the Student Advisor said, GIRLS OFTEN GIVE UP, IT'S NOTHING TO BE ASHAMED OF. Books were bastards. I could no longer listen to music. There was only one thing for it. Teaching.

On teaching practice, I turned up at school in trousers and was sent home. This troubled me a bit but it wasn't new. I could handle it. Eager as a squirrel, I taught happily for ten years. I got into trouble for not taking my register seriously enough and teaching stuff outside the syllabus to the 'wrong' age group some-times, but the children were very forbearing. I was a good teacher, the Head informed me one day, but not promotion material. He wasn't sure why. Maybe I needed my wings clipped. I thought he had a point. I wanted to stick with this job. I enjoyed the children, their enthusiasm and inventive cheek. I did not like the book shortages but teaching was fine. I still cried off and on and took to writing the odd poem, but wary I was heading down the primrose path of SHOWING OFF all over again, concealed them as much as I could. Occasionally I caught myself gazing down the stairwell, at the bland, blank walls. One day, a propos of nothing, I caught myself glaring at a child. WHO DO YOU THINK YOU ARE? a voice roared, terrifying from the back of the classroom. SOMEBODY SPECIAL? And the voice was mine. This troubled me a lot.

Bizarrely, it led me to reading. I re-read the curious woman who had writ-ten the equally curious BRODIE, then everything else I could run to ground. I read Carver and Kafka. I read Duras and Carter. I read Machado de Assis and Mansfield and Carswell and Borges and Woolf and chewed up national anthol-ogies of stories – any country's – whole. I fell over Gray's big book about Glasgow that is also a big book about everywhere, and something clicked, not just from Alasdair's work but from everybody's. It was the click of the hereto-fore unnoticed nose I'd just found on my own face. It was astounding, a revelation. For the first time since I learned how to pronounce MOZART, I realised Something Big. I had the right to know things. Me. I had the right to listen, to think; even godhelpus to join in. A tentative glimmer of freedom started squirming around beneath the sea of routine shame and I remembered being another way. I remembered being wee. I remembered the Saltcoats Library and the living room fireplace. I remembered Elvis. And I knew three things. I knew:

a) that all Art is an act of resistance;

b) that the fear of SHOWING OFF would kill me if I let it; and

c) the words WHO DO YOU THINK YOU ARE? stunk like a month-old kipper.

My mother was dead.

I had not seen my sister for years.

Reader, I started writing.

ADOPTION

Jackie Kay, 1961–62

Poet and novelist Jackie Kay stood out in her hometown of Bishopbriggs from the start, and not just because of her outgoing personality. A black child in a very white society, she was adopted by staunch Communist parents, John and Helen, who refused to lie to the adoption board and say they were regular churchgoers. As a result, their hopes of finding a baby of their own looked slim, until a chance remark changed everything.

After my parents finally got accepted by the Scottish Adoption Agency, and found a lovely woman who they felt was on their side, they went to a meeting where they were asked more questions. On the way out of this meeting, my mum remarked, and it was an almost casual, throw-away remark, 'By the way, we don't mind what colour the child is.' And the woman said, 'Really? Well, in that case we have a boy in the orphanage; we could let you see him today.' And if my mum hadn't thought to say that, just as she was leaving, my brother might have remained in the orphanage for the rest of his life and so might have I, because having one 'coloured child' they decided to adopt another, to keep him company, which was forward-thinking, I see now looking back, for the sixties. 'To think they didn't even think to mention Maxie to us,' my mum says, still outraged at this, 'that he wasn't even thought of as a baby.' . . .

My parents took my brother home on the 18th September 1959. They always remember the day they got him home because it was the same day as the Auchengeich Colliery Disaster, when forty-eight men lost their lives. 'It was terrible. Just dreadful! And when the anniversary of that came round, I always remembered that was the day we got our Maxwell home.' My mum's father had been a miner from Lochgelly and had twice been buried alive down the pits, and twice survived, and she had grown up in a house full of miners. She remembered being offered a penny for washing the backs of her mining uncles when they sat in the steel tub bath, and how by the weekend they would also ask for their penny back to go dancing . . .

Shortly after the day they brought my brother home, a minister arrived at my parents' house. "'I've heard that you've done a kind act and adopted a coloured child," he says to me,' my mum said. "'We at the Church just wanted to know if we could be of any assistance," as if he were thinking of you both as noble savages. I sent him packing,' my mum told me, 'I'll tell you what's savage, the Scottish Presbyterian Church!' I don't know if this really happened, the minister on the doorstep, or if it's apocryphal, but my mum used to insist that it did, though I also know that I have inherited, if inherited is the word, and perhaps it is, her gift for exaggeration . . .

A couple of years after they adopted my brother, my mum had a call from the same woman at the Scottish Adoption Agency. 'There's a woman who has come down from the Highlands, and the father of the baby is from Nigeria. We thought we'd let you know since you told us you wanted another child the same colour.' So, months before my birth mother gave birth to me, my mum knew that she was going to have me. 'It was the closest I could get to giving birth myself,' she's told me often. 'I didn't know if I'd have a girl or a boy, if you'd be healthy or not, the kind of thing that no mother knows. It was a real experience. It felt real. I remember waiting and waiting for news of your birth and phoning up every day to find out if you'd been born yet. Finally, I was told you had been born, you were a girl, but you were not healthy. And they advised me to come in and pick another baby, because you weren't expected to live. The forceps had caused some brain damage, and also left a gash down your face. The brain damage still shows,' my mum said, laughing. I like hearing this fairytale; I've heard it often. My mum wouldn't pick another baby; she'd become attached to the idea of me in the months of ghost pregnancy, where she'd shadowed my birth mother in her own imagination, picturing, perhaps, her belly getting bigger and bigger. She already felt like I belonged to her. She visited every week, or every month, depending when she's telling the story, driving the forty miles from Glasgow to Edinburgh, with my dad, and she had to wear a mask, so as not to infect me, and got to pick me up and hold me. Perhaps this interest, this love, is what made me survive against the odds. The doctors were apparently amazed at my recovery.

Then after five months she was finally allowed to take me home. My brother was told they were going to collect his baby sister, and he was excited about it, my mum said. 'And protective from the word go. He'd guard that big navy Silver Cross pram, and if anybody peered in, he'd announce that you were his sister. We had to feed you a special diet – it worked! by Jesus, it worked all right! – porridge and extra vitamins, to build up your strength. A few weeks later, the woman from the Agency rang again saying your birth mother had requested a baby photograph.'

'Did she?' I asked.

My mum nodded. 'She did . . . But I never heard anything back. I know that they sent it on because she was reliable that woman, and kind. A while later I received a wee knitted yellow cardigan for you in the post that had been knitted by your birth mother.'

'You did?'

'I did,' she nods.

'I don't remember you ever telling me that before.'

'No? Probably just forgot. Maybe I've even made it up. Maybe I thought she should have knitted you something. You get all mixed up with what's the truth and what's not. I know she went back up to the Highlands. She lived with her grandmother. I imagined she'd been encouraged to have her baby adopted, put it that way. It wouldn't have been the norm in those days, a black man with a white woman. It must have been a hell of a lonely journey back to that wee Highland town of Nairn. I was told her address there was Ivy Cottage.'

When I was seventeen and my mum was the age I am now, we went on a wee holiday, just the two of us, staying at various B and Bs in the north of Scotland. We passed through Elgin and into Nairn. 'Why don't we try and find that Ivy Cottage, just to see,' my mum said, excitedly. 'We can do our Columbo.' We went into a red phone box and looked up the surname Fraser. We found so many Frasers it was staggering, Fraser the butcher, Fraser the baker, Fraser the plumber, but only one that lived at an Ivy Cottage. 'You hide behind the corner, in case they see you,' my mum said. Then she knocked at the door, and said she was looking for an Elizabeth Fraser, that she used to nurse with her. (She'd known that my mother was a nurse.) 'Whoever answered the door wasn't very friendly,' my mum told my dad when we got back to Glasgow.

'And no bloody wonder,' my dad said, angrily. 'That was irresponsible of you. What if it had been her? What might you have walked straight into? You don't know what kind of can of worms you might have been opening.'

My mum shrugged as if my dad's response bored her. 'We thought we were playing at being detectives,' my mum said, as far as she was concerned it'd all just been a bit of fun, and he was being a real stick in the mud.

'You're out of your mind!' my dad said. 'And having Jackie hide round the corner! Honestly, Ellen! Who knows what could have happened?'

'But there was definitely something she wasn't telling us,' my mum said. 'She knew an Elizabeth Fraser, that's for sure. She was hostile. Why should she be hostile? All I was doing was saying I used to work with an Elizabeth Fraser, nothing more.'

'You're a stranger on her doorstep. Naebody likes strangers on their door-steps, least of all folk with something to hide,' my dad said and hid behind his

Morning Star in a fury. My mum rolled her eyes at me. I was her accomplice and her daughter. We had both wanted to find my mother just out of curiosity, we told ourselves. Neither of us had given proper thought to what might have happened next had my birth mother answered the door. My dad was right, we'd acted irresponsibly, it was a trail we were on, but we hadn't seriously considered where it might have ended.

STALKED IN THE CORRIDORS OF WESTMINSTER
Winnie Ewing, 1967–68

Winifred Margaret Ewing's triumphant return as SNP MP in the Hamilton by-election in 1967 was greeted with fanfares, and has been credited as the starting point for Scottish devolution, and the rising fortunes of the SNP. Her famous catchphrase, 'Stop the world, Scotland wants to get on' continues to resonate. Yet when she reached Westminster, and the noise of the pipe bands and cheering crowds faded, the reality was less thrilling. From the outset, Ewing encountered fierce sexism and heckling, notably from the likes of Willie Hamilton, Labour MP for Fife: 'I must have been second only to the Queen on his personal hate list. Tam Dalyell, however, ran him a close race in terms of abuse, though, being Tam, he was always a little more gentlemanly. Norman Buchan, Hugh Brown and Archie Manuel were also particularly offensive.' But their jibing was never personally threatening and she grew used to comments such as 'The Honourable Lady should be on at the London Palladium' or 'The Honourable Lady should see a psychiatrist'. There was one individual, however, who behaved in a decidedly sinister manner, as she describes here. Although coping with all this took a toll on her health, Ewing prevailed. A couple of years after the events described here, the Speaker told her that he thought no one in the history of the House of Commons had been treated the way she had 'day after day, week after week'.

I was under constant barracking from Scottish Labour benches, but an important plus for me was the scrupulous fairness of the Speaker, Horace King. Sometimes some particularly obnoxious Labour MPs would try and complain about what they thought was favourable treatment being meted out to me, as I was called quite often to speak. Horace King, totally unruffled, would merely say, 'The House knows my attitude is to be fair to minorities.' He also quoted Winston Churchill on at least one occasion, responding to a Labour member with the words, 'A civilisation can be judged by the way it treats minorities.' I certainly was an expert at being in a minority, for there was only me . . .

I was interrupted whenever I spoke, I was regularly insulted and I was even defamed once or twice . . . I was even stalked by a Labour MP, though as he is still alive I shall not name him. That memory is not one on which I want to dwell too much in any case, because the whole experience was very frightening. The problem started following a speech I made at the Bannockburn Rally when I said the enemies of Scotland were not the English but 'Scots traitors within the gate'. This infuriated some Labour MPs who took the remark personally, though why they should I don't know, unless they had a guilty conscience. One of them seemed to become unhinged by it. I first noticed the problem in the Select Committee on Scottish Affairs. Wherever I sat this MP sat opposite. If I changed seats, he did so also. Then I noticed that he had started to follow me along corridors, appearing behind me without saying anything. It got so bad that on one occasion I stopped dead in the corridor as an old Tory, Boyd Carpenter, went past and complained to him that this man – pointing behind me – was following me everywhere. He was horrified and told the MP to clear off and not do it again. But later I had to complain again in the library, where he sat staring at me.

Emrys Hughes and Willie Baxter, in whom I confided, told me to complain to the Leader of the House, Fred Peart, as it was becoming very disquieting for me. I spoke to Fred after a vote one night and he was very sympathetic and said he would have a word and make sure it stopped. Fred was also very hospitable and after I had told him about it invited me for a drink in his office behind the Speaker's Chair, where he often entertained his staff. I declined as I wanted to go home. Off I set through the dark Chamber and into the Public Lobby to go to the stairs leading to the Members' Entrance, from where I could ring for a taxi. However, as I left the Public Lobby, I saw the door swinging in front of me. I felt afraid but I went on through the door and down the steps, with the sound of my high heels clicking loudly on the stone. As I turned a bend on the stair, there was my stalker right in front of me, looking very sinister indeed. I tried to humour him as I wanted to reach the cloakroom – where there was an attendant – without having anything happening. He kept staring and following me, but I made it and breathlessly told the cloakroom attendant what was going on. Then I rushed back up the stairs to Fred Peart's room, which I must have stumbled into, ashen faced. He just looked at me and immediately realised what had happened, saying sympathetically, 'Not again?' The Leader of the House took prompt action and I got a written apology – and, equally importantly, the stalking stopped.

❧

STAND-UP AND BE COUNTED

Elaine C. Smith, 1970s

Born in Baillieston, Glasgow, in 1958, and qualified as a teacher, Elaine C. Smith soon jettisoned her original career to become a stellar panto dame, and a stalwart of sitcoms and comic sketches with a strong Scottish accent. Her role as Mary Doll, the forbearing wife of Rab C. Nesbitt, assured her reputation as a national treasure. Yet as she explains, given the prejudice of the time, aspiring to be an actress and comedian was the hardest line of work she could have chosen.

I had watched too many movies when that small town girl made it all the way. I was trying to be different and the same all at once – never an easy thing to pull off. To have a showbiz career while staying close to the places and the people that I loved and respected was what I wanted, the drawback was that everything around me kept telling me that I couldn't do it and shouldn't even try.

In reality, we all know that even in the safest, most perfect of lives, things go terribly wrong. Those girls who played by the rules that have now changed, who conformed, who dieted for Scotland and kept their mouth shut must be raging now cos disaster still bloody happens, ladies! Divorce, affairs, cancer and sudden death turn up at the door anyway – life and death are random and no one is ever truly safe. But we all bought it, well, most of us did – and I certainly did for a while. The fantasy of the good life that was peddled throughout my early years, from the 1960s onwards. In every magazine, TV show, advert, by every political party or organisation and by every restrictive practice that existed in all the small villages and towns in Lanarkshire, in beautiful Scotland – land of my birth, my hame!!

Bonnie Scotland. A land with a psyche and soul made up of a heady cocktail that drives its population to drink. A toxic blend of Calvinist Presbyterianism, severe Catholicism, massive ego, even bigger inferiority complex supported by insecurity, all settling within strict boundaries of conformity and general sexism. What a place, with of course a hell of a lot of rain to water it down and make it more palatable. You can get ice too if needs be!

Throw into that formula a city like Glasgow, with all its wonderful madness, violence, sectarianism and poverty – where a sense of humour is a necessity, as well as a great weapon, in the struggle to keep body and soul together. When the wagging finger of the men in authority (from John Knox's statue over the city shouting 'Don't!') told women to 'shuttit!' Not an ideal world for a lippy woman like myself to thrive in, and if truth be told, not an easy world for anyone different – male or female – to thrive in . . .

Though the great irony in Scottish culture is that most women are pretty opinionated but we try our best to hide it, so as to maintain order, and to be accepted and play the game. Well, until we get pished and then the truth spills out and results in a 'rammy'. A favourite gag of mine is the one where the wee boy comes home from school all excited that he has got a part in the school show. When his mother asks what part he's playing, he says, 'I've got the part of the Scottish husband.' His mother is outraged and tells him to get back to the school and 'Tell that teacher to give you a speaking part!' The messages from authority however, and from the powers that be in the late '50s and early '60s, were very powerful about a woman's place, and what and where that should be.

The propaganda from the movies with my idols like Doris Day didn't help either. They sent a very strong message to women about who they were supposed to be. The '50s woman would ideally be beautiful, coiffed and even though she may have had a career, in reality she was just waiting for her man to come along, make her life complete and give all that nonsense up and have babies. Gone were the movies of the '30s and '40s with women like Bette Davis and Joan Crawford who were seen as strong and liberated, untameable and vibrant. In '70s Lanarkshire to me those messages felt just as strong. And in a way they drove women like myself out of our minds. On the one hand we wanted to have good jobs and independence, but on the other we were being told to just love our man.

My heroine was Billie Holiday. I loved what I have since dubbed 'victim songs'. The ones describing how much you love your man and how you will die if he leaves. Lady Day summed it up in the song 'My Man' with ' . . . he isn't true, he beats me too, what can I do?' From my perspective now I would say 'phone the "polis". If he hits you once, he'll hit you again.' But then it just seemed to be that if you sacrificed your very soul it meant you truly loved your man . . .

Men were funny, from Eric Morecambe to Bob Hope, and even though Doris Day could deliver a great comedy performance she always had to get her man in the end. Women just weren't that visible in anything but the 'looks' department. Watching old Doris in *Calamity Jane* one night on telly changed my life. It gave me hope. My dad said, 'This is a great film, doll,' and I thought to myself, 'Aw naw, that means it'll be a cowboy or a war picture with John Wayne or Audie Murphy and I will have to listen to my dad's commentary all the way through telling me details about cowboy life or the war and explaining everything!' My mum maintained that during the '60s and '70s my dad watched so many of these movies that if we took the back off the telly all that would fall out would be horseshit and bullets! My heart sank. But then, there she was, Doris on top of a stagecoach singing 'The Deadwood Stage' and that was it, I was hooked.

I have always had that dilemma within me: the desire to conform on the one hand and then to be irreverent, funny and rebellious. I was the feminist who wore make-up and thigh-length boots, I was the politico on every march from supporting the miners to anti-apartheid and women's rights, who didn't want to offend too much, who wanted to be liked, and who always saw the other point of view. Hopeless! I was the woman who wasn't supposed to have opinions about football, politics and comedy. I was supposed to sit and listen while the men talked – well, a pile of 'shite' – about football, politics and comedy. And God, I have endured hours listening to total 'balloons' talk rubbish about football while the other men all play along, pretending they agree. That assumption that a man is born with his brain genetically programmed to understand the offside rule and a woman isn't drives me insane. It ain't rocket science and if an 8-year-old boy running about a park can understand it then why can't I? I demand the right to talk as much 'pish' about football as men do . . .

Being a woman and funny with lots of opinions about, well, everything isn't easy anywhere. But it's twice as hard in the land of the macho funny man that is Bonnie Scotland.

LOVE IN A COLD CLIMATE

Rhona Cameron, 1979

As a teenager in Musselburgh, Rhona Cameron had relationships with boys, but found girls much more alluring. On a school skiing trip in the Italian Alps, where British school groups converged, she met a Welsh schoolgirl who seemed ideal in almost every respect. She decided to declare her feelings.

She was very beautiful and very mature. We hung out for a while, although I have no idea why because I quite clearly wasn't like her other friends. I should have realised that she wasn't available to the likes of me, because she appeared to have pulled the Italian ski instructor, who was quite old (nineteen), muscled, and constantly wore white lip cream to stop sunburn.

Nevertheless, I suddenly decided I fancied her rotten. I couldn't think of anything else. This was the new crush. It replaced all previous crushes in an instant. She was the biggest thing in my life . . .

As with all the others, I somehow convinced myself that she knew how I felt, and that she probably felt the same way . . . For a couple of days I would go up to her and say, 'I have something very important to say to you, but I can't tell you what it is. It's a very important thing, but I'll tell you another time.' Maybe I was hoping that she'd catch my drift and say, 'Oh, I do hope that you love me, because I love you too.'

The day before we were due to leave I stepped up my campaign by telling her more often – about every twenty minutes or so – that I had something important to tell her.

She may never have learned what it was if I hadn't realised that night, while lying awake thinking of her, that this was my last chance. A ridiculous impulse kicked in and I leapt out of my bed. With everyone asleep and the whole skiing complex dark and quiet, I sneaked out of my room and made my way to hers on the other side of the lodge. The Welsh wing.

I nervously knock on the door. She opens it, and greets me with a smile. This is all going well. In the other two beds, her roommates are asleep. Perfect!

'What was this thing you have to tell me?' she asks as soon as I walk through the door.

'I'm not sure I can tell you now,' I say.

'It's OK, I don't mind. You can tell me.'

'It's very hard to explain. I'm very nervous.'

She seems warm and friendly and understanding. I am convinced she knows what is really on my mind.

'I'd rather write it down on a piece of paper.'

'Fine.'

I get a scrap of paper and a pencil, think for a moment, and write:

Dear Jacqueline, I think you are so beautiful. I have fancied you ever since I first saw you. When we are together, the moments I cherish with every beat of my heart, to touch you, to hold you, to feel you, to need you. There's nothing to keep us apart.

p.s. Can I kiss you now?

I smile as I hand her the note.

She takes it from me and sits down on the edge of her bed, back to me, one long leg folded over the other. Very grown up and womanly.

She takes a long time to read the contents of my note. Maybe two or three minutes. I watch her and prepare myself for the beautiful moment when another warm smile will appear, far warmer than the others. She'll look up at me, reach out her hand to mine, and give it a long reassuring squeeze.

Instead she looks up at me, reaches out her hand to fend me off, opens her mouth, fills her mighty Welsh lungs and gives a long, most unreassuring scream. And she carries on screaming. At the top of her voice. The only other circumstances under which screaming at that volume could possibly be valid would be a rape or a fire. It is definitely an over-the-top reaction to a corny love letter from a small, confused, Scottish lesbian.

SCOTLAND'S WORLD CUP WINNER
Hugh MacDonald, 1984

There is little imminent likelihood of the Scotland squad matching Rose Reilly's record as the only Scottish footballer to have played in a World Cup-winning team. Born in 1955, Reilly played for the Scottish and Italian national teams, and for clubs such as Reims and AC Milan, where she made her name. She is a member of the Scottish Football Hall of Fame and the Scottish Sports Hall of Fame. Yet when she was growing up in Stewarton, East Ayrshire, football was an all-male affair, and girls who wanted to play were chased off the pitch as if they were contagious. Women's football is gradually gaining ground, but those who think it is still taking too long might find inspiration in her attitude to the game.

There is a tattoo in the shape of Sicily on the arm of Rose Reilly. It is a physical, tangible reminder of where her heart lies, but what precisely shaped this remarkable woman must remain mysterious.

The Reilly story has its recognisable signposts on the journey to becoming a great footballer on foreign shores.

There is the three-year-old escaping from mum and finding her way to a football pitch, the seven-year-old pretending she was a boy in a bid to be signed for Celtic, the child swapping a Christmas doll for a ball, the practised player nutmegging an infuriated Lorenzo Amoruso in a bounce match.

But there is more. This is a woman of substance. She gained fame, glory, medals and money by her exploits on the pitch. These include eight *scudetti*, four Italian Cups, a World Cup winner for her adopted Italy and league titles in France. But it is her very character, the strength of her conviction, that is her greatest triumph.

The story of how Reilly went abroad to work and the tale of why she came back is the most convincing testimony to her personality.

At 62, Reilly retains much of her youthful exuberance and all of her determination which may, in terms of her native Stewarton, be described as thrawnness.

But there is a softness, too. Reilly left for professional football because she was carried off by a love of the game. She returned because she bowed to her love of her mother.

Of her early career abroad that started at 17, she says of her exile: 'I used to speak to myself in the mirror at night because there was nobody to talk to.'

Of her return three decades on, she says briskly: 'My mother was sick in hospital. So we flew back home, abandoning my sports shop in Italy. My mum said: "Don't leave me". I didn't. She lived on for nine years and we are still here.'

The 'we' is Reilly's husband, Norberto, and the 'wee miracle' Meghan, the daughter she had 17 years ago.

The Stewarton lassie was a phenomenon. Her career in Italy encompassed Reims, AC Milan, Catania, Lecce and Tranni. She would play with Lecce on a Saturday then fly to France to play for Reims on a Sunday. Predictably, she won league titles with both clubs in the same season.

'I never kept my medals. I always gave them away to guys or women at the side of the pitch,' she says. 'I never dwelled on what I won. I moved on to the next match.'

This is the precise definition of the insatiable winner. But where did it come from?

'It's in my genes,' she says blithely. But its origin is more difficult to divine precisely. Dad was a football fan but not a formidable player, mum had no interest in football. The passion for the game alighted on Rose at three. It has never left her.

'I nearly got burned at the stake,' she says of the reaction in 1950s Ayrshire on discovering a girl who would not substitute a ball with a doll or a football strip for a blouse.

At three, she found the local pitch. At seven, she was playing for the local boys' club, attracting the attention of a Celtic scout. 'The trainer told me I had to change my name and change at home,' she says. 'I scored eight goals one day and there was a Celtic scout. He wanted to talk to me but was told I was a wee lassie and so that was that.

'I just thought: "How can I not play for Celtic?" I was devastated.'

She was an excellent athlete but football was a constant love. 'I was training for the pentathlon but was told not to practise football because it was thickening my thighs. I lasted a week,' she says of a time in her teens.

This passion for football has defined her. But so has the drive to make the most of her talent. With the help of a journalist, she discovered that professional football for women flourished in France.

'I went over to Reims for a trial and I ran riot,' she says flatly but accurately. Within six months AC Milan signed her.

'As soon as I came off the plane, it was like a mother embracing me, I fell in love with Italy,' she says. It was a romance that came with problems. 'There was no communication back home then, no mobiles or email. Phone calls would have been out of the question. It was down to airmail.

'I bought myself a dictionary and I learned three words every day because I thought four words a day would bamboozle me,' she says.

This is an indication of her determination to master the practicalities of life abroad. Her faith in what she could do on the park, however, never required any bolstering.

'Nothing fazed me,' she says. 'I remember walking out on to the pitch at San Siro just after I signed. I walked up to one of the goals and said: "I am going to score in that". Then I walked up to the other end and said: "I am going to score in that". I was mentally prepared. I was physically ready.'

She adds: 'It's not being big-headed. You must have belief.'

This confidence had enough reserves to enable Reilly to conjure up a nutmeg of a young Lorenzo Amoruso, a future captain of Rangers, in a bounce game in southern Italy. 'He was not too pleased and stormed off in a huff after trying to put me up in the air,' she says with a smile.

But this mental and physical strength was needed to take her from Stewarton to the very top of the woman's game and then back to Ayrshire. 'I remember as a kid I had this Stanley Matthews book and I would follow every instruction in it,' she says.

'I used to sleep with the window open because he talked of the importance of fresh air. There was five of us in the one room and my four sisters used to howl at me to close the window as an icy Ayrshire blast came in. I used to tell my mum that I had to have steak too. She would just reply that I would have mince and tatties once a week and get on with it.'

And she got on with it. A peerless professional career was followed by meeting Norberto, a political refugee from Argentina, and setting up a sports shop in Trani. The physical bond with Italy was broken when her mother's illness necessitated a return to Ayrshire.

There are no regrets. 'I am content. I did what I had to do,' she says simply.

She now lives in a Scotland where the women's team can qualify for major finals. 'My thought is that is absolutely fantastic. But there is so much more to be done.

'There has to be more football for girls in primary schools. There is a shocking lack of PE in primary schools and we have to address that. I am so proud that there is a [women's] league in Scotland and of the success of the national team. That is great.

'It is a big, beautiful, blossoming tree but there are no strong roots. If a tree has not got roots it can wither. Get them young, get them interested and take it from there.'

She sips her macchiato and her fingers slip to touch the remembrance of Sicily on her arm. 'I love it still,' she says. She could be talking about football or Italy. She is probably speaking about both.

THE 'OOTLIN'

Jessie Kesson in conversation, 1985

Jessie Kesson was one of Scotland's most admired mid-century writers. Her first and acclaimed autobiographical novel, The White Bird Passes, *published in 1958, was a thinly disguised version of her own early years as the illegitimate child of an occasional prostitute. Born in 1917, and raised in Elgin, Kesson later combined various jobs, including with the BBC, with writing for page and radio and stage. Nine years before her death she agreed to this recorded interview with Isobel Murray, of the University of Aberdeen. Professor Murray has made it her life's work to conduct in-depth conversations with writers as a record for posterity. As a result, Kesson's vivacity, honesty and north-east accent come alive once more. You can see why one acquaintance described her as 'a one-woman riot'. This is all the more remarkable given the stigma attached to those born out of wedlock. As is implied here, it was a prejudice that coloured all her writing.*

21 August 1985. Present: Jessie Kesson, Isobel Murray and Bob Tait [Murray's husband]

Isobel Murray: Jessie, we are anxious to talk to you for our archive because it seems to me that one of the things that future generations will simply not know about you is your voice, and I'd like them to hear it. Anybody who knows anything about you inevitably knows a wee bit about your life, but could you start just by giving us a few minutes about your upbringing – the kind of story that you tell in *The White Bird Passes* really. You were born in Inverness, yes?

Jessie Kesson: Yes, yes, I was born in Inverness. That was a bit o' an accident. I dinna think I was meant to be born in Inverness but you know, as you know, I was illegitimate and in Scotland in those days it was an awfa' thing for respectable folk like fit my grannie and the oe wis, so that my mother obviously took awa' fit they wid cry in those days her shame, and went to the nearest place and went to Inverness. But since this is for the Archives, this is something that winna maiter if I tell you it now, to be used maybe when I'm nae there to care aboot it. I knew I was born in Inverness, but, until I went to the orphanage you know, I was never known as Jessie. I was nine when I went to the orphanage but I was never called Jessie – because I was named for my grannie, and my grandfather objected very much to it being used and it never was used. And my mother – I was aye known as Ness and my mother said, 'You're Ness,' she said. 'Never mind about the Jessie, we'll nae bother aboot the Jessie.' Because obviously when I went to school I had tae hae the two names: she said to forget aboot the Jessie; we're niver to use it! She said, you see . . . she told me that she couldnae use the name. She said, 'Eh, you see,' she said, 'You was born in Inverness,' and she said, 'We'll call you Ness because a town canna object!' So the name Ness was my name. In fact, now I'm beginning to feel a wee bit like Queen Victoria fin Prince Albert died – I don't know if you know what she said and I can well believe it. When he died she said, 'There's nobody left to call me Vicky now!' So I've just about two cousins, one in Erskine and another still up Morayshire and they're the only two that it's always 'My Dear Ness'.

Now, the funny thing about that, the other part of it, Inverness, which is not, never been in biographies or nothing, I really got the address of my birthplace when we went to sit the Eleven Plus, the Qualifying it was called in that days, at the Skene school that I went at, and wanted my birth certificate. And for the first time I saw exactly where I was born. 82–84 Old Edinburgh Road, Inverness. Now, Mrs Elrick, the Matron, her daughter lived in Inverness and every summer she would go there for her holidays. So this particular summer she wis gaun awa' for her holidays to Inverness and I said, 'Mrs Elrick, when you're up in Inverness will you look for my hoose?' Oh, she would look for my hoose. So, back she come, and she had looked for my hoose and she described it – a big house, with a big avenue leading up intil't, and trees and lots of geraniums and a' this – God I wis right set up, wisn't this something! I wis born – and I went aboot cocking up – I wis born in a big hoose, I'm telling the rest of the kids, and of course nobody could gainsay that cos Mrs Elrick said it and she didna tell lees. It really set me up! Well the thing is, I never saw that hoose till I was married, and I got married in Inverness actually; and I thocht I'll hae a keek along and see it, and I saw it. Everything she said was right – it was a big hoose – and there was an avenue leading up till't. It wisna geraniums, it was in the autumn: I think it was chrysanthemums – that was the only difference fae her story – except that she didna' tell me it was the workhouse!

Isobel Murray: Wasn't that nice?

Jessie Kesson: That says an awful lot for her, doesn't it? I realised she knew it was the wrong time to tell me, and she probably realised that when I saw it for mysel it widna maiter, and to be quite honest, it never did! But the only reason that this little part of biography has niver come out is because every time I hiv onything on, and especially wi' my last television play – they emphasise 'prostitute's daughter' and the orphanage, forever this orphanage, and I thought, my God if they only got the ither bit I'd nae hae a life o't at a'. They'd be workhouse – orphanage and everything else! And that is exactly, nae that I'm getting dumpy about that, but I knew that this wid be anither thing – 'born in the workhouse' – that wid be a right added thing. Because none of these things really maiter you know. Nae tae me. It's nae that I've ever been the least ashamed of that. But I thought, God it was bad enough with the orphanage withoot adding a workhouse on top! [Laughs] This is what I thought, and I jist thocht, well I'm nae saying a word aboot it, but now when this ever goes on it winna maiter!

Isobel Murray: And you've never been one for respectability and hiding things. I think your writing is very remarkable for the confessional aspect of it. The way you lay yourself open; you make yourself vulnerable to your readers.

Jessie Kesson: Aye, yes. But the ither thing . . . You know how folk often say – reviewers and thesis writers when they're analysing – (I read two theses on my work already) – and I know that their folk had gane to a great lot o' bother obviously and certainly daen their homework, everything – even my short stories – but I do sit back efter they've come to a conclusion and think God, was that really what I was writing aboot? [Laughs]

. . . But I realised myself what I was writing aboot. At long last. And I'll tell you what it wis. You mightna' agree. But I actually put it in [one of my novels, *The White Bird Passes*] in one line – wi' one of the characters! And I thocht that's it, that's really what everything I've ever written is aboot – queer fowk! Queer afore it had its current meaning. 'Queer fowk, who are oot, and niver hiv ony desire to be in!' Every work I've ever written contains ae 'ootlin'. Lovely Aberdeenshire word. Somebody that never really fitted into the thing.

And that is when I think o' it everything – *The White Bird, The Glitter o' Mica*, Sue Tatt and Hugh Riddel himself, and if you think on even my short stories it's always aboot people who don't fit in!

OPEN CASKET

Sue Black, 1987

Professor Sue Black is one of the world's foremost forensic anthropologists. Her career began with a weekend job in an Inverness butcher's shop. As a student studying anatomy at the University of Aberdeen she spent a year dissecting a corpse and learning everything it had to tell her. Nevertheless, this did not prepare her for the death of her beloved Uncle Willie. She was still a student when he died, and when her father asked her to 'Go and check Uncle Willie is OK' in his open casket, she was filled with trepidation, unsure about what she would find and how she would feel.

The dead are not as they are depicted in the movies by actors lying perfectly still as if in a deep sleep. There is a void in them which serves somehow to weaken the certainty of the bonds of identification. We cannot recognise the person easily and of course the explanation for that is so simple – we have never seen them dead before. Dead really is dead, it is not just sleeping or lying motionless.

My duty should have entailed nothing more than a quick glance into the coffin to verify that the man lying there was indeed my great-uncle and that he was suitably dressed and looking smart, as he would have wanted, before being laid to rest. However, in my youthful enthusiasm to do things properly, I went overboard. I slipped into a pompous analytical mode worthy of Monty Python's Flying Circus. No dead parrot in this sketch, though – only poor old dead Uncle Willie.

Had any of the funeral staff walked into the room they would have questioned my sanity and possibly even have had me escorted from the building for disturbing the peace of the dead. Certainly no other corpse in the history of that highly respected highland funeral home can ever have left the premises with such a rigorous MOT.

First I made sure that he was dead. Yes, really. I felt for a radial pulse at his wrist and the carotid one at his neck. Then I placed the back of my hand on his forehead to check his temperature. How on earth I could imagine he might show any signs of life or warmth after being in the funeral home fridge for three days, I don't know. I noted that there was no bloating of his face, no skin discolouration and no advanced odour of decomposition. I examined the colour of his fingers to ensure that the light embalming fluid had fully taken, and his toes, too (OK, I admit it – I took off one of his shoes). I gently prised open an eyelid at the corner to check that his corneas had not been removed illegally and opened a button of his shirt to rule out any evidence of an improper postmortem incision. I knew one should never overlook the possibility of the theft of body parts. Honestly? In Inverness? Not exactly the epicentre of the international black market in stolen organs. Then, perhaps worst of all, I checked his mouth to establish that his false teeth were in place. Who would have wanted to steal Willie's wallies? One careful owner, free to a good home . . .

Noticing that his watch had stopped, I instinctively wound it up and placed his hands across his large tummy. Did I seriously think he was going to want to know what time it was when he was in the ground at Tomnahurich Cemetery, and perhaps ponder how long he had been lying there waiting? For what? In the unlikely event that he woke up, he wouldn't have been able to see his watch without a torch anyway and I hadn't thought to bring one of those, had I? I moved an errant lock of Brylcreemed hair that had strayed across his face and patted him gently on the shoulder. I thanked him silently for being who he had been and, with a crystal-clear conscience, returned to my father and reported that all was well with Uncle Willie. He was certified fit to bury.

I crossed many boundaries that day, and without much logical justification. Although I look back on my actions with incredulity, of course I understand now that death and grief do strange things to a mind. It had been a first experience for me and I had handled it in the only way I felt I could. And it was an important milestone. It confirmed that I could compartmentalise: as well as bringing compassion to my dealings with the bodies of strangers, I could manage the emotions and memories involved in viewing the mortal remains of a person I had known and loved while accessing the detachment required to inspect him professionally and impartially without falling apart.

In no way did this diminish my grief but it showed me that such a compartmentalisation of emotions was not only possible but permissible. For that lesson, I have Uncle Willie to thank and also my father, who simply assumed that this was a service I was equipped to perform and did not doubt for a moment my ability to do it. And I am glad that I did. My reward from Father was a curt nod of the head that told me he accepted my word. From that moment on, I have experienced no fear of death in the many forms she takes, though I have unquestionably come to respect her.

RUNNING FOR OLYMPIC GOLD

Adrianne Blue, 1988

Scotland's finest-ever woman runner, Liz McColgan, a Dundonian, had proved herself a formidable athlete by taking gold in the 1986 Commonwealth Games in Edinburgh, when she was twenty-two. Crossing the line twelve seconds ahead of her closest rival she was only the third woman to run this distance in under thirty-one minutes. In future years she was to win countless races and set as-yet unbroken Scottish records, among them gold in the 10,000m 1991 World Championships, and three marathons, including her debut in New York City. Nothing matters more, however, than an Olympic title. In 1988, in the inaugural Olympic women's 10,000m race in Seoul, there were justifiably high hopes of her performance. After losing closely to Norwegian star Ingrid Kristiansen in Rome the previous year, but beating her just three months earlier in Oslo, McColgan felt she now had her measure. As she crouched in the starting blocks, it seemed likely that she would soon be celebrating another gold medal.

As they stood on the start line, Liz's face fell into its characteristically dour pre-race pout. She looked miserable, but she was just concentrating.

The world champion looked all right and was as usual wearing white cotton gloves. They were not to keep Ingrid's hands warm, they were to wipe away the sweat of her brow. Liz had no intention of letting her get away this time as she had in Rome. But no matter what happened, Liz planned to run her own steady race, regardless of anyone else's tactics. Ultimately the tortoise, she believed, would prevail over the hare.

As the race began Liz tucked into fourth place, behind the world champion. The pace at first was leisurely, 75-second laps, even one of 77 seconds.

On lap six, looking stiletto-sharp and with no sign of injury, Kristiansen made the break, a fast 69-second lap carrying her away from the pack. She seemed every bit her speedy old self.

Remembering Rome, they tried to catch her. Two laps later the German and the two Russians were gaining, but certainly not overtaking, when suddenly Kristiansen jolted to a stop. Wincing with pain, her right foot having truly given out, she stepped gingerly off the track and was carried away on a stretcher.

Kristiansen's unexpected departure left Kathrin Ullrich the unwilling race leader by ten metres. With no other option, the twenty-one-year-old Berliner who had won bronze at the World Championships now put on the steam, upping her lead by twenty metres.

On her tail were the two red-vested Russians. But Liz, still running her own race, was slowly but surely closing on the three of them. She passed the Russians and caught the big German just before the halfway mark of the race.

With 5,200 metres to go Liz was leading the two Russians staying in spiking distance right on her heels, Ullrich worn out and trailing.

Running from the front is the hardest way to win a race. But Liz had no intention of letting anyone past now. Knowing that she would be unable to outsprint either of the Russians to the line, for they both had better kicks than hers, she ran steadily but slightly faster on each lap. If she could make the race pace too fast for her pursuers' comfort, if she could get too far away for them to be able to make up the ground at the end, the gold would be hers. She wanted it badly.

The 10,000 is a gruelling distance to race at, and she ran the next dozen laps at a gruelling pace. It was lonely at the front of the field, even with the Russians crowding her.

With three laps left, Liz put in a 73-second lap – fast since they had already come a long way. That burned off the most dangerous of the two Russians. Yelena Zhupiyeva, the world silver medallist, dropped back and settled for Olympic bronze.

Only Olga Bondarenko followed. With the whole track available to her, Bondarenko ran in Liz's shadow, almost in Liz's vest. It was intended to be intimidating, and it was. The dark-haired, twenty-eight-year-old European silver medallist from Volgograd had a powerful physique. Her strength, allied with that other asset, her lightness, were a dangerous combination. Bondarenko stood a mere five foot one inches and weighed in at a scant six stone six. She looked bigger. She ran bigger too.

Liz tried to shake her off, but she couldn't go any faster and she could see that Bondarenko knew it. But it is never over until it is over. As the Russian kicked past Liz on the last lap, Liz tried first to go with her, then tried to catch her, pumping her legs and slashing the air with those pointed elbows in an effort to propel herself forward faster, but her muscles wouldn't respond. She had nothing left.

Liz had done all the work of the race, had seemed on the point of winning the Olympic gold medal, only to be cruelly demoted on the very last lap to silver.

[Her coach, John] Anderson appeared from nowhere, putting his arm around Liz's dejected shoulders. The photograph of Liz that would go round the world depicted an athlete's calvary. An Olympic silver medal, people would tell her over and over again, was something to be proud of . . .

Liz would soon speak of her second place in the Olympics as the moment she had arrived as a top world contender. It was. But some part of her would regard it for ever as a great disappointment.

❦

DON'T LOSE THE JOY OF LIVING IN THE FEAR OF DYING
Maggie Keswick Jencks, 1993

When garden designer Maggie Jencks was diagnosed with breast cancer, she was appalled at the thoughtless and rushed manner in which she and other patients were treated. After being informed she had cancer, for instance, she was asked if she would mind taking a seat in the busy corridor. When the disease returned, and proved incurable, she was encouraged to keep a journal. An honest and emotional account of her last two years, it in time became a blueprint for her visionary ideas. Maggie died in 1995, at the age of forty-three. The following year her architect husband, Charles Jencks, put in train the plans she had been working on until the day before she died. The result was the first Maggie's Centre, at the Edinburgh Western General. It was revolutionary in design and ethos: a place where patients and their families and friends could find professional practical and emotional support, and also a sense of peace. It set a standard for cancer healthcare, and since then, twenty Maggie's Centres have been built in the UK and abroad. They bear testimony to one woman's determination to leave the world a better place.

Hospital waiting areas could finish you off
In general hospitals are not patient-friendly. Illness shrinks the patient's confidence, and arriving for the first time at a huge NHS hospital is often a time of unnecessary anxiety. Simply finding your way around is exhausting. The NHS is obsessed with cutting waiting time, but waiting in itself is not so bad – it's the circumstances in which you have to wait that count. Overhead (sometimes even neon) lighting, interior spaces with no views out and miserable seating against the walls all contribute to extreme mental and physical enervation. Patients who arrive relatively hopeful soon start to wilt.

Waiting time could be used positively. Sitting in a pleasant, but by no means expensive room, with thoughtful lighting, a view out to trees, birds and sky, and chairs and sofas arranged in various groupings could be an opportunity for patients to relax and talk, away from home cares. An old-fashioned ladies' room – not a partitioned toilet in a row – with its own hand basin and a proper door in a door frame supplies privacy for crying, water for washing the face, and a mirror for getting ready to deal with the world outside again. There could be a tea and coffee machine (including herb teas) for while you're waiting, and a small cancer library, as well as BACKUP and other leaflets, for those who want to learn more about their disease.

More ambitiously there could be a TV with a small library of cancer-informing tapes and, to cheer you up, a video laughter library. Norman Cousins' book, *Anatomy of an Illness*, makes a good case for laughter not only as escape but as a therapy to relax the patient physically, leading to less pain and better sleep.

At the moment most hospital environments say to the patient, in effect: 'How you feel is unimportant. You are not of value. Fit in with us, not us with you.' With very little effort and money this could be changed to something like: 'Welcome! And don't worry. We are here to reassure you, and your treatment will be good and helpful to you.' Why shouldn't the patient look forward to a day at the hospital?

Above all what matters is not to lose the joy of living in the fear of dying. Involvement in one's own treatment is an empowering weapon in this battle. I believe it will be proved in time to make a difference in mortality, but meantime there is a reasonable body of evidence to suggest that patients who eat healthily, keep active and take steps to deal with stress and fear, feel fewer symptoms and less pain even in the final stages of their disease. At a complementary cancer care conference at Hammersmith hospital, a young girl spoke of how her mother had continued aerobic and dance classes to within a few weeks of her death, delighting in remaining fit and virtually pain-free – 'She was,' said her daughter with real happiness and pride, 'so well when she died'.

I have no deep illusions of long survival. My chemo-remission, if I perform according to the median, is likely to end in about six months. As the surgeon who put in my Hickman line reminded me, early warning of further metastatic activity is not known to prolong survival. But if the next AMAS [anti-malignin antibody serum] test shows positive again and the map we've made so far no longer works, there are still other things to try – and most of them work maybe twenty per cent of the time. Choosing the less expensive (no point in bankrupting my family), those that least disrupt how we want to live, and as many of them as possible, I mean to keep on marching, down the tail of the statistical curve and on, into the sunset, and then, when eventually I must die, to die as well as possible.

❧

RAPE

Helen Percy, 1995

The Church of Scotland prided itself on ordaining its first woman minister in 1969, thereby proving itself more liberal-minded than many Christian churches. But for one minister, no liberality or compassion was shown when scandal broke. After one of her congregation raped her – and admitted it, both to her and his wife – Helen Percy found herself on trial by Kirk and media. She also felt she had no choice but to have an abortion. Unable properly to defend herself, she was obliged to resign her post, thereby appearing to be the guilty party. It was one of the most unjust and unkind decisions the Kirk has made in modern times, leaving Percy, who had been sexually abused by her father throughout her childhood, alone to fight her corner. A long battle to win a case for sex discrimination ended in victory in 2006, though the sum the Church was obliged to pay her – £10,000 – was paltry and insulting. Today, Percy makes her living as a shepherd. The title of her memoir, Scandalous, Immoral and Improper, *is taken from the Kirk's judgment upon her.*

1st December 1995
I am feverish. My head hurts if I turn on the pillow, and my bones ache. I've left the door undone since crawling out to throw food to the animals. You couldn't do that in a town. Here, neighbours know just to come in. Gigha barks if someone knocks first, but wags her tail if they let themselves in.

I don't want the soup Moyra has sent up with Sandy. I call out to leave the pot on the cooker. He puts his head round the bedroom door to see if there is anything else I need.

'Just boiled water, please.'

Sandy puts down the mug of water.

Then, unbidden, he sinks down on the side of the bed.

Resisting, or leaping away from him, is no more an option than it was when I was a child. I do what I learned to do then: hold my breath and black out.

All I ever recall of those early incidents was 'waking up' with a great weight on top of me struggling to breathe again. I absented myself mentally until it was all over. Afterwards, I couldn't remember what had happened. It was as if I hadn't been there . . .

Now I experience the same dissociation between mind, sensation, and memory. I am paralysed. I can neither move nor feel. A switch trips in my brain. It is the reaction of the deer at the moment its predator seized it. From then on it feels no pain. It isn't dead but it seems so. The lion tears at its flesh but it does not quiver.

Sandy goes to the door. 'That was just a bit of rape wasn't it?' Strange words and an embarrassed apology. I don't answer. I should feel anger. I am numb . . .

Was I raped? There wasn't violence. But there was violation. There is not a bruise on my body and yet the dynamics of the power between us were unequal. I believed our relationship was 'safe'. I held affection for him and trusted him. He has experience of life. I am a young woman, still peculiarly childlike at times. He is old enough to be my father and is a 'ruling elder' in the church. Though a minister, I have not taken up the authority generally associated with that role.

Conversations with dozens of women come back to me: 'It's not the first time I've had sex when I didn't want it,' I hear one friend saying, 'but I could hardly go to the police and say I was raped.' Another, 'There's nothing different about me from millions of women. You don't even have to have been abused in the past in order for this to happen. Most of us have had the spirit knocked out of us some way: all of us as girl children have been brought up to be obliging and nice to people and say, "Yes" to whatever's wanted of us.' A third. 'He was my husband. Rape within marriage was still legal in the last decade.'

A terrible keening sound rises from the depths of my being.

DUNBLANE'S DARKEST DAY

Kareen Turner (with Peter Samson and Alan Crow), 13 March 1996

Nobody will ever forget the hour when news came of a shooting in Dunblane Primary School in Stirlingshire. A disgruntled former Scout leader, Thomas Hamilton, entered the school gym and gunned down a primary one class of four- and five-year-olds. He killed sixteen children and their teacher, before committing suicide. The worst mass shooting in Britain, it will go down in history as one of the most cowardly massacres ever known. The horror and pointlessness cannot be put into words, but the experience of Kareen Turner and her family is a reminder of who, and what, was lost that day.

The morning of Wednesday, 13 March, was typical of most in the Turner household. Kareen and husband Willie were up first, anxious to get a head start before waking Megan and her little brother Duncan. They were both working that day. Kareen, a trainee nursery nurse, was starting a week's placement at Borestone Primary School in Stirling. Willie was getting ready for work at Kareen's dad's electrical business in Dunblane.

Breakfast television was babbling away in the living-room, but there wasn't time to watch it. Too much to do. Kareen began pouring out two bowls of cereal for the kids. It was 8 a.m. Time to get them up.

Megan jumped out of her top bunk, brushing aside the mini-mountain of teddies and soft toys. Her school clothes were on the radiator as usual. She loved to dress herself in the morning, although sometimes mum would give her a hand if she was a bit slow.

She pulled on her blue polo shirt, wriggled into her new grey pinafore with her cardigan on top, and put on a bright red pair of tights and a pair of Pocahontas socks. She bounded down the stairs for breakfast.

'I think we were running a bit late that morning,' recalled Kareen. 'We all had to be out of the door by 8.30 a.m. and it was a real rush to get Duncan ready to go next door to our childminder, Amanda.

'Mornings are usually pretty eventful in our house. There's always some-body moaning or chirping away about something or other.'

There was snow on the ground that day and it was pretty cold, so Megan put on her coat and her special Batman wellies before leaving the house.

'Megan got the bus to school and she would usually meet a couple of her pals outside the house and walk with them to the bottom of the road. That morning they came out of their front doors just as Megan was leaving.

'I remember shouting to her that she would have to hurry to catch the bus, as she was a little late leaving the house and she and her two friends were dawdling a bit going down the road. She'd been going to school on the bus since her second day there. On her first day I took her in the car, but on the second she was adamant she wanted to go in the bus, so I let her, but I followed in the car, parked near the school and spied on her just to make sure she was all right.

'Megan loved school, but it was always a big secret with her. You never really knew what was going on at school because she rarely told you. "We did nothing at school today," she'd say. She was in the second-top reading group and she had a new reading book home with her that week. I've still got it in a drawer somewhere.

'She loved drawing and colouring in. She was always drawing people. She would draw me, her dad and Duncan.'

Once Megan had got on the school bus, Willie left for work and Kareen ran next door to Amanda's with Duncan.

'I was due to start work at 9 a.m., so after I put Duncan next door, I drove to the school in Stirling. I was working with a Primary One class that morning, helping the teacher. I remember we were doing some printing work.

'I remember thinking there was something unusual going on because the teacher had left the classroom a couple of times. Around 11 a.m. the class teacher, Mrs Devine, came back into the classroom with the head teacher and they asked me to come with them. I remember thinking: "I've done something wrong. I must have made a mistake." Looking back now there was definitely something strange going on that morning because the school secretary had come in to sit with my class at one point, and that was very unusual. They'd obviously been trying to find out information all morning.

'They took me into the teachers' room and told me there had been a shooting at Dunblane and that it was a Primary One class that was involved, but they couldn't find out any other information. They said they thought it was a gym class and I was sure that Megan didn't have gym that day, but I couldn't remember.

'I went to the office to phone, but all the numbers to Dunblane were engaged. I remember what went through my mind when I realised that Megan may have been at gym. I just thought: "Oh my God, it will be Megan. She would be up there at the front. She would have been jumping about doing somersaults and cartwheels. She'd be in full view." One half of me was saying, "It's impossible, it can't be"; the other half realised she would be there doing her handstands and cartwheels out in the open. I just thought: "No, it can't be; no, it can't be." My head was spinning with all these thoughts and possibilities. It was a nightmare . . .

'It must have been around midday and as I drove to Dunblane I remember thinking that the roads were incredibly quiet. It should have been busy at that time of the day.

'It was strange, but I never thought to put the radio on. I was just intent on getting to Dunblane. I had to get to Megan.

'When I arrived in Dunblane, I jumped out of the car and asked the guy behind me: "Have you got a mobile phone? I have to phone. There's been a shooting in Dunblane." He said: "I know. Everybody knows." I just kept on thinking: "This is terrible. How could anything like this happen in Dunblane?"

'At that point I just knew there had been a shooting, but I didn't know there had been children injured or killed. Then I saw someone I knew and I shouted over to her and asked her what was happening. She shouted back: "It's okay. Megan's okay. It's Mrs Mayor's class."

'She thought Megan was in another class. She didn't know Megan was in Mrs Mayor's class.

'My heart just sank. My stomach was churning. It's hard to describe what was going through my head. I just couldn't take it in. It was just so unbelievable.

'Then I saw someone else I knew and I just screamed at her: "It's Megan's class. It's Megan's class."

'I drove on to get nearer the school. I stopped a policeman and said my daughter was in Mrs Mayor's class. He told me to get up to the school as quickly as possible on foot.'

When Kareen arrived at the school, Willie and her mum were already there. They were taken the short distance to the school staffroom, along with the other parents.

'The room was noisy, but it wasn't hysterical noise. It was incredibly calm. People were just trying to find out what was happening. My mum had heard that 12 children had been killed and others had been injured. She was saying this, but I wasn't really taking it in.

'It was like a bad dream. We just weren't getting any information and people were getting angrier and angrier. I just kept thinking: "Where's Megan? How is she? Is she hurt?" I just wanted to be with her. They kept us waiting for so long. All sorts of things were going through my mind. The ministers who were there just didn't know what to say to us.'

Then support teams comprising policemen and social workers took families away from the staffroom one by one to tell them the grim news.

'I find it hard to describe what it was like in that room waiting for your name to be called out. Not knowing what you were going to be told. Hoping for the best, but fearing the worst.

'When our name was called we were taken to the school music hut. The policewoman asked us to sit down. She held my hand and told me Megan had been killed.

'Strangely, I felt anger. I was angry that I'd been kept waiting for so long. I was furious that it had taken them hours to tell me my daughter had been murdered.

'I just wanted to see Megan. I wanted to be with her, wherever she was. If she was still in the gym, I wanted to be there. I just needed to be beside her.'

The distraught couple returned home to prepare themselves for the ordeal of formally identifying Megan's body in Stirling Royal Infirmary's Chapel of Rest.

'She looked as if she was sleeping. I touched her. She was cold. I didn't want her to be cold. I don't remember saying anything to her, but I probably did.

'It had been such a long, long day we just wanted to get back home again. We were numb . . . so numb at everything that was going on round about. We just sat in the house, stunned. We had the news on and we found ourselves watching what had happened to US. We just couldn't believe it. Only hours earlier we had waved goodbye to Megan as she went for the school bus. Now it just didn't seem real. It felt like we were in a dream. How could this happen here? We could see pictures of Dunblane on the news, pictures of the school . . .

'But it did happen. We'd been to the school and we'd gone to identify our child, but it still didn't seem like it was really happening to us.'

BARBIE IN THE MOSQUE

Leila Aboulela, 1997

The daughter of Sudan's first female demographer, and brought up mainly in Khartoum, Leila Aboulela became a writer after she married and moved with her husband to Aberdeen in 1990. She has since won several awards for her fiction. Her Muslim faith informs much of what she writes, as in this snapshot of a sometimes confusing multi-cultural and pluralistic society.

I grew up in Khartoum where there were no Barbie dolls. Now in my house in Scotland there is Action Man and Biker Mice for my sons, no doll with long hair to comb. So when I see Barbie in the mosque I pick her up and hold her on my lap, rest my back on the wall, and smooth her hair. It's the month of Ramadan, it's a Saturday. Everyone has broken their fast and we are now waiting for the Isha prayers. The doll belongs to Aisha's daughter, who is play-ing with my son and the other children. They run around in the free space of the prayer hall, no furniture to bump into, nothing in the way except us women sitting on the floor.

Aisha puts the tea tray near me. The cups tinkle when the tray hits the carpet. Then she is off to yell at a child or change another or mop up the kitchen floor. She is always marching around doing things or making sure that things get done. The men in this mosque are afraid of her. 'Brother, . . .', she would start her complaint and in alarm they would stare down at the ground, subdued under her voice. I look at Barbie's face, her cheekbones, the way her hair sticks up from her scalp and then falls. Her body is hard; I remem-ber my dolls back home, soft and malleable.

I hear the children and the blur of Turkish; one woman is breast-feeding a huge baby, the other has a mole on her cheek. They are louder than the

Bengali woman and her sister. I can understand neither Turkish nor Bengali and this soothes me. It is as if I am a child, too young to understand what my mother is saying to her friends. I want to braid Barbie's hair; I split it into three parts.

'You haven't given anyone tea,' Aisha glares down at me, hands on her hips. Her denim dress reaches her ankles. She is wearing a scarf with blue and red flowers. It covers her hair which is blonde and straight down to her waist, like Barbie's.

I put Barbie away and start to lay the tea cups in a straight line. Aisha sits on her heels and pours the delayed tea. 'Laid-back Leila,' she sighs.

'Serene,' I say, 'not laid-back, serene.'

She rolls her blue eyes up to the ceiling. She is not fooled; I can't hide my faults in this place. The light is too bright and we are pared down, without our shoes, without chairs to lift us off the ground.

Outside is a city that knows little about us. Outside is a Europe uneasy with our presence. Outside they speak in a different way. Enter a newsagent, pick up a paper and read: *It is ironic that most British converts to Islam are women, given the widespread view that Islam treats women poorly.*

I try and imagine Aisha before she became a Muslim. Long hair swaying under the disco lights of Glasgow. She was a Catholic then. Things she said to me; she was closer to her step-mother than to her real mother, she had a boyfriend, a mechanic who one day walked in angry from work and wiped his hands on her pink mini-skirt – black grease marks that made her cry.

Yesterday, Aisha and I took our children and their friends to the park. Flowers on her daughter's dress, a Barbie umbrella. I sat on a bench and watched Aisha and the children play ball. Aisha running, black head-scarf, long coat, and me mesmerized by the children; Sudanese, Lebanese and half-Bengali, speaking in the Scottish accent of Froghall and Tillydrone. 'It's his turn now,' Aisha shouted, her smile that needed no lipstick. She had never been outside Britain, not once, yet she was closer to the world than those who go abroad On Holiday every year.

We've passed the tea, I've finished braiding Barbie's hair and now Aisha sits next to me. 'You must have been real pretty when you were young,' I say.

She frowns. 'I was banned from a baby competition, I kept winning every time.'

I laugh because she makes beauty sound like a burden.

'But when you were a teenager,' I say, 'when you were older, it must have been nice.'

'No', she says, guarding some pain, guarding stories she hasn't told me. 'No, it wasn't nice.'

'But you must have got loads of attention,' I persist. 'Lots and lots of admirers?' My questions reveal my sheltered background, my curiosity about this friend, who is so unlike me.

So she tells me what is worse than a mechanic rubbing grease on her short skirt. She tells me about neglect and about crime. I listen, the doll slight in my hands, as if I'm not carrying anything. I listen wishing she were exaggerating or not telling the truth. She speaks until we hear the azan and then it's time to stand up and pray.

STANDING UP TO SECTARIANISM
Cara Henderson, 1999

In 1999, high-profile lawyer Donald Findlay QC was filmed singing 'The Sash', a provocative anti-Catholic song, and had to resign from the board of Rangers FC. It was a sharp reminder that sectarianism, the bigotry between tribal Catholics and Protestants – often expressed by rivalry between supporters of Rangers and Celtic football teams – is not confined to the uneducated or criminal classes. In response, nineteen-year-old student Cara Henderson wrote a passionate denunciation of Scotland's scourge in a letter to The Herald. *Henderson was to make her name the following year as the founder of Nil by Mouth, an anti-sectarian charity dedicated to educating young people in particular about the evils of ignorant prejudice. Her motives were altruistic, but also deeply personal.*

St Hugh's College, St Margarets Road, Oxford. June 2.
Dear Sir
Donald Findlay, QC, the former vice-chairman of Rangers Football Club, a man raised to an eminent position in society, has seen in person the devastating consequences of sectarian violence. In 1996, in his capacity as a Queen's Counsel, he defended Jason Campbell, the accused murderer of Mark Scott, 16. Mark, my friend, had just watched his favourite team Celtic beat Partick Thistle, and was walking through Bridgeton in a large crowd of fellow Celtic supporters on their way into the centre of Glasgow.

Campbell, a notorious Rangers fan, randomly selected Mark as his victim, and came from behind him and slit his throat. Mark died on the street as he tried to stem the flow of blood pumping from his body. The sectarian motive for the attack was later confirmed when Campbell unsuccessfully tried to secure a transfer to the Maze prison in Northern Ireland, supposedly as a political prisoner.

The following year Findlay also defended Thomas Longstaff, a close friend of Campbell, accused of the attempted murder of another young Celtic fan, in an attack that was described by Detective Sergeant Shaw – the man leading the hunt – as a 'carbon copy' of the previous murder. Findlay, a devout Rangers fan himself, has therefore seen the extremes to which this fanaticism swings. He has seen the consequences of those who act upon this entrenched tribal hatred. He has read the case notes on the murder of Mark Scott, my friend, the 16-year-old Glasgow Academy schoolboy, who walked down the wrong street at the wrong time, supporting the wrong football team. And yet in an atmosphere of euphoric celebrations over a successful season's football, he can still stand up and chant sectarian songs, that have offensive, threatening, anti-Catholic lyrics:

'We're up to our knees in Fenian blood,

Surrender or you'll die,

We're the Bridgeton Boys.'

It was a 'Bridgeton Boy' who murdered Mark, and it was on a Bridgeton street that Mark stumbled and finally fell. I take extreme offence at the language of such bigoted songs, and I take extreme offence at the actions of Donald Findlay, QC. One has to wonder how an intelligent man such as he, holding such anti-social prejudices, can represent the law in an honourable and respectful fashion.

As for myself, I am left now, in the wake of Findlay's revelations and last weekend's spree of violence, with the sick hollow emptiness that once was anger but now is just futility. The rational mind tries to but cannot comprehend such mindless violence. Sectarianism provides a superficial reason, but it is no excuse. What cost shall we continue to pay for the liberty to chant such violent, anti-social, anachronistic lyrics, in response to a game of football?

It has been argued in recent years that with so much control of Scottish industry passing out of local hands, those who wanted to be bigots no longer had the power to reward their own. Discrimination at work was therefore rare. Moreover the political associations that used to divide across confessional lines are, in the modern political context of Scotland, irrelevant.

Cardinal Winning seemed to allay Catholic long-standing fears about an independent Scotland last year, when he announced his belief that Scottish nationalism represented a modern future that could embrace all of its citizens irrespective of ethnicity or blood-lines. It seemed therefore that with its major economic and political underpinnings removed, sectarianism was a spent force.

Unfortunately the later half of the '90s has seen sectarianism surface in a new and more gratuitously violent form. Its centuries-old tribal roots remain intact, nourished each week by the sectarian chants and post-pub banter that are so infused in both the working and middle-class west of Scotland culture. But what in this arena seems like a controlled means of satisfying man's tribal instincts to belong – identified as they are by who they are not – seems, on the other hand, to trigger, or at least to provide some sort of sanction for, the violent actions of a sub-working-class section of society.

Perhaps these murderous assaults would have taken on another form, had there not been the pretext for violence in the songs that record a history of hatred. The fact remains though that the pretext, whether or not it be the civilised rational pretext which most adhere to, is there and ready for this violent sub-society to exploit.

PRODIGY OF THE YEAR

Brian Donnelly, 4 May 2004

Nicola Benedetti was sixteen when she became the first Scot to win BBC Young Musician of the Year. It was the start of a career that has seen her become one of the most sought-after musicians in the world. Working with conductors such as Vladimir Ashkenazy, Stéphane Denève and Kristjan Järvi, and with orchestras including the London Symphony Orchestra and the New York Philharmonic, in 2017 Benedetti became the youngest recipient of the Queen's Medal for Music. She performs on the Gariel Stradivarius, made in Cremona in 1717, during the violin-maker's golden period, and estimated to be worth £6.3m. It is on long-term loan to her by the banker Jonathan Maules. Below is an account from The Herald *of the night she became famous.*

She has been playing violin since she was four, at eight she was leading the National Children's Orchestra of Scotland, one year later left home to study at the Yehudi Menuhin Music School in Surrey, and at 14 she was named Prodigy of the Year. Now 16-year-old Nicola Benedetti has become the first Scottish musician to win the coveted title of BBC Young Musician of the Year.

The violinist, from West Kilbride, Ayrshire, scooped the award for her stunning rendition of Szymanowski's Violin Concerto No. 1, much to the delight of the audience in the Usher Hall, Edinburgh. Local favourite Nicola, now enjoying a schedule that has taken her to New York, triumphed over four other finalists, who collectively formed the youngest group of musicians to reach the final in the competition's 26-year history.

Asked after her performance whether she had been nervous, she said: 'I was much less nervous than I expected. I thought I was going to be shaking but I was kind of fine, I think most of my nerves were got rid of last night because I was really nervous but today I was okay I think.'

Nicola shook her head and covered her face when the result was read out by John Sessions, the actor and chairman of the seven-member jury. She smiled and waved to her cheering friends and family in the audience before accepting the award from the Duchess of Kent, patron of the competition. The duchess presented Nicola, dressed in a floor-length ivory gown, with a trophy specially designed by John Rocha for Waterford Crystal. As well as the coveted title she also received a BBC Young Musician Travel Award to promote her musical studies.

A former pupil of Wellington School in Ayr, she is the daughter of Francesca and Gio, an Italian-born businessman. Her older sister, Stephanie, 19, and also an orchestral violinist, is studying at the Royal College of Music in London.

Nicola has already obtained four good GCSEs and plans to do A-level music and possibly French, but she says she wants to do music for the rest of her life and does not intend to go to college or university. Her debut as a soloist came with the Scottish Ensemble on their BAA Scottish Airports High Flyers tour, during which she performed compositions by Craig Armstrong, fellow Scot and Oscar-nominated Moulin Rouge composer.

With the Scottish Ensemble she was described as working at the sharp end, and the highest level, of public performance. As well as playing solo, she will also partner Clio Gould as joint soloist in Alfred Schnittke's Moz-Art à la Haydn. Last month, it was reported that several record companies were offering Nicola a record deal worth more than £1 million.

STAGE FRIGHT

Judy Murray, November 2004

A promising tennis player who won sixty-four titles in Scotland, Judy Murray became national tennis coach for Scotland in the late 1990s. Her charges included her sons Jamie and Andy, who also happened to be the most talented players the country has ever known. Andy's breakthrough came in 2004 when he won the US Junior Open

Championship in New York. Over the years, Murray and her then husband were to make many sacrifices to help their boys embark on their careers, not least financial, but few were as memorable or difficult as the night she describes below.

At the end of November that year, we were told Andy was going to be awarded Junior Player of the Year at the Scottish Sports Awards. It was a big awards ceremony held at a fancy hotel in Glasgow. It was also the type of event where the women wore a lot of sparkle – long dresses, heels, bling, that sort of thing.

Andy was away playing at a tournament in Spain so he wasn't around to pick it up, and none of us wanted his achievement to go unnoticed on the night, so I went with my dad and picked up the award for him. I was hugely nervous about the event in general, but especially about having to get dressed up and sit with people that I didn't know. The whole thing was entirely out of my comfort zone: my job had been performed in sportswear for over a decade, and I simply didn't own the kind of clothes that were expected at a do this formal. More importantly, I certainly didn't have the budget to buy something appropriate.

I could hardly rock up in a shell suit though, so I did my best. And my best was a smart, pale green corduroy jacket from Marks & Spencer. It was £29.99 and that was absolutely every penny that I had to spare. As such, it left me with no leeway to buy anything else, so I wore it with a longish denim skirt and some pretty ancient black boots. . . .

As the evening progressed, I paid close attention to the mood and the layout of the room so I could avoid as much embarrassment as possible when it was my turn to head up to the stage. The evening's presenter was Tam Cowan, a well-known Scottish comedian and football pundit. He was a perfect after-dinner speaker for an event in front of a bunch of men. It was a pretty male-dominated room, but it was not an event for men. It felt like it though, with the underlying atmosphere of 'sport equals men'. But this kind of laddish banter was nothing I hadn't heard before, and I wanted to show the room that I could meet their tone and hold my own in the company there that night. I knew Andy's award wasn't coming up until the second half of the evening, so I had a little bit of time to prepare a comeback for whatever inevitable quip came my way.

It had only been a couple of months since the success in New York, but we had quickly learned that the one question that now would be a constant in our lives was: 'So, when's Andy going to win Wimbledon then?' And it looked like that night would be no different. I was pretty sure Tam would ask me that, so I paid close attention and established that his home football team was a mid-table team called Motherwell. I felt ready to answer back if he gave me any grief about Wimbledon, and focused on navigating the stage to avoid tripping up the steps or wandering off out of the wrong exit.

When I went up and collected the award, his remark followed the congratulations like clockwork.

'Never mind the US Open,' he said with a grin, 'when's Andy going to win Wimbledon then?'

The crowd laughed.

'Well,' I replied with a raised eyebrow, hoping I was playing along and showing the crowd that a mum could meet banter with a sense of humour, 'I think he has more chance of winning Wimbledon than Motherwell do of winning the European Cup.'

The laughter continued. A smile broke across my face. But not across Tam's. He looked me up and down pointedly.

'Could he not have bought you anything decent to wear tonight then?'

The laughter turned to the roar that a rush of blood to the head can create, as I felt my face turn crimson. I had no reply now. But even if I had, I wouldn't have had a chance to use it, as Tam gave me no opportunity to answer back this time. He grinned at the crowd, then returned to his script quickly, leaving me to be ushered, mortified, from the stage.

It would be impossible to understate the impact that one moment had on me. I'm almost embarrassed to admit how much it affected me. I just wanted to get off the stage and stay off stages for ever. It compounded every anxiety I had ever had about dressing up and going to a public event like that. It made me avoid them wherever possible for years. After years of being a confident, adventurous spirit, I began to dread and then to avoid, walking into rooms where I didn't know anyone. I turned down countless events, which should have been fun, for fear of not having the right clothes or not knowing what to say when put on the spot.

C-SECTION

Chitra Ramaswamy, 6 August 2007

A subject kept under wraps for centuries, or talked about only between women, childbirth is the last great taboo. In this graphic description, journalist Chitra Ramaswamy does not hold back. After conceiving by donor, throughout her pregnancy she was determined to have a home birth. When she went into labour, she and her partner Claire

*thought everything was going to plan but, after hours of contractions, when nothing was
happening, it became clear there were serious complications. The midwife Gillian called
an ambulance, and helped Chitra make the gruelling climb down the steep stone stairs
of her Edinburgh tenement flat. After that things happened quickly.*

1.30 am Inside the labour ward I kicked and screamed and swore and demanded
an epidural. From home birth to Hollywood in one fell swoop. More amniotic
fluid burst out of me when I was deposited on the bed and this time it was
flecked with meconium. The baby's first faeces, dark green and algae-like. A
sign that he was in distress, although I have also heard it is not uncommon for
overdue babies to be born with some meconium in their waters. Everyone
shouted at me to calm down. I felt hands all over my body. The drama felt
almost choreographed in its extravagance, like some overblown and tasteless
piece of site-specific contemporary dance. I yowled on like a wildcat. A doctor
arrived. There was also a young, sweet-faced midwife who was very sympathetic to my frenzy and let me pummel her. Then Gillian dropped a bombshell.
She told me that she would have to leave. Her shift had long finished and she
was handing over to the doctors and midwives at the hospital. She was going
home. I was appalled. 'Don't leave,' I whimpered, as though she was a lover
about to walk out on me for good. 'I have to,' she said. And then I hardened,
grew defiant, got sick of all the begging, adoration and abasement that had
characterised our night together. 'Well fuck off then,' I hissed in her face. And
that was that. She left without another word.

I was instructed to sit on the edge of the bed and stay completely still.
Between contractions, which by now were virtually constant, I locked eyes
with Claire, unblinking and savage, while an epidural was plunged into my
lower back. I felt nothing. Emotionally, however, I was soon euphoric. The
prospect of the contractions being cut short was nothing short of miraculous. There was no disappointment, fear or distress. Only delight as the
drugs went to work and slowly, sublimely, I began to feel nothing from the
waist down. The black force dulled. The machine turned not off but down
to an imperceptible level. The sheer relief and joy of becoming myself again.
I apologised to everyone in the room for arriving in such an unhinged
state . . . I turned to Claire and saw her, properly, for the first time all night.
She looked dreadful. 'Are you all right, darling?' I asked. She burst into tears
and threw up in my sick bowl . . .

I lay on the bed, monumental and passive as a beached whale, while a
procession of doctors and midwives shook my hand then looked between my
legs. I felt like a giant MacGuffin, filled with something bright and precious
that I, mere audience rather than participant, would never be permitted to see.

All I got were the expressions on their faces as they peered inside the cavern of my womb.

An electrode with a tiny wire was inserted into my cervix and placed onto the baby's head to monitor his heart. I felt so sorry for him. His soft new scalp, pricked and prodded. After a while his heart rate returned to normal, though it kept increasing whenever the cocktail of drugs being passed through a drip into my body was topped up. I hated them too, they made me shake uncontrollably. The drugs were reduced. He calmed down. The shaking abated. I was left then checked, left then checked. I kept telling everyone I still wanted to have as natural a birth as possible . . . We signed forms about C-sections, epidurals, forceps, episiotomies . . .

Finally, for the second time that night, I was pronounced fully dilated. And so, lying on my back with my legs open, I leaned forward and pushed as hard as I could. The midwife and Claire cheered me on. Told me I was a brilliant pusher. I became a warrior again, red-eyed and resolute. There was nothing, literally nothing, I wouldn't do to get this baby out of my body. I pushed until I thought my eyes would pop out of my skull. I felt nothing but a blissed-out doggedness and great pride at being the centre of attention. The consultant kept putting her hand inside me to check. I pushed again. The baby would not descend. I pushed again, angry with him now. My contractions were so strong, my pushing so A-grade. Still, he refused to budge. He was well and truly stuck.

Theatre. A room so white and dazzling it looked like the end of life . . . I was profoundly moved by the sight of an anaesthetist, registrar, consultant, nurses and Claire, small and pale as a ghost in her scrubs, gathered here for me . . . One by one they introduced themselves to me, an NHS formality that made me weep tears of gratitude. I told them how wonderful they all were. Praised the fortitude of the National Health Service. Implored them to take good care of us. Gazed up at the brilliant white of the ceiling and talked and talked in a monologue that felt scripted it was so seamless and long. Claire wept beside me, silently, holding my hand as though she were the child and I the mother.

First I was numbed all over again . . . A little white curtain was erected halfway down my body. The anaesthetic made me retch repeatedly. The anaesthetist stroked my hair and called me darling. The tears rolled in a deluge from the corners of my eyes onto the bed. I was neither sad nor scared, just unspeakably moved . . .

I had insisted on a C-section as a last resort so the consultant tried forceps first. The baby was still relatively high up in my pelvis so they were rotational forceps, giant salad servers out of a joke shop inserted deep inside me and turned this way and that to manipulate the baby's head into a better position. The consultant tugged me down the bed. It worked. The baby's head turned. But, still, even with forceps, he would not be pulled out any more than he would be pushed. . . . And now, for the first time, there was real danger. Urgency. The baby was in distress. The swift response of a medical team who know what they're doing but no longer have the time to share it with you. It was a C-section, and now.

I was sliced open expertly, routinely, felt nothing. The world seemed reduced to a series of small, astonishing facts in the way a single word, when placed on a line, becomes poetry. I was told not to worry if he didn't cry when he was pulled out because he might have too much fluid in his lungs. But then, in spite of this warning, came a cry, bold and loud, not belonging to this disinfected and orderly place but belonging so absolutely to him. 'A big healthy boy,' someone pronounced. 'Lots of hair.' It was 7.02 am on 6 August. Claire sobbed. I felt more deliciously, orgiastically exhausted than I have ever done in my life.

The baby was shown to us quickly but I was still heaving into my bowl and barely saw him. Oily black hair slicked to a head. Big white hands around a robust pink baby body. Little chicken legs pulled up. He was whisked away to have his lungs cleared. Perhaps this should have worried me, but I was so tired and relieved that he was out of me I lay there in a kind of flittering ecstasy. The doctor told me he would have to stitch me up as I had a small tear from the forceps. It was only then that I wept tears of devastation for myself, that my labour had ended like this, that I was a body that required stitching back together. I felt very alone for a while as Claire retreated to the back of the room to vomit into another sick bowl and, though I did not know it, hold our baby boy. I lay there, drifting in and out of sleep, or perhaps consciousness, veering from relief to shock to awe at what I had just done. I had tried everything. I had seen myself in a way I had never done before. I felt very brave and sorry for myself. I didn't think much of the baby but of my own body and what it had just been through. What it might start to feel like in the hours and days to come. How I might survive.

And then he was brought into the room. The same baby who had been wedged inside me all these hours was now being presented to me swaddled in a pale blue hospital blanket with a hand-knitted mint-green hat. He weighed 8 lb 6 ounces and was 58 cm long. Here and there his hat was encrusted with patches of blood, already turning brown. His or mine, I do not know. Ours. He was placed on my chest, his little mouth working already at the smell of me. I craned my neck forward, unsure of how to hold him. His skin was dry and the top of his head smelt like biscuit dough. His eyes were closed. I made an effort to notice him more but I was so exhausted it was an act of will rather than desire. His skin was sallow, more pale than I expected. He had my big squashy nose, my father's nose, and a dainty rosebud mouth, the top lip slightly overhanging. I saw elegant long fingers. A serious expression. A life.

I said nothing, lay back stunned on the gurney. We were wheeled out of theatre to the recovery room. Claire walked behind us, her slow footsteps squeaking on the gleaming floors. The baby lay still, settled, and precious on my chest. I watched the panelled ceiling race away from us as we moved forward slowly, tenderly, ceremonially. A little life procession down a hospital corridor at the start of another day. A beginning, after all.

WOMEN VOTERS

Lesley Riddoch, September 2014

As campaigning ahead of the Referendum on Scottish Independence gathered momentum, it began to look as if women might tip the balance towards a Yes result. A few days before the ballot, Lesley Riddoch, a tireless Indy Ref commentator, explained why women, who had been slow out of the blocks, were increasingly drawn towards casting a Yes vote on 18 September. The final outcome – 44.7% Yes, 55.3% No – proved her optimism misplaced, but while Independence supporters may have been gravely disappointed, the months of debate and conversation witnessed a marked increase in women's interest and involvement in political issues which seems to have been maintained. From that perspective at least, Riddoch's conclusions remain instructive.

So what happened to the gender gap in the Scottish independence polls? The weekend's seismic YouGov poll not only put the yes campaign in the lead for the first time – by 51% to 49% (excluding don't knows) – but showed support for independence among women was up 14 points in a month to 47%. In other words, the long-running gender gap in the yes campaign – which has ranged from 9–22% – appears to have been practically eliminated. How come?

First, the more that voters engage, the more likely they are to vote yes. According to research by Edinburgh University, 'Provision of information does affect [the likelihood to vote yes] mainly by reducing indecision . . . especially when a balanced set of arguments is presented, since the "change" option is the one which carries more uncertainties compared to maintaining the status quo.'

It seems women were more disengaged at the start of the campaign. This is partly because arguments seemed technical and abstruse, partly because debating styles were aggressive and aimed at winning plaudits from the usual suspects – male supporters and commentators – and partly because the editorial line of most papers in Scotland has been pro-union, making 'a balanced set of arguments' hard to find.

That's changed dramatically over the past six months, with the nation-wide emergence of grassroots campaigns, often organised by women with no party political involvement or experience in formal politics. Women for Independence has thousands of members and has organised more relaxed 'women-friendly' events, at community centres near schools before pickup time, outside shopping malls and at weekend coffee mornings. There have been fewer 'sages on the stage' and far more informal mass chats. I spoke at a Women for Indy afternoon event in the large, deprived, peripheral housing estate of Castlemilk, near Glasgow. The main attraction was the local woman, standup comedian and BBC Scotland soap opera star Libby McArthur. That strategy – of celebrities talking informally in their home towns – has been a big success with women. Street stalls have distributed free, in-depth analysis in publications such as the *Wee Blue Book*, produced by web campaigner Wings Over Scotland and a small mountain of YouTube videos and websites.

Second, as the penny dropped that women, not men, held the key to a yes vote, the focus of the wider yes movement changed to give more prominence to powerful female speakers such as the actor Elaine C. Smith and Business for Scotland director Michelle Thompson. Artwork has also featured images of women, not men – the *Spirit of Independence* has become the iconic image of the campaign.

Third – as commentators like myself suggested some time ago – women have always been less likely to be 'heart nationalists', more likely to admit if they don't know and more open to quiet discussion and persuasion, not heated Punch and Judy argument. In a testosterone-fuelled world of political analysis, that type of engagement was wrongly dismissed as dithering and indecision. It wasn't.

Finally, the general vibe has changed. Female voters now sense optimism about the possibility of real change, where there was previously a sense of uncertainty and difficulty. That is partly due to a change in tone by the once ebullient Alex Salmond, who stopped shouting, opened up a wider set of issues than currency – including health, poverty, bedroom tax, austerity and Trident – and scored with female voters in the first TV leaders' debate, despite being judged the loser by political commentators.

Salmond's wider subject choice, combined with the new, less smug tone produced a victory among all groups in the final televised debate, and was a game-changer.

However, all of that overlooked the contribution from the Deputy First Minister, Nicola Sturgeon, whose calm, surgical dissection of the former Scottish Secretary, Michael Moore led to his replacement by the more bullish Alistair Carmichael – himself demolished by the impressive Sturgeon in a subsequent TV debate. Sturgeon's approval ratings in Scotland have topped those of all male performers including Salmond for more than a year – in a less sexist society, she would unquestionably have been named Person of the Match.

More than all these slugging contests involving professional politicians though, the positive, creative energy generated by the wider yes movement has been its greatest achievement – even attested to by unionist commentators such as the *Spectator*'s Alex Massie, who said: 'This vigorous political carnival . . . has been a revolt against politics as usual: a cry, from the heart as much as from the head, for a different way of doing things.' The recent YouGov poll supports that view – 60% of those sampled thought the yes campaign was more positive than negative, while views of the no campaign were precisely the other way around.

Relentless positivity, combined with well-constructed arguments by local, articulate, non-party-political female yes volunteers, and a less aggressive tone from yes-supporting men, has made yes a more attractive proposition.

Of course with a week to go, there is still plenty to fight for – indeed one new poll puts the no campaign back in front. But there's a dedicated and well-organised band of female yes volunteers in every town ready to make sure the mould of Scottish politics is well and truly broken next Thursday – in more ways than one.

❦

FIRST AMONG EQUALS: NICOLA STURGEON, FIRST MINISTER

Mandy Rhodes, 5 September 2016

Ending Scotland: Her Story *with an interview with First Minister Nicola Sturgeon is not a party political choice, although it is political in the wider sense. When the First Minister spoke publicly for the first time of the personal tragedy she had endured, Holyrood was dominated by women party leaders. As well as Sturgeon there was Ruth Davidson at the head of the Scottish Conservatives and Kezia Dugdale of Scottish*

Labour. It was a situation unthinkable just a few decades earlier, but by 2016 so common-place as to be almost unremarkable. How far Scotland had come. Sturgeon's reflections on the different and sometimes unfair ways in which male and female politicians are judged is applicable to many professions, of course, even if they are especially acute in this most public of arenas. In the course of conversation, her assessment of the challenges that continue to face women, particularly when juggling private and family life with a high-profile and all-consuming job, are what make this insight into life at the top both interesting and inspiring.

Saturday, 2 January, 1971, is remembered as the darkest day in Scottish footballing history. Around 80,000 people left for the traditional Old Firm Ne'erday match at Ibrox that morning, but 66 Rangers fans would never return – crushed to death on stairway 13 at the Copland Road end of the ground. No one is quite sure what happened, but as the fans left the stadium at the end of the match it seems likely that someone fell, creating a domino effect, a barrier collapsed and thousands of people were trapped in a desperate battle for life. The disaster, which left 66 dead and more than 140 injured, changed Scottish football for ever.

Four decades later, thousands of people gathered at the ground on 3 January, 2011, to mark the anniversary of the disaster. Rangers players past and present, including John Greig, the captain on the day of the tragedy, were joined by family and friends of the dead as well as Scotland's religious leaders and leading politicians. Among them was the SNP's deputy first minister, Nicola Sturgeon, whose constituency of Glasgow Govan covered Ibrox.

It was a grim occasion and, looking back now at pictures from that day, Sturgeon appears tired and pale. Some images show her with her eyes tightly shut and, while the occasion was undoubtedly sombre, she looks to be in real pain. The cause of which was something beyond the commemoration. In fact, as she sat on the terraces that day, Sturgeon was going through her own very personal anguish. She was miscarrying a baby. She should have been at home in her bed, being looked after by her husband, Peter Murrell, chief executive of the SNP, and not sharing in what was a public grief. But it was her public duty to be there, so there she was.

Over the years there has been much speculation about the fact that Sturgeon, now 46, has not had children. In interviews she had been constantly asked when she would be starting a family, questions that she deftly deflected. Nevertheless, assumptions have been made and opinions have been formed. I knew only by accident – a slip of words over lunch – that being childless had not been an entirely conscious choice for Sturgeon and it has made me reflect on how much female political leaders, in particular, wrestle with what they expose of themselves and why.

Sturgeon is, despite outward appearances, an intensely private person and our relationship has been a slow burner. Not long after the 2011 election, in which the SNP won by an historic majority, we were having lunch. The conversation turned to a mutual friend who had lost a baby, when I realised that Sturgeon was also talking about herself.

She chose, as is her prerogative, not to talk about the miscarriage publicly, and I have respected her need for privacy, but with the passage of time she has become less adamant that it stays a secret and has allowed me to refer to it now. It is important because it says something about the pressures on and the conjectures made about women in leadership positions. Crucially, it also says something about the impact that all of that scrutiny and speculation has had on her and how she manages it.

In December 2010, Labour was polling way ahead of Sturgeon's own party in Scotland. There were serious questions about whether the SNP could hang on to power – they had formed a minority government in 2007, having beaten Labour by just one seat – and Sturgeon knew she had a fight on her hands.

Had she not lost the baby, she would have been almost 41, and six months pregnant going into the formal election campaign and, while clearly happy about being pregnant, she would also have been anxious about how it might affect not just the election campaign but also her role in any future Cabinet. And while these are normal feelings for any woman with a career to think about, for some-one as politically programmed as Sturgeon, who would also never have wanted something as personal as a pregnancy to see her accused of exploiting a personal situation for political gain during an election, they would have been paramount.

Being prepared and in control is what has powered Sturgeon – turning the gauche, unsmiling teenager that first stood on a platform for the SNP at the age of 16, where she was derisively dubbed the 'nippy sweetie', into the powerhouse politician that she is now. Being vulnerable and powerless are not positions Sturgeon likes to be in.

Why does any of this matter in the context of political leadership? It matters because Sturgeon is cognisant of the responsibility that she has as a role model. As the first female first minister, she is acutely aware that some young girls will look at her and think that, as a woman, you have to sacrifice part of your life to climb the career ladder. And in that respect, it is important to understand that being childless was not always a conscious choice for Sturgeon. She is also aware that women in politics are afraid to show vulnerability, as if revealing emotion in the male-dominated world of politics is seen as a weakness that would reflect adversely on their ability to lead. And that, too, is wrong.

It also puts into some context the repeated accusations that she has had to endure, both in and out of the parliamentary chamber, that, as a political leader without children, she could not understand some of the concerns that parents might feel about the impact of her political decisions.

'Speaking as a mother' is a phrase frequently used by politicians with the presumption that being a parent gives you a shortcut to authenticity and normality. As if not being a mother makes you less of a person – abnormal. One very senior female Labour politician once described Sturgeon to me as 'ruthlessly ambitious', all because she assumed that, given that she had no children, she had put career first.

For a female politician, being childless becomes a much more defining characteristic than it ever does for a man. In July 2015, *New Statesman* magazine ran an article entitled 'The motherhood trap' and on the front cover pictured Sturgeon along with Theresa May, Liz Kendall and Angela Merkel standing by a cot, empty bar a ballot box. It asked the question: 'Why are so many successful politicians childless?' Sturgeon later praised some of the content of the article, but had initially tweeted, 'Jeezo . . . we appear to have woken up in 1965 this morning!'

The article cited research that showed 45% of female MPs were childless compared with just 28% of men, and raised a fundamental question about how we perceive our female politicians. However, it also made fundamental assumptions about why women may or may not have children.

For Sturgeon, there have been moments, for instance, during her appearance on Radio 4's *Desert Island Discs* in 2015, when it seemed that she was almost on the verge of making public what was clearly a very private matter, but at the last minute decided against it. Instead, on questions over why she and Murrell did not have children, she said: 'That can be hurtful, if I am being brutally honest about it, because people make assumptions about why we don't have children. The assumption that people sometimes make is that I have made a cold, calculated decision to put my career ahead of having family, and that's not true. Sometimes things happen in life, sometimes they don't.'

Sturgeon hasn't been public about her own circumstances before because, clearly, while the miscarriage was a highly personal experience that will always be with her, it is not something she wants to be defined by. She is acutely self-aware and knows how things like this can be viewed or even manipulated.

Despite her overwhelming public popularity, Sturgeon retains a very definite personal boundary. And despite the outward appearances of being incredibly comfortable with the cult of personality – the selfies, the informality on Twitter, the public shows of affection and so forth – when it comes down to actually talking about herself or sharing intimacies she is much less comfortable, even with close associates.

She is naturally a bit of an introvert: this is the woman who admits that, as a child, she hid under a table at her own birthday party. She wasn't unpopular at school but neither was she in with the in-crowd. She has few lifelong friends and most of the people that might describe themselves as close – and whether she shares that view is debatable – are of and from the party.

Ironically, as Sturgeon's public appeal has grown, her closest relationships have diminished to a handful: her husband, her family and, to some extent, Shona Robison, Scotland's health secretary, who is often quoted as a close friend. There is no real inner circle – something that she is attracting criticism for and the Sturgeon/Murrell wife–husband combo at the top of the party has led to some misgivings internally that there is no real avenue for criticism, constructive or otherwise, of the party leadership.

Sturgeon and Murrell are very self-contained as a couple. They have known each other since she was 18 [and] started going out properly in 2003, having become particularly close during that year's election campaign, when they were living in adjacent flats on Edinburgh's Royal Mile, lent to them by other party members. They can sit for hours in silence just reading and rarely socialise as a couple. She doesn't seek his counsel on major political decisions; in fact, she says that most decisions that she takes on a day-to-day basis he will know nothing about. However, crucially, she says she can't imagine doing the job without him.

Despite her reputation as being a bit frosty, Sturgeon herself has a quick wit, a risqué sense of humour and she laughs a lot more than she is credited for. One profile described her as someone you wouldn't see on a girls' night out, but that is just not true. She is very much a woman's woman – depending on the woman – and can talk as enthusiastically about shoes and fashion as she can about fighting inequality. She has become adept at giving the impression of being just like you and me, elevating 'being normal' to an art form. This is undoubtedly the secret to her recent popularity. In her younger political days, she was – by her own admission – 'a bit po-faced'. If there is one bit of advice she would give her younger self it would be to smile more. And, despite much speculation to the contrary, there was never any big image makeover, just a simple evolution over time and with maturity. The 'nippy sweetie' of her youth, she says was 'probably not [me] being the real me', but a persona she adopted because she believed it would help her fit better into the political arena. Now she is not so sure: 'It's a cliché, but all the things that are seen as positives in men can be seen as negatives in women.'

In accepting the role of first minister, Sturgeon, a working-class woman from Ayrshire, referred to her eight-year-old niece, Harriet, and said she hoped her appointment sent a strong and positive message to girls across our land. 'If you are good enough and if you work hard enough,' she said, 'the sky is the limit – and no glass ceiling should ever stop you from achieving your dreams.'

Sources and Permissions

Note: Every effort has been made to trace the rights-holders for the material which appears in this book. The Author and Publishers will be happy to correct any omissions in future editions.

'The final letter written by Mary, Queen of Scots', NLS: Adv.MS.54.1.1

'Awake for sin' by the Venerable Bede, from *Historia Ecclesiastica* IV 25 vol. 1, in *Scottish Annals from English Chroniclers* by Alan Orr Anderson (David Nutt, 1908; republished Paul Watkins, 1991, ed. Marjorie Anderson)

'Viking invaders are repelled', from *Chronica Majora* by Matthew Paris, in *Scottish Annals from English Chroniclers* by Alan Orr Anderson (David Nutt, 1908; republished Paul Watkins, 1991, ed. Marjorie Anderson)

'Queen Margaret's saintly ways' by Turgot of Durham, from extracts of 'The Life of St Margaret Queen of Scotland', in *St Margaret, Queen of Scotland* by Alan J. Wilson (John Donald, 1993)

'Matilda reluctantly wears the veil' by Edmer, from *Historia Novorum*, in *Scottish Annals from English Chroniclers* by Alan Orr Anderson (David Nutt, 1908; republished Paul Watkins, 1991, ed. Marjorie Anderson)

'A house full of lepers' by Aelred of Rievaulx, from *Epistola*, in *Scottish Annals from English Chroniclers* by Alan Orr Anderson (David Nutt, 1908; republished Paul Watkins, 1991, ed. Marjorie Anderson)

'A much-maligned wife' by William of Malmesbury, from *Gesta Regum* vol. II, in *Scottish Annals from English Chroniclers* by Alan Orr Anderson (David Nutt, 1908; republished Paul Watkins, 1991, ed. Marjorie Anderson)

'A nursemaid witnesses horror' by Orderic Vital, from *Patrologia* by Jacques-Paul Migne, in *Scottish Annals from English Chroniclers* by Alan Orr Anderson (David Nutt, 1908; republished Paul Watkins, 1991, ed. Marjorie Anderson)

'King Malcolm's mother goes too far' by William of Newburgh, from *Chronicles of Stephen*, in *Scottish Annals from English Chroniclers* by Alan Orr Anderson (David Nutt, 1908; republished Paul Watkins, 1991, ed. Marjorie Anderson)

'Queen Margaret's ongoing influence' by Roger Hoveden, from *Chronica* vol. IV, in *Scottish Annals from English Chroniclers* by Alan Orr Anderson (David Nutt, 1908; republished Paul Watkins, 1991, ed. Marjorie Anderson)

'A queen runs for home', from *Flores Historiarum* vol. II, in *Scottish Annals from English*

Chroniclers by Alan Orr Anderson (David Nutt, 1908; republished Paul Watkins, 1991, ed. Marjorie Anderson)

'Rules for ale women', from *Leges Quatuor Burgorum*, in *Scottish Pageant* vol. 1 ed. Agnes Mure Mackenzie (Oliver & Boyd, 1949)

'The Maid of Norway's fate is feared' by Bishop William Fraser, in *Scottish Historical Documents* by Gordon Donaldson (Neil Wilson Publishing, facsimile edition, 1998)

'Warrant for the Countess of Buchan's capture', from Tower MSS (original in French), in *Scottish Pageant* vol. 1 ed. Agnes Mure Mackenzie (Oliver & Boyd, 1949)

'Wedding list' in the Exchequer Rolls of Scotland, I, Records of Elgin, NLS

'A mother's impossible choice' by John Major, from *A History of Greater Britain as well as England and Scotland*, 1521, translated from Latin by Archibald Constable (Scottish History Society, Edinburgh, 1892)

'Black Agnes defeats the English' in *Liber Pluscardensis*, 1338

'Murder of James I' by (?) One of Queen Joan's ladies-in-waiting, 20 February 1427, in *Scottish Pageant* vol. 1 ed. Agnes Mure Mackenzie (Oliver & Boyd, 1949)

'Bold women' by Don Pedro de Ayala, in *Early Travels in Scotland* ed. P. Hume Brown (Edinburgh, David Douglas, 1891)

'Royal wedding' by John Young, in *Scottish Pageant* vol. 1 ed. Agnes Mure Mackenzie (Oliver & Boyd, 1949)

'A lonely bride writes to her father' by Margaret Tudor, in *The Days of James IV: Scottish History by Contemporary Writers* by G. Gregory Smith (David Nutt, London, 1890)

'After Flodden', in a Proclamation by the Town Council of Edinburgh, 10 September 1513, in *Scottish Pageant* vol. 1 ed. Agnes Mure Mackenzie (Oliver & Boyd, 1949)

'Dowager queen stands her ground' in a letter to Lord Dacre, in *The Monstrous Regiment of Women: Female Rulers in Early Modern Europe* by S. Jansen (Palgrave Macmillan, 2002)

'A prioress's double life' by the Marquis of Dorset, in *Scottish Pageant* vol. 2 ed. Agnes Mure Mackenzie (Oliver & Boyd, 1949)

'Mary of Guise is mocked' by John Knox, from letter to the Queen Dowager, Regent of Scotland, from *Selected Writings of John Knox: Public Epistles, Treatises and Expositions to the Year 1559*, in *A Source Book of Scottish History* ed. William Croft Dickinson, Gordon Donaldson and Isabel A. Milne (Thomas Nelson and Sons, 1954)

'Mary Stuart's first wedding', from *The Marriage of Mary Queen of Scots to the Dauphin: A Scottish Printed Fragment* ed. Douglas Hamer (Bibliographical Society, London, 1932)

'Young Mary's beauty' by Pierre de Brantôme, from Pierre de Brantôme's memoir, published in 1924 as *The Lives of the Gallant Ladies*, in *Scottish Pageant* vol. 2 ed. Agnes Mure Mackenzie (Oliver & Boyd, 1949)

'Mary, Queen of Scots and her turbulent cleric' by John Knox, from *History of the Reformation in Scotland* by John Knox (Thomas Nelson and Sons, 1949)

'David Riccio's assassination' by Sir James Melville, from *The Memoirs of Sir James Melvil of Halhill: Containing an Impartial Account of the Most Remarkable Affairs of State During the Sixteenth Century, Not Mentioned by Other Historians*, in *Scottish Diaries and Memoirs, 1550–1746*, ed. J.G. Fyfe (Eneas Mackay, Stirling, 1928)

'Secret cure for smallpox scars' by Mary Stuart, in *Scottish Pageant* vol. 2 ed. Agnes Mure Mackenzie (Oliver & Boyd, 1949)

'Elizabeth I hears of Mary Stuart's newborn son', from *The Memoirs of Sir James Melvil of Halhill: Containing an Impartial Account of the Most Remarkable Affairs of State During the Sixteenth Century, Not Mentioned by Other Historians*, in *Scottish Diaries and Memoirs, 1550–1746* ed. J.G. Fyfe (Eneas Mackay, Stirling, 1928)

'Relations improve between Mary and Darnley' by Thomas Crawford, in *Calendar of the State Papers* vol. 2 ed. Joseph Bain (London, 1900)

'Darnley's murder' by Barbara Mertine and M. De Clarnault, in *Calendar of the State Papers* vol. 2 ed. Joseph Bain (London, 1900)

'Marriage of Mary and the Earl of Bothwell', in *Diurnal of Occurents*, in *A Source Book of Scottish History* ed. William Croft Dickinson, Gordon Donaldson and Isabel A. Milne (Thomas Nelson, 1954)

'Queen in captivity' by Mary Stuart, in *Letters of Mary, Queen of Scots and Documents* by Agnes Strickland (London, 1842)

'A pension for John Knox's widow', General Assembly of the Church of Scotland, in *Scottish Pageant* vol. 2 ed. Agnes Mure Mackenzie (Oliver & Boyd, 1949)

'The execution of Mary, Queen of Scots' by Robert Wingfield, in *The Tragedy of Fotheringay* by the Hon. Mrs Maxwell Scott (Edinburgh, 1905)

'The North Berwick witches', from *Newes from Scotland* (1591)

'James VI's view of witches', from *Daemonologie* by King James The First (1597), in *Elizabethan and Jacobean Quartos* ed. G.B. Harrison (Bodley Head, 1922–26)

'Prenuptial contract', in *Women in Scotland c.1100–c.1750* ed. Elizabeth L. Ewan, Maureen M. Meikle and Rosalind K. Marshall (Tuckwell Press Ltd, 1998)

'On beasts and women', from *A Description of Scotland* by Sir Anthony Weldon, in *Early Travellers in Scotland* ed. P. Hume Brown (Edinburgh, 1892)

'An unexpected night-time visitor' by John Taylor, in *Early Travellers in Scotland* ed. P. Hume Brown (Edinburgh, 1892)

'Edinburgh style', from *Travels in Holland, the United Provinces, England, Scotland and Ireland* by Sir William Brereton, in *A Source Book of Scottish History* ed. William Croft Dickinson, Gordon Donaldson and Isabel A. Milne (Thomas Nelson and Sons, 1954)

'The Book of Common Prayer is roundly rejected' by Henry Guthrie and Robert Baillie, in *Scottish Diaries and Memoirs, 1550–1746* ed. J.G. Fyfe (Eneas Mackay, Stirling, 1928)

'Dinner ruined' by John Lauder, Lord Fountainhall, from *Lauder of Fountainhall's French Journal*, in *Scottish Pageant, 1625–1707* vol. 3 ed. Agnes Mure Mackenzie (Oliver & Boyd, 1949)

'Hiding from the law' by Grizel Murray, in *Scottish Diaries and Memoirs, 1550–1746* ed. J.G. Fyfe (Eneas Mackay, Stirling, 1928)

'Soldiers' wives' by Sir James Turner, from *Pallas Armata* by Sir James Turner (1683)

'Abduction!' by the Privy Council, in *Scottish Pageant* vol. 3 ed. Agnes Mure Mackenzie (Oliver & Boyd, 1949)

'Martyrs on the mudflats' by Patrick Walker, from *Biographia Presbyteriana* ii by Patrick Walker, in *A Source Book of Scottish History* ed. William Croft Dickinson, Gordon Donaldson and Isabel A. Milne (Thomas Nelson and Sons, 1954)

'Waiting for love' by Alexander Allardyce, in *Scottish Pageant* vol. 3 ed. Agnes Mure Mackenzie (Oliver & Boyd, 1949)

'The Tumbling Lassie', Court of Session, from *Dictionary of Decisions* by William Maxwell Morison, under the title 'Pactum Illicitum' (Edinburgh, 1802)

'A servant's religious awakening' by Elizabeth West, in *Scottish Pageant* vol. 3 ed. Agnes Mure Mackenzie (Oliver & Boyd, 1949)

'Famine' by Patrick Walker, from *Biographia Presbyteriana* ii by Patrick Walker, in *A Source Book of Scottish History* ed. William Croft Dickinson, Gordon Donaldson and Isabel A. Milne (Thomas Nelson and Sons, 1954)

'Choosing a wife' by Sir John Clerk of Penicuik, in *Scottish Diaries & Memoirs, 1550–1746* ed. J.G. Fyfe (Stirling, 1927)

'School fees' by Elisabeth Stratoun, in *A Source Book of Scottish History* vol. III ed. William Croft Dickinson and Gordon Donaldson (Thomas Nelson, 1961)

'Rape in the Highlands', Anonymous, in 'Women of the Gaidhealtachd and their songs to 1750', an essay by Anne C. Frater in *Women in Scotland c.1100–c.1750* ed. Elizabeth Ewan and Maureen M. Meikle (Tuckwell Press, 1998)

'Household accounts' by Sir John Lauder, in *Scottish Diaries and Memoirs, 1550–1746* ed. J.G. Fyfe (Eneas Mackay, Stirling, 1928)

'Queen Anne's common habits' by Sir John Clerk of Penicuik, in *Scottish Diaries and Memoirs, 1550–1746* ed. J.G. Fyfe (Eneas Mackay, Stirling, 1928)

'A Flying Woman' by Robert Wodrow, in *Scottish Diaries and Memoirs, 1550–1746* ed. J.G. Fyfe (Eneas Mackay, Stirling, 1928)

'A Jacobite wife springs her husband from the Tower of London' by Winifred Maxwell, Countess of Nithsdale, from *Genuine Account of the Escape of Lord Nithsdale* by Winifred Maxwell (NLS manuscript archive)

'Regulations for midwives', St Cuthbert's Parish, Edinburgh, in *Sin in the City* ed. Leah Leneman and Rosalind Mitchison (Scottish Cultural Press, 1998)

'Well-bred girls' by Elizabeth Mure, in *Scottish Diaries and Memoirs, 1550–1746* ed. J.G. Fyfe (Eneas Mackay, Stirling, 1928)

'Fornication', Aberdeen Kirk Session records, in *Sin in the City* ed. Leah Leneman and Rosalind Mitchison (Scottish Cultural Press, 1998)

'Nursekeepers' by Elizabeth Mure, in *Scottish Diaries and Memoirs 1550–1746* ed. J.G. Fyfe (Eneas Mackay, Stirling, 1928)

'Like an overgrown coachman' by the Rev. Alexander Carlyle, in *Scottish Diaries and Memoirs, 1550–1746* ed. J.G. Fyfe (Eneas Mackay, Stirling, 1928)

'Captive on St Kilda' by Rachel Erskine (née Chiesley), Lady Grange, in *The Prisoner of St Kilda* by Margaret Macaulay (Luath, 2009)

'Two days after Culloden' by Mrs Robertson of Inches, from *The Lyon in Mourning* by Rev. Robert Forbes (Scottish History Society, 1895)

'Saving Prince Charles' by Flora MacDonald, www.nationalarchives.gov.uk

'Pipe-smoking' by George Ridpath, in *Scottish Diaries and Memoirs, 1550–1746* ed. J.G. Fyfe (Eneas Mackay, Stirling, 1928)

'Brussels lace and other fashions' by John Ramsay, in *Scottish Diaries and Memoirs, 1550–1746* ed. J.G. Fyfe (Eneas Mackay, Stirling, 1928)

'How to kill time while men drink and gamble' by Elizabeth Mure, in *Scottish Diaries and Memoirs, 1746–1843* ed. J.G. Fyfe (Eneas Mackay, Stirling, 1942)

'Happy Sundays' by Lady Anne Barnard, in *Scottish Diaries and Memoirs, 1746–1843* ed. J.G. Fyfe (Eneas Mackay, Stirling, 1942)

'Houses and hovels' by George Robertson, in *Scottish Diaries and Memoirs, 1746–1843* ed. J.G. Fyfe (Eneas Mackay, Stirling, 1942)

'Begin the world again' by Flora MacDonald, www.nationalarchives.gov.uk

'Dr Samuel Johnson makes an impression' by Lady Anne Barnard, in *Defiance: The Life and Choices of Lady Anne Barnard* by Stephen Taylor (Faber & Faber, 2017)

'Upskirting' by Edward Topham, in *Scottish Pageant* vol. 4 ed. Agnes Mure Mackenzie (Oliver & Boyd, 1949)

'Far-sighted Mrs Somerville' by Thomas Somerville, in *Scottish Diaries and Memoirs, 1746–1843* ed. J.G. Fyfe (Eneas Mackay, Stirling, 1942)

'The problem with hoops' by Robert Chambers, from *Traditions of Edinburgh* by Robert Chambers (W&R Chambers, 1824)

'Excellent Scotch old ladies' by Lord Henry Cockburn, from *Lord Cockburn, Memorials of His Time* (New York, 1856)

'Hats like balloons' in *The Lounger* (1785)

'Clarinda struggles with her conscience' by Agnes Maclehose, in *Clarinda* by Raymond Lamont Brown (Martin Black Publications, 1968)

'Convict Ship' by John Nicol, in *Scottish Pageant* vol. 4 ed. Agnes Mure Mackenzie (Oliver & Boyd, 1950)

'An abused wife' by Mary Eleanor Lyon Bowes, Countess of Strathmore, from *The Confessions of the Countess of Strathmore: Carefully Copied from the Original, Lodged in Doctor's Commons* (London, 1793)

'Robert Burns's wife remembers' by Jean Armour, in *Dirt and Deity* by Ian McIntyre (HarperCollins, 1995)

'Robert Burns's last letter to Jean', 14 July 1796, in *Dirt and Deity* by Ian McIntyre (HarperCollins, 1995)

'The first Female Benefit Society' by Eliza Fletcher, in *Scottish Diaries and Memoirs, 1746–1843* ed. J. G. Fyfe (Eneas Mackay, Stirling, 1942)

'An Aberdeen breakfast' by the Rev. Donald Sage, in *Scottish Diaries and Memoirs, 1550–1746* ed. J. G. Fyfe (Eneas Mackay, Stirling, 1928)

'The farmer's wife' by Ian Niall, from *To Speed the Plough* by Ian Niall (Heinemann, 1977). Copyright © the Estate of Ian Niall. Reproduced by permission of Andrew McNeillie

'The gunner's wife' by John Nicol, in *Scottish Pageant* vol. 4 ed. Agnes Mure Mackenzie (Oliver & Boyd, 1950)

'A church service in the Highlands' by Elizabeth Grant, in *Memoirs of a Highland Lady* by Elizabeth Grant, ed. Andrew Tod (Canongate Books Ltd, 2006)

'Miss Baillie sees too much' by Elizabeth Grant, in *Scottish Diaries and Memoirs, 1746–1843* ed. J. G. Fyfe (Eneas Mackay, Stirling, 1942)

'A child's view' by Marjory Fleming, in *Scottish and Irish Diaries* by Arthur Ponsonby (Methuen, 1927)

'The Strathnaver Clearance' by the Rev. Donald Sage, in *Scottish Diaries and Memoirs, 1746–1843* ed. J. G. Fyfe (Eneas Mackay, Stirling, 1942)

'Waterloo blue' by Elizabeth Grant, from *Memoirs of a Highland Lady* by Elizabeth Grant, in *Scottish Diaries and Memoirs, 1746–1843* ed. J. G. Fyfe (Eneas Mackay, Stirling, 1942)

'Edinburgh welcomes King George IV' by Mrs Fletcher, in *Scottish Diaries and Memoirs, 1746–1843* ed. J. G. Fyfe (Eneas Mackay, Stirling, 1942)

'Flirting without a licence' by Lord Henry Cockburn, from *Memorials of His Time* by Lord Cockburn (New York, 1856)

'Experimenting on a child' by Elizabeth Storie, from *The Autobiography of Elizabeth Storie* by Elizabeth Storie (1859)

'A publisher congratulates his author' by William Blackwood, in *Memoir and Correspondence of Susan Ferrier* by Susan Ferrier, ed. John A. Doyle (John Murray, 1898)

'Celestial mechanics' by Mary Somerville, in *Queen of Science: Personal Recollections of Mary Somerville* by Dorothy McMillan (Canongate Books Ltd, 2010)

'Sir Walter Scott's anxious daughter' by Anne Scott, in *Memoir and Correspondence of Susan Ferrier* by Susan Ferrier, ed. John A. Doyle (John Murray, 1898)

'The well-dressed thief' from Anderston Case Book, 1810–32, Strathclyde Regional Archives

'Maternity hospital rules and regulations', from 'Rules and Regulations of the Glasgow Lying-In Hospital and Dispensary (as agreed on by the Committee)', 6 October 1834 (Glasgow University Archives)

'A schoolmistress's tragic tale' by Janet Kemp, from *The Life Story of Aunt Janet* by George Lewis (Selkirk, 1902)

'Servant trouble' by Jane Welsh Carlyle, in *I Too Am Here: Selected Letters of Jane Welsh Carlyle* ed. Alan and Mary McQueen Simpson (Cambridge University Press, 1977)

'Testimony of coal workers' by Janet Cumming, Janet Allen, Jane Johnson, Isabel Hogg, Jane Peacock Wilson, Katharine Logan, Helen Read and Margaret Watson, in *Sair, Sair Wark: Women and Mining in Scotland* by Lillian King (Windfall Books, Kelty, 2001)

'Marriage' by Jane Welsh Carlyle, in *I Too Am Here: Selected Letters of Jane Welsh Carlyle* ed. Alan and Mary McQueen Simpson (Cambridge University Press, 1977)

'The sex trade' by William Logan, from *An Exposure, from personal observation of Female Prostitution* by William Logan (1843)

'Marital harmony restored' by Jane Welsh Carlyle, in *I Too Am Here: Selected Letters of Jane Welsh Carlyle* ed. Alan and Mary McQueen Simpson (Cambridge University Press, 1977)

'The factory girl' by Ellen Johnston, from *Autobiography Poems and Songs of Ellen Johnston, The Factory Girl* by Ellen Johnston (Glasgow, 1867)

'Cholera' by James Maxwell Adams, from *Observations on the Epidemic Cholera of 1848–9, chiefly as it prevailed in the 13th Medical District of City Parish Glasgow* by James Maxwell Adams (Edinburgh, 1849)

'A missionary's mother-in-law protests' by Mary Moffat, in *Wives of Fame* by Edna Healey (Sidgwick & Jackson, 1986)

'Letter to a doomed youth' by Madeleine Smith, Mitchell Library Archive, Glasgow

'I nursed my husband night and day' by Margaret Oliphant, from *The Autobiography and Letters of Mrs M.O.W. Oliphant* ed. Harry Coghill (New York, 1899)

'Cook's hot temper' by Janet Story, from *Mrs Story's Early Reminiscences* (James Maclehose and Sons, 1911)

'A right-minded woman', *Ardrossan and Saltcoats Herald*, 14 May 1864

'Giving birth on the street', Board of City of Edinburgh Poorhouse, March 1866, in *Government and Social Conditions, 1845–1919* ed. Ian Levitt (Scottish History Society 1988)

'A room of one's own' by Margaret Oliphant, from *The Autobiography and Letters of Mrs M.O.W. Oliphant* ed. Harry Coghill (New York, 1899)

'Lewd practices' by the Board of Inveresk Poorhouse, in *Government and Social Conditions, 1845–1919* ed. Ian Levitt (Scottish History Society, 1988)

'O pioneer!' by Susan Allison, in *A Pioneer Gentlewoman in British Columbia: The Recollections of Susan Allison* ed. Susan Allison and Margaret A. Ormsby (University of British Columbia Press, 1976)

'Highland tragedy' by Queen Victoria, in *Victoria in the Highlands, the Personal Journal of Her Majesty Queen Victoria* ed. David Duff (Muller, 1968)

'How to be a domestic goddess' by Margaret MacKirdy Black, from *Household Cookery and Laundry Work* by Margaret MacKirdy Black (1882)

'Orphans in the snow', in 'Report of Parochial Board Sub-Committee, and other witnesses', in *Government and Social Conditions, 1845–1919* ed. Ian Levitt (Scottish History Society 1988)

'Newhaven fishwives' by Janet Story, from *Mrs Story's Later Reminiscences* by Janet Story (James Maclehose and Sons, 1911)

'Stays and parasols' by Catherine Carswell, from *Lying Awake* by Catherine Carswell (Secker & Warburg, 1950). Copyright © the Estate of Catherine Carswell. Reproduced by permission of Canongate Books Ltd

'Mary Slessor's babies' by Mary Kingsley, in *A Voyager Out: The Life of Mary Kingsley* by Katherine Frank (Tauris Parke, 2006)

'Death of a beloved son' by Mrs Margaret Isabella Balfour Stevenson, from *Letters from Samoa 1891–1895* by Mrs M. I. Stevenson (New York, 1906)

'Combinations' by Naomi Mitchison, from *Small Talk: Memoirs of an Edwardian Childhood* by Naomi Mitchison (Bodley Head, 1973). Reproduced by permission of the Estate of Naomi Mitchison

'Black house' by Alexandra Stewart, from *Daughters of the Glen* ed. Innis Macbeath (Leura, 1986)

'Force-feeding suffragettes', medical officers of Perth and Barlinnie prisons, National Archives of Scotland, HH55/327

'Votes for women – dangerous', *Greenock Telegraph*, December 1909, from typed pamphlet entitled 'Greenock and the Suffragettes' by Charles McGuire

'War begins' by Annie S. Swan, from *My Life: An Autobiography* by Annie S. Swan (Ivor Nicholson & Watson, 1934)

'Working at the pithead' by Margaret Davie, from *Voices from Work and Home* by Ian MacDougall (Mercat Press, 2000). Copyright © Ian MacDougall. Reproduced by permission of Birlinn Ltd

'Rent strikes' by Grace Kennedy, from *Voices from War* by Ian MacDougall (Mercat Press, 1995). Copyright © Ian MacDougall. Reproduced by permission of Birlinn Ltd

'The lady tram driver has arrived', *People's Journal*, December 1915

'Cooking for Elsie Inglis's Russian unit' by Mary Lee Milne, in *Between the Lines: Letters and Diaries from Elsie Inglis's Russian Unit* by Audrey F. Cahill (Pentland Press, 1999)

'The Russian front line' by Elsie Inglis, in *Between the Lines: Letters and Diaries from Elsie Inglis's Russian Unit* by Audrey F. Cahill (Pentland Press, 1999)

'Married love' by Marie Stopes, from *Married Love: A New Contribution to the Solution of Sexual Difficulties* by Marie Stopes (A. C. Fifield, London, 1918). Copyright © the Galpin Institute. Reproduced with permission

'*Iolaire* widow asks for help' by Kate Morrison, in *When I Heard the Bell, The Loss of the Iolaire* by John McLeod (Birlinn, 2010)

'Kept in the dark' by Fiona McFarlane, from *Dutiful Daughters* ed. Marjory Spring Rice, Jean McCrindle and Sheila Rowbotham (Penguin, 1979). Reproduced by permission of Penguin Books Ltd

'A marked woman' by Mary Brooksbank, from *No Sae Lang Syne* by Mary Brooksbank (Dundee Printers, 1968)

'The night washing' by Molly Weir, from *Shoes Were for Sunday* by Molly Weir (Penguin, 1977). Copyright © the Estate of Molly Weir. Reproduced by permission of Penguin Books Ltd

'A thrashing' by Maggie Fuller, from *Dutiful Daughters* ed. Marjory Spring Rice, Jean McCrindle and Sheila Rowbotham (Penguin, 1979). Reproduced by permission of Penguin Books Ltd

'A sexual harasser meets his match' by Ann Flynn, from *Voices from Work and Home* by Ian MacDougall (Mercat Press, 2000). Copyright © Ian MacDougall. Reproduced by permission of Birlinn Ltd

'Fictional sex' by Annie S. Swan, from *My Life: An Autobiography* by Annie S. Swan (Ivor Nicholson & Watson, 1934)

'A country school' by Alexandra Stewart, from *Daughters of the Glen* by Alexandra Stewart ed. Innis Macbeath (Leura, 1986)

'Bringing Burns out of the mist' by Catherine Carswell, from *Lying Awake* by Catherine Carswell (Secker & Warburg, 1950). Copyright © the Estate of Catherine Carswell. Reproduced by permission of Canongate Books Ltd

'The hockey party' by Christian Miller, from *A Childhood in Scotland* by Christian Miller (originally published in *The New Yorker*, 1982; subsequently published by Canongate Books Ltd, 1989)

'Blin' drift on the Cairngorms' by Nan Shepherd, from *The Living Mountain: A Celebration of the Cairngorm Mountains of Scotland* by Nan Shepherd (Aberdeen University Press, 1977). Copyright © the Estate of Nan Shepherd. Reproduced by permission of Canongate Books Ltd

'Mill work' by Betty Stewart, from *Voices from Work and Home* by Ian MacDougall (Mercat Press, 2000). Copyright © Ian MacDougall. Reproduced by permission of Birlinn Ltd

'Making ends meet', Anonymous, *Aberdeen Free Press*, 1930s

'Sex – damned thing' by Maggie Fuller, from *Dutiful Daughters* ed. Marjory Spring Rice, Jean McCrindle and Sheila Rowbotham (Penguin, 1979). Reproduced by permission of Penguin Books Ltd

'Edinburgh women in their prime' by Muriel Spark, from *The Prime of Miss Jean Brodie* by Muriel Spark (Macmillan, 1961). Copyright © Administration Ltd. Reproduced by permission of David Higham Associates

'Storming Stirling Castle', *Glasgow Herald*, 27 June 1932

'Greyhounds for breakfast, dinner and tea' by Cicely Hamilton, from *Modern Scotland* by Cicely Hamilton (J. M. Dent & Sons Ltd, 1937)

'The famished prostitute' by Ralph Glasser, from *Growing Up in the Gorbals* by Ralph Glasser (Chatto & Windus, London, 1986). Reproduced by permission of David Higham Associates

'The Spanish Civil War observed' by Katharine Stewart-Murray, Duchess of Atholl, from *Working Partnership: Being the lives of John George, 8th Duke of Atholl . . . and of his wife Katharine Marjory Ramsay* (A. Barker, 1958)

'Fish gutters' by Cicely Hamilton, from *Modern Scotland* by Cicely Hamilton (J. M. Dent & Sons Ltd, 1937)

'Teashops' by Cicely Hamilton, from *Modern Scotland* by Cicely Hamilton (J. M. Dent & Sons Ltd, 1937)

'Health, husbands and housekeeping' by Margery Spring Rice, from *Working-Class Wives* by Margery Spring Rice (Pelican Books, 1939). Reproduced by permission of Penguin Books Ltd

'Operation pied piper', *The Bulletin*, 2 September 1939

'Lights going out all over Europe' by Marion Crawford, from *The Little Princesses: The Story of the Queen's Childhood by her Nanny* by Marion Crawford (Orion, 2003). Reproduced by permission of the Orion Group Ltd

'Stillbirth' by Naomi Mitchison, from *Among You Taking Notes: The Wartime Diary of Naomi Mitchison 1939–1945* ed. Dorothy Sheridan (Phoenix, 2000). Reproduced by permission of David Higham Associates

'Land girls' by Mona McLeod and Una A. Stewart (née Marshall), from *Scotland's Land Girls* ed. Elaine M. Edwards (NMS, 2010)

'A Day in the Life of . . .' by Irena Hurny, from *Voices from War* by Ian MacDougall (Mercat Press, 1995). Copyright © Ian MacDougall. Reproduced by permission of Birlinn Ltd

'Sales assistant', Anonymous, from *Friday Night was Brasso Night* (Workers Educational Association, South East Scotland District, 1987)

'Growing old' by Catherine Carswell, from *Lying Awake* by Catherine Carswell (Secker & Warburg, 1950). Copyright © the Estate of Catherine Carswell. Reproduced by permission of Canongate Books Ltd

'Advice to sons' by Maggie Fuller, from *Dutiful Daughters* ed. Marjory Spring Rice, Sheila Rowbotham and Jean McCrindle (Penguin, 1979). Reproduced by permission of Penguin Books Ltd

'Genteel war-work' by Catherine Carswell, from *Lying Awake* by Catherine Carswell (Secker & Warburg, 1950). Copyright © the Estate of Catherine Carswell. Reproduced by permission of Canongate Books Ltd

'The landlady' by Christopher Rush, from *A Twelvemonth and a Day* by Christopher Rush (Aberdeen University Press, 1986). Copyright © Christopher Rush. Reproduced by permission of Canongate Books Ltd

'National Health Service' by Mary Brooksbank, from *No Sae Lang Syne* by Mary Brooksbank (Dundee Printers, 1968)

'A Protestant girlhood' by Liz Lochhead, in *Jock Tamson's Bairns* ed. Trevor Royle (Hamish Hamilton, 1977). Copyright © Liz Lochhead

'Measuring out a life in percolated coffee' by Margaret Tait, from *Margaret Tait: Poems, Stories and Writings* by Sarah Neely (Fyfield Books, 2012). Copyright © Margaret Tait Reproduced by permission of Carcanet Press Ltd

'A croft at Christmas' by Katharine Stewart, from *A Croft in the Hills* by Katharine Stewart (Birlinn, 2009). Copyright © the Estate of Katharine Stewart. Reproduced by permission of Birlinn Ltd

'Day one at the National Library of Scotland' by Margaret Deas, from *Voices of Scottish Librarians* by Ian MacDougall (The Scottish Working People's History Trust, in association with John Donald, 2017). Copyright © The Scottish Working People's History Trust. Reproduced by permission of Birlinn Ltd

'An Italian Scottish wedding' by Mary Contini, from *Dear Alfonso: An Italian Feast of Love and Laughter* by Mary Contini (Birlinn, 2017). Copyright © Mary Contini. Reproduced by permission of Birlinn Ltd

'A new way of travelling' by Jess Smith, from *Jessie's Journey* by Jess Smith (Mercat Press, 2002). Copyright © Jess Smith. Reproduced by permission of Birlinn Ltd

'The long journey towards myself' by Jo Clifford, specially written for this book. Copyright © Jo Clifford. Reproduced by permission of the author

'No. 1 Catterline' by Joan Eardley, in *Joan Eardley* by Christopher Andreae (Lund Humphries, 2013). Reproduced by permission of Lund Humphries

'Jean Redpath wows New York' by Robert Shelton, *New York Times*, 15 November 1961

'Gang members' by Lulu, from *Lulu: I Don't Want To Fight* (Time Warner Paperbacks, 2003). Copyright © Lulu. Reproduced by permission of Little, Brown Book Group

'Who do you think you are?' by Janice Galloway, in *Spirits of the Age: Scottish Self Portraits* ed. Paul Henderson Scott (Saltire Society, 2005). Copyright © 2005 Janice Galloway. Reproduced by permission of the author

'Adoption' by Jackie Kay, from *Red Dust Road* by Jackie Kay (Picador, 2010). Copyright © Jackie Kay. Reproduced with the permission of the Licensor through PLSclear

'Stalked in the corridors of Westminster' by Winnie Ewing, from *Stop the World: The Autobiography of Winnie Ewing* by Winnie Ewing (Birlinn, 2004). Copyright © Winifred Ewing. Reproduced by permission of Birlinn Ltd

'Stand-up and be counted' by Elaine C. Smith, from *Nothing Like a Dame: My Autobiography* by Elaine C. Smith (Mainstream Publishing, 2009). Copyright © Elaine C. Smith

'Love in a cold climate' by Rhona Cameron, from *1979: A Big Year in a Small Town* by Rhona Cameron (Ebury Press, 2004). Copyright © Rhona Cameron

'Scotland's World Cup winner' by Hugh MacDonald, *Scottish Daily Mail*, 1984

'The 'Ootlin'' by Jessie Kesson, in *Scottish Writers Talking* ed. Isobel Murray (Kennedy & Boyd, 2008). Reproduced by permission of Kennedy & Boyd

'Open casket' by Sue Black, from *All That Remains* by Sue Black (Doubleday, 2018). Reproduced be permission of The Random House Group Ltd (© 2018)

'Running for Olympic gold' by Adrianne Blue, from *Queen of the Track: The Liz McColgan Story* by Adrianne Blue (Hf and G. Witherby, 1992). Copyright © Adrianne Blue. Reproduced by permission of the author

'Don't lose the joy of living in the fear of dying' by Maggie Keswick Jencks, www.maggiescentres.org

'Rape' by Helen Percy, from *Scandalous, Immoral and Improper* by Helen Percy (Argyll Publishing, 2011). Copyright © Helen Percy. Reproduced by permission of the author

'Dunblane's darkest day' by Kareen Turner (with Peter Samson and Alan Crow), from *Dunblane: Our Year of Tears* by Peter Samson and Alan Crow (Mainstream Publishing, 1997). Copyright © Scottish Daily Mail and Sunday Mail Ltd

'Barbie in the mosque' by Leila Aboulela, original version in *Being Scottish* ed. Tom Devine and Paddy Logue (Polygon, 2002). Copyright © Leila Aboulela. Reproduced with the permission of the Licensor through PLSclear

'Standing up to Sectarianism' by Cara Henderson, *The Herald,* June 1999. Reproduced by permission of Herald & Times Group

'Prodigy of the year' by Brian Donnelly, *The Herald,* 4 May 2004. Reproduced by permission of Herald & Times Group

'Stage fright' by Judy Murray, from *Knowing the Score* by Judy Murray with Alexandra Heminsley, (Chatto & Windus, 2017). Reproduced by permission of The Random House Group (© 2017)

'C-section' by Chitra Ramaswamy, from *Expecting: The Inner Life of Pregnancy* by Chitra Ramaswamy (Saraband, 2016). Copyright © Chitra Ramaswamy. Reproduced by permission of Saraband (Scotland) Ltd

'Women voters' by Lesley Riddoch, *The Guardian*, September 2014. Copyright © Guardian News & Media Ltd, 2018

'First among equals: Nicola Sturgeon, First Minister' by Mandy Rhodes, in various soures, incl. *Scottish National Party Leaders* ed. James Mitchell and Gerry Hassan (Biteback, 2016). Copyright © Mandy Rhodes. Reproduced by permission of the author

Index